The Last of Marian

"Marian?"

Parker reached for his daughter with hands that trembled, despite his silent promise to be brave. He called her name again; still no response. It struck him that she seemed too small, somehow. . . . He thought perhaps her knees were drawn up to her chest.

As Perry Parker swept his daughter up into his arms, he realized that he was wrong. Not only was the blanket-swaddled figure shorter than it should have been, but it was also much too light. Marian weighed 100 pounds fully dressed, but now . . .

"Marian?"

The earth seemed to tilt on its axis as Parker eased his daughter's limp body back to the asphalt. Tears stung his eyes as he fumbled with the blanket, drawing back one corner, then the other. For a frozen moment he could only stare in shock.

Then he began to scream.

STOLEN AWAY

Books by Michael Newton

Daddy Was the Black Dahlia Killer
Waste Land: The Savage Odyssey of Charles Starkweather and
    Caril Ann Fugate
Rope: The Twisted Life and Crimes of Harvey Glatman
Stolen Away: The True Story of California's Most Shocking
    Kidnap-Murder

Published by POCKET BOOKS

STOLEN AWAY

The True Story of California's Most Shocking Kidnap-Murder

MICHAEL NEWTON

POCKET **STAR** BOOKS

New York   London   Toronto   Sydney   Singapore

An *Original* Publication of POCKET BOOKS

 A Pocket Star Book published by
POCKET BOOKS, a division of Simon & Schuster, Inc.
1230 Avenue of the Americas, New York, NY 10020

Copyright © 2000 by Michael Newton

Photographs courtesy of University of Southern California, on
behalf of the USC Library Department of Special Collections.

ISBN: 0-671-01748-9

First Pocket Books printing November 2000

10 9 8 7 6 5 4 3 2 1

POCKET STAR BOOKS and colophon are registered
trademarks of Simon & Schuster, Inc.

Front cover photo montage by Lisa Litwack; front cover photo
courtesy of the author

Printed in the U.S.A.

for Feroze Mohammed

Failure or success seems to have been allotted to men by their stars. But they retain the power of wriggling, of fighting with their star or against it, and in the whole universe the only really interesting movement is this wriggle.

—E. M. Forster

What is madness? To have erroneous perceptions and to reason correctly from them.

—Voltaire

Contents

Contents

Preface

Shortly after 10:00 P.M. on Tuesday, March 1, 1932, twenty-month-old Charles A. Lindbergh Jr. was abducted from the nursery of his home in Hopewell, New Jersey. A note left at the scene demanded $50,000 ransom for his safe return. The price was met on April 10, but all in vain. A month later, on May 11, the young child's badly decomposed remains were found by searchers in a field close by the Lindbergh home.

It was the Crime of the Century, in an age before that phrase had been flogged to death by tabloid journalists. It took authorities more than two years to find a suspect, in September 1934, and another nineteen months to execute him in the Garden State's electric chair. By that time, Congress had responded to a groundswell of national outrage by passing a federal statute imposing the death penalty for ransom abductions. Henceforth J. Edgar Hoover's G-men would be on the job.

Hero-pilot Charles Lindbergh's celebrity made that case significant, but it was not unique—far from it. Ransom kidnapping of children in America dates back at least to July 1874, when another Charles—four-year-old Charley Ross—was snatched from his home in Philadelphia and held for $20,000 ransom. (The kidnappers never collected, and their victim was never seen again.) Twenty-three years later, in August 1897, five-year-old John Conway was kidnapped in Albany, New York, his abductors vowing that he "would be killed the same as Charley Ross" if they did not receive $3,000 from the family. Fifteen-year-old Eddie Cudahy, kidnapped in Omaha, Nebraska, while running an errand for his parents in December 1900, was safely returned after payment of $25,000 in gold. Philadelphia hosted another notorious abduction in June 1906, when a jeweler's son, seven-year-old Freddie Muty, was held for a paltry $500 ransom. The March 1909 kidnapping of eight-year-old Willie Whitla in Sharon, Pennsylvania, prompted brief agitation for a federal statute punishing such crimes, but the boy's safe return four days later, followed by the arrest of his abductors that same afternoon, stalled efforts to involve Uncle Sam in the manhunt.

Lloyd Keet, fourteen months old, was murdered by the men who stole him from his wealthy Springfield, Missouri, family in May 1917, and his abductors nearly followed him to the grave before the sheriff managed to disperse a lynch mob. Three years later, in June 1920, the Pennsylvania kidnap-slayer of thirteen-month-old Blakely Coughlin narrowly saved himself from the gallows with a bargained plea on charges of second-degree murder. In March 1927, two-year-old Virginia Jo Frazier, of Chattanooga, Tennessee, was safely returned after payment of a curious $3,333 ransom.

And then, ten months later, there was the case of twelve-year-old Marian Parker, abducted and savagely murdered in Los Angeles by William Edward Hickman, a young man barely seven years her senior.

The Parker case, preceding the Lindbergh tragedy by four years and three months, was a sensation in its day. The crime, if such things may be quantified, was even more atrocious than the murder of young Lindbergh. Like the New Jersey case, the 1927 kidnapping made headlines from coast to coast, but it was solved in something close to record time with an arrest before the week was out, and the killer was executed barely ten months later. Also, in this case, unlike the Lindbergh kidnapping, there was no doubt concerning the defendant's guilt, no indication of a possible conspiracy.

Because all memory is transitory—and perhaps because the Parker family did not include global celebrities—the grim deeds of December 1927 are largely forgotten today. And yet the kidnap-slaying's legacy endures, marking the first test of a modern statute that defined the limits of a criminal defense based on insanity. This is a controversy that continues to divide attorneys, legal scholars, jurors, and Americans at large, from John Hinckley's attempted murder of President Ronald Reagan in 1981, to the trial of Unabomber Theodore Kaczynski in 1998.

Before commencing research on this book, I was aware of William Edward Hickman's crime, as each of us know many things. It was a factoid, filed away, collecting dust, until a valued friend and fellow author, David Frasier, offered a suggestion that the case deserved a closer look. My editor at Pocket Books, Linda Marrow, agreed, and Dave provided further critical assistance, as he has so often in the past, by helping me obtain newspaper coverage of the case on microfilm, through the library at Indiana University, in Bloomington. I also owe heartfelt thanks to the research staff of the California State Archives, for providing me with the 1,600-page transcript of Hickman's murder trial, plus some 500 pages of correspondence related to the case; to Joy Marlow, at the Columbus (Ohio) Metropolitan Library, for documenting Hickman's early crimes in that city; and to John T. Duncan, with the Kansas City Board of Education, for supplying abstracts of my subject's years in public school. As always, Nancy Yost, my agent at Lowenstein Associates, provided support and encouragement from drawing board to final draft.

I'm often asked about my choice of subjects: What attracts me to the sordid subculture of crime? And why, within that murky realm, am I inexorably drawn to the most lethal and depraved inhabitants? It is, I think, because they teach us more about our so-called civilized society than does the average sneak thief, pimp, or drug-dealing "gangsta." A segment of the human race, worldwide, has always thrived on fraud, theft, trafficking in contraband; it always will. The human predators among us, though, have been so largely an American phenomenon, and have increased in numbers so dramatically in the past four decades, that examining and understanding them has advanced from an academic hobby to a critical survival skill.

In the case of William Edward Hickman, as with other brutal predators I have examined in the past—Carroll Edward Cole, George Knowlton, Charles Starkweather, Harvey Glatman—there were early warning signs of trouble, noted but dismissed by family and friends, before he ever turned to violent crime. There is at least a chance that timely intervention, in those early days, might have diverted Hickman from the course that ultimately claimed at least three lives, while leaving untold others trashed beyond repair.

Random murderers who prey on strangers time and time again have always posed a special problem for law enforcement. Through the late 1940s, when criminologist James Reinhardt dubbed them "chain killers," they were relatively few and far between, an average of two per year reported in America. By 1966, when British author John Brophy coined the term "serial killer," the domestic incidence had increased to one new case per month. Today that rate has nearly tripled, and there is no end in sight for what one FBI analyst describes as "an epidemic of homicidal mania" in the United States. Even a downward trend in violent crime across the board, widely reported at the end of 1997, had no impact on the ever-rising murder rate, and homicides by total strangers—once a tiny fraction of the yearly butcher's bill—today account for nearly half of all reported murders.

What, if anything, can yet be done to turn the tide?

It is too late for William Edward Hickman, certainly, too late for those he killed, too late for the relatives and loved ones who were traumatized. He may still be of service, though, even in death. If he can teach us something—how to spot the warning signs, avoid the critical mistakes of apathy and negligence—his life may not have been a total waste.

It may not be too late for those who follow after him.

It may not be too late for *us*.

1 ✦ The Drop

A stolen child is every parent's nightmare. Not a *missing* child, whose absence without leave may be explained by any of a hundred logical, innocuous hypotheses. Children are sometimes known to dawdle coming home from school. They get distracted on an errand to the store, lose track of time and place. Sometimes they stray on purpose, out of pique or spite. Most often they come home again with no harm done.

A *stolen* child is something else entirely. The solution of one mystery begets another, infinitely more extreme, more sinister. Uncertainty gives way to panic, consternation spirals into terror. Time slips out of joint. The future is transformed from hope and light into a thing of dread.

By 7:55 P.M. on Saturday, December 17, 1927, Perry Parker thought he had learned everything there was to know about the nightmare. Fifty hours of unrelenting fear, with his wife, Geraldine, pacing her room like a caged animal, barely conscious of who or where she was. The letters that demanded cash and threatened death. Phone calls. Two days of hell on earth, and Perry Parker would have said that nothing could surprise him now.

But he was wrong.

The Parker family nightmare had begun on Thursday shortly after noon. A well-dressed dark-haired man, described as twenty-five or thirty years of age by those who met him, had appeared in the attendance office of Mount

Vernon Junior High School on West Seventeenth Street in
Los Angeles. He introduced himself by name, but no one
thought to write it down. It was his errand that the secretary focused on, as he had known she would.

The stranger said he worked at First National Bank,
where Perry Parker was employed as chief cashier. He also
knew the Parker home address, on South Wilton Place,
reciting it from memory. Mr. Parker had been gravely
injured in a traffic accident, he said, and was calling for his
daughter to attend him at the hospital.

The secretary told him there were two Parker girls
enrolled at Mount Vernon, sisters Marjorie and Marian. The
stranger only wanted Marian. He specified "the youngest
one."

Why only one? the secretary asked.

The stranger shrugged. Perhaps, he guessed, because she
was the baby of the family.

In fact, the Parker girls were twins, but that escaped the
secretary in her moment of confusion. Rattled by the break
in her routine, she called on teacher Mary Holt, who was on
her way to lunch, for some advice. The stranger, sensing
their hesitation, offered the bank's telephone number. They
should call and double-check, he said, if they had any
doubts at all.

No need for that. The young man had a banker's look
about him, and a wounded man had a right to decide
whom he wanted at his bedside. Together the three of them
went to fetch twelve-year-old Marian Parker from home-
room, interrupting a class Christmas party. The stranger
broke the news of her father's accident, assuring her that
they would reach the hospital in no time. Marian was so
anxious to go that she left without her coat and didn't think
to ask if her sister was coming. Mary Holt watched the man
and child drive off in a dark-colored coupe.

And no one had seen them since.

It was unusual for Marjorie Parker to come home alone.
She hadn't a clue as to what had become of her sister, and
Geraldine Parker was fretting by the time her husband got

home from work, at 4:45 P.M. He found a Western Union telegram waiting for him, sent from Pasadena two hours earlier. It read: "Do positively nothing till you receive special delivery letter. Marian Parker."

Bewildered and worried, Perry Parker followed orders, doing positively nothing. The next communication he received was not a letter, though. It was another telegram, this one dispatched from Alhambra, California: "Marian secure. Use good judgment. Interference with my plans dangerous. George Fox."

The name meant nothing to Perry or Geraldine Parker, but it dashed any faint hope that their daughter had sent the first wire of her own volition. They were dealing with a kidnapper, uncertain what he wanted yet, terrified by the thought of their child in a cruel stranger's hands. Prompted by the second telegram, young Marjorie recalled a stranger in a dark-colored car who had tried to stop the girls and speak with them while they were on their way to school that morning. They had passed on by, ignoring him, as they had been taught to do with strangers.

Nothing in his life had prepared Perry Parker for this, but twenty-six years in banking had taught him to keep a clear head under pressure. He wasted no time in contacting police, and a pair of detectives drove out to the house on South Wilton Place. They were there, asking questions, when a special-delivery letter arrived. Inside the envelope, Parker found a single page covered with tidy handwriting, headed with the word "Δeath"—a Greek letter delta in place of the D. The letter read:

P. M. Parker:
Use good judgment. You are the loser. Do this. Secure 75 $20 gold certificates U.S. Currency 1500 dollars at once. Keep them on your person. Go about your daily business as usual. Leave out police and detectives. Make no public notice. Keep this affair private. Make no search. Fulfilling these terms with the transfer of the currency will secure the return of the girl.

Failure to comply with these requests means no one will ever see the girl again except the angels in heaven.

The affair must end one way or the other within 3 days. 72 hours.

You will receive further notice.

But the terms remain the same.

Fate

Across the bottom of the letter, "Fate" had written, "If you want aid against me ask God, not man."

A note from Marian was enclosed with the kidnapper's letter:

Dear Daddy and Mother:

I wish I could come home. I think I'll die if I have to be like this much longer. Won't someone tell me why this had to happen to me. Daddy please do what this man tells you or he'll kill me if you don't.

Your loving daughter,
Marian Parker

It was clearly too late for the Parkers to "Leave out police and detectives," but they struck a bargain with LAPD to keep quiet about the kidnapping, so far as the press was concerned. That way, with any luck at all, authorities might have a fighting chance to trace the kidnapper and rescue Marian. Meanwhile, Perry Parker set about following the abductor's instructions by collecting $1,500 in twenty-dollar bills.

The ransom demand was curious, almost trifling, and it puzzled police. Six years earlier, in California's first known kidnapping for ransom, $50,000 was demanded for the safe return of Gladys Witherall. Four years later, in 1925, a $200,000 ransom plot concerning actress Mary Pickford had been foiled at the outset, the would-be kidnappers packed off to prison for ten years to life. By 1926, in the wake of evangelist Aimee Semple McPherson's bizarre kidnapping hoax, many Californians had come to regard ransom abductions more as publicity stunts than as credible threats.

Still, Perry Parker was taking no chances. He would pay on demand, ignoring official advice, if only "Fate" would tell him where and when.

There was no sleep for Parker or his wife on Thursday night, as they attempted to console each other, waiting for the telephone to ring. Friday, December 16, seemed to creep by in slow motion, Perry going off to work as "Fate" had ordered him to do, returning home again that afternoon to find that there had been no word of Marian.

Police had visited Mount Vernon Junior High, meanwhile, to question Mary Holt and the attendance secretary. They had a description of the kidnapper, but could not share it with the press. As for the dark coupe, it could be anywhere. L.A. was already a city on wheels, with thousands of cars on the streets. Without a license number, officers could never hope to trace the vehicle.

Three times on Friday afternoon the phone rang at the Parker house, but there was no one on the line when Perry answered. Only dead air for a moment, followed by a click, and then a dial tone. Wrong numbers? Or was he being tested by the kidnappers?

At 8:00 P.M., the fourth call came. This time, when Parker picked it up, a male voice spoke: "I'll call back in five minutes."

Half an hour later, his nerves stretched like piano wires, the banker picked up instantly, before the telephone could finish one full ring. It was the same voice, asking if he had the money. Parker did. He was told to leave the house immediately and alone, drive north on Wilton Place to Tenth Street, turn right onto Tenth, and park on Gramercy. If he obeyed instructions to the letter, someone would stop by to trade his daughter for the cash.

The banker followed orders, carrying a hefty wad of twenties in his pocket, taking the route dictated by the caller. After half an hour parked on Gramercy, eyeballing each car and pedestrian that passed him by, Parker began to fear that something had gone wrong. He sat and waited till 11:45 P.M. before he gave up, dejected, and drove home.

It was only later, after he had missed the drop, that Perry Parker learned he had been followed by police. They had his house staked out, prepared for anything. If they could only spot the kidnapper when he retrieved his payoff, they could trail him to his hideout—or, if Marian was liberated on the street, they would arrest him on the spot.

Parker was stunned and furious, but no more so than Marian's abductor. News of the kidnapping broke on Saturday morning, with a front-page story in the *L.A. Times.* That morning a second special-delivery envelope arrived at the Parker home, with two letters folded inside. The first was again headed "Δeath," with the now familiar Greek *D* and an arrow pointing to the next line down: "DEATH APPROACHING NEARER EACH AND EVERY HOUR." The body of the letter read:

P. M. Parker:
    When I asked you over the phone to give me your word of honor as a Christian and honest businessman not to try a trap or tip the police you didn't answer— Why?—Because those two closed cars carefully followed your car north on Wilton to 10th and stopped shortly off Wilton on 10th and then proceeded to circle the block on Gramercy, San Marino, Wilton and 10th. I knew and you knew—what for? One was a late model Buick and the other had disc wheels. Then later, only a few minutes I saw a yellow Buick police car speeding toward your neighborhood. Of course you don't know anything about these facts—and that is sarcasm!
    Mr. Parker, I'm ashamed of you! I'm vexed and disgusted with you! With the whole damn vicinity throbbing with my terrible crime you try to save the day by your simple police tactics. Yes, you lied, and schemed to come my way, only far enough to grab me and the girl too. You'll never know how you disappointed your daughter. She was so eager to know that it would only be a short while and then she would be free from my terrible torture and then you mess the whole damn affair.

Your daughter saw you, watched you work, and then drove away severely broken hearted because you couldn't have her in spite of my willingness—merely because you, her father, wouldn't deal straight for her life.

You're insane to betray your love for your daughter, to ignore my terms, to tamper with death. You remain reckless, with death fast on its way.

How can the newspapers get all these family and private pictures unless you give them to them? Why all the quotations of your own self, Marian's twin sister, her aunt and school chums? All this continues long after you received my strict warnings.

Today is the last day. I mean Saturday, December 19-year-1927 [sic].

I have cut the time to two days and only one more time will I phone you. I will be two billion times as cautious, as clever, and as deadly from now on. You have brought this on yourself and you deserve it and worse. A man who betrays his love for his daughter is a second Judas Iscariot—many times more wicked than the worst modern criminal.

If by 8 P.M. today, you have not received my call—then—hold a quiet funeral service at your cemetary [sic] without the body—on Sunday, the 18th—only God knows where the body of Marian Parker would rest in this event. Not much effort is needed to take her life. She may pass out before 8 P.M. So I could not afford to call you and ask you for your $1500 for a lifeless mass of flesh.

I am base and low but won't stoop to that depth, especially to an ungrateful person.

When I call, if I call, I'll tell you where to go and how to go. So if you go don't have your friends following. Pray to God for forgiveness for your mistake last night. Become honest with yourself and your blood. If you don't come in this good, clean, honest way and be square with me—that's all.

Fate—Fox

The letter bore a familiar postscript: "If you want aid against me ask God, not man."

A note from Marian was enclosed with the kidnapper's furious letter:

Dear Daddy and Mother:

Daddy, please don't bring anyone with you today. I'm sorry for what happened last night. We drove wright by the house and I cryed all the time last night. If you don't meet us this morning you'll never see me again.

> Love to all,
> Marian Parker

P.S. Please Daddy: I want to come home this morning. This is your last chance. Be sure and come by yourself or you won't see me again. Marian

The kidnapper apparently relaxed a little as the day wore on. A second special-delivery envelope, containing two more letters, arrived in early afternoon. The first adopted a weary but patient tone:

P. M. Parker:

Please recover your senses. I want your money rather than to kill your child. But so far you give me no other alternative.

Of course you want your child but you'll never get her by notifying the police and causing all this publicity. I feel however, that you started the search before you received my warning, so I am not blaming you for the bad beginning.

Remember the 3-day limit and make up for this lost time. Dismiss all authorities before it is too late. I'll give you one more chance. Get that money the way I told you and be ready to settle.

I'll give you a chance to come across and you will or Marian dies.

Be sensible and use good judgment. You can't deal with a master mind like a common crook or kidnaper.

                    Fox—Fate

One again, across the bottom of the page was written, "If you want aid against me ask God, not man."

A second note from Marian's abductor bore the familiar heading, "Δeath," once again with a Greek delta in place of the *D*. The author seemed determined to drive home his point:

P. M. Parker:

Fox is my name. Very sly you know. Set no traps. I'll watch for them.

All the inside guys, even your neighbor Isadore B., you know that when you play with fire there is cause for burns. Not W. J. Burns and his shadowers either—remember that.

Get this straight! Remember that life hangs by a thread and I have a Gillette ready and able to handle the situation.

Do you want the girl or the 75 $20 gold certificates U.S. Currency? You can't have both and there's no other way out. Believe this, and act accordingly. Before the day's over I'll find out where you stand.

I am doing a solo, so figure on meeting the terms of Mr. Fox or else.

                    Fate

And yet again, like a mantra at the bottom of the page: "If you want aid against me ask God, not man."

Around sundown, the telephone rang. It was the same male voice, reminding Parker that his daughter's life was hanging in the balance. He would have one final chance to pay the ransom. If he failed, or if police showed up, Marian would die. The banker understood and said so; he was startled when the line went dead.

It was 7:15 P.M. before the stranger—Fox or Fate—called back. The time had come, he said. Parker should leave the house immediately and drive north on Wilton Place to Fifth Street. He was to turn right at the intersection, drive another three blocks to the east, and park at the corner of Manhattan Place. His car was known and would be recognized.

It was now or never.

The rendezvous was six miles north of the earlier designated meeting place, which meant a longer drive. It also gave the kidnapper more time to shadow Parker and find out if he was being followed by police. While he was driving north on Wilton Place, the banker checked his rearview mirror constantly, trying in vain to figure out if the cars behind him were tailing him. He had been stern with the police, insisting they make no attempt to follow him, and yet . . .

He made the drive in twenty minutes, give or take, parked on Manhattan Place, and switched his engine off. It was a residential neighborhood, the streetlights few and far between in 1927, mostly dark. Once more, the banker settled in to wait.

It was approximately 8:15 when headlights flashed in Parker's rearview mirror and a dark Ford roadster pulled up close beside him. Parker recognized it as the same car that had passed by without stopping, ten or fifteen minutes earlier. The driver leaned across the front seat, and even in the darkness Parker saw he was disguised, some kind of cloth—a handkerchief, perhaps—masking his lower face.

Like Jesse James.

A sawed-off shotgun nosed across the roadster's windowsill, twin muzzles aimed at Parker's face. "You see this gun?" the stranger asked.

"I see it," Parker said.

"Well, did you bring the money?"

Parker took the stack of twenties from his pocket. "Here it is."

"Give it to me," the masked man ordered.

Parker hesitated, caution kicking in. "Where's Marian?" he asked.

"Right here," the stranger answered. "She's asleep."

As proof, he reached down with his free hand, lifting, while the shotgun never wavered. Parker glimpsed his daughter's face, a pallid oval in the shadows. He could not tell if her eyes were open, and she did not speak. A heartbeat, there and gone, before she slipped back out of sight, reclining on the passenger seat.

"All right, now the money."

As Parker leaned out his window to pass it across, the masked man reached over Marian to receive it. Their hands were mere inches apart as he grasped the bundle of twenty-dollar bills, the shotgun less than two feet away from Parker's face. At that range, if the kidnapper fired . . .

Parker swallowed his fear and focused on Marian. "Are you going to give her to me?" he asked.

"Yes," the stranger replied, "just as I said. Wait here just a minute."

"How far are you going?" asked Parker.

"Not far."

The Ford nosed forward, perhaps 200 feet, and stopped again at number 432 Manhattan Place. Parker tried to make out the license number, but both ends of the plate were bent over, hiding the first and last digits. Giving up, he concentrated on the driver, waiting for him to emerge. Instead, the passenger door swung open for a moment, then slammed shut again. The Ford accelerated suddenly and vanished into darkness, northbound.

Frightened of a trick, Parker edged his car cautiously forward, peering over the dashboard to scan the curb where the roadster had stopped. At first he thought the bundle lying in the gutter was a bag of trash, but then he saw the face in profile and recognized his daughter lying wrapped up in a blanket, with her head against the curb.

Parker braked but left the engine running as he leaped from the car, stumbling in his haste. He knelt on the rough pavement, calling out Marian's name, but she did not respond.

Her eyes were open. He could see that now, but there was something dull and flat about them. Something wrong with her eyelashes, too, though he could not be sure what it was.

"Marian?"

Parker reached for his daughter with hands that trembled, despite his silent promise to be brave. He called her name again; still no response. It struck him that she seemed too small, somehow. Marian stood 4 feet 6 in her stocking feet, but at a glance he thought perhaps her knees were drawn up to her chest, from lying on the car seat.

As Perry Parker swept his daughter up into his arms, he realized that he was wrong. Not only was the blanket-swaddled figure shorter than it should have been, but it was also much too light. Marian weighed 100 pounds fully dressed, but now . . .

"Marian?"

The earth seemed to tilt on its axis as Parker eased his daughter's limp body back to the asphalt. Tears stung his eyes as he fumbled with the blanket, drawing back one corner, then the other. For a frozen moment he could only stare in shock.

Then he began to scream.

2 ✦ Born Dead

Paul and Rebecca Buck were odd. You couldn't hide that fact in tiny Hartford, Arkansas, a town whose population peaked at around 600 in a crowded year. Located in Sebastian County, 20 miles south of Fort Smith and 5 miles from the Oklahoma state line, it was—and is today—the kind of town where everyone knows everybody else . . . even if they are not on speaking terms.

The Bucks were easy to avoid. They had a hard-luck farm a few miles out of town, kept mostly to themselves except for shopping days, or when they sent the kids to school. Still, stories do get around, sometimes exaggerated in the telling, and the more bizarre a story is, the longer it endures.

The old man, Paul, was a religious sort, almost fanatical about it, even for the Bible Belt. He didn't just say grace at every meal and spend his free time studying the Bible and various religious tracts; he also sat the family down for worship at the kitchen table each and every night. Still, even that would not have set Paul Buck apart, particularly, if it had not been for stories about his *other* side.

Paul had a temper. Everybody said so, and there seemed to be no rhyme or reason to his outbursts. One of Paul's grandsons, Alfred Hickman, would later describe him as "very irrational," possessed of "a rather eccentric nature." Despite Paul's incessant study of religion—or perhaps because of it—"there were times when the smallest thing would incite him and he would become very nervous and become violent and swearing and blackguarding, and things of that sort." The old man was prone to whip his livestock when such fits came over him, said Alfred, and he wasn't shy of venting rage on "anyone who was around him," though he stopped short of striking his neighbors and kin.

What would set him off? "Just small things," Alfred said. "Somebody didn't give him the right answer, or the answer that he liked, and he would get angry, wasn't satisfied. Maybe he wasn't in a jovial mood, and it would excite him, and he didn't like it." At such times, Alfred recalled, Grandpa Paul "went into swearing fits [and] told me he wanted to leave the city." He "was always very nervous and irrational and did not seem able to control his temper at all."

It was all for the best, then, that Paul Buck kept to himself, except when relatives came visiting. Of course, he snapped and swore at them, the same as anybody else, but they were family.

More than anything, Paul seemed to enjoy the company of his grandchildren. He was willing to baby-sit whenever he was needed. In fact, it seemed there were always one or two grandkids around the Buck place. "He saw to that himself," Alfred recalled.

Rebecca Buck was the polar opposite of her husband. Where Paul lashed out at the world, she imploded, lapsing into black depressions tinged with paranoia, convinced that her neighbors and even members of her own family were scheming against her and "talking her down." Irvin Harris, a neighboring farmer who had known Rebecca since childhood, described her as "an awful nervous person," prone to "imagine everybody had it in for her and she didn't have a friend in the world." Indeed, at times, Harris agreed, "It was a fact." Her own behavior led the people of Hartford to avoid her like the plague. "She had lots of troubles and she was nervous," Harris recalled, "and if you would go there one time, she would be crying and telling you her troubles."

The Bucks had four children, but the oldest of them, Johnny, died in February 1891. Future son-in-law Tom Lewis had arrived in Hartford the month before Johnny's

death, noting that Rebecca's "mind was not right" even
then. In fact, he thought her mind "was weak as a little
child's." Lewis lived with the Bucks for a year after marrying
their daughter Minnie, and bought their farm in 1906.
Throughout their acquaintance, he said, Rebecca "would
talk foolish at times, and acted queer—strange. You could
get up a conversation with her and she would talk a little
while, and then get off on something else." More to the
point, she would "imagine things," including fantasies that
"everybody had it in for her." The plotters included Lewis
himself. "There were times she would treat me pretty
good," he said, "and other times she would kind of get it in
for me. She would draw up ideas that I had it in for her, and
she would think lots of times that her children had it in for
her."

At times, Lewis said, Rebecca would lapse into silence for
three or four days at a stretch, possessed by "ideas in her
head that we didn't have any use for her." Embittered and
depressed, she "would sit around and cry half the time." Her
health suffered, and grandson Alfred recalled that "she was
always ill," but no one seemed overly impressed with her
sporadic threats of suicide.

Today, Rebecca's condition would probably be diagnosed
as manic depression, perhaps paranoid schizophrenia. Both
forms of mental illness have been linked to chemical imbal-
ance and are treatable in many patients with the proper
medication. They are also viewed by most physicians as
hereditary problems, and there is persuasive evidence that
the famous Buck family "nerves" were passed on with their
blood.

Sometimes the trouble skipped a generation, as with
grandson Otto Buck, whom the kinfolk called Ottie. He
seemed just plain odd to others in the neighborhood, subject to fits that were later diagnosed as epileptic seizures.
Brother-in-law Benjamin Bailey recalled that the seizures
were "pretty frequent," lasting ten or fifteen minutes each,
during which Otto would "crawl around considerably, wallow around," or simply "groan and grunt and take on." Irvin

Harris, who had observed one such incident, in nearby Oliver, Arkansas, described how Otto "would chew his tongue, and was liable to kill himself."

Most epileptics can live perfectly normal lives if their seizures are controlled with medication, but even between fits, Ottie Buck was . . . well . . . strange. Irwin Harris considered him "insane to a certain extent," and Tom Lewis agreed that his mind was "no good." In fact, Lewis judged, "He was kind of foolish. He didn't have any mind." Attempts to speak with Otto produced a "kind of foolish conversation," much like his grandmother's, skipping from one disjointed subject to another. Ottie worked odd jobs around the county, sometimes in the fields or at a sawmill, but he "had no management" and barely made a living. When the great flu epidemic took him in 1918, some said it was a blessing in disguise.

Eva Margaret Buck was not among them. Born in 1880, the younger daughter of Paul and Rebecca, she had her own demons to contend with, firsthand experience of what nephew Ottie had suffered. Eva was not epileptic, but she had her mother's moods, a textbook case of manic depression passed down from parent to child. Tom Lewis, her uncle by marriage, remarked that Eva "always acted curious to me," from the first time he met her. "Anything just flustrated her, and she was nervous," he said, falling back on the favored adjective. "She would break down over anything." Health weakened by a childhood bout of typhoid, Eva was described by future sister-in-law Ida Hickman as someone who "didn't act just exactly like other people." In Ida's view, Eva had "always been a strange-acting woman."

Another future sister-in-law, Mrs. Artie Smith, agreed, pronouncing Eva "a little high-strung and nervous." Like Rebecca, Eva suffered dramatic mood swings. "In some instances," Mrs. Smith recalled, "she would be talkative and talk like everything for a while, and then she would get sullen—we always called it pouting—melancholy, and worry, and cry. And sometimes she would wring her hands." The crying jags, in replication of her mother's bleak depressions, sometimes lasted three or four days at a time.

It was a wonder, some in Hartford said, that Eva ever found herself a man, but so she did. Young William Thomas Hickman, a handsome devil with a reputation as a ladies' man, worked as a day laborer for the Central Coal and Coke Company. We may assume that Eva hoped to tame him, but their marriage on December 5, 1900, did nothing to correct William's roving eye.

The newlyweds started having trouble six months later, while Eva was pregnant with the first of five children. Relatives and neighbors recall a series of violent quarrels, beginning in the early summer of 1901 and continuing, more or less unabated, until William finally deserted his family sixteen years later. Long after the fact, a court-appointed psychiatrist blamed those fights on "the mental condition of the mother," and while Eva's mental state doubtless contributed to the deterioration of her marriage, there was also a more obvious cause.

William Hickman—sometimes called Bill—was cheating, and had been, perhaps, from the start. Tom Lewis recalled his brother-in-law as being "just that kind. He was looking for something all the time." Eva kept the embarrassing fact to herself, refusing even to discuss it with her sister Minnie, but Lewis remarked that "we could hear others talk." Despite his prior judgment of Eva's mental state, Lewis was willing to admit, "Of course, that woman I guess for ten or twelve years was miserable because Hickman was in and out, and he kept bad company."

William's infidelity was no secret around Hartford and environs. Dr. W. J. Hunt had treated members of the Hickman family at various times from 1912 to 1920, and he knew William was cheating. So did Dr. H. P. Routh, a company doctor for Central Coal and Coke: he called William's philandering "a very flagrant case," naming a local waitress whom Hickman visited several nights a week as soon as he could get off work. Ida Hickman agreed that Eva "worried quite a bit" about her husband's dalliances with other women, described by Ida as "just a general course of conduct, most all the time." Before he started stepping out, Ida said, Eva "got along all right" at home; afterward, upon discovering his infidelity, Eva was frequently reduced to tears.

But there was anger, too, verging on mayhem. Bill Hickman told his family that he awoke one night to find Eva standing over the bed, a butcher knife clutched in her hand. He blamed the episode on mental instability, denying any provocation on his part, and while blood relatives of Hickman still denied his adultery twenty years after the fact, neighbor Mae Forrester confirmed that William "had that reputation" as a playboy. Neighbor Sarah Slankard, on the other hand, explained Eva's curious behavior in ethnic terms. The women had met in 1904, with Sarah pronouncing Eva "nicely behaved" but "a little bit queer." The reason, in Sarah's opinion: "She was German, and I thought she was kind of funny-turned."

Bill Hickman, decades later, offered yet another explanation for the trouble in his household. Eva, he told a California court in 1928, "always had a horror of such things as sexualities or married relations, and always claimed she did not ever want to have children." In fact, she produced five babies in ten years, though William claimed that each time she was pregnant, she asked him "to get her out of it." When he replied that there was nothing he could do, Eva allegedly threatened—not once but "hundreds of times"—to disembowel herself with a kitchen knife.

Whatever their cause, Eva's "troubles" grew worse as her marriage to William dragged on. She bore their first son, Paul, in 1901; Horace followed in 1903, Alfred in 1905. Tom Lewis noted that Eva "was always uneasy about her children" and would never leave them at home alone. Whenever she left the house, to go shopping, visit her family, or, years later, to work in the fields picking cotton, she would always take the kids along. Lewis still diagnosed her as "foolish and queer," noting that "anything would tear her nerves all to pieces." He recalled that, "Any kind of a piece of work, if it didn't go right, she would just quit. Her nerves would get all torn up."

It was Rebecca all over again.

Dr. Hunt, drawing on eight years of sporadic observation, offered the first professional assessment of Eva's condition, diagnosing her as "a melancholy type of person," depressed one moment, while "at times she was flighty." Her "morose and sullen" moods would often pass quickly, he noted. "Maybe right after, she would get up and fly around the house, and then she would be sullen again."

Eva was also an apparent hypochondriac, complaining at various times of undetectable problems with her heart, stomach, and kidneys. She developed "whole strings of imaginary troubles," Dr. Hunt reported. "I never could make out what the troubles were. At times I would be called out there at night, and when I got there she would cry and relate her troubles." Hunt watched Eva weep inconsolably for half an hour at a time some nights, unable to describe exactly what was wrong.

At one point, William Hickman summoned Dr. Routh, from Central Coal and Coke, to have a look at Eva. She suffered from hallucinations, William said, imagining nocturnal prowlers in the house, bent on harming the children. Dr. Routh found her emaciated, with a "general appearance of ill health," which he linked to a systemic infection following the recent birth of her latest child. Depending on when he was asked, Routh variously diagnosed her problem as "extreme melancholia," a "mild puerperal mania condition," or "dementia praecox of the melancholia type." In any case, he thought—incorrectly, as it turned out—that the condition would resolve itself once Eva was cured of her infection and returned to health.

Eva's third son, Alfred, offered a more mundane explanation for her mental condition, noting his father William's frequent absence from the home. "The conditions, as far as I felt, were not what the average home was," Alfred later said. "It seemed always that the only person to lead any of us, up to the time we got where we were of the age where we had to lead ourselves, more or less, the only person with any responsibility was Mother." As a result, he observed, Eva "was always worried" about one thing or another. "She was naturally, I thought, inclined to take on spells when she would not be just natural. She would become very nervous and affected by those things, as the average mother would."

But even so, at times, Alfred described her as "insane."

Her problems were exacerbated during pregnancy. While carrying Paul, it was observed that Eva "became melancholy, morose, despondent, irritable, and had ungovernable spells or outbursts of temper, during which she would threaten to destroy herself and her husband." With each successive pregnancy, her symptoms became "more aggravated." Eva would sometimes disappear from home, hiding in various spots on the farm. When found, she "would resist efforts to pacify her and would not give any explanation of her actions." By June 1907, Eva was pregnant with her fourth son, and Ida Hickman recalled that for the next eight months "her and her husband got along very badly. She worried quite a bit." The cause of that worry? "It was over him being around with other women," Ida said.

Today's physicians understand that any serious, prolonged emotional disturbance during pregnancy may affect fetal development, since hormonal fluctuation can cause a wide range of problems for the child. Coupled with the hereditary manic depression and other ailments that dogged the Buck bloodline, Eva's fourth pregnancy was a recipe for disaster.

To make matters worse, the baby arrived a month early. He was improperly positioned in the womb, and Eva would later describe "two days and nights" of grueling labor, including sedation with chloroform, climaxed by what was believed to be a stillbirth on February 1, 1908. Bill Hickman described his son's birth in traumatic terms: "He was just as black as anything you ever saw. They worked with him about an hour, almost, it seemed to me like that long, anyhow, before they ever got any life into him." The infant remained "very delicate," described by one observer as "greatly emaciated," over the next two or three months.

"After that," Eva said, "he seemed to grow and was healthy, as healthy as could be expected under the circumstances."

His parents named him William, but he was known within the family by his middle name, Edward, or simply Ed, to avoid confusion with his father. In Eva's case, one William Hickman in the house was probably enough.

Two years to the month after Edward's arrival, in February 1910, Eva bore her fifth and final child. It was a daughter this time, christened Mary, and Eva's last pregnancy was the worst of all. At times she raved, barely coherent, threatening harm to her family and herself. On one occasion, brandishing a hatchet, Eva drove her cheating husband from the house.

By her tenth anniversary with William, Eva had threatened suicide so often that no one took her seriously any more. It was something the Buck women did for attention, people said, or because they "weren't right in the head." Just look at Rebecca.

Still, there was no doubt of Eva's depression, her bleak outlook on life. Mae Forrester remembered her as "the most despondent woman I ever saw. I called it brokenhearted, at the time." Speaking of Eva's husband, William, Mae recalled, "She said he didn't care anything about her, and she thought it would be best for her to be out of the way, that he might take better care of the children if she was out of the way."

One Saturday morning in the spring of 1911, Mae Forrester said, "I had gone by [Eva's] house to go to my mother's, and she was walking in the yard. She called me and asked me . . . if I had any carbolic acid, and I told her no. And then she broke and said, 'You look so happy, and I wish I could be as happy as you are.' And then she told me what she planned to do with the medicine."

Eva didn't get carbolic acid from Mae, but she found it somewhere. Two days later, Dr. W. C. Chambers was called out to treat her for symptoms of self-inflicted poisoning, the apparent result of a suicide attempt. Sarah Slankard, visiting Eva three days later, believed Eva had taken leave of her senses. "I didn't think she knew what she was doing," Sarah said. "She acted crazy to me." Asked why she had tried to kill herself, Eva referred vaguely to "the way Bill treated me."

No immediate action was taken in response to Eva's attempted suicide, and her condition continued to deteriorate. Mrs. Artie Smith later testified, "I saw her do things that made me feel anxious about the children. One day she took a spell of dancing all over the house. The children were all at school and I felt uneasy about the children, and I stayed out and watched to see that nothing happened to them." The mood swings continued unabated. At times, Mrs. Smith noted, Eva was "just laughing and singing and happy as a lark," but the change could come without warning and "She would sit around and cry, just down and out. She didn't say anything then," for two or three days at a stretch.

Matters grew worse in 1913, when Eva's mother, Rebecca, was partially paralyzed by an apparent stroke. Rebecca was bedridden for the last four years of her life, in need of perpetual care, and Eva shouldered much of the burden. It was finally too much for William, juggling his girlfriends and a crazy wife. By that July, he had decided something had to give. Records from the State Hospital for Nervous Diseases, in Little Rock, reveal what happened next:

STATE HOSPITAL FOR NERVOUS DISEASES
IMPORTANT DATA

NAME: Mrs. Eva Hickman   CASE NUMBER: 6840
   Held as special guest until July 22, 1913
   See Special Dictation
ADMITTED: July 2, 1913   COUNTY: Sebastian
DATE OF PRESENTATION AT STAFF MEETING: July 22, 1913
DIAGNOSIS: PROVISIONAL—Simple Depression
SPECIAL DICTATION

   Dr. Greene: This patient came to the hospital July 2, 1913, in company with the Sheriff of her county, her husband and Dr. W. C. Chambers without any commitment papers, and it was understood and agreed that a full set of papers would be sent by mail within the next few days. It was concluded that the patient would be held as a guest pending the arrival of the regular commitment papers, and after a vigorous correspondence with the County Judge and the husband, they finally reached the institution on the morning of July 22, and the patient was regularly committed on that date.

That "vigorous correspondence" with Bill Hickman and Sebastian County's probate court resulted in the following order of commitment for Eva Hickman:

WARRANT OF COMMITMENT OF INSANE PERSON TO THE STATE LUNATIC ASYLUM AT LITTLE ROCK

State of Arkansas
County of Sebastian
Greenwood District
In the matter of Mrs. Eva Hickman,
    An insane person.
    State of Arkansas to_____   Greeting:
    You are hereby commanded to receive forthwith into your custody Mrs. Eva Hickman by me adjudged to be insane and safely and speedily deliver her to the superintendent of the Arkansas State Lunatic Asylum at Little Rock, Arkansas, and take his receipt thereof.
    Of this writ you will make the due return:
    Witness the hand of the Judge of the County and Probate Courts in and for Sebastian County, Greenwood District, and the seal of said courts, at Greenwood, this 1st day of July, 1913.

Ezra Hester
County and Probate Judge

It is a mystery why Judge Hester's order, dated two days *before* Eva's arrival in Little Rock, took another three weeks to reach the state hospital, but she spent the time as a "special guest" of the state. In addition to the police escort, she arrived in company with sworn statements from her husband and physician, attesting to her precarious mental state.

STATE HOSPITAL FOR NERVOUS DISEASES
NAME: Mrs. Eva Hickman
STATEMENT BY: W. T. Hickman
(Husband)

The first indication I had that there was anything wrong with her was about two months ago. She seemed to be run down in health; her periods were irregular; at times she appeared to be unnerved and would become frightened at every little thing: She has made threats to destroy her life but has never attempted it but once about two years ago she had an attack like this and attempted to take carbolic acid. At times she seems all right and then again she seems to be wrong mentally, she has a very melancholy disposition and worries about little things that do not amount to anything.

STATEMENT BY DR. W. C. CHAMBERS

She is in a melancholy state most of the time but sometimes this alternates with periods of slight exaltation. She gets up at night and rambles about the house when everyone else is asleep. She says that she does not think that there is any use living. About two years ago she had a similar attack and at this time she attempted suicide by taking carbolic acid.

A staff physician, Dr. Murphy, examined Eva the day after her arrival in Little Rock, and prepared a report of his findings.

PHYSICAL EXAMINATION

ANTHROPOLOGICAL DATA AND GENERAL APPEARANCE: This patient is about 33 years of age; complexion is florid; hair is light brown, oily; there is no seborrhea present;

cranial contour shows no irregularities, sutures and
fontanelles are normally closed; eyes are gray and on
unequal planes, the left being slightly higher than the
right; the nose is medium sized; left side of the face
seems to be fuller than the right; ears are fairly well
formed and on equal planes and set close to the head;
tongue is large, broad, slightly coated and protrudes
slightly to the right; the dentures show no irregularities; there are several teeth missing in both dentures;
mouth shows recent neglect; there is present a slight
degree of pyorrhea alveolaries; there is noticed over the
face several small pimples; thyroid gland shows no
abnormal enlargement; cervical glands are not palpa-
ble; skin is clean, moist and there is present over the
chest, back and shoulders a papular eruption; bone
frame is rather small but strongly built; the muscles are
well developed and firm in character; general nutrition
of this patient seems to be about normal; there is no
Gordon, Babinski or ankle clonus; no tremors, tics, or
spasms; coordination tests are well performed; pulse
rate sitting posture is 78 with full volume and medium
tension; there was no undue hardening of the radial
arteries.

GENERAL MANNER AND ATTITUDE: The nurse states that
on admission this patient was put to bed and remained
in bed for one day. Since then, she has been up and
quiet, giving no trouble whatever. She does not sleep
well, and the patient stated that she assisted with the
ward work today. During the examination she was
quiet, answering all questions readily. She seemed to be
interested in the examination.

MENTAL STATUS: This patient states that she had fever
for three weeks in May, at which time she tried to do
her own house work, and at times she was in bed. She
would go to bed some days then would get up and try
to carry on her household duties. During this time she
thinks she lost in weight and strength. She states that
she heard bells and roaring in her ears which she could

not account for. There were no visual hallucinations or delusions of any character expressed. She states that there has been times when she knew her mind was not right during the past five years. When these spells would come on her, she would be inclined to roam away from home, not having any cause for doing it. She stated that she felt like she wanted to die and get out of the way but when she would stop and think about this, she would change her mind, stating that she did not want to die or be killed. She states that she never left home but would talk to her husband about it when these spells would come on her. She states that at times she would get to thinking about her children and herself which would worry her and she would become depressed. The patient states that at times she would get mad and go off to herself and scream, and that she wanted to fight and hammer the walls of the house. Orientation, memory and impressionability show no disturbance. Her fund of acquired knowledge is fair for her opportunities. She is able to read and write and compute simple sums correctly. She has partial insight.

PROVISIONAL DIAGNOSIS: Simple depression

A staff meeting on Eva's case was held on July 22, following arrival of the commitment papers from Sebastian County. The minutes read as follows:

STAFF MEETING REPORT
July 22, 1913　　　　　　　　　　8:15 A.M.

PRESENT: Dr. Green[e], Dr. Darnall, Dr. Arkebauer
　　Dr. Doyne, Dr. Thompson, Dr. Murphy, Dr. Roberts
ABSENT: Dr. Fletcher
CASE PRESENTED: Mrs. Eva Hickman　　By Dr. Murphy
PROVISIONAL DIAGNOSIS: Simple Depression

Dr. Murphy: I couldn't get much out of her. I don't know how to classify her.

Dr. Greene: Assuming that the statements made by the patient are true, and there is no apparent reason for doubting her veracity, the history would suggest a recurrent depression, and since there is present now an emotional tone of sadness without retardation, apparently she has not deteriorated. I believe that the patient is suffering from simple depression, recurrent in character.

Dr. Roberts: From the history and your questioning, I believe that she is psychogenic.

Dr. Greene: At any rate the dominating feature at this time is a depression. There is something [in] back of the case which she will not tell.

There was indeed: no mention from Eva or Bill of his flagrant infidelity spanning at least a dozen years; no reference to the mental illness of her parents and nephew; no indication of recent stress, in the form of her mother's disabling illness. Statements from Eva's attending physicians in Hartford, likewise, glossed over the long-standing background of her problems with bland denial. The interrogatories filled out by Dr. W. C. Chambers provide an example:

21. Has she experienced any great shock or strain of mind recently? *Ans. No*

22. Were her parents or grandparents, or any of them, ever intemperate, insane, or subject to fits? *Ans. No*

23. Is there now, or has there been, any one of her immediate relatives insane, intemperate, epileptic, or hysterical, to a marked degree? *Ans. No*

Dr. H. P. Routh provided negative answers to the same three questions, and while his ignorance of Eva's background may be excused, Dr. Chambers, as her family physician, should certainly have been acquainted with Paul and Rebecca Buck, not to mention Eva's nephew, Otto.

Student nurse Stella Mann observed Eva in custody and later testified, "She was in a state of melancholia, a deeply depressed state, most of the time. At times she would talk, and at other times she would sit for hours staring, and would not want to speak at all. We would speak to her several times, and she wouldn't speak. She would take to crying spells for hours at a time." On other occasions, Mann recalled, "She was a little stubborn. Lots of times we wanted to give her a bath, or sometimes when I wanted to give her medicine, she wouldn't take it. She would want to knock the medicine glass from my hands."

Dr. Darnall, a staff physician at the hospital, obviously missed those episodes. His report on Eva, dated September 2, 1913, notes that "Almost from the beginning she has shown a decided interest in everything going on about her, has expressed a willingness to assist in any kind of ward work, has been pleasant and agreeable and for several weeks past has been rendering efficient service as an assistant in the employee dining room. If we may judge her true mental state by the observations made here, there is reason to believe that she is at this time in a state of practically normal mental health."

September 2 was the day Bill Hickman came to visit Eva and, in Dr. Darnall's words, "being so favorably impressed with the improvement which he noted both in her mental and physical condition, made a request that she be given a trial at home on parole." Because she had been formally committed by Judge Hester, yet another legal pleading was required:

STATE HOSPITAL FOR NERVOUS DISEASES
LITTLE ROCK, ARK., SEPTEMBER 2, 1913

To the Superintendent of the Arkansas State Hospital for Nervous Diseases:

Believing that Eva Hickman, my wife, is improved and in condition to be removed from the hospital, I have requested that she be granted a parole. I agree to faithfully care for the patient, or to have some responsible person do so, both day and night, and to exonerate the management of the State Hospital should she commit any act of violence while away from the institution.

I also agree to return the patient to the hospital should I not be able to fulfill my agreement, and I further agree that a report of the patient's condition shall be made in writing to the superintendent of the hospital for a period of six months, and I further agree, if at the expiration of the period of this parole, it is thought necessary to do so, or if at the expiration of this parole, it becomes necessary to do so, I will return the patient to the State Hospital for Nervous Diseases without expense to the said hospital or to the county in which the patient resides.

W. T. Hickman

Eva was released "as improved" the same day, and while she never returned to the Little Rock asylum, her period of supervision on parole was extended for another six months, until September 2, 1914, at which time she was formally discharged from state custody.

There was bitter irony in Bill's promise to "faithfully" watch over Eva—his philandering continued without letup—and there was a question also as to how much she had actually improved while she was locked away. Back in Hartford, Sarah Slankard "never talked with her about her troubles" after Eva was released, and while Dr. Hunt agreed that Eva was "apparently normal as anyone," he also recalled "a time or two" when he observed her and believed she was irrational.

Edward Hickman was five years old when his mother went away to Little Rock. It is difficult to assess the impact of such incidents on one so young, but we do have some clues. He started school a year later, in Hartford, and Edward's first teacher, Mable Bright, recalled him as "a nice but peculiar boy," adept at his lessons but frequently caught up in mischief. When chastised for some prank or other, Edward would "cry out in bitterness for the rebuke, or sob outright." At such times, in Bright's opinion, he displayed "abnormal nervousness"—the same description offered by so many close acquaintances of Edward's mother and maternal grandparents.

No detailed description of his school yard mischief has survived, but years later, when Edward made headlines from coast to coast, childhood associates described some of his more unusual behavior *after* school. Several Hartford youths claimed that "a mania for capturing and torturing stray dogs and cats possessed the boy from an early age," and while those accusers remained anonymous, one girl from Edward's class provided further specifics. Mrs. C. E. Meister, a resident of Washington State when she spoke to the press, recalled that Edward "was in the habit of wringing the necks of her family's chickens." He also "took apparent delight" in strangling her pet kitten.

Whatever the truth of those stories, Edward seemed normal enough around home. He attended the Baptist church with his mother and siblings every Sunday, plus weekly prayer meetings and biweekly Bible school. Baptized at age twelve, Edward thereafter "showed great zeal and interest in all matters pertaining to religious subjects and also great zeal and interest in religious organizations." In that respect, at least—and perhaps in his treatment of animals as well— he was the spitting image of his grandfather.

Between the ages of seven and nine, Edward contracted the usual childhood diseases—measles, mumps, and whooping cough—surviving each in turn with no apparent ill effects. The same could not be said for other members of the family, however. Grandma Buck died in 1917, after four years as an invalid, and Edward's cousin Ottie followed a year later, swept away by the influenza epidemic that killed 550,000 Americans and millions more around the world. Edward himself caught the bug in 1919, but he managed to survive.

By that time, Eva and the kids were on their own, deserted by William in 1917. Accounts would differ on the reason for his bailout. Recalling the event in 1928, William testified that "We never lived together as man and wife any more after our last child was born. Of course, I was there with them all the time for three years [*sic*], but we was not like man and wife. We was just kind of like brother and sister, more than anything else." Some two months before he left, Bill recalled, Eva had resumed her habit of creeping into his room after lights-out, making him fear for his life. "I could not sleep of nights," he said. "I was uneasy all the time, afraid I would fail to wake up some time and she would muster up nerve enough to go through with what it seemed like she had on her mind to do."

Even so, Bill later claimed, he was willing to stick it out, haggard and terrified, until his siblings urged him to abandon Eva and the children. Eva treated the children much better, his brother and sisters advised him, when he was away from the house. As Bill remembered it, "They told me they believed the best thing I could do would be to get out of the way, just get up and leave her." With nothing but the best intentions, therefore, he signed the farm over to Eva and fled to New Mexico, looking for work.

Predictably, another version of the story was told by neighbors and acquaintances who did not share the Hickman bloodline: Bill had run off with his latest girlfriend, leaving Eva and the children to fend for themselves.

In retrospect, Alfred Hickman would say that Eva "tried to be" a good mother after Bill deserted her: "She made all the sacrifices she could to that extent." And yet . . .

A new physician, Dr. William Grigsby, arrived in Hartford from Oklahoma in 1918, settling on property next to Eva's and treating her occasionally as a patient. Ten years later he testified, "I wouldn't consider her absolutely [of] sound mind. She was slightly subnormal mentally." Dr. Grigsby found Eva "very emotional" and noted that her hypochondria continued. "She imagined that she had some organic trouble. . . . She talked a great deal about her trouble and her physical condition—more than a person would that would be perfectly normal mentally, I think." In fact, the only ailment Dr. Grigsby ever diagnosed in Eva was chronic constipation, but he prescribed medication "for what I thought was neurasthenia and exhaustion of the nervous system."

Part of that nervous exhaustion could have been Edward's fault, for he had turned to petty theft by age eleven, pilfering candy and other small items from shops in town, sometimes helping himself to the property of neighboring farmers. On one occasion, after he and several friends were caught with stolen watermelons, he recalled that "Mother talked to us then and told us it was wrong, and we cried." The incidents seemed trivial in 1919, merely childhood pranks, but when combined with the reports of Edward's sadism toward animals, they had the makings of a pattern—and revealed a sharp divergence from his outward Christian zeal.

Two years later, in the spring of 1921, Eva Hickman was ready to make a new start, away from Hartford and its ugly memories. She packed the children up and moved 250 miles due north, to Kansas City, Missouri.

They had some crazy little women there, according to the song. With any luck at all, one more should do just fine.

3 ✦ "An Unusually Kind, Good Boy"

Kansas City was "Tom's Town" in the 1920s, the Tom in question being Thomas Joseph Pendergast. Presiding over a ménage of gamblers, bootleggers, and politicians with their hands out, Missouri's premier political fixer was still years away from sending Harry Truman to the U.S. Senate, but he already had the local scene well in hand. If elections got rowdy from time to time, hired muscle was always available to mop up at the polls. When gambling dens and speakeasies began to operate so flagrantly that locals suffered an embarrassing attack of virtue, Pendergast himself organized the grassroots reform movement, cleaning up just enough for appearance's sake. Fugitives on the run could always cool off in K.C., though—for a price. Police were paid to look the other way, run independent operators out of town, and keep the city's blacks in line.

None of which meant anything to Eva Hickman in the spring of 1921 when she settled with her children in a modest house on Euclid Street. School was out, which gave the kids some breathing room, and they appeared to make friends easily. One of Edward's early comrades in K.C. was Vincent Doran, who lived just across the street. The two boys played together "nearly all the time," Vincent's mother later recalled, and Edward seemed well behaved.

Money was tight, but Eva found work where she could, and Bill sent small amounts of cash along from time to time. Another friend of Ed's, Don Johnstone, described the

Hickman family as living in "moderate circumstances," noting that Edward's mother "had a hard time raising him and putting him through high school." In later years, the children helped out with jobs when they could—Alfred, for example, returned to work the fields around Hartford during his summer vacations—but for the moment, Eva was glad of her break with the past. Her father's unexpected death, barely a month after she moved her brood to Kansas City, was an affirmation of the change her life had undergone.

September 2, 1921, marked the beginning of a new academic year, and Edward Hickman started school in Kansas City as a "pre-freshman" at Central Junior High. The school was housed within Central High School—K.C.'s largest, with an average enrollment of 2,500 students per year—and it must have been a shock to Edward, after the modest facilities in Hartford. It might have daunted some, but Edward took to Central like a duck to water, making an instant impression on all who knew him. Don Johnstone recalled Ed as "one of the most popular students in school," while classmate Baylor Sutton described him as "very steady and [a] faithful plugger." John Proudfit claimed to know Edward in "an intimate way, I should say," calling him "a leader among the boys" who "mixed as well as the average boy does." Howard Hibbs found him "a very steady person and a brilliant student." Joe Tiffany noted Edward's "brilliant record as a student and a leader." Another classmate, C. M. McFarland, led the field in superlatives: "As a student, Mr. Hickman was the most upright student that I have ever become acquainted with. At all times he attended to his duties, and was recognized by the students as being a brilliant scholar. He was known to study hard, and was known to be morally straight. His actions at no time indicated otherwise."

The faculty at Central Junior High agreed. Edward seemed "greatly interested" in his schoolwork, and he finished out the year with perfect attendance and straight E's (for "excellent")—the equivalent of a 4.0 grade point average.

Brilliant. Steady. Upright. Morally straight.

It was a far cry from Hartford, where Edward was known to his teachers and classmates as "nice but peculiar," "abnormally nervous," a strangler of kittens and hens. From all appearances, the boy was making progress.

One thing that did follow Ed from Hartford to K.C., though, was his interest in religion. He remained a steady churchgoer, and joined the Boys High School Club—Hi-Y, sponsored by the YMCA—at the start of his freshman year, quickly winning election as a club officer. There is no indication that his petty thievery continued while Edward was enrolled at Central High.

Marion Huscher recalled Ed fondly as a pupil in his mechanical drawing class. "He was an excellent student and attended to his own business," Huscher said. "He didn't give me any trouble at all." A test administered in April 1923 pegged Ed's I.Q. at 111, which placed him in the "superior" range. After hours, he remained involved with the Hi-Y Club, and Sunday mornings found him listening attentively in church.

Sometime during 1923, Ed's father visited his family in Kansas City. Bill was divorced from Eva by that time and had remarried in New Mexico. We have no details of that visit, but five years later, on the witness stand, he insisted that he had found Eva "still insane."

Edward was fifteen years old at the beginning of his sophomore year, in September 1923, and his final grade point average would slip a fraction of a point that year, from 4.0 to 3.9, after he received a G (for "good") in one of his classes. While brother Alfred recalled "a very slight drop in [Edward's] scholastic standing" as a sophomore, he also noted that "that was very well made up after the opening or beginning of the extracurricular activities." Besides the Student Council and Hi-Y Club, Edward was "very prominent" in the Central Webster Club, according to fellow member Joe Tiffany, and he still had time for the Central Thucydides Club (named for the Greek historian, c. 460–400 B.C.).

In the summer following his sophomore year, despite excellent grades, Edward apparently flirted with the notion of quitting school to work full-time. He had a summer job at James Parker's grocery store on Woodland Avenue, and Parker recalled him as "an awful good boy, just about the best boy I ever had." In fact, Ed fell short on the job in only one respect—an ironic failure, in light of statements from childhood acquaintances in Arkansas. "There was one thing that he would not do," Parker said years later. "He would not kill a chicken. It was that boy's place to kill chickens and dress them, and he would not do that." Instead of firing Edward, however, Parker kept him on and gave the killing chores to another youth, who "liked to do it." When summer ended, Parker said, "I hated to see him leave. He wanted to stay and work and make money to help his mother on, but his mother wanted him to go to school and get a schooling, an education. That is the reason he left."

Going into his junior year at Central, Edward was described by sidekick Howard Hibbs as "a happy, carefree, normal boy in every respect." Both boys remained active in the Hi-Y Club and the Central Webster Literary Club, while Edward also cultivated membership in the Classics Club and a spot on the staff of Central's yearbook, the *Centralian*. In May 1925, despite another slip in his GPA, to 3.3—the equivalent of a B+ average—Ed was elected president of Central High's National Honor Society chapter, one of only five juniors who rated membership. In the spare time remaining to him, Hickman also joined the football team.

Summing up Ed's junior year, Principal Otto Dubach later said, "We judged him to be rather sensitive." Pressed for an explanation of that diagnosis, Dubach could not be specific, "except he seemed to be rather sensitive about his winning and losing."

Nowhere was that sensitivity more evident than in Edward's interest in forensics, as a member of the Central High debating team. Alfred Richmond, who coached that team during Ed's junior year, recalled, "There is nothing in my memory that would designate him as being any different from the average pupil, with the possible exception of one thing. In our successes through our debating work, it was my observation that he did not respond to these successes as the other boys did." More specifically, Richmond noted that Edward "did not seem to get the enjoyment of self-satisfaction out of his winning, as some of the other boys seemed to do. That seemed to be—I don't know whether you would call it an emotional state or not." Still, Richmond conceded, "as far as preparatory work is concerned, he worked slavishly and promptly. He did his work excellently, but after the whole thing was over, it did not seem to satisfy him, as I remember the case."

Charles Edwards, a former chief of police, recalled Ed Hickman visiting his home almost daily, befriending Edwards's son (also named Charles), and frequently discussing his progress on the debate team. Chief Edwards had attended some of the debates and was impressed enough to lend the team a hand, arranging appearances before the K.C. Chamber of Commerce and the Sanford Brown Post of the American Legion. Edward Hickman seemed to enjoy the experience, and it helped him prepare for the intramural debates in March 1925, when his team trounced Manual High School on the topic of Philippine independence.

The real focus of Edward's attention that spring, however, was the upcoming National Constitutional Oratorical Contest, sponsored yearly since 1895 by the *Kansas City Star*. School competitions offered only medals to the victor, but the *Star* was offering $500 for top honors for a speech entitled "The Higher Patriotism." Members of eight literary societies at Central High would compete for the cash, in what Don Johnstone called "the biggest event of the year." Ed won the competition in the Webster Club—beating even his brother Alfred—to represent that body in the finals, although his close friends later disagreed about his aim. Howard Hibbs thought Edward entered the contest "not with the idea of winning but rather with the idea of gaining experience for the following year." John Proudfit, conversely, found Hickman "possessed of great ambition to win the contest."

In fact, Ed was so intent on winning that he started making preparations for the contest a full year in advance. Rebecca Tomlin, a teacher at Central, had coached the winner in Ed's sophomore year, and Hickman approached her that spring, asking her to help him prepare for next year. "You know," he told her, "Al and I will have to dig for ourselves when we start in to the university, because we haven't got a dad to help us, and I would like to make some money, if I could do it, toward my college education."

Tomlin agreed to help out, and Edward came back in the fall of 1925 with a prepared speech, ready for coaching. Tomlin recalled him as "a very serious, constant worker," although he "had some very peculiar little habits. He was overanxious, you see, to get his delivery down to a fine point. He was nervous. He gesticulated too much. He moved about the stage too much. He was too nervous about the whole thing, and I tried to stop that." In Tomlin's view, the cash prize offered by the *Star* put undue pressure on contestants, creating "too much rivalry among the boys."

Not satisfied with just one opinion, Ed tried his speech out on Chief Edwards's wife, not once but several times. "I said I thought it was very good," Mrs. Edwards recalled, "but I did tell him I thought his size was against him, because he was so short."

Such criticism failed to make a dent in Hickman's zeal. Brother Alfred noted that Ed's practice for the intersociety contest involved "more time than he spent on his own studies, taken up not only [by] his own efforts but by coaching and everything of that sort, and just absolutely trying to win those things, daily building up for it." Classmate Don Johnstone agreed: "I know [Ed] spent many hours of work on this night and day, in addition to his lessons, and really seemed to have worked too hard. It seemed to be his one interest of that year, was the winning of that contest. He was completely wrapped up in it."

All in vain.

In the finals that April, Edward faced "a very brilliant orator at Central," and came in second best. He regarded his five-dollar prize as a virtual slap in the face.

All of Ed's friends and relatives marked a dramatic change in his character, beginning from the moment of his public embarrassment. Don Johnstone found him "very much crushed" but "thought he would get over it right away." That didn't happen, though, and while his friends tried to cheer Edward up, Johnstone recalled that "he seemed to feel that he was out."

Mrs. Edwards also noted the change, remarking that Edward seemed "very much depressed" in the wake of his loss, which had "cut him terribly." She later testified that "From that time, it seemed to me he avoided the companionship that he had been enjoying with the boys that came to our house. He would come as far as the steps and then go on home, just as if he didn't want to mingle with the boys any more."

Alfred Hickman also noted the change in his brother. "After that event," Al said, "he seemed to adopt the feeling that, well, 'Not much use for me to try to do anything, anyhow; I guess I really wasn't meant to do these things.' He became much more reserved in his actions and in his dealings with other people. He seemed to want to be more by himself, and spent more of his time in studying over things, which I thought was a great change in his conduct and in his feelings."

Reserved he may have been, but Edward was not giving up, by any means. Howard Hibbs recalled that "After he was defeated in this contest he worked like a Trojan, starting in immediately to prepare for the following year, to prepare for this oratorical work, and for his constitutional oration work."

Edward found another summer job in 1925, taking tickets in a dance hall at Winwood Beach, but he felt no strong attraction to the work, as he had at Parker's grocery. When September rolled around, he was anxious for school to resume. Eager to pursue the dream deferred.

At first glance, it may have seemed that Edward had recovered from his April disappointment. Back at Central for his senior year, he went to work for the student newspaper, the *Luminary*, and was chosen to serve as business manager, soliciting ads. Edward also resumed his work on the *Centralian*, the school's yearbook. G. Leslie Smith, who taught printing at Central from 1922 through 1926, recalled that Hickman "had a brilliant turn of mind and won his position on the *Centralian* staff by competition in which his requirements were the submitting of written papers." A panel of three teachers had selected Ed's work over that of several other competitors.

If those activities were not enough to demonstrate school spirit, Edward also served on the Student Council for the third straight year and was elected vice president of the senior class. He made the football squad again, but played for only "a short time," before dropping out.

Of course, the football team was not the only thing Ed quit that year. On closer examination, it is evident that he was disconnecting from his former life, piece by piece, one step at a time.

The clubs went first. Edward was elected secretary of the Hi-Y Club during his senior year, but he held that office only briefly. That fall, he attended a YMCA gathering at Washita, and returned in a funk. "After that time," Don Johnstone recalled, "his interest dropped completely in the organization and he did no work as secretary. After about ten weeks I was required to ask for his resignation, and did so in a very matter-of-fact way, letting him know at the same time that nobody personally held anything against him, but right away he became enraged. That was the first time I had seen him lose his temper. He snatched a pen and wrote a very fiery note of resignation, saying that he hated the whole damn bunch, not personally but as an organization, and thought we were all hypocrites. The reason the note sticks in my mind is that I showed it to two or three other members, and all of us decided that it was of such a nature that we shouldn't make it public. So we destroyed the note and wrote out a formal resignation for him to sign."

Fellow Hi-Y member Howard Hibbs had another take on Ed's split from the group. "He told me that he did not seem to be able to get along with the adviser or the club," Hibbs said, "and that the adviser had something against him, although I don't believe it was so, by any manner or means, and he was rather, well, just plain sore, and took it out in this letter that he wrote to the adviser of the club and offered his resignation from office." As for the offending note itself, Hibbs said, "He wrote a letter to the secretary [sic], which the secretary handed to the president, Don Johnstone, and which was read to the members of the inner circle, instead of the adviser to the club, because of the nature of the letter. The letter was totally unnecessary, I believe . . . and declared that the members of the club were hypocrites, not being the true Christians they professed to be in the club, and . . . he seemed to denote this by his rather surly attitude, which cropped out at times."

Yet another view of the Hi-Y split comes from C. S. Matthews, a Central High junior who "never was very familiar" with Hickman, but knew him from club meetings. According to Matthews, "Ed had very high ideals." In one of their brief conversations, he recalled, "Hickman stated that he did not think he could live up to the ideals of the club, and he didn't think he ought to remain a member."

Around the same time, Edward also parted company with the Webster Club. Fellow member Joe Tiffany recalled, "Ed was very prominent there the first year and a half that he was a member, and was elected president for the senior year. Then, shortly after that, he dropped out of the club for the reason of lack of interest, as far as I know, and didn't become a member again until about March or April 1926. In other words, he was out four or five months; then he became a member again, more at the insistence of several friends who were members than because of any desire of his own."

Or perhaps because club membership was required to participate in the *Star*'s annual speech contest.

Hickman's off-and-on relationship with clubs he once found fascinating was a symptom of his altered personality. Howard Hibbs tried to nail down the source of the change. "In September 1925," he said, "when we entered upon our senior year together, there seemed to be something different about him. He was not the same carefree boy. He seemed to be worried and rather brooding at times, and that change, I believe, took place some time during the summer. What he did during the summer, I don't know. But it seems to me that he did grow more and more so . . . , this becoming noticeable in a series of incidents which occurred during his senior year, his apparent lack of interest in some things, and noticeable interest in others."

Girls, for instance. Baylor Sutton noted that Edward "very seldom" spent time with female classmates. Otto Dubach agreed, later testifying that Ed "didn't have what we would call in school serious cases. He went with girls occasionally." Pressed for names, Dubach cited three, including a junior clerk on the *Luminary* staff, but insisted that Hickman "didn't go with any girl regularly." Howard Hibbs disagreed with the majority view, noting that during his senior year Edward "was interested in a young lady at Central." However, Hibbs noted, "That interest seemed to grow less and less, and the split came, and this seemed to affect him a great deal, although he did not mention it so much to me."

Hickman himself would comment on his love life for the first time in December 1927, following his arrest on murder charges. In a written statement to police, he claimed to be a virgin, noting, "I have never been in any corrupt conduct with the female sex." A month later he told Dr. Victor Parkin, a court-appointed psychiatrist, "Last year in high school, for a short time, I was in love with a girl. I got jealous of her, because she had so many other fellows." Those statements notwithstanding, another psychiatrist, Dr. Thomas Orbison, told the court in 1928 that Edward "had an ordinary sex life, perfectly ordinary, no suppressions or complexes or anything of that nature." As to whom he may have had that "ordinary sex life" *with*, there was no clue.

Some of the changes displayed by Edward in his senior year looked like the Buck bloodline asserting itself: "surly" moods and depression, "nervousness," an unsupported sense that others "had it in for him." Aside from his humiliation in the April 1925 speech contest and his breakup with the unnamed girlfriend, though, there was at least one other source of stress in Edward's life that year. Across the street, his good friend Vincent Doran had been diagnosed with tuberculosis in 1924. He was bedridden by October 1925 with barely four months to live. Edward visited as often as he could, Vincent's health permitting, and on his final visit, he presented Vincent with his favorite ukelele as a kind of parting gift. Vincent died on February 22, 1926. Two years later, with Edward on trial for his life, Vincent's mother still recalled their neighbor's "gentle, kind, loving personality." "As near as I know," she said under oath, "he was an unusually kind, good boy."

At school however, Edward's personality change produced some uncharacteristic behavior. He signed up for Alfred Richmond's course in commercial law, but the Central High debating coach barely recognized his former star pupil. "His attitude in the class was not the same as . . . before," Richmond said. "I—it worried me somewhat, because I expected of an E student better work, and I talked to him several times about it, and went to his brother on some two or three different occasions and asked him what he could do, what was the matter with Ed that he wasn't doing better work. Now, I can't say whether that was due to any particular change, but at least there was a reaction in my work. Instead of the promptness that he had always displayed in his other work, he was now indifferent."

That indifference resulted in Edward receiving a grade of P+ in Richmond's class, the equivalent of a D. It was the worst grade of his academic life, to date.

If Ed was indifferent to commercial law, he seemed to be fascinated by chemistry, but even there his interest took a peculiar turn. Joe Tiffany later testified, "There was one thing Mr. Hickman did in the last year that was rather queer. He was taking chemistry, and he carried a little box about two inches by four inches by two inches, full of little vials of chemicals, and he kept that down in the *Luminary* office—the school paper. And we asked him time after time what he wanted with it, but he always evaded the question, and said he was going to play around in chemistry. We objected to it because it created an awful odor."

Ed may have been interested in "playing around" with chemistry, but he was obsessed with the *Star*'s oratorical contest. "When he came back to school in the fall of 1925," Don Johnstone said, "he seemed to cease to be interested in anything but that. He spent practically all of his spare time on it. He had been very interested in athletics and sports, but he dropped this and paid more attention to working on that oratorical contest." At the same time, however, Johnstone remembered Ed's sense of futility. "I don't think it will do any good," Hickman remarked on one occasion, prompting Johnstone to conclude that he was "rather irrational."

Howard Hibbs saw just the opposite attitude, remarking that Edward "had a pretty definite notion he would win" the contest in his senior year. The topic was "French Pioneers of America," and while Ed, coached once more by Rebecca Tomlin, made it to the finals, the showdown on April 16, 1926, saw him relegated to second place once again, pocketing a five-dollar prize while the winner walked off with five hundred.

Classmates and teachers at Central High disagreed about Ed's reaction to the loss. John Proudfit recalled that Hickman "seemed perfectly satisfied that the best man had won the contest." Howard Hibbs would later say that Edward kept his feelings to himself, "but his general attitude was probably the main evidence of his disappointment." Joe Tiffany, meanwhile, found Edward "much disappointed" by his defeat, while Don Johnstone noted the most dramatic reaction of all. "It seemed to affect him—depress him," Johnstone said. "Hickman told me several times afterward that it seemed as if he wasn't good for anything."

Baylor Sutton found Ed "somewhat crushed" by his loss, but viewed the reaction as simply part of Hickman's personality. "He seemed to take things a great deal more seriously than the rest of us," Sutton recalled. "If we failed, we just let it go and thought we would take it up some other time. He thought it was a failure, and talked about it for quite a length of time." In fact, Sutton regarded Edward as "eccentric" before the *Star* contest, and decided he was "crazy" after his final defeat.

In the wake of the contest, Rebecca Tomlin said, "[Edward] avoided me. I suppose it was because of his extreme disappointment." Still, she blamed the system more than Edward. "The winner in those contests is the hero of the school," she said. "I am sorry to say that there is too much emphasis, I really believe, placed on it for the good of the boys."

In any case, it seemed to be the final straw. Don Johnstone noted a "very pronounced" change in Edward's demeanor. "I believe that in his senior year he was a great deal more reserved," Johnstone said. "Where formerly he seemed to want companionship, he rather drew away and was retiring and serious-minded."

Baylor Sutton also noted the change: "In his first three years [at Central] he was regular in his attendance and high in his scholastic record, and very popular. And during his [last] year his attendance was very irregular and his grades suffered, and his popularity decreased." Overall, Sutton testified, Edward "neglected his schoolwork, his school attendance, his friends, and his jobs." John Proudfit recalled that in those months Edward's "interests seemed to be different than they had been during previous years," and Joe Tiffany noted that "His restlessness was apparently shifting from job to job, but I learned that from others."

Alfred Richmond said of Edward, "It is unusual for a boy of that type to make that sudden change, and for that reason I was worried about it, as the average teacher, I think, is, when they know they are not getting the best out of the students, and having done E work for me the whole year."

Rebecca Tomlin, meanwhile, clung to her high opinion of Edward. "Had I been asked to pick out the five finest Central graduates of that class of boys, the boys with the finest prospects, the best minds, and the highest principles," she said, "I would have chosen Edward as one of the five."

Edward did graduate in June, although his grades had slipped dramatically. Instead of straight E's, he boasted only two, with four G's and one P dragging his average down to an all-time low of 3.0—equivalent to a B. There was stinging irony in his selection by senior classmates as Best Boy Orator of the year.

Edward had been thinking of his future long before graduation, as evidenced by his conversations with Rebecca Tomlin. When the dream of winning his college tuition from the *Kansas City Star* fell through, he tried another tack, approaching Chief Charles Edwards for help. "In April 1926," Edwards later recalled, "he came to see me and said that he would like to continue his education, but he said, 'I have no money.' And I said, 'Well, Edward, go up to Park College. I lecture up there a little, and if you would like to go to Park College, I will see what I can do to get you in there.' "

Park College was a local institution that prepared students for the ministry, among other careers. It catered to the poor and charged no tuition, but students were required to work half-days, a system that stretched the normal four-year curriculum out over eight years of study. Edward promptly agreed to the plan, and Chief Edwards wrote a letter to Dean Walter Sanders on May 19, 1926:

Dear Sir:

   With reference to Edward Hickman, I am glad to state that I have known this young man for about five years and have become well acquainted with him. During this time his character and standing in the community have been above reproach.

   Edward is a hard worker and ambitious to improve himself. I know him to be an honest, upright, clean living, Christian young man. He will be a student of whom Park College will be proud. Any assistance you can give him will be well deserved.

Dean Sanders wrote back to Edwards a week later, on May 26.

My Dear Mr. Edwards:

Permit me to acknowledge your letter of recent date with reference to Edward Hickman. We are very much interested in this young man, and if possible we shall attempt to make room for him next year. As you probably know, we have a long waiting list and it became necessary for us frequently to refuse young men who are very worthy.

I am sending under separate cover a recent copy of our catalog.

Very truly yours,
W. F. Sanders, Dean

Despite the hopeful tone of that response—and a curious note in Edward's Kansas City school records, claiming that he "entered Park College on 6/24/26"—Chief Edwards remembered that "when I told him to make arrangements to go up [to Park], he decided he didn't want to go." The reason: "He said that that would be too long; eight years was too long, he thought."

It was the first sign of the change Chief Edwards noted in the boy who had always been so steady and dependable. "The only thing I noticed," Edwards later testified, "would be that he was restless, inasmuch as he would come over to talk to me about his future, and when I would go ahead and arrange for him to do something, he would back out." Park College was only the beginning. "I couldn't seem to get him to center on any one thing," Edwards said. "As soon as I would line up something for him, he would turn it down. He didn't seem to know what he wanted to do."

Park College had appealed to Edward, at least in part, for the theology courses it offered. Baylor Sutton recalled that

Ed "was going to be a minister at one time." Don Johnstone had a similar memory: "He first thought of going to college and entering the ministry. Then he got another job, and then he dropped it, and from that time on [he] switched from one thing to another."

Within two weeks of hearing from Dean Sanders, Chief Edwards received another letter concerning Ed Hickman. This one was dated June 9, addressed to Edwards from the Schmelzer Company, a Kansas City sporting goods distributor.

Dear Sir:

Edward Hickman, 3524 Euclid Avenue, has applied to us for a position, and has given us your name as a reference, as to his character, ability, etc.

We would greatly appreciate any information you may be able to give us concerning this party, and assure you that same will be held strictly confidential. . . .

Yours very truly,
The Schmelzer Company
M. Stipp
General Office

Chief Edwards replied on June 11, with a virtual carbon copy of his earlier note to Dean Sanders at Park College.

Gentlemen:

In reply to your communication of June 9, in regard to Edward Hickman, who has applied to you for a position, [I] have to advise you that I have known this young man for about five years, and have become well acquainted with him. During this time his character and standing in the community have been above reproach.

Edward is a hard worker and ambitious to improve himself. I know him to be an honest, upright, clean living Christian young man. Believe he would prove efficient in whatever department you might place him. Any assistance you can give him will be well deserved.

In fact, according to subsequent testimony from Charles Harper, office manager for the Schmelzer Company, Edward had been hired on June 8, had held the job for one day less than two months, and then had resigned for unspecified reasons on August 7, 1926. Chief Edwards would later recall the Schmelzer job as one of "at least six" for which he provided glowing references over the next six months.

Ed's friends from Central High were also conscious of his seeming inability to hold a job that summer. From Schmelzer's, he shifted to a local restaurant, the Unity Inn, then quit after two weeks "for no apparent reason." Don Johnstone recalled that Ed "bought and sold cars" for a while, and it was during this time that Baylor Sutton became convinced that his onetime classmate was "absolutely insane."

Sutton later testified, that Edward "came out in a Ford coupe, which he had just bought, and he was hard up, and I thought he was going to enter Park College. Then he told me he wasn't, and he said he didn't have enough money. I told him I thought it was a free institution, that he could enter and pay his way by working. And that night we went over to Chief Edwards's house, and then [Edward] said he was going to sell his Ford. He had just bought it a couple of days before, and paid all the money he had for it, and all he had saved up of his savings—just wanted to get rid of it. At that time is when I began to think he was off."

Sometime late in August 1926, moonlighting as a life insurance salesman, Alfred Richmond visited the Hickman home to speak with Ed and Alfred. It was an easy sale—both boys purchased small policies—but Richmond was struck by Edward's curious behavior.

"We began to talk on the subject of college," Richmond testified in 1928, "and I was interested in the boys. They asked me for advice, what I thought probably would be the best place for them to go to college, and Al, of course, was settled—that is, he had a definite thing to do—but Ed was undecided. But I attempted to work out his problem, and it was during this course of probably over two hours that we spent on that subject that I observed certain reactions in Ed that I had never observed before. He didn't know what he wanted to do and didn't know what college he wanted to attend. Al and I would start working out the proposition, and while we were getting it partly worked out, Ed would go over to one side of the room, apparently fingering a book. . . . He would then come back and ask two or three intelligent questions, and then walk away over to one side of the room and to the other side. He did this repeatedly, throughout the entire evening, when we would be trying to decide something. He was evidently so undecided in his own mind, I would term it—he was having some sort of a conflict in his mind—he was under, or in a state of indecision."

At length, Richmond said, "We finally decided that the best place would be [Kansas City] Junior College," a part of the public school system. According to subsequent testimony from President Edward Bainter, Hickman entered the junior college on September 7, 1926, and lasted exactly nine days. He failed to report for classes on Monday, September 20, and his file was marked "withdrawn on account of absence" one week later.

Unknown to his professors, Edward had returned to work at the Schmelzer Company on September 20, working half days, but that was another false start, and he quit for good on October 1. Three days later he went to work at the Kansas City Public Library, also part-time, where the chief of staff, Grace Hudson, recalled that he was "supposed to be going to junior college." Baylor Sutton, who had seen Ed once at the library, recalled that "he seemed to have his whole heart in it, but then he gave it up immediately." He was gone by October 23, after less than three weeks on the job. As Grace Hudson remembered it, "He left us to go to the Kiger Jewelry Company because he wanted all-day work."

Ed had changed directions once again, this time with the assistance of J. L. Laughlin, the vice principal of Central High. Laughlin later recalled that he had received a call from Kiger Jewelry, a local wholesaler, who asked him "to send one of our graduates, one of the best boys I could," to fill a job opening. Days earlier, by chance, Laughlin had met Alfred Hickman on the street and had learned that Edward intended to drop out of college. "So when this call came to me," Laughlin said, "I felt that Ed would be a fine boy for the position; and knowing that he expected to quit school, I called Al Hickman up and asked him to send Ed to this company."

Ed got the job, and Baylor Sutton saw him again, a few days later. "I was going to school on the streetcar one morning," Sutton said, "and I saw him on the car and asked him where he was working. He said he was working at Kiger's jewelry store, and I asked him how he liked it, and he said, 'Fine.' Then he quit four or five days after that." Perhaps embarrassed, J. L. Laughlin came looking for answers. "I asked him why he quit that jewelry company, and he said he quit because of the morals of some of the men over him. He said they drank and gambled, and he didn't want to be mixed up with that kind of people."

The truth was rather different, though. During his brief employment at the library, Edward had become acquainted with a fellow worker, Welby Hunt, a high school dropout four years his junior. They had nothing in common, but still hit it off. By the time Ed quit his job at Kiger's, they were hanging out together regularly, and they were up to no good. Ed's brother Alfred later remarked that he saw Welby Hunt only once—"for about five minutes" in the fall of 1926—but the new friendship would have a profound effect on Edward's life.

By the time November rolled around, Ed Hickman was unemployed and going nowhere fast. His uncle Tom Lewis later testified under oath that Ed joined his mother and sister for a holiday visit to Hartford, arriving in plenty of time for Thanksgiving dinner on November 25. According to Lewis, the trio stayed for "three or four days or a week," which included a jaunt to Fort Smith. Tom took the opportunity to note that his sister-in-law was "still insane."

As certain as he was, however, there is a problem with Lewis's testimony. Ed Hickman himself later admitted to being in Kansas City on Friday, November 26. He recalled the date particularly, since it marked the occasion of his first armed robbery.

"I went out with two fellows in Kansas City," Hickman later told police. "Welby Hunt and I went to a confectionery store and held up a woman with guns and got seventy dollars, the other fellow sitting in the car. We made a clean getaway."

He needed money for the road.

A few days later, sometime in the first week of December 1926, Hickman and Hunt put Kansas City behind them. They had wheels and guns, a little money, and the nerve to pick up more, if they ran short. Ed was out on his own for the first time in his life.

Headed west.

4 ✦ Easy Money

California was the dream. America had coveted the future Golden State enough to fight a two-year war with Mexico for ownership, and it had paid off with the discovery of gold at Sutter's Mill. The wagon trains and railroads, Model Ts and buses had been rolling westward ever since, bringing new pilgrims to the nation's last frontier. Sunshine and palm trees. Beaches. Orange groves. Earthquakes. Hollywood.

Los Angeles was still a sleepy pueblo when the mass migration started, back in 1849. Even then, the town was spared the worst of the gold rush, boasting a population of less than 12,000 souls in 1883, when the Southern Pacific railroad arrived. That changed everything, with a national advertising campaign and tickets as cheap as one dollar enticing thousands of tourists, would-be settlers, and shady land speculators. By 1887, the population of L.A. was climbing toward 100,000 and real estate sales had broken the $100 *million* mark.

That human flood continued for the next three decades. Overwhelmingly Caucasian, Protestant, and Midwestern, L.A. would become the "white spot" of the nation, tolerating its minorities as cheap labor and "local color" without permitting them to rock the boat. The native Indians and Mexicans had learned that lesson in the 1840s. Asian immigrants were forcefully reminded of it in the Chinatown Massacre of 1871. If residents of color happened to forget their place in future, the "regulators" were always happy to instruct them in the facts of life. And after 1881, those lessons would be taught officially, by members of the new Los Angeles Police Department.

Despite its later reputation as a launching pad for motorcycle gangs, new drugs, and spaced-out cults, Los Angeles—at least, behind the flash and glare of Hollywood—was for decades an ultraconservative city. In 1902, voters overwhelmingly supported an ordinance limiting the number of saloons to two hundred. By 1913, a law banning sex between unmarried adults had passed and was strictly enforced. Civic groups like the Anti–Saloon League, the Anti–Racetrack Gambling League, and the Sunday Rest League hounded LAPD to enforce midwestern morality at any cost. William Huntington Wright, writing for *Smart Set* in 1913, described L.A. as possessed of "a stupid censorship so incredibly puerile that even Boston will have to take second place. . . . Los Angeles is overrun with militant moralists, connoisseurs of sin, experts of biological purity." Sixteen years later, in a successful race for mayor, Iowa transplant John Porter would take such criticism as praise, describing his city as "the last stand of native-born Protestant Americans."

It sounded perfect to a boy who found the Central Hi-Y club too sinful for his taste.

We have no record of the path Ed Hickman and his traveling companion followed on their trek from Kansas City to the coast. Welby Hunt thought the trip took "about a month, or maybe a little better," but only one incident stuck out in his mind. "I don't know the conversation, how it came up," he testified in 1928, "but [Edward] made the statement one time that it was his wish to get someone and chop them up all in little pieces, he said, and throw them along the highway, I believe was the words he used." Fourteen months later Hunt could not recall his answer to that startling admission, but he said, "I just thought it was a foolish idea myself, and I didn't really think he took it seriously."

Upon arriving in Los Angeles, the boys made a beeline for suburban Alhambra, in the San Gabriel Valley, where

Hunt's maternal grandparents lived. A. R. Driskell and his wife, Connie, welcomed the new arrivals into their home on Birch Street. Any friend of Welby's was a friend of theirs. Ed Hickman, meanwhile, had kept in touch with his mother "often, all along while he was gone," and after settling with the Driskells in Alhambra, he sent another letter off to her "most every week."

He did not tell her everything that he was up to, though.

Sometime before Christmas Eve, Hickman and Hunt began prowling L.A., casing targets, looking for someplace to score. They rented a room at the Alto Hotel to serve as their base of operations, keeping Hunt's grandparents out of the loop. By December 24, they were starting to get anxious, ready to try anything.

"We needed money," Edward later told police, "and that afternoon we saw this place as we drove by, and we said we would come back and get it that night."

"This place" was a pharmacy owned and operated by Clarence Ivy Thoms, known as Ivy, in the L.A. neighborhood of Rose Hill. It was a lucky break to find the shop still open when they came back after dark on Christmas Eve.

Lucky for Hunt and Hickman, anyway.

On this job, they had no driver to wait outside, so both teenage bandits went into the store, wearing masks, waving pistols. They found Thoms and his wife still at work, three customers waiting for prescriptions to be filled. Talking tough and brandishing their weapons, Ed and Welby herded their startled captives toward the rear of the shop.

"There were two doors in the back of the store," Hickman later recalled, "one on each side, and my partner went through the door to the right. Welby Hunt backed the druggist and his wife ahead of him, and I went through the door to the left with the customers, forcing them inside the little room in the back of the store."

And found LAPD Patrolman D. J. Oliver waiting for them there. The beat cop had stopped in to say hello, a common practice in those bygone days when most of L.A.'s Finest still patrolled the town on foot. Today the visit might be termed community relations. On that Christmas Eve in 1926 it spelled disaster.

Edward got the drop on Oliver, had him covered when Welby arrived on the scene. Ed told his partner to disarm the cop, and Hunt was stepping forward to obey the order when the whole thing went to hell.

Oliver pretended to surrender, half-raising his hands, then whipped out his .38-caliber service revolver. Hunt was closer, and the patrolman fired at him first, jerking the trigger, forgetting to squeeze, as they had taught him on the pistol range, firing two shots at one target before he swung toward the other.

"He started firing his gun at me," Hickman said, "and just at the same time I started firing at him, and Welby Hunt started firing. I was firing directly at the policeman, as far as I knew, and I judged that Welby Hunt was firing at the policeman, although I did not have time to watch him."

Edward was too busy running out through the front of the shop, Welby lurching behind him. They both fired more rounds toward the back room of the pharmacy, stalling pursuit before they fled into the night. One of their bullets struck Patrolman Oliver in the abdomen; another drilled Ivy Thoms through the chest, mortally wounding him.

Welby was whimpering and moaning by the time they reached the Alto Hotel, slipping in the back way to avoid the clerk. Ed helped his sidekick remove his shirt and jacket, which were stained with blood. On Welby Hunt's right shoulder, there were superficial scratches from a bullet graze, but a second round had drilled through his left shoulder.

Ed had to clean and bind the wound, a through-and-through, because physicians, then as now, were required by law to report bullet wounds. He must have done a fairly decent job, since Welby Hunt survived and suffered no long-term disability. We have no details of his convalescence, but Hunt was apparently able to conceal his wound from the Driskells and get on with daily life.

Back in Alhambra, while his partner healed, Ed Hickman was becoming a familiar face among his Birch Street neighbors and the local merchants. He shopped often in M. K. Wadley's Main Street grocery and was a regular at Walter Price's service station. Next-door neighbor Frank Thompson, like everyone else who met Hickman that winter, deemed Edward normal "from his general appearance and conversation." A cousin of Mrs. Driskell's, Percy Beck, saw Edward often at the house on Birch Street, sometimes playing cards with him, and later told the court, "I always considered him an exceptionally bright young man."

Of course, they didn't know about the robberies—and now the murder—that Edward and Welby had committed.

Soon after the Rose Hill fiasco, Hickman and Hunt decided to try their hand at honest work, more or less. On January 18, 1927, both young men were hired as pages for the First National Trust and Savings Bank at the corner of Seventh and Spring in downtown L.A. They were assigned to do a little bit of everything: run errands, carry messages, sometimes stamp checks for the tellers.

Hickman had once again used Chief Edwards as a reference, and Edwards soon received a letter from one George Nern, manager of the bank's employment division, inquiring into Hickman's character. Chief Edwards wrote back to Nern on January 22, with a response virtually identical to his other wasted letters of recommendation. By that time, Ed was already on the job, surrounded by money.

No one who encountered him at work found Edward strange, or even worthy of a second glance. His immediate superior, head page Mark Traugott, later told the court, "I was with him every day while he was at the bank." As for his demeanor, Traugott said, "At the time I knew him, he was sane." Assistant teller Edward Brewster agreed, having watched Hickman stamp checks in his cage "every day for a couple of hours." L. S. Gilhousen, an assistant cashier at First National, who recalled that "I would see him come and go most every day," concluded from Hickman's demeanor that he possessed "more than average intelligence." The bank's assistant chief clerk, Walter Rappold, likewise observed Hickman "every day at various intervals." A year later he would testify that "During my contact with him he always conducted himself in a very normal and sane manner."

One must wonder if Rappold's boss, chief clerk Perry Parker, even noticed Edward. He had more important things on his mind than watching the pages. It is doubtful that he would have known Ed Hickman if they had met each other on the street. A Los Angeles resident from early childhood, transplanted with his family in 1887, Parker had graduated from high school in 1901 and had gone to work at First National soon afterward. He enjoyed working with numbers, moving money, secure within his office, and he rose steadily through the ranks during twenty-six years of loyal service. Parker and his wife, son, and twin daughters by 1927 were comfortable rather than wealthy.

By early April, Edward had once again begun to hear the siren song of easy money. He started forging checks—small sums, nothing that would attract attention. Forgery was safer than armed robbery—perhaps too safe for one who had enjoyed the thrill of blazing guns and running for his life. Still, there were other ways of getting cash that coupled kicks with the reward.

On May 24, A. R. Driskell withdrew a "large sum" of money from the bank where his grandson, Welby Hunt, was employed. Bright and early the next morning, Driskell's broken body was found beneath the Colorado Street bridge in Pasadena, a suicide hot-spot with several high dives in its history. Driskell's money was gone, and he had explained his sudden exit in five suicide notes—something of a local record, with one found on the bridge above his corpse, four others in his pockets. The messages alluded to financial problems that had lately spun out of control, but there was something odd about the notes: it was evident to police graphologists that they were produced by two different hands.

Driskell's death was peculiar, at best, but LAPD had more pressing concerns in the Roaring Twenties. Another seven months would pass before investigators sought an alternative author for the suicide notes, announcing that some of the numerals, at least, had been penned by Edward Hickman.

On June 10, flush with cash from one source or another, Ed purchased a .380-caliber automatic pistol from a pawnshop on South Main Street. He gave his name as Albert Matthews, with a false address on Bronson Avenue. A short time later, three blocks down the street, he bought a 6.35mm Spanish revolver from the Herden Hardware Company, this time giving his true name and address.

Four days later the roof fell in.

Unknown to Edward, the accountants at First National had finally noted his illicit withdrawals—more than a dozen bogus checks, some $400 overall—and called the police. Edward was arrested on June 14 by Detective E. M. Hamren of the forgery squad. He confessed his thefts in the course of a ninety-minute interview, leaving Hamren with the impression that his prisoner was rational and "very intelligent."

Notified of Ed's trouble, Eva Hickman came west to console him, with daughter Mary in tow. They presented a loving family portrait at his trial in juvenile court, and presiding Judge Carlos Hardy let Ed off the hook with the wrist-slap of probation.

Incredibly, Ed applied for reinstatement to his old job at First National, where he had been terminated on June 15. The bank turned him down flat.

On July 22, six months to the day after Chief Edwards had written his last recommendation for Hickman, probation officer A. L. Mathews wrote to the retired Kansas City lawman:

Dear Mr. Edwards:

I am writing you in reference to a boy by the name of Edward M. Hickman [sic] of 2523 Birch Street, Alhambra, California. Edward has been working in the First National Bank of Los Angeles since January and has been involved in the forging of signatures on checks that he cashed. This was not a great amount and the boy has impressed the writer with the fact that he might be a boy who has just made a mistake and this will be the last one.

I would very much appreciate it if you would kindly give me the boy's history as you know it.

Chief Edwards replied on July 26:

Dear Sir:

In answer to your letter of July 22nd, regarding Edward Hickman, I wish to state that I have known the above party for about eight years.

He is one of five children whose father deserted them and their mother a number of years ago. The mother has worked hard and faithful in the raising of these children.

Edward, the boy I refer to, is a graduate of Central High School in this city, and was a member of the Honor Society for several years. He was an outstanding Christian boy. I noticed during the last year of his high school life at times he was restless and strange in his manners and not like any of the other children. He had the wonderlust [sic] and a roaming disposition.

I feel like you do about the matter—that this is his first mistake and he should be given a chance. If he should desire to return to this city, I shall be glad to assume the duty of watching over him and assisting him in his future.

In the wake of his trial and subsequent rejection by First National, Edward apparently renewed his interest in the ministry. It was admittedly an odd choice, for a thief and murderer, but he was not deterred by circumstance. L.A.'s chief probation officer, W. H. Holland, sent Ed to his own minister—the Reverend Dr. J. Hamilton Lash, pastor of the Hollywood Congregational Church—for advice on how to become a man of the cloth. As Lash recalled their interview,

"The boy asked me whether he should stay in Los Angeles and study at a Bible institute or return to Kansas City. I advised him to go back to Kansas City, as he had something to live down in Los Angeles."

Eva Hickman agreed with the minister's advice. "I thought it was best," she later testified, "to take him back where I had the rest of the family and his friends."

Around the same time, on August 1, Central High Vice Principal J. L. Laughlin received a letter from Edward, postmarked in L.A. As Laughlin described the note, "He condemned himself bitterly for violating the trust that his friends had placed in him, stating he wanted to go back to Kansas City and get an honest job. He said he would be willing to do any kind of work, just so it was honest, that he would be glad if I would even get him a job as a janitor of the school building, if I could do it. He said he would be in as soon as he returned from California, to see me."

On August 8, probation officer A. L. Mathews wrote to Chief Edwards once more:

Dear Mr. Edwards:

I have your letter of July 26th in regard to Edward Hickman. He was granted probation by the Juvenile Court, and afterwards in talking with his mother, she has decided that it was best that she and the boy and girl return to Kansas City, as they have friends there and he will be able to get work. They have left Los Angeles on the bus, and should arrive in Kansas City very shortly. I have asked Edward to go and see you when he gets there, and if you will interest yourself and try to get the boy on his feet again, I think it will be a very great piece of work along this line.

It is unclear exactly when the Hickmans left L.A., but we know from later testimony, at his murder trial, that Ed found work in Kansas City on August 20, 1927, as an usher at the Linwood Theatre. Don Johnstone saw him there, their first meeting since graduating from Central, and he later recalled that Ed "told me he was studying to become an assistant manager, and that the manager told him he would take him in when he learned the fundamentals of the business. And I later learned that that wasn't so at all." The lie led Johnstone to conclude that Ed was "crazy."

Back in his old haunts once more, there was a definite change in young Edward's demeanor. Eva saw it, later remarking that her son was "different" following his half year in Los Angeles. "He didn't seem to care for me like he always had," she complained, "and he was restless. He never seemed to know what he wanted to do. He would talk about certain things that he wanted to do, when he would make plans that he would do those things, and then before he could settle down he would change to something else."

Chief Edwards had noted the same attitude the previous summer, but it was now more obvious. Alfred Hickman reported that his brother "acted kind of sullen, to himself. He didn't engage in the sociabilities around there like he did on previous occasions when he was there." When he met Mrs. Edwards on the street one day, she recalled that "he ran from me. He didn't talk to me." She later told the court, "I didn't think anything about it," but acknowledged she was "hurt that he wouldn't speak to me."

Edward did speak briefly to Howard Hibbs when they met on August 30 at a dinner given at the Ivanhoe Country Club by one of their high school friends. As Hibbs described his former classmate, "He was not the same happy, carefree boy he was in his junior year of high school. He seemed to be rather pale. He was unfriendly that night, not to any degree of hurting anyone there intentionally, but he did not have the same slap-on-the-back and happy smile and remark for you that he did have in his junior year of high school. He just did not seem to be the same Hickman at all."

They spoke for barely fifteen minutes, but Hibbs recalled the gist of the conversation months later. "I asked him why he preferred to stay out of school and work," Hibbs testified, "and he said that he really didn't know which was the better thing for him to do. He said he could learn a great deal by working, and he proposed to do that and then enter school eventually again."

The next morning, Ed met with Vice Principal J. L. Laughlin at Central High. Once again he made a curious impression on a former trusted friend. "I asked him what he was doing," Laughlin recalled, "and he said he had a job at the Linwood Theatre in the evening, and he expected to either go to school in the daytime or get another job—I mean another job to work in connection with this evening job. He said nothing about his trouble in California until I questioned him about it; and I asked him how it happened that he had forged the checks, and he told me that he had to travel from one bank to another, that he had no transportation except the streetcars, and that he forged these checks so as to get money enough to get a motorcycle. When he was talking to me, he seemed to have no regret about what he had done. He didn't indicate in his conversation that he had any regret for it. He told me that everybody had been free with advice, and he indicated he was pretty well 'fed up'—I think that is the expression he used—on advice. The thing that impressed me about the conversations was this: I expected him either to come to me for some sort of advice or help, or else come to me to see if I could get him a job. He intimated that he didn't want any advice, that he already had a job, and apparently had no reason whatever for coming to see me. And I was impressed by the lack of the old sincerity that I used to notice when he was in high school."

In his subsequent sworn deposition, Laughlin said, "The only thing that impressed me at the time was the fact of his untruthfulness, and the fact that when I had known him before he was perfectly sincere, and conveyed that idea." In retrospect, it is unclear what Laughlin thought Ed was untruthful about; if anything, the youth seems to have been brutally frank in expressing contempt for his elders.

"There was one more peculiar fact about this visit," Laughlin recalled. "When he left me, he went into the outer office, which is connected to my office, and asked the clerk for a transcript to the Teachers College in Kansas City. He asked her not to mention the fact to anyone that he was going to this school. That is a girl's school. As far as I know, only one boy has ever attended it. [Edward] never entered that school, and as far as I know the transcript was never used."

Whatever Ed Hickman did with his life from that point on, he was clearly not bent on becoming a teacher and molding young minds. That August visit marked the last time he would see his onetime friend and counselor. The next time J. L. Laughlin heard Ed Hickman's name, it would be linked to kidnapping and multiple murder.

5 ✦ "I Mean Business"

Confusion surrounds Ed Hickman's last stab at Kansas City Junior College, in the late summer of 1927. His permanent record, on file with the local school board, states that he enrolled on August 31. John Proudfit had a different memory five months after the fact, stating under oath that "I helped him enroll a few days after the regular term began at Junior College." Don Johnstone agreed that Ed signed up on September 7 or 8—that is, one or two days after school started—and remained in school for a week or more. They met twice on campus, once for a brief conversation, the second time when Johnstone "just passed him in the hall." In his sworn deposition, Johnstone said, "He told me he had trouble with his French lessons."

In fact, there were no French lessons . . . or lessons of any other kind, for that matter. The school's president, Edward Bainter, testified in 1928, referring to transcripts in hand, that Hickman enrolled and paid his five-dollar registration fee on September 2, 1927. Four days later, on the first day of class, he officially withdrew, and his money was refunded. He attended no classes, received no grades, and presumably was not on campus chatting with his high school friends.

Another mystery.

In September 1927 the corpse of an unidentified man, shot once in the temple, was found in a roadside ditch near Cottonwood Falls, Kansas, 110 miles southwest of Kansas

City. The victim had been dead about two weeks when he was found, and while police never learned his name, they guessed that he was in his seventies. A car believed to be the victim's, stripped of license tags, was found in Topeka, 60 miles northeast, suggesting that the killer may have traveled back in the direction of K.C. The dead man, whoever he was, had last been seen with a wavy-haired youth. Three months later, when Ed Hickman's photos were published in connection with another homicide, residents of Cotton-wood Falls noted his striking resemblance to the suspect in their own unsolved murder.

Edward, of course, had been working nights at the Linwood Theatre since August 20, but he didn't work *every* night, and there were days off, besides. The round trip to Cottonwood Falls would have taken him four hours, give or take, at a steady 60 miles per hour, but his possible involvement in the case remains a mystery. Edward never confessed to the crime, and if he was questioned about it, no records of the session have survived.

Whatever his movements in September, Ed was coming to the end of his tenure at the Linwood Theatre. A report in the *New York Times*, published twelve weeks after the fact, quoted co-worker Philip Fournet as saying that Hickman was fired on September 30 "because of unsatisfactory work." Don Johnstone, meanwhile, recalled seeing Ed on the job in "the early part of October," and Dr. A. L. Skoog would later peg the date of Edward's dismissal as October 10.

Alfred Hickman only spent a few days with his brother that summer, between Edward's return and Al's departure for college, but it was time enough to note the change in Ed's personality. "He seemed to be brooding over something," Alfred later testified, "would not talk much, would not talk with the folks at home. He seemed to be thinking about something, about something that he did not want to tell us or let us know. Of course, when he came back home, the people that had been interested in him were glad to know he was back and wanted to see him, wanted to run around with him. I gave him the phone number that had called up [sic], and to my knowledge he was not with them more than once or twice during that time. He did not go with me, did not want to go with me any, which I thought very peculiar, because he seemed to have a common interest in things that I did."

As summer wound down, Ed Hickman was primarily interested in resuming his life of crime. According to his later statements, he began with a car theft, dawdling near the corner of Thirty-fourth and Euclid one night, when he saw a young man dropping off his date. Edward waited in the dark, until the youth returned from walking the girl to her door, then flashed his .380 automatic and made off with the car. Three days later, Ed recalled, he robbed a pharmacy at Twenty-ninth and Brooklyn, followed by another the next night, at McGee and Thirty-fourth. Drugstores had become his favored target, and he robbed three more that month, although his later statements were vague about details.

Edward may have imagined that the police in K.C. were watching him, following his string of holdups, but it made him nervous, all the same. He wanted to get away from there, and that meant he needed wheels.

On the night of October 7, he accosted James H. Cook, a traveling shoe salesman from Independence, Missouri, and relieved Cook of his Chrysler coupe. Either Ed did not think to take the salesman's cash and jewelry, or he simply didn't care.

Hickman would later tell police he "drove directly to Chicago" in the stolen Chrysler, but there is a ten-day gap between the theft and his appearance at the Paradise Arms Hotel on West Washington Boulevard in Chicago, where he registered under his own name and paid eleven dollars for one week's rent. It is entirely possible that Hickman found some other lodgings before the Paradise Arms, but why would he lie, when the date could be so easily checked?

One possible answer comes from Milwaukee, some 80 miles north of Chicago, where a young girl was strangled to death on October 11, 1927. In the wake of that murder, police sought a young man matching Hickman's general description, driving a vehicle thought to be a Ford coupe. Eleven weeks later, following Edward's highly publicized arrest for kidnapping and murder of another child, Milwaukee authorities asked LAPD to question their prisoner about the October slaying. Hickman never admitted the crime, and the Milwaukee case remains officially unsolved.

Morgan Armstrong, a clerk at the Paradise Arms, remembered Ed Hickman as a tenant who "was well behaved and paid his bills." There was another side to Edward, though: a face he showed only to his victims. One was a Chicago grocer, robbed of twenty dollars at gunpoint, and Hickman would later mention "several other" holdups in the city, without providing specifics.

One mysterious incident from this period involves Edward's reported appearance at the Weiss Employment Agency, in Pasadena, California, on October 15. The agency's proprietor, Mrs. Ernest Weiss, positively identified Ed as the young man who had visited her office that day. She said he filed an application for work, listing his preferred occupation as bookkeeper. The address on his application—the local YMCA—turned out to be false. When Mrs. Weiss remarked on Ed's youthful appearance, he replied, "I can give you good references." He was accompanied on that first visit, said Mrs. Weiss, by a taller, older man who sought work as a secretary or stenographer. "Hickman" returned several times, asking for work, but the agency never found him a job.

The report is intriguing, but almost certainly false. No application bearing Hickman's name was ever produced, and while a two-day drive from Pasadena to Chicago is conceivable, Hickman's subsequent travels make no allowance for the follow-up visits described by Mrs. Weiss. From all appearances, her report to the press, if not entirely fabricated, was a case of mistaken identity.

Back in Chicago, the real Ed Hickman was getting restless, ready to move on. He drove eastward through Michigan, stopping long enough to steal new plates for the Chrysler, then pushed on through Ohio and into Pennsylvania. After passing through Pittsburgh, Ed later recalled, he played Good Samaritan by offering a lift to a stranded member of the state police. "You can check on this," he later told authorities, "for he rode with me more than twenty miles."

Check it out they did, locating Private Joseph Connell at the Nemacolin substation. His car had broken down during an investigation, Connell said, and a youth who gave his name as Farrell had driven him from Pitcairn to Greensburg.

"I told him I was from Detroit," Hickman said, "although I had never been in Detroit. He surprised me by saying that he had a brother who was an officer in Detroit and that he had visited him several times. Fearing that he might learn that I was unfamiliar with Detroit, I avoided making any comments about the city."

Private Connell, for his part, recalled young "Farrell" saying that he had set off to drive from Detroit to Philadelphia on a bet with his father, the old man doubting his ability to make the trip alone.

On arriving in Greensburg, Hickman later said, the officer invited him to stay for dinner. "He bought me a good steak, and before I left he took a road map and spent fifteen minutes telling me how to get to Philadelphia. He told me that if I returned that way he would like to show me through the barracks."

Ed drove through Philadelphia, but the city didn't appeal to him—"I did not like the apartments or the one-way streets"—so he turned west and drove across the southern part of the Keystone State.

On the evening of October 29, 1927, fifty-three-year-old James O. Claire was shot and killed during a robbery at the gas station where he worked as night manager in Chester, Pennsylvania, a Philadelphia suburb. The shooter's description "generally" resembled Ed Hickman, and he became a suspect in the murder two months later, after his face made front pages from coast to coast. Pennsylvania authorities requested a more detailed description of Edward from

LAPD, and while his known itinerary placed him in the area when Claire was shot, Hickman was never charged.

From Philadelphia, Edward drove west to Gettysburg and paid two dollars for a guided tour of the battlefield. Then, steeped in history, he drove south through Baltimore to Washington, D.C. The nation's capital did not impress him terribly, so he turned north again. At Jersey City he took the ferry to Manhattan and rented a furnished room on West Fifty-fourth Street. Two nights in New York were all Edward could stomach, and he started for home on the third day, driving through Pennsylvania and West Virginia into Ohio. Entering Columbus on November 1, he rented a small room on Broad Street and went out to scare up some cash. That night, within a span of thirty minutes, Edward robbed three different shops on the east side of town.

His first target, around 8:00 P.M., was Morris Helman's confectionery shop on East Mound Street. Unmasked, Edward entered the shop wearing a white slouch cap and a long dark overcoat and asked the proprietor for some cakes. As Helman started to ring up the sale, Ed drew his pistol and demanded money. Placing his cap on the counter, he watched Helman fill it with some twenty dollars from the register. Unsatisfied, he seized Helman's wallet, found it empty, and relieved his victim of a gold pocket watch. As he was leaving, Helman also started toward the door, but Edward aimed the pistol at his face and cautioned, "You had better stop." The candymaker, mindful of his handicapped son watching from the shop's storeroom, backed off and did as he was told.

From Helman's shop, Edward drove to Oak Street and the pharmacy owned by F. H. Buck. Unknown to Hickman, the Columbus Police Department's chief of detectives, one W. C. Shellenbarger, had left the shop moments earlier, but Ed's luck was holding. Inside the drugstore, he found Buck and two other men, Arthur Mayo and H. E. Sutton, making small talk at the counter. After ordering a tube of tooth-paste, Edward drew his automatic, doffed his cap, and ordered Buck to fill it from the register. Edward got $31.49

from the cash drawer, another $10.00 from Buck, and $3.00 from Sutton, overlooking the money hidden in Mayo's pocket.

Speaking softly as he pocketed his loot, Ed asked the druggist, "What are you going to do when I leave?"

"Nothing, brother," Buck replied.

"You'd better not," Ed warned him. "I have two others in a machine outside, and we mean business."

A short time later, on Grant Avenue, Hickman entered the Community Grocery, owned by Joseph Grant. Again Ed flashed his gun and emptied out the register, then relieved the grocer of his gold watch and some pocket change before locking him inside the walk-in freezer. By the time another customer arrived and released Frank, the bandit was gone.

Edward was proud of his achievements in Columbus. "I think I set a record for the town," he later told police. "There was a good write-up about me in the papers the next morning." In fact, his one-man crime wave was covered in three local papers, one of which described "a youthful bandit, attired in the latest collegiate style." Victims from all three holdups believed the gunman was a student, said the article: "They further said it was apparently his first job and that although he conducted himself in a businesslike manner, he was apparently frightened over what he was doing."

Perhaps. But if the holdups frightened Ed, he clearly wasn't scared enough to stop.

From Columbus, Edward drove through Indianapolis and on to Saint Louis, stopping there to commit several more robberies. In Julius Sager's pharmacy, Ed was especially nervous, twice dropping his pistol. Sager and his customers had begun to think the gun was empty and their assailant was bluffing when Ed fired a shot into the floor, saying, "I'm going to show you guys I mean business."

Back at last in Kansas City, Edward left the stolen Chrysler in a residential neighborhood and threw away the keys. When the car was found and returned to James Cook, days later, it had 4,000 extra miles on the odometer.

Ed did not tell his mother he was back in town. For all she knew, he had spent the past month in Chicago, working at some nonexistent usher's job in yet another theater. Ed saw no point in speaking to his family, since he did not plan to remain in town.

On Monday, November 7, Dr. Herbert Mantz left his home on Olive Street in Kansas City, en route to his office. A respected physician and a former director of the Jackson County Tuberculosis Hospital, Dr. Mantz was better with people than with machines. He was having some trouble starting his Chrysler coupe, when a young man slid into the passenger seat, uninvited. Before he could speak, Mantz felt a rigid object prod his ribs.

"That's a gun you feel," the stranger informed him, "and it's likely to go off if I see anything to get nervous about. Now start the car and go straight ahead."

Mantz did his best, but the engine was cold, and it died a block from his house.

"What's the matter with you?" the young man snapped.

"A little nervous," Mantz replied.

The youthful gunman smiled at that. "That's funny," he replied. "I'm not."

Mantz got the car running again, and they traveled barely half a block farther before he was ordered to "hop out and run along." Obediently, Mantz pulled over to the curb, switched off the engine, and stepped out of the car. The gunman handed him his medical bag, surprising Mantz by making no demand for cash.

"I hope you don't have far to go," the young man said, then asked some questions about the Chrysler's controls, leaving Mantz with the impression that the car thief knew very little about automobiles. Relieved to see the young man drive away, Mantz turned back toward his house to summon the police.

Ed was on the move again. He drove west across Kansas until a sudden premonition of danger made him double back all the way to Saint Louis. From there he drove southwest through Missouri and Oklahoma and into Texas. He passed through Fort Worth and stopped in El Paso long enough to buy a .45-caliber pistol, before continuing on his way through New Mexico and Arizona. In Phoenix, Ed was startled by fuel prices of thirty cents a gallon, ruefully noting that "gasoline cost as much as milk did at home."

From Yuma, Ed crossed into California and motored up through the Imperial Valley. He reported being stopped by federal agents there, part of a search for smugglers or illegal aliens, but the agents did not find his guns and probably would not have bothered Hickman if they had. No warrants had been issued in his name, at that point. He was free to travel when and where he liked, armed to the teeth.

Having reached Los Angeles on or about November 18, Edward celebrated his arrival by holding up a pharmacy on Sunset Boulevard. It was another penny-ante job, no more than thirty dollars taken from the till, but he had simple needs. Instead of settling in, he drove the stolen Chrysler north to San Francisco, where he felt a sudden urge to play the trombone.

On a whim, Ed walked into a music store and scrutinized the merchandise. He chose the best horn in the place, priced at a whopping $365, and informed the eager salesman that his father planned to buy it for him as a Christmas gift. There was a catch, however: they would have to let his father see the horn, and that meant driving back to Edward's house. The prospect of a fat commission made the salesman vulnerable. He followed Ed outside and got into the Chrysler, swallowing the bait.

"I got him out a little ways," Ed later told Detective R. J. Lucas, in Los Angeles, "and I took my gun and I stuck him up and told him to get out of the car." According to Edward, the salesman took it in stride, telling Ed he was "all right," reaching out to shake hands, but "I told him not to get anywhere near me at all." Ed left him standing on the curb and drove back to Los Angeles with his hot trombone.

There he spent a full day looking at apartments, finally renting number 315 at the Bellevue Arms on Bellevue

Avenue, on Wednesday, November 23. He paid landlady Ethel Broderick a month's rent in advance, under the name Donald Evans.

The next day was Thanksgiving, and Ed treated himself to an outing, driving south to San Diego for the day. While there, he later told police, he met and was befriended by a couple, Andrew Cramer and June Dunning, who needed a lift to L.A. Happy to oblige, Edward dropped them off at their hotel. Before they parted, Hickman claimed that Cramer agreed to meet him two days later, on November 26, to plan a string of robberies.

"I was lonesome," Hickman later told authorities, "and wanted to get someone's company. You see, I have had everyone against me for so long. I have not had a date with a girl for over a year. You can see how easy it would be for me to be fooled by him."

Perhaps.

We know this much: On Sunday night, November 27, Hickman entered K. D. Jackson's pharmacy on Sunset Boulevard, unmasked, and flashed a pistol. He demanded anesthetics, specifying chloroform or ether, and was told that Jackson had none in stock. Ed made the druggist lie down on the floor while he searched the place, finally making off with $80.00 in cash and a supply of sleeping tablets.

Why the sudden need for sedatives?

"During the past six months," Ed later told police, "the idea of kidnapping a young person and holding it for ransom came to me as a means of securing money for college."

On the night of December 5, Ed raided two more pharmacies, both on Glendale Boulevard, not far from his apartment. In each case, the drill was the same: Edward demanded chloroform or ether and threatened to kill the druggists if they failed to comply. Harry Packer had no anesthetics on hand, but Edward scooped $120 from the register. Before he fled, Packer spotted the getaway car, a Chrysler coupe, parked at the curb outside, with another man at the wheel.

Ed got lucky at his second stop on Glendale. Druggist L. D. Welch had chloroform in stock, and with a pistol pointed at his head, he briefed the gunman on its use. Appearing satisfied, Ed left with the chloroform and $36.00 in cash.

Five days later, with or without his accomplice, Hickman invaded another drugstore, this one on Hollywood Boulevard. It was a bust: a young girl screamed when he drew his pistol, and an old man bolted from the store. Hickman fled empty-handed, worried that someone might have seen his license plates. The snafu frightened him so badly that he drove straight on to San Diego, where he stole another set of license plates before returning to Los Angeles.

Despite his repeated attempts to steal chloroform, Ed later told authorities, "At this date I had no definite plans to kidnap, but on Monday, December 12, I decided to locate Mr. Harry Hovis, chief teller of the First National Bank of L.A., and arrange to take his young child." Hickman thought of Hovis first, believing the chief teller could easily meet any ransom demand, since "he is a chief officer of the bank and handles hundreds of thousands of dollars. While I was in the bank, I saw all the money shipments come in and used to go around the vaults and any place in the bank, and I knew practically everyone in the bank."

Still, something didn't feel right to Edward. "I wasn't satisfied with the situation," he later explained, deciding that the chief teller's child was too young. "I was afraid it would be harder to handle her," Ed explained. "She was a baby and would probably cry." As an alternative, he said, "I then thought of Mr. P. M. Parker, because I had seen a young girl with him one day at the bank, while I was employed there as a page." It was nothing personal, he insisted. "I thought either Mr. Hovis or Parker, either one would have sense enough to consider $1,500 an easy settlement in consideration of their own daughter. I meant no harm to either one, but I thought it would be easier to handle the older girl than the little child."

On Wednesday afternoon, December 14, Ed drove to South Wilton Place and staked out the Parker residence, watching as the girls returned from school and as their father came home from work. It wasn't much, in terms of planning an event that would inevitably change his life, but Edward reckoned it would do.

He was ready to go.

6 ✦ Stolen Away

Ed Hickman was up bright and early on Thursday morning, December 15. Twelve-year-old Lorna Littlejohn, a classmate of the Parker twins at Mount Vernon Junior High, later recalled a dark-haired man in a coupe who eyed her as she passed him on her way to school. It was around 7:00 A.M., she later told police, and he was parked at the corner of Wilton Place and Sixteenth Street.

Around that same time, the Parker girls, Marian and Marjorie, were also on their way to school. As later summarized by LAPD homicide detective R. J. Lucas, Hickman said he "watched them when they left [home], and followed them to the Red Car line on Venice Boulevard, and they took a car there and rode out for a few blocks, and he followed them until they went to the Mount Vernon School, and then he left."

Marjorie Parker had a somewhat different memory of the event. She later told police, "We got the [street] car at the corner of Wilton Place and Venice Boulevard, to go to school. We were sitting together on one of the car seats when the man drove alongside the car, about Third Avenue and Venice Boulevard. He smiled at us several times and motioned to us to get off the car and go with him. We looked the other way, but finally saw him turn off at Fourth Avenue. That's the last we saw of him until he took Marian away from school."

Of course, Marjorie didn't *see* her sister abducted from school, and the kidnapper was still unidentified. No photographs had been published at the time she made her statement to authorities on December 16. She was guessing—accurately, as it turned out—at the connection between Marian's disappearance and the young man in the dark coupe.

Hickman, who had worked his cover story out overnight, knew it would make no sense if he went to the school before Perry Parker left for work at First National. Instead of proceeding to the junior high immediately, therefore, Ed told authorities that he "went downtown" for a while, killing time. His movements are uncertain, but we know from Lucile Greene, proprietor of an Alhambra employment agency, that Edward stopped by "shortly before" the kidnapping—apparently sometime before noon—to ask about getting work. Greene had no jobs to suit him, but he did not seem particularly disappointed when he left.

Hickman later told homicide investigators, "I returned to this school later, from my apartment at the Bellevue Arms. I entered the attendance office at approximately 12:30 and asked for Mr. Parker's daughter, saying that her father had been in an accident and wished to see her."

Mount Vernon's male students were eating lunch when Hickman arrived; the girls were in their homerooms. Principal Cora Freeman had gone off campus for lunch, so secretary Naomi Britten was the first to see Hickman, afterward recalling him as "quiet and courteous." His request confused her, since there were two Parker girls at the school, and Britten turned to teacher Mary Holt for advice on how to proceed.

"I gave my name as Cooper," Hickman later said, "and assured the teacher that I was a friend of Mr. Parker's and worked at the First National Bank. I was asked if the girl's name was Marian, since . . . Mr. Parker had two daughters at the school. I replied in the affirmative and emphasized that it was the younger daughter for whom the father was calling."

Indeed, Edward had no way of knowing which twin was younger, by a matter of minutes, but Mary Holt confirmed his statement to police, recalling that he said, "It is Marian, the younger one, that is wanted." Like Naomi Britten, Holt remembered "Mr. Cooper" as "very calm and courteous" throughout their brief encounter.

"There was only a slight wait," Hickman told authorities, "and Marian was called from her class. I told her to come with me, repeating what I had said to the teacher. The young girl did not hesitate to come with me, and we left the school immediately. I drove east on Venice Boulevard to Western Avenue, north on Western to Beverly Boulevard, east on Beverly Boulevard to Temple Street, on Temple to Glendale Boulevard, out Glendale Boulevard through the city of Glendale."

By that time, Edward's passenger had grown suspicious. "I stopped the car on a quiet street out in this vicinity," he recalled, "and told Marian that she had been deceived. I told her that I would have to hold her for a day or two, and that her father would have to give me $1,500."

Moments later the girl was blindfolded, bound hand and foot. "Marian did not cry out or even attempt to fight," Hickman said. "She pleaded with me not to blindfold or tie her, and promised not to move or say anything. I believed her and took off the blindfold and the bandages from her arms and ankles. I explained to Marian what a chance I was taking. I warned her that she would be hurt if she tried to get away, and I showed her my .380 automatic revolver [sic]. Marian said she understood and that she didn't want to be shot."

So far, so good.

"I started the car," Ed told police, "and we drove back to Los Angeles, to the main post office, where I mailed a special-delivery letter to Marian's father. Marian sat right up in the seat beside me and talked in a friendly manner. I was very nice to her, and I could see that she believed and trusted me for her safety. When I left the post office, I drove out to Pasadena. Here I stopped at the Western Union office on Raynold Avenue and left Marian perfectly free in the car while I sent a telegram to her father. I wanted to warn Mr. Parker not to do anything until he got my letter, and [I] told him that his daughter was safe."

In fact, the Pasadena telegram contained no assurance of Marian's safety, although it was signed with her name. By the time Ed completed that chore, some two hours and fifteen minutes had passed since the kidnapping. So far, no one knew the girl was missing.

"Marian and I left Pasadena," Hickman continued, "and drove out Foothill Boulevard beyond Azusa. We talked and had a jolly time. Marian said she liked to go driving, and she went so far as to relate to me that she had had a dream just a few days before that someone called for her at the school and in reality kidnapped her. Before dark came, I turned back and we stopped in Alhambra, where I mailed a second telegram."

Employees Helen Seelye and Dorothy Snyder would later identify Hickman as the young man who stopped at the Western Union office on North Garfield to dispatch a second wire to the Parker home at 6:20 P.M.

According to police in Long Beach, Edward's statement to LAPD omitted a three-hour period on Thursday afternoon, during which he cashed bad checks at three local shops. Butcher Loren Temple and grocer Herbert Woods, both on East First Street, were taken for $5.00 apiece, after which Ed cashed another check—for $3.00 this time—at Daleys, Inc., on East Fourth Street. Another witness placed him in Culver City, some twelve miles away, where Ed swapped his gray overcoat for five gallons of gas at a local garage. Ironically, the garage was owned by Captain C. T. Truschell, a Culver city motorcycle cop.

By the time Perry Parker reported his daughter's abduction on Thursday evening, Los Angeles police already had five missing youngsters on their books. Robert Leslie, age fifteen, had left his home on West Sixty-sixth Street at 8:30 A.M. on December 7, bound for school, and had yet to return. Lillian Runyon, seventeen, had disappeared three days later. She was last seen by her mother, pulling away from the house with "a strange young man in a dark coupe." Thirteen-year-old Harry Arnold Jr. had been missing since he left for school on Wednesday morning, December 14, but police gave that a low priority because

Harry had several times threatened to run away from home. The same could not be said of fifteen-year-old Hazel Warner, who vanished Thursday afternoon on her way home from an after-school music lesson. Also missing on the day of Marian's abduction was twelve-year-old Bern-hard Blossom, but the errant child returned home later in the evening, after being AWOL to go to the movies.

In addition to the rash of missing children, local lawmen were baffled by a mysterious cache of clothes and school-books found in a hollow oak tree in suburban San Dimas, northeast of Los Angeles. The garments included a brown-and-white cotton dress, a wide-brimmed white cloth hat, a one-piece suit of pink silk underwear, silk stockings, and ruffled pink garters. No shoes were found, but L.A. County sheriff's deputies reported the discovery of several text-books, one bearing the name Douglas W. Kerr. It was assumed the books had been reissued to a female student for the current year, and while they were eventually traced to an intermediate school located at Jefferson Boulevard and University Avenue, in Los Angeles, staff members there were unable to identify their present owner.

None of it would help police find Marian.

For Edward Hickman, so far, the kidnapping had been a lark, more like a date than a felonious enterprise. Once he had sent the second telegram, it was time to relax.

"At seven o'clock," Edward later told investigators, "we went to the Rialto Theater in South Pasadena, and saw the picture entitled *Fathers Don't Lie*, with Esther Ralston. Marian enjoyed the picture, and we both laughed very much during the vaudeville which followed the picture. We left the theater about ten P.M. and drove directly to the Bellevue Arms Apartments. Marian, I could see, was a little worried and was also sleepy."

There was a problem at the Bellevue Arms, however. As described in court by R. J. Lucas, based on his interrogation of Hickman, there were people in the lobby and around the front of the apartment house, as if a party was just breaking up or about to begin.

"We sat in the car by the side of the apartment for about thirty minutes," Ed recalled, "and saw a chance to enter without being seen. I told Marian that my room was on the third floor and cautioned her to follow just a few steps behind me. No one saw us go to my apartment, and when we were inside, Marian went to sleep immediately. She chose to sleep on the couch and only took off her shoes, and used a pillow and a heavy blanket which I gave her for cover. I placed a reading lamp by the door and left it lighted so that it cast a dim light over the room. I slept in the bed and retired shortly after Marian. I stayed awake for some time, to see that the girl would not attempt to leave the apartment."

Friday's sunrise took the shine off of Edward's adventure. "Next morning," he told police, "Marian was awake by seven o'clock. She was sobbing and didn't say much. I got up and prepared breakfast, but she said she wasn't hungry."

The weeping child began to get on Edward's nerves. "After a while," he said, "I began to talk to Marian and tried to console her. I told her that she could write a letter to her father, and that I would, also. So then she stopped sobbing and wrote the note, and didn't cry any more that day. About 9:30 A.M. I left the apartment for about thirty minutes. I went downtown, where I got the newspapers and mailed the second special-delivery letter, which included Marian's note. I tied Marian to a chair while I was gone, but I used cloth bandages, and she was not cut or bruised in any way. I did not blindfold or gag her, and she promised to keep quiet."

Marian kept her word and seemed perfectly docile when Edward returned from his errand. The morning newspapers carried no report of his crime, a circumstance that Hickman found encouraging. Perhaps Perry Parker was following orders. With any luck at all, Ed would collect the cash that night.

First, though, he had to keep his hostage in a cooperative mood. "Marian didn't want to stay in the apartment all day," Hickman said, "so I promised to go out driving again.

We left the apartment about noon and drove out through Alhambra and San Gabriel, past the Mission Playhouse to San Gabriel Boulevard, and turned on the highway toward San Diego, near Whittier. We drove through Santa Ana, and while we were stopped there for gasoline at a Richfield station, I noticed that the attendant looked at Marian very closely."

Perhaps, but it had nothing to do with her abduction, since police were still keeping the crime under wraps. Ed's paranoia was showing, but he still went ahead with the outing.

From the gas station, he told police, "We drove on beyond San Juan Capistrano and stopped to rest the car a while before we turned back. We were about seventy miles out of Los Angeles, and it became dark before we got back to the city. I secured some evening papers, and Marian read them to me as I drove. About seven o'clock, I stopped the car just south of Seventh Street, on Los Angeles Street, and left Marian in the car while I went to the P.E. [Pacific Electric] Station at Sixth and Main Street and called her father over the telephone."

According to Perry Parker, there had already been three other calls that afternoon, but no one had spoken when he answered. Dead air. Was it the kidnapper? Or some awkward soul dialing a wrong number?

On this attempt, Edward struck out. "I called twice," he said, "but the line was busy each time. I told Marian so, and we then drove up Los Angeles Street to Sunset Boulevard, and out Sunset to a drugstore near Angeles Temple."

Perry Parker had been busy, meanwhile, collecting the $1,500 ransom in twenty-dollar bills and recording the serial numbers. It was eight o'clock, give or take, when the telephone rang once again. As Ed recalled their conversation, "I called Marian's father and talked to him. He said he had the money and wanted me to bring his girl back to him. He said he'd meet me anywhere, and I said I'd call him back."

Edward could almost smell the money.

"I called the second time from a drugstore at Pico and Wilton Streets [sic], at about eight-thirty," he said, "which was about thirty minutes later than the first [call]. I told Mr. Parker to get in his car alone and drive north on Wilton to Tenth and turn to the right one short block to Gramercy and park on Gramercy, just north of Tenth. Marian and I were parked on Pico, between Wilton and Gramercy, and we both saw Mr. Parker drive by. There were two other cars following his, and I feared that some detectives were planning to trap me, so Marian and I drove directly back to my apartment and didn't go by her father."

This time, the apartment house was quiet. "We got back inside without anyone seeing us," Hickman told investigators. "Marian sobbed a little because she couldn't go home that night, but she saw everything and was content to wait till the next morning. Marian slept the same way Friday night as Thursday, and we both were awake and up by seven-thirty the next morning."

The news of Marian's abduction broke on Saturday. Her photograph and a description of the kidnapper were featured on the front page of the *Los Angeles Times*. Police reported the interrogation of one George Carciak, a resident of South San Pedro Street, but the grilling "failed to enlighten" lawmen, and the suspect was released. LAPD Chief of Detectives H. H. Cline, undaunted by the setback, assured reporters that "arrests are due before daylight." Marian's parents were portrayed as grief-stricken but hopeful. Even Patsy, the family dog, was said to be traumatized; she was photographed for page two on the seat of a double scooter owned by Marian and Marjorie. Geraldine Parker told a *Times* reporter, "I have an idea that when her abductor realizes the effort that is being made to find her, he will be frightened and will release her. She isn't the type of child whom anyone would wish to harm."

Frightened he may have been, but Edward was also enraged. First, the bungled trap on Friday night, and now this, headlines flouting his orders to keep the kidnapping quiet. The self-described mastermind was not a common thief, to be treated with such disrespect.

"When Marian saw her pictures and name in all the papers, she felt sorry," Edward told authorities, "because she didn't want her father to give out the news of the kidnapping, because I had told her of all my plans. Later, however, she seemed to like to look at her picture and kept reading the account of her abduction."

She would not have long to revel in her new celebrity.

Saturday the seventeenth would be Perry Parker's last chance. Hickman had promised him seventy-two hours, but the near-miss on Friday night demanded punishment. Besides, it put too much strain on Edward's nerves. The longer he kept Marian at his apartment, the more likely he was to be caught.

On Saturday morning, Ed recalled, "I told Marian to write her father that he must not try to trap me, or something might happen to her. She wrote the note in her own words and very willingly, same as the first note, since she knew my plans as well as I did and read all of my letters. I told Marian all along that I would have to make things look worse to her father than they really were, so that he would be eager to settle right away. Marian knew that I wrote her father that I would kill her if he didn't pay me, but she knew that I didn't mean it and was not worried or excited about it. In fact, I promised Marian that even though her father didn't pay the money, I would let her go back unharmed. She felt perfectly safe."

Edward was determined to crush Perry Parker's resistance. "I wrote my third letter to Mr. Parker," he said, "and put it with Marian's note in the same envelope. I told Marian that I would go downtown again and get the newspapers, and mail the special delivery letter. I said I would return in less than half an hour, and then we would get in the car and meet her father somewhere that morning. I went ahead and tied her to the chair as I did Friday morning, except that I blindfolded her this time, and made ready to leave the apartment. She said to hurry and come back."

But Ed had changed his mind. He wasn't going anywhere.

"At this moment," he told police, "my intention to murder completely gripped me. I went to the kitchen and got out the rolling pin, meaning to knock her unconscious. I hesitated for a moment, and changed my mind. Instead, I took a dish towel and came back to where she was sitting on the chair, pushed back in a small nook in the dressing room, with her back turned to me. I gently placed the towel about her neck and explained that it might rest her head, but before she had time to doubt or even say anything I suddenly pulled the towel about her throat and applied all my strength to the move. She made no audible noise, except for the struggle and heaving of her body during the period of strangulation, which continued for about two minutes."

In fact, Edward later tried to convince authorities, "The tragedy was so sudden and unexpected that I'm sure she never actually suffered during the whole affair, except for a little sobbing which she couldn't keep back, for her father and mother."

Then again, in Edward's frenzied mental state, he was not the best judge of another's suffering.

"When Marian had passed to unconsciousness and her body stopped its violent struggle," he continued, "I untied the bandages and laid her on the floor. I took off her shoes and stockings, her sweater and dress, and placed her in the bathtub. I got a big pocket knife which I had in the apartment, and started cutting. First, I cut a place in her throat to drain blood, but this was not sufficient. I then cut her arms in two at the elbows and washed and wrapped them in newspaper. I drained the blood from the tub as I cut each part, so that no stain would be allowed to harden. Next, I cut her legs in two at the knees. I let the blood drain from them and then washed and wrapped them in newspaper, also. I put the limbs in the cabinet, in the kitchen, and then took the remaining undergarments from the body and cut through the body at the waist."

Dismembering his victim took more time than Edward had anticipated. "As I cut the limbs and body," he recalled, "there were heavy issues of blood and jerks of the flesh to indicate that life had not completely left the body. I drained the blood from the midsection and washed and wrapped this part in newspapers and placed it on a shelf in the dressing room. I washed the blood from the tub and separated some of the internal organs from the body and wrapped them in paper. Then I tied a towel about the neck and tied another towel to it and left the upper part of the body to hang until the blood had completely drained from it. I placed a towel up in the body to absorb any blood or anything which had not dried. I took this part of the body and, after I had washed and dried it, wrapped the exposed ends of the arms and waist with papers and tied them so that the paper would not slip. I dressed the body and placed it in a brown suitcase. I combed back the hair, powdered the face, and laid a cloth over the face when I closed the suitcase. I put the suitcase on a shelf in the dressing room and then cleaned up the bath, trying not to leave traces of blood anywhere."

His cleanup finished, Edward told police, "I went to the writing desk and wrote a second part to my third letter, which I called the final chance terms. I opened the envelope, which I had sealed, and put this third part with Marian's second note and my third letter. I went downtown and mailed this letter special delivery to Mr. Parker about one o'clock. I then went to Loew's State Theatre, but I was unable to keep my mind on the picture and wept during the performance."

His tears were apparently a result of the letdown after Edward's manic slaughter of his victim at the Bellevue Arms. A week later, when he was in custody, he told Detective Lucas that the murder was impulsive, sparked by paranoia. "I saw everybody looking at me," Hickman said, and he was "getting pretty scared" that the police would track him down. "If they had looked in there, if they had come and looked through the hotels and apartments and found me in there, I would have been in jail."

Strangling his victim, a child, was more difficult than gunning down a druggist. "I am not very strong," Ed told

Lucas, "so I put all my weight right into it." Dismembering the corpse was a matter of convenience rather than pathology; he simply thought it would be easier to carry Marian in pieces than intact.

Perhaps the worst part of Ed's statement to Detective Lucas was his frank admission that Marian was still alive when he went to work with the knife. "I started to bleed her," Hickman explained. "I reached down and cut her in the neck, but I could see that I didn't get the jugular vein. At this time, she kind of came to, started to get up," Hickman said, but he pushed her back into the tub and cut off her left forearm, followed by the right. That seemed to do the trick, Edward insisting that "the heart was still," although Marian's blood "was coming by spurts."

In fact, Ed's statement to Detective Lucas makes it clear that he had no idea when Marian expired. Both legs were severed at the knees, Hickman said, and he had opened the apartment windows for better ventilation, to disperse the stench of body fluids, before he started to bisect the child's torso. When he cut the spinal cord in two, Ed told Lucas, "the upper part of the body still jerked." Detective Lucas, clearly repulsed by Edward's litany, would later testify, "He said he didn't know anything [about] why the body jerked. Either she wasn't dead, or else it was the nerves that were jumping, but he said the top part pretty near jumped out of the bathtub when he cut the spinal column."

Ed was vague about the time involved in butchering his victim. It was half past nine, he thought, when he began to strangle Marian, and sometime after 1:00 P.M. before he reached the theater.

Now it was time to dispose of most of the evidence. Ed needed part of Marian—the upper half—for his exchange with Perry Parker, but the rest was excess baggage, a one-way ticket to the gallows, if police should find the grisly relics in his room. "I returned to my apartment about five-thirty P.M.," he later said, "and took all the parts of Marian's body downstairs to a car waiting by the side entrance. No one saw me, and I hurried out Sunset Boulevard and turned to the right at Elysian Park, where within a hundred yards along the road I left all of these parts."

It was dusk when he entered Elysian Park—later home to the Los Angeles Police Academy—and began to dispose of the remnants. Driving aimlessly through the park, Ed pitched the paper-wrapped parcels from his car—arms, legs, intestines, pelvis and thighs. One package tumbled into a roadside ravine near a house. "I thought that the folks in this place heard this thing drop," he told Detective Lucas, "because somebody looked over that way, but it was pretty dark then. I do not think they could see me."

If they did, no one investigated. There was no discovery, no call to the police.

Returning to his apartment around six o'clock, Edward had another brainstorm. Removing Marian's upper body from the suitcase where it rested, he stitched her eyelids open, to present an appearance of life. As Dr. A. F. Wagner later testified, following his autopsy on Marian, "The tongue and eyes were normal, except that the eyelids had been raised by a black thread tied around the hair and brought back and tied to a cloth that was wound around the neck."

That gruesome chore completed, Hickman said he "took the suitcase with the upper section and drove to Sixth Street and Western Avenue. Here I called Mr. Parker and told him to come to Manhattan Place and park just north of Fifth Street. I drove around in that neighborhood to see that no police cars were coming. Before I met Mr. Parker, I stopped between Sixth and Fifth Streets, on Manhattan Place, and took the body from the suitcase. I left the suitcase outside the car, and before I got back inside, I turned one number back from each end of the rear license plate."

Edward left the suitcase in the gutter in front of a home on Manhattan Place while he placed Marian's truncated corpse in the passenger seat of the Chrysler, lying down on one side.

"About eight o'clock," he continued, "I saw Mr. Parker's car where I had told him [to park], and as I approached, I tied a white handkerchief about my face. I drove up to the side of his car and stopped. I had a sawed-off shotgun in one hand, and I raised it up so that Mr. Parker would see it, and cautioned him to be careful. He asked for his daughter, and I raised the head of the child so that he could see its face. He asked if it was alive. I said, 'Yes, she is sleeping.' I asked for the money and he handed it right over to me. I said I'd pull up ahead of him about fifty feet and let the child out. I pulled up ahead and stopped, but only leaned over and placed the body on the edge of the fender, so that it rolled over onto the [parkway], and then I speeded east on Fourth Street and downtown, where I parked the car at Ninth and Grand."

Behind him, Perry Parker was living a nightmare. "[Hickman] drove up a short distance and slowed down, or paused," Parker testified in court, "and then drove on. I followed, up to where he had stopped, there, looking for her, and I expected she would be lying on the parkway. I could not see anything at all, and then I saw some kind of a bundle of trash in the gutter which, upon closer view, I saw was my girl. I could see her white face, and I stopped and picked her up." A frozen heartbeat later, unwrapping the blanket that swaddled Marian's form, he found that "the body was not complete."

LAPD Detective George Contreras was one of the officers who reached the scene "seven or eight minutes from the time the call came into headquarters." He found Perry Parker standing beside his car, parked on Manhattan Street. "I walked up to him and asked him where the little girl was," Contreras testified, "and he said, 'There she is, sitting in the car. Go and look at her. God bless her little heart.' And he could talk no more, and this friend of his had to take him away. So, I immediately went over to the car, and the little girl was sitting up with her little head leaned over to the right, and the first thing that attracted my attention was the thread that was fastened over each eyelid and across the forehead and right back over the head and down around the neck, and sewed onto a white piece of linen that went around the neck. I lowered the little cloth, and there was a cut there, so I did not touch it any more, on account of getting finger marks on it."

As for the body's condition, Contreras testified, "She had, as I say, this linen around her neck and a sweater on, buttoned up, and sat in that position. I made an examination and lifted the body up, and told Inspector Taylor that all of the body wasn't there. He came over and made an examination, and talked to Parker and searched the automobile, and searched the block. And when the coroner came, I carried the body out of the automobile and put it in the wagon, and we came on down to the morgue with it."

Dr. A. F. Wagner was waiting to perform the first phase of the autopsy, with *L.A. Times* photographer George Watson on hand to photograph the corpse. Dr. Wagner had no difficulty identifying the victim, since he had lived next door to the Parker family for the past four years. It was after 9:00 P.M. when he began his postmortem examination, later described under oath at Hickman's murder trial.

"On the first evening," Wagner said, "I found part of the body, consisting of the head, the trunk down to an inch and a half below the navel, with the arms intact, but the forearms disarticulated at the elbows. I examined that part of the body. I found that there was also a cut made by a knife on the left—on the top of the left shoulder. This cut was two and a half inches long. There were a very few superficial marks around this cut, especially between the cut and the head, which I could not determine at the time as to their cause. They were merely very superficial marks. There were no other marks upon that part of the body at all. There was no discoloration of the face. There were no contusions about the neck."

Before opening the torso, Dr. Wagner noted that the eyelids had been stitched open. "I examined the organs of the body," he reported, "the lungs and the heart, the trachea, and I found everything without any evidence of contusion or blow. That included also the stomach, the liver, kidneys, which were all intact, all in perfectly normal, healthy shape."

In addition to the towel that had been thrust into Marian's abdominal cavity, Dr. Wagner extracted part of a man's shirt, with the name Gerber printed inside the collar. That name was a red herring that would initially divert police from the true identity of their quarry.

Ed Hickman had worked up an appetite by the time he dropped the Chrysler off at Ninth and Grand. "I then went to the Leighton Café," he said, "in the arcade on Broadway, between Fifth and Sixth Streets. I passed one of the twenty-dollar gold certificates when I paid for my meal." On a whim, as he paid for his food, he spoke to the cashier: "I kidded her and told her, I said, 'You would be surprised if you knew who I was.' " Later, looking back from the perspective of a jail cell, he told Detective Lucas, "I would like to see that girl. I bet she got a thrill when she found out it was me."

His hunger sated, Edward left his car in the public lot and caught a streetcar back to his apartment, where he promptly went to sleep.

Meantime, LAPD was on the job. Within an hour of the ransom pickup, patrolmen had located Ed's Chrysler coupe and learned from the parking lot attendant that the driver, a young dark-haired man, had promised to return for the car on Sunday. Swearing members of the press to secrecy, detectives staked out the Chrysler and settled in to wait.

7 ✦ Fox and Hounds

The Sabbath brought no rest for Hickman or the homicide detectives who were hunting him. Unnoticed by Edward and unknown to members of the press, the towel that he had stuffed into the gaping void of Marian's abdomen bore a Bellevue Arms label. It took some time for LAPD to discover that clue, but once they had it, there was no delay in follow-up. Ed woke to find the Bellevue Arms surrounded by police.

"On Sunday morning," he would later say, "detectives from the police department searched my apartment for towels, but made no arrest." It must have been a harrowing moment, supposing it happened, but Edward told a different story in his jailhouse conversation with Detective R. J. Lucas.

As Lucas recalled it in court, Edward told him that "in the morning, before he was up, or [as] he was just getting up, they surrounded the Bellevue Arms Apartments. . . . He talked to two or three of the officers and asked them what they were doing there, and they said they were looking for the kidnapper of Marian Parker. He said that he told them, 'I sure hope you get that fellow. Is there anything that I can do? I will be glad to do anything I can do.'"

In Ed's first version of the incident, he told Lucas, "I kidded the coppers right out of it. They didn't have any idea it was me at all." As Lucas recalled that initial statement, "He said they seemed to be looking for towels, but they never looked for any towels in his place at all."

It was just as well, for Ed. Inside the flat, he had a sawed-off shotgun "lying in the window," his two pistols hidden in the kitchen stove. The remaining ransom money, $1,480 in all, was stashed behind an ironing board that folded up into the wall.

When the police left, Hickman said, "I took my guns and the ransom money and checked them at the P.E. station near Sixth and Main. I also checked a black handbag and a suit box at the station. I went to the Tower Theatre early in the afternoon."

While Ed sat munching popcorn in the dark, Los Angelenos were recoiling from the grisly details of his crime. That Sunday's *L.A. Times* carried the headline KID-NAPED CHILD SLAIN BY FIEND, with Marian's portrait front and center, flanked by details of the "gigantic search" for her killer. The crime eclipsed Charles Lindbergh's visit to Mexico City and the sinking of a U.S. Navy submarine off Provincetown, Massachusetts, with thirty-seven crewmen aboard.

The news was bad, but there was worse to come.

William Britton was miles away from his home in suburban Downey, strolling through Elysian Park on Lilac Terrace, when he found four newspaper-wrapped parcels scattered along the roadside. Opening one of them, he found a small human arm, severed at the elbow, and rushed to call police. Upon their arrival at the scene, detectives found the other parcels to contain the second arm and lower legs. About an hour later and 150 yards farther east, two boys hiking through the woods found another package lying at the bottom of a gully, where it had come to rest when tossed from Hickman's car. Inside was the pitiful remainder of Marian's body, truncated at the waist and knees.

Police found tire tracks on the muddy shoulder there, where Edward had pulled over to the side. They made a cast, which matched the tires of the coupe then under guard at Ninth and Grant.

And still the driver did not show himself.

That Sunday morning brought detectives back once more to Manhattan Place. Margaret Root had found a suitcase standing in the gutter in front of her house, a block from the point where Marian's body was dumped by the man known as Fox. The suitcase was imitation leather, cheaply made. Inside it police found one clean towel, two bloody newspapers, a writing tablet that appeared to match the two notes penned by Marian to her father, and a spool of black thread identical to the stitching in Marian's eyelids.

Dr. Wagner was waiting at the morgue when the rest of Marian's corpse arrived. As he would later tell the court, "On the morning of the next day, the other parts of the body had been brought in, in separate pieces, each arm, and each leg from the knee down, and also the other part of the body, ranging from an inch and a half below the navel down to the knees. I examined these parts very closely. I could find no evidence of contusion or abrasion or scratches upon the ankles, except very slight, superficial abrasions. The lower part of the body that was brought in contained the genital organs, which were all intact." Despite the absence of apparent mortal wounds to head or torso, Dr. Wagner logically concluded that his young neighbor had suffered a "violent homicidal death."

The dismemberment invited psychiatric speculation about the killer's motives, and one of the first to speak out was Dr. Paul Bowers, a professor of legal medicine at Loyola College and former superintendent of the Indiana Hospital for the Insane. Bower deemed Marian's murder the work of a sexual sadist, the ransom demand a mere smokescreen to disguise a crime "planned and carried out . . . for the gratification of the abnormal sexual impulse." The killer "is not a moron," Bowers said, but rather "more or less conventionally well educated." Local psychiatrist Victor Parkin agreed, suggesting that he had selected the paltry sum of $1,500 because it "would just about cover his expenses in making his escape." The typical sadist, according to Dr. Parkin, possessed a "high degree of cunning and egotism." Marian's killer might well appear normal in everyday life, perhaps holding employment as a trusted office worker.

Dr. Joseph Catton, a psychiatrist in San Francisco, generally agreed with his colleagues to the south, profiling a killer "with an emotional disturbance which probably affects his sex life." At the same time, though, he warned against imagining the man was legally insane. No bleeding heart, Dr. Catton told the press, "Society's impulse to do away with this type of offender, sane or insane, should be acted on. In this Christian age we are inclined to want to remove from our reactions to such offenses as these all elements of vengeance, but I feel that this case cries out for vengeance."

Ed Hickman was still at the movies when authorities received their first false lead in the case. A tailor in Alhambra, S. A. Nemeth, told LAPD that two men and a woman had entered his shop on Saturday morning, around eleven o'clock. One of the men "resembled" Marian's still-unidentified killer. He carried an overcoat and two loose buttons, and asked Nemeth to sew them back on. The tailor noted "dark spots which looked like bloodstains" on the coat, but when he tried to scratch them off, the nervous young man brusquely ordered him to leave the stains alone and reattach the buttons. Nemeth's description of the woman and the second man was vague, but homicide detectives were impressed with his report. "As a result of this," the *New York Times* declared, "instead of hunting for one man, the Los Angeles search is for three, possibly four persons."

And there seemed to be no shortage of suspects. One of those questioned on Sunday was the twenty-five-year-old son of a local physician, "known in the past to have committed offenses against young girls." Detectives said the unnamed man "was in a position to know intimate details of the Parker family life," but he produced an airtight alibi and was quickly released.

Suspect Lewis Wyatt, a lumber salesman from Terre Haute, Indiana, drew attention to himself on Sunday when he paid for an eastbound bus ticket with a twenty-dollar gold certificate. Detectives swarmed the bus depot, but Wyatt had already left for Las Vegas on a Red Feather coach. Instead of checking the serial numbers of the twenties against their list of ransom bills, the manhunters commandeered two private airplanes and overtook the bus when it stopped for fuel. Wyatt was briefly detained in the Clark County jail, but the lawmen found him too old and "too stocky" to pass for their quarry, and he was soon on his way back to Terre Haute.

Twenty-one-year-old Joe Montgomery, back in Pasadena, had a rougher time of it, but he brought the trouble on himself. Montgomery was out riding his motorcycle with a female companion when he approached an LAPD roadblock on the outskirts of the city and decided not to stop. Police gave chase and peppered him with gunfire, but Montgomery eluded them cranking his cycle up to a breathtaking 68 miles per hour. Somewhere along the way, he ditched his date, but officers were waiting for him at 2:30 A.M., when he visited Pasadena Emergency Hospital to have a bullet removed from one heel.

In all, that Sunday, Pasadena detectives questioned five suspects "resembling" the killer, but all were soon released. The net had come up empty on its first broad sweep.

While LAPD pursued shadows and roped off a block of South Wilton Place, to spare the Parkers any more harassment from the press, rewards were offered for information leading to the kidnapper's arrest. Lieutenant Governor Buron Pitts got the ball rolling, with a telegram to Governor C. C. Young.

Without any doubt the murder of Marian Parker is the most vicious and atrocious crime in California history. California has been stirred as never before, and in view of the nature of the crime most strongly urge if legally possible that the State of California immediately offer a thoroughly substantial reward for the apprehension and conviction of the murderer. Suggest that the reward be divided, one-half for information leading to arrest and conviction and the other half for the actual arrest. Authorities feel that crime was undoubtedly committed by degenerates and in view of frequency of these crimes recently in Los Angeles on other children and the fact that the criminal is still at large, and the danger from their activities, the State should be the first one to initiate and contribute its share to the apprehension of these degenerates for the future protection of its children. Unquestionably, the offer of a substantial reward by the State of California and the co-operation with local agents will be one of our most effective weapons in the hands of police authorities.

Governor Young was inclined to agree, but state law restricted such rewards from his office to a maximum of $2,500 every two years, with $800 of that amount already pledged in other cases. Radio station KMIC in Inglewood, however, unconstrained by statutes, took pledges of $4,000 in reward money, and evangelist Aimee Semple McPherson—who had faked her own kidnapping the previous year—called on her disciples for donations to the fund. William Bonelli, president of the L.A. city council, pledged $5,000 toward the killer's arrest, a sum that was instantly matched by Sidney Graves for the county board of supervisors.

The object of all their attention, meanwhile, was preparing to get out of town. "Shortly after five P.M.," he later told police, "I rode out on Hollywood Boulevard on a P.E. car and got off at Western Avenue." The stolen Chrysler was a write-off; its discovery reported in the Sunday morning papers. As Ed informed Detective Lucas, "I wanted to get a car and get out of town."

The car he chose was a Hudson driven by Frank Peck, a Los Angeles dealer in wholesale building supplies. Hickman watched Peck drop off his wife in front of a shop on Hollywood Boulevard, near Western, and start looking for a place to park. "He was a big fellow," Edward recalled. "I thought maybe he was a policeman."

The thought didn't stop Ed from sliding into the Hudson's passenger seat and pointing a blue steel automatic at Peck. "You see what this is?" he demanded.

"Yes, sir."

"You are going to do just as I tell you to do, won't you?"

Another yes from Peck, his eyes still on the pistol.

"You are not a plainclothesman, are you?" Hickman asked.

"No, sir," Peck replied.

"All right," said Hickman. "Start your motor." When Peck had obeyed, he issued further instructions. "Drive to Western and up Western. Turn to the right on Western."

Peck did as he was told, following directions to a point on Russell Street where Edward ordered him to stop in the middle of the block.

"Have you got a gun on you?" Ed asked him.

"No, sir."

Ed leaned across the seat and patted his captive down. Satisfied at last, he sat back and said, "Give me your money."

Peck dug into his pocket, producing fifteen dollars, which he handed to his uninvited passenger. It wasn't much, but Peck was hoping it would save his life.

"All right," said Hickman. "I will do the driving now. You sit still, however. I am going to get out of the car and walk around the front. You sit still until I get around there."

Peck nodded agreement, and Edward circled the Hudson's nose, keeping his pistol trained on Peck through the windshield. Opening the driver's door, he told Peck to scoot over, and he slid in behind the steering wheel.

"Has this car got an emergency brake on it?" Hickman asked.

"Yes," Peck replied, "on the left."

When Ed twisted the ignition key, he was immediately answered by a high-pitched squeal from underneath the hood. "What's that?" he asked.

"A fan belt squeak," Peck said. "I just put a new fan belt on, and it's probably slipping."

As Ed turned onto Franklin and crossed Normandie to Melrose, he grilled Pike about the Hudson's gauges, how much gas and oil he had, and how far the car would go before the engine needed to be drained.

"Where are you taking me?" Peck asked.

"Never mind," Hickman said. "I will let you out when I get ready."

Peck tried to talk him out of taking the car, but Hickman was adamant. He needed wheels. "Have you got it insured?" he asked.

"Yes."

"Well, then, you are all right."

Edward drove through a red light on Normandie, catching himself too late, and said, "Gee! I've got to watch my step." He stopped at the next light, then peeled away with a squeal from the tires, testing the machine. "Gosh," he told Peck, "this car has got a lot of pep and power, hasn't it?"

"Yes," Peck said, "it will travel all right." The salesman had begun to worry as he watched Edward steer with his right hand while holding the pistol steady in his left. "Where are you taking me?" Peck asked again. "We are getting out in the sticks now."

"Well, I will let you out down here," Hickman replied. "You needn't worry."

He stopped a half-block north of Melrose, with the engine idling, and ordered Peck out of the car. A robe was lying on the back seat, and Peck asked if he could take it with him.

"No, leave it there," said Hickman, frowning at him. "I know just exactly what you are going to do when you get out of this car. You are going to call the cops."

Peck saw no point in denying it. He was waiting for the bullet when Hickman ordered him out of the car, then told him to first roll down the passenger window. "I might want to shoot out there."

Peck did as he was told, got out, and watched his Hudson disappear into the night.

"This occurred about six o'clock Sunday evening," Hickman later told authorities, "and shortly after seven I had secured my packages and grip [suitcase] from the P.E. station and was on my way out of Los Angeles on Ventura Boulevard. I drove overnight and arrived at San Francisco [on] Monday, about one P.M."

Police in San Francisco were already waiting for him, according to the *Los Angeles Times*, an alert having been triggered by reports that a man resembling Marian's killer and flashing a large roll of cash had boarded a Southern Pacific passenger train "at Zelzah," north of L.A., and disembarked "at Hasson" before the train was stopped and searched in Santa Barbara. (Curiously, no such towns or any reasonable sound-alikes exist in California.)

Some 400 miles to the north, in San Francisco, Chief of Detectives Duncan Matheson warned residents to be prepared for the worst. "Having accomplished what he did with such comparative ease and safety," Matheson told reporters, "it is more than likely that the murderer's courage will be so buoyed up that he will attempt to duplicate the crime with only minor changes in his plan." Parents should be vigilant, the chief declared, and warn their children of the threat posed by strangers.

Chief Matheson need not have worried. Hickman checked into the Herald Hotel on Monday afternoon, registered as "Edward J. King" of Seattle, and spent the night in room 402, preparing to leave in the morning. He had no interest in San Francisco's children. All that mattered now was escape and survival. After a good night's sleep, he would head north.

Behind him, in Los Angeles, he left chaos. Another threatening letter had been found on Sunday afternoon, tucked into a fire alarm box at the corner of Hobart and Melrose. It read:

P. M. Parker:
   For the trouble you have caused, Marjorie Parker will be the next victim. Nothing can stop the Fox and they who try will know the penalty. If you warn anyone of this second success, it will mean you next.

Try and get me. I am the Fox. You will never know
the rest of my success. You will miss her at 12 o'clock.
                    The Fox

Security at the Parker home was doubled, but even superficial handwriting analysis told investigators that the latest
message was a hoax. Coverage of the manhunt in the *Los
Angeles Times* included front-page announcements of increased rewards "for [the] monster's capture," plus an editorial headlined "This Fiend Must Not Escape":

> Staggering to the imagination, abhorrent to every
> human instinct, are the incredibly horrible circum-
> stances surrounding the murder and mutilation of
> twelve-year-old Marian Parker, lured from her school-
> room last Thursday, subjected by her kidnapper to
> unknown and unnamable horrors, slain, dismembered
> and—as a crowning, frightful touch to the hell-born
> scheme of a fiend incarnate—the pitiful fragments of
> her hacked-up body wrought into the ghastly guise of a
> living child and delivered to her father in return for
> $1,500 "ransom."
>
> The police are doing everything possible to apprehend
> this fiendish slayer, but this is not a job for the police alone.
> Every citizen of Los Angeles, every resident of the South-
> west, must assist. If every pair of eyes within the area of
> the murderer's possible movements is vigilantly alert for a
> man of his description, for his car and for the numbers of
> the bills paid him for the little girl's shattered corpse, his
> chances to elude the gallows will be scant indeed.

There followed a description of a clean-shaven man with
wavy brown hair, believed to be twenty-five or thirty years of
age. Serial numbers of the twenty-dollar gold certificates, ranging from K68016901 to K68016975, were also noted, for the
benefit of anyone who might do business with the fugitive.

A coroner's jury convened on Monday morning to examine Marian's case. Dr. Wagner, the first of three witnesses

called, chilled the panel with his admission that he could not determine a specific time or cause of death; more to the point, Wagner testified, "I cannot say whether she was killed before her body was so horribly mutilated." There was no evidence of chloroform or any other anesthetic being used, he said, leaving the jury to imagine Marian suffering the torments of the damned.

Mary Holt, the teacher, was next, with her description of the kidnapper. "He seemed very well educated," she said, "and was very courteous and calm. He completely convinced me, and I am always very careful about excusing children, even questioning parents as to identity and reason for the desired absence. I shouldn't have let her go if I had questioned him in the least." Detective Lieutenant W. W. Warren from the LAPD closed the show with a recap of the events since Thursday afternoon, and the panel wasted no time in returning its judgment that "Deceased came to her death at the hands of a person or persons unknown to the jury, acting with homicidal intent."

America was less litigious in the 1920s than it is today, but Los Angeles school board officials already knew the value of covering their backsides. Mary Holt was still on the witness stand when Superintendent Susan Dorsey issued this statement to the press:

Mrs. Holt [Dorsey said] had no authority to excuse any child from school. That is done by our vice principal, and then only at the request of the child's parents or guardian. But in this case there appeared to be an emergency when the man rushed in and claimed that there had been an accident and the child's father was calling for her.

I talked to Mrs. Holt and am satisfied that I would have acted as she did if I were confronted with the same circumstances. At that time the vice principal, who is the person in authority entitled to excuse a child from class, was busy with the Christmas program and could not be reached in the few minutes that elapsed.

The fact that nothing has ever befallen our school-children in the past is evidence in itself that they are as safeguarded as is humanly possible.

If this assurance from the brass was not enough to calm anxious parents, the *Times* also announced that fifty supervisors of attendance and child welfare from the city school system were being mobilized to join the manhunt.

All too late.

A private funeral service for Marian Parker was held on Monday afternoon at Forest Lawn Cemetery's Little Church of Flowers in Glendale. Dr. Herbert Booth Smith, pastor of Immanuel Presbyterian Church, officiated at the service, in a chapel described by the *L.A. Times* as "a perfect bower of flowers and potted plants." Following the closed-casket service, which concluded shortly after 5:00 P.M., Marian's remains were cremated.

And the search for her killer went on.

Three "suspects" were in custody by Monday afternoon. Earl Smith, age twenty-three, identified as a "manufacturing dentist," had been jailed on Saturday for grand larceny, and police also grilled him about the kidnapping, apparently for want of anything better to do. A second prisoner, Gaylord Barnaman, was arrested at a downtown hotel after he identified himself as "the Fox" and demanded radio time for a public statement. By Monday afternoon, police were ready to dismiss him as "a psychopathic case."

The third and most promising suspect, twenty-two-year-old telephone operator Lillian Padley, was arrested in the predawn hours of Monday morning, after neighbors complained of a loud disturbance at her rented quarters near the corner of Fifth Street and Manhattan Place. Officers surrounded the house, whereupon Padley ran outside, reportedly screaming, "I didn't kill her! I didn't kill her! They did!" An unnamed man was found asleep inside the house, but he produced an iron-clad alibi and was released, while Lillian went downtown to pay a ten-dollar fine for drunk and disorderly conduct. A search of the premises turned up a "grotesque picture of Judas Iscariot," mentioned by name in one letter sent to Perry Parker by "the Fox," plus "sharp heel prints on the carpet, etched in blood, a man's undergarment splotched with blood, and several washed towels which appeared once to have been bloodstained." It all smacked of sinister intent, but ultimately came to nothing. As the *Times* reported, "While it is doubted whether this house had any connection with the butchery of Marian's body, the young woman is to be detained until further developments."

Police also searched a second house in L.A., after neighbors reported that two men and a woman had moved out "several days ago." A torn and crumpled piece of paper was found on the floor, marked with the name "Marian." Curiously, the *Times* reported that "Although the scrap of paper is of no particular significance, the investigators said, it is believed it is a portion of a draft of one of the ransom notes." Detectives failed to explain how such a clue could be *in*significant, but their search of the house yielded no helpful evidence.

In fact, the police were spread too thin, attempting to search everywhere at once. Near Saugus, well after sundown, two deputies routed a suspect "resembling" the kidnapper from a northbound Southern Pacific freight train. They chased him into the foothills, firing at him with shotguns, but he gave them the slip. He later eluded a posse of lawmen and 250 vigilantes drafted from the nearby Barker Ranch. Police in Santa Monica were stopping cars at random, looking for drivers who fit the kidnapper's description, after one nervous resident phoned in a possible license number. The L.A. County sheriff's office broadcast an alert for a recent San Quentin parolee, convicted of raping his own daughter, but the suspect's name and description were curiously omitted from press reports.

It was a free-for-all, with rewards totaling $50,000 by Monday night. The city of Los Angeles was in for $10,000, plus $5,000 from the county supervisors, an embarrassing $1,000 from the governor's office, and $400 from Sister

Aimee's Angelus Temple, but the real money came through private pledges, some $32,500 having been phoned in to three local radio stations. On the side, J. Bruce Goddard, president of the Co-operative Apartment and Hotel Owners Association of Southern California, appealed to all landlords to aid in the search by scrutinizing their tenants.

Another child went missing on Monday afternoon: twelve-year-old Rose Neritue was last seen around 2:00 P.M., selling tickets to a school fair at Evergreen Playground, near her Eagle Street home. Authorities, meanwhile, were still concerned about the possibility of an organized conspiracy behind Marian's murder. One of the victim's classmates, Adeline Howard, told police on Monday that a man had lured her into his car three months earlier, on September 27, but released her on learning her name. "I'm looking for a girl named Marian Parker," the stranger allegedly said, as he shoved her out of the car.

Still, there *was* some progress in the manhunt. A nationally broadcast description of the Chrysler coupe recovered on Saturday night put detectives in touch with its owner, Dr. Mantz, in Kansas City, and his description of the thief fit their elusive subject to a tee. More to the point, although his name would not be mentioned in the press before Wednesday, police had clearly begun to focus on Ed Hickman as a suspect by Monday. That afternoon, probation officer Warren Prescott fired off an urgent telegram to Charles Edwards, in Missouri. It read: "Was Edward Hickman in Kansas City all last week? Answer immediately."

Edwards wired back at 1:01 P.M., Central time: "Telegram received. Will check party referred to immediately and report."

Chief Edwards spoke to Eva Hickman and later reported the gist of their conversation to the court. "She informed me," Edwards said, "that the last time that she heard from him, that he was in Chicago, and handed me a letter that she had received from him. When his mother told me that she did not know where he was, other than the information conveyed in the letter, I took the matter up with Chief of Detectives Toyne of the police department."

Distinctly uneasy by then, Chief Edwards wired Prescott again on Tuesday morning: "Edward Hickman has not been seen since October in this city. Have taken matter up with Chief of Detectives L. R. Toyne. Wire fully if we can be of any assistance to you."

It was the last Chief Edwards would hear from out west until Wednesday morning, when national headlines named Ed as prime suspect in Marian's death.

Unknown to Hickman, by the time he checked out of the Herald Hotel on Tuesday, around 9:30 A.M., he was a hunted man. The self-styled fox and mastermind had failed to wipe the Chrysler down for fingerprints before he abandoned it on Saturday night. Police had missed him in their first search of the Bellevue Arms apartments, but they tried again on Monday, and this time they found no. 315. In his haste to evacuate, Edward had left his breakfast on the table, complete with fingerprints on a milk bottle and sugar bowl. Upon comparison, they matched prints from the Chrysler—and his booking card from the arrest in June. Amid the clutter of his life—golf balls and clubs, a portable phonograph, partly burned notes—investigators found the broken shell of a Brazil nut and matched it to a similar fragment retrieved from a pocket of Marian's dress.

The Los Angeles district attorney's office formally charged Ed with kidnapping and murder on Tuesday, December 20. Municipal Judge Baird signed a bench warrant for his arrest, to facilitate extradition if Hickman was captured outside California. Before the afternoon was out, druggists K. D. Jackson, L. D. Welch, and Harry Packer identified Edward from mug shots as the "chloroform bandit" who had robbed their stores in November.

The news stunned Edward's parents and acquaintances back east. "It is a terrible mistake," his mother told reporters in Kansas City. "This crime is the work of a fiend. My boy is a good, clean boy. I'll never believe it until I hear it from his own lips." Ed's father, interviewed in El Paso, was equally skeptical, but he took a harder line. Whoever was responsible for the murder, Bill Hickman said, "ought to be punished to the full extent of the law." Ed's former teachers, from Hartford to K.C., were unanimous in voicing shock that such a polite, studious youth could be accused of kidnapping and murder. Dr. Mantz, when shown a photograph of Hickman, was unable to identify him as the carjacker who had stolen his Chrysler nearly two months earlier.

Reactions to Edward's ID in Los Angeles were something else, again. In June, Charles Downing had briefly shared a cell with Hickman at the county jail, and he remembered Edward's talk of keeping surgical instruments at home. He also reported that the youth was "interested in poisons."

Perry Parker, for his part, appeared to entertain no doubts once he had been informed of the killer's identity. "After the search through employees' records, the photographs and incidents that have been revealed by the work of the police," Parker declared, "I recall the unusual manner in which Hickman talked with me about his discharge for forgery. I remember how he asked me for his position again after being granted probation—which probation I protested—and his replies to questions, and the calm manner and voice I heard over the telephone, and lastly the coolness and nerve displayed Saturday night when we met for the exchange, and I am convinced that Hickman was at the other end of the telephone and that he took the $1,500."

As for motive, Parker said, "I cannot call to mind any words of madness or revenge that passed while I was talking with Hickman, but I do remember that his reactions to the forgery charges did not seem to me to be usual. He evinced no nervousness and showed very little concern over the seriousness of his actions. This impressed me very much at the time, but no thought of his planning to harm me or members of my family in return for his discharge entered my mind."

Of course, Perry Parker had no way of knowing that by June 1927, Edward had already killed at least one person, possibly several. The banker had believed that he was dealing with a wayward child.

Alleged sightings of the fugitive proliferated once Hickman was identified. Also, the reward for information leading to his capture topped $62,000 by Tuesday afternoon, when $500 was wired in from the Rotary Club in Milford, Delaware. Possemen around Saugus were still combing the hills, without result, for the train-jumping suspect who had dodged them on Monday, and the Kern County sheriff posted men along the Ridge Route from L.A., to prevent Edward from escaping north to Bakersfield. At 1:00 A.M. on Tuesday, a young man fitting Hickman's description used the pay phone in a drugstore at Forty-eighth and Arlington, in Los Angeles; the pharmacist overheard him telling someone on the other end of the line to "Lay low, for God's sake! Lay low!" Four hours later and a few blocks distant, in downtown L.A., pump jockey John Ward reported filling Hickman's gas tank, whereupon the fugitive fled without paying his bill.

It seemed that Ed was everywhere—and nowhere—all at once. In San Louis Obispo, a man "who looked like Hickman" was reportedly seen motoring through town, accompanied by a middle-aged male passenger. L.A. traffic officers scrambled in pursuit of a suspect in a blue Cadillac, losing him downtown before he ditched the Caddie in San Bernardino, stole another car, and drove on to Redlands, where he crashed the second vehicle and fled on foot, successfully eluding his pursuers. Howard Mitchell, an attorney and officer of the Automobile Club of Southern California, said he had spotted Hickman outside Pomona; the suspect was riding a motorcycle, conspicuous in a white sweater and high-top boots, "as though prepared for travel in rough country." Homer Mays, a black barber in Monrovia, recalled a rare Caucasian customer entering his shop around 8:00 P.M. on Monday, ordering a shave and heavy hair dressing to flatten his wavy locks. "You look like Hickman," Mays remarked. "There's a lot of money on his head." To which the frowning white man had replied, "You don't know how close you are to getting it."

By that time, twelve thousand American Legionnaires were mobilized in southern California, prepared to join in the manhunt, and Hickman fever had spread nationwide. Police in San Francisco found themselves on renewed alert Monday night after one Leslie Russell reported a strange encounter in the Mission District. He was sitting in his auto with the engine running, Russell said, when a young man answering Hickman's description approached him on foot and "mumbled something about having come from Los Angeles and wanting to 'lie low' until the 'excitement died down.'" Russell sped off to find a patrolman, but the Hickman look-alike was gone when he came back with reinforcements. Meanwhile, patrons at a local post office reported Edward or his twin mailing a package off that afternoon, to Kansas City.

Farther north, at Yreka, within a twenty-minute drive of the Oregon state line, a waitress swore that she had served the fugitive on Monday night. He was extremely nervous, she reported, once dropping his coffee cup from a tremulous hand. In the other direction, away to the south, California authorities urged Mexican police to keep diligent watch for a kidnapper headed their way. Baja California Governor Abelardo Rodriguez deputized a special force of *rurales* to patrol 150 miles of border around the clock, scouring the desert and scrub for Hickman. Elsewhere, police were on alert from Denver to Portland, Oregon. Charles Edwards and Chief Toyne promised help in Kansas City, if the fugitive came their way, and lawmen were alert in Hartford, Arkansas, in case Ed returned to his birthplace.

Revisiting the family homestead was the last thing on his mind, however, as he headed north, bound for Seattle. Ed knew police were looking for a young man traveling alone, and he elected to improve his odds by finding company along the way. He found his first passenger thumbing rides outside Davis, east of Sacramento, and drove the man as far as Redding, where they separated after dining in a coffee shop. The other patrons were talking about the reward being offered for information about Marian Parker's killer— $65,000 and counting by then. The talk made Hickman nervous, and he rushed through the meal, eager to be on his way.

About 20 miles farther north, approaching Dunsmuir, he spotted two more hitchhikers around 8:00 P.M. James Nelson and Irwin Mowrey were on their way to Portland to spend Christmas with relatives, and Hickman told them he could take them all the way. The young men noticed that Ed kept a .45 automatic close at hand, either resting on the seat beside him or tucked into a pocket on the driver's door. One of them asked about it, and Ed explained that he carried it for protection, worried that he might be stopped and robbed somewhere along the way. Vaguely aware of the manhunt in Los Angeles, his riders had paid no attention to descriptions of the murderer and never guessed that they were riding with the state's most wanted fugitive.

It was close to ten o'clock when they approached the Oregon state line, near the hamlet of Hilt, California, and Ed began looking for a place to park off the highway. Nelson and Mowrey asked what he was doing when he nosed the Hudson into darkness on an unpaved logging road. Taking a gamble, Ed told them he had heard police were stopping drivers at the state line, and he didn't want to take a chance because he had two gallons of illegal whiskey in the car. They would rest till midnight, when he thought the lawmen would relax their vigil.

Shortly after twelve o'clock they started north again, with Nelson driving, Mowrey riding in the shotgun seat. Keeping one hand on his automatic, Hickman stretched out in back and feigned sleep as they approached the state line. He had been wrong about the roadblocks breaking up at midnight. They were stopped and examined briefly, but the officers were looking for a single youth, not three men on the road. They waved the Hudson through, and Hickman relaxed after they had put a few more miles behind them.

It was half-past noon on Wednesday when they pulled into Portland, where Ed dropped his passengers off downtown, in front of the Imperial Hotel. He stepped out of the car to stretch his legs, embarrassed when his pistol clattered to the sidewalk at his feet. Retrieving it without a word, he got back into the car and drove away, leaving Nelson and Mowrey at the curb. It was midafternoon before the young men saw a newspaper with Hickman's photographs and telephoned police. LAPD broadcast a description of the stolen Hudson and its California license number, 1-350-391, from coast to coast, and officers in Portland went on the alert. A gas station attendant called to say that he had filled a Hudson's tank that afternoon. He readily selected Hickman's L.A. mug shot from a group of eight, and lawmen scrambled to cover the roads out of town, alerting departments along the North Bank and Columbia highways.

Too late.

Ed was gone. He had already crossed into Washington.

Ironically, instead of narrowing the search, the news from Portland seemed to pass unnoticed while a steady stream of sightings poured in from points far and wide. Three bus station employees in Medford, Oregon claimed to have seen the fugitive "or his twin brother" at the depot's breakfast counter, early Wednesday morning, but he had fled without finishing his meal, after he saw them studying a newspaper. Police in Medford gave the report "little credence," but still warned their colleagues in Roseburg to search incoming buses. In Salt Lake City, meanwhile, patrolmen chased a phantom motorcyclist who resembled Hickman. Officers in Boise, Idaho, thought Ed had stopped off in their city long enough to cash a rubber check. No fewer than three witnesses placed Hickman in Tulsa, Oklahoma, where various observers saw him at a coffee shop, a gas station, and the post office.

In Kansas, J. H. Trothman identified Ed's photo as a likeness of the young man who had thumbed a ride with him from Wichita to Newton, saying he was on his way home to Kansas City, from Los Angeles. That was bad news for Dr. Mantz, already under guard by two detectives since the L.A. killer was named as the man who had stolen his Chrysler in November. At 3:00 P.M. on Wednesday, the doctor's secretary reported an incoming long-distance call.

"Do you recognize my voice?" the caller asked, when Mantz came on the line.

Mantz frowned and answered, "No, I don't."

"I'm the fellow who took you for a ride," the caller said. "Do you recognize my voice *now?*"

Mantz signaled the detectives lounging in his outer office, and they scrambled in a vain attempt to trace the call.

"I wouldn't be in all this trouble if it were not for you," the stranger told Dr. Mantz. "I'm going to get one of your girls. You know what will happen to her."

Mantz tried to stall, keeping the line open for a trace, but the connection was severed moments later. Operators told police they were unable to determine where the call had come from. Hours later, another anonymous call was placed, this one to the editorial desk of the *Kansas City Star*, announcing new developments in "the Hickman case."

Pressed for details, the caller said, "I'll give you a tip. Dr. Mantz knows a lot about it. He has had contact with that fellow. He [Hickman] was in Kansas City yesterday [*sic*] and threatened Dr. Mantz. He [Mantz] is scared to death. Dr. Mantz has two detectives guarding him. They're private men, I think."

Asked for his name, the caller replied, "You wouldn't know me, but I just wanted you to get this angle." The call *was* traced this time, to a pay phone in the lobby of a Saint Louis bank, but there the trail went cold, police dismissing both calls as the work of a crank.

In Omaha, that same afternoon, railroad detectives thought they had captured Hickman when they grabbed a young man disembarking from a livestock train, where he had stowed away to ride for free. They were mistaken, but ironically they had come closer than anyone else to date. In custody, nineteen-year-old Wallace Boardman admitted to being a former classmate of Hickman's at Central High School.

Scattered reports notwithstanding, police in Los Angeles still behaved as if they expected to find their quarry close to home. Their optimism was encouraged by callers like C. F.

Kaufman, from Pomona, who once worked with Ed at First National Bank and who now reported that his former co-worker had stopped by to ask for directions to Tijuana, Mexico. Dorothy Taylor, a teenage waitress jailed for writing bad checks in L.A., told police that Hickman resembled her best girlfriend's "sweetie." Yet another lead, from Realtor William Ryan, had Hickman and an unidentified companion house-hunting in Chico on Sunday afternoon.

And speaking of accomplices, detectives in Los Angeles were still searching for the "other man" allegedly seen with Hickman on Saturday night, loading packages into a car behind the Bellevue Arms. As for the apartment itself, an exhaustive search had persuaded Chief Cline—erroneously—that Marian Parker had been murdered at some other site.

"I am convinced," Cline told reporters from the *Times*, "that the apartment was not used to slay the child, although it is possible, but not probable. Later developments, I am certain, will show that she was killed elsewhere. It is possible her body was taken in the apartment after the killing."

Wholesale arrests of young dark-haired men continued in Los Angeles, even after Cline and company heard from the Portland police that Hickman had been sighted in Oregon, headed north. The *Times* reported "dozens" of arrests, some accompanied by threats of mob violence, as would-be vigilantes lined up to settle the score for Marian's murder. Hickman look-alike Richard Pleaux, arrested on suspicion in Tucson, displayed an LAPD "parole card" to investigators there, and while Chief Cline denied that such cards existed, his men *were* issuing hastily printed "exemption certificates" to suspects who had already been questioned and cleared. Nothing seemed to help Michael O'Neil, though: by Wednesday afternoon the wavy-haired twenty-seven-year-old had been arrested no less than five times by different patrolmen.

Although the suspect remained elusive, armchair detectives were hot on the trail of explanations for Ed's heinous crime. An uncle, Oklahoma barber J. D. Hickman, told the press about Eva's suicide attempt and subsequent commitment to a sanitarium. She responded with a furious denial from Missouri. Judge Allen, of Orange County Superior Court, meanwhile blamed the murder on the coddling of criminals by the state parole board. In future, Allen told reporters, he would place all convicted defendants on probation instead of sending them to prison, with the singular condition that they serve the probationary term confined to county jail. "No use sending them to the state prison to be paroled," Allen told the *Times*. "I am going to sentence them so they will stay sentenced."

How would that solution have affected Hickman's case? "If it's a check case, for instance," Allen said, "the state law provides an indeterminate sentence of from one to fourteen years in state prison. The State Prison Board then fixes the exact length of time to be served and can parole the defendant at any time. When such a case comes before me, henceforth, I shall grant probation and then send the defendant to jail for such period of time, between one and fourteen years, as I think the case merits."

Such bluster aside, detectives in L.A. were still no closer to their man by Wednesday night. Chief Edwards, in Kansas City, tried to help with an appeal for Ed to write or call. Published in the press from coast to coast, it read:

To William Edward Hickman:
   Your mother is prostrated. Brothers and sisters wish you to get in touch immediately with your friend "Cap" Edwards, who you know will see that you are justly and fairly treated. Wire, telephone or write me at my expense at my home, 3418 Bellefontaine Avenue, Kansas City, Mo., day or night, or at my office, 701 Bryant Building.

                                   "Cap" Edwards

If Ed saw the appeal, he was unmoved.
He reached Seattle shortly after 6:00 P.M. on Wednesday, and his first stop was a movie theater. He spent one of the

twenty-dollar gold certificates to buy his ticket, pocketing the change. It was a foolish risk, but maybe Ed was far enough away from southern California that he didn't think it mattered.

Then again, perhaps he *wanted* to be caught and punished for his crime.

Hickman denied involvement in the act, but *someone* mailed a letter from suburban Bryn Mawr that Wednesday, addressed to Seattle's chief of police, William Searing. It was almost rejected for insufficient postage—the sender had made do with a single one-cent stamp—before a clerk made note of the addressee and the word "Fox" that was written on one corner of the envelope. The letter read:

> I am tired of this. Will I be given fair play if I surrender? I did not intend to kill Marian. I did not mean to harm her. I only wanted to put her to sleep. I did not want her to suffer, as she was a good girl. She was not afraid of me at any time and did not suffer. She only wanted to go home and would have left in safety if my plans had not failed. Will this make any difference?
> This is the truth.
> The Fox

It certainly *sounded* like Edward, but if he did write the letter, he evidently changed his mind about waiting around for an answer. Emerging from the theater around 8:30 P.M., he watched a squad car pass and calculated that police were hunting him. (In fact, the letter to Chief Searing had not been delivered yet, and no one at the theater ever acknowledged receiving one of the ransom bills.) He also felt Seattle's biting cold and went in search of a men's clothing store, to reinforce his winter wardrobe.

It was pushing 8:50 P.M. when he found a store open to serve him. He selected a hat, heavy gloves, and a suit of thermal underwear. The bill came to five dollars, and instead of using his change from the theater, Ed produced another twenty-dollar gold certificate. This bill—serial number K-6801970—*would* be reported to police, and the sales clerk would identify Ed's mug shot from Los Angeles. "As quick as I looked at that fellow," Ed later told police, "I knew he recognized me."

As Hickman walked back to his car in the cold, his paranoia kicked into high gear. He saw a newsboy trailing him, imagined hot pursuit, hurried to the Hudson, and drove off as quickly as the traffic would allow. Whatever thoughts he may have had about surrender in Seattle vanished instantly, his focus shifting to evasion and escape.

By 9:30 P.M., Ed was leaving Seattle behind, doubling back toward Oregon. His mastermind was working overtime, telling him that any manhunt would be concentrated to the north. If the police had tracked him this far, they would surely think he was headed for Canada. He was sure he could outfox them by retreating, charting his course as he went along.

In Kent, Washington, he stopped for gas and spent another ransom bill. "I had plenty of money," he later told authorities. "I don't know why I paid that man off with a twenty-dollar bill. They were looking for me up north and did not expect I would double back over my trail like that, but I gave him the twenty-dollar bill, and as quick as I gave it to him I knew he recognized me."

Or maybe not.

Some 60 miles south of Seattle, he stopped in Olympia long enough to discard the Hudson's California license tags and steal a set of local plates from an unattended Ford. Ed felt a little better, then, although the Hudson was distinctive in its own right. He should have ditched it for a less conspicuous model, but Hickman calculated rightly that his normal style of carjacking would be a greater liability just now than sticking with the car he had.

He made it back to Oregon without getting stopped, and by daylight Thursday morning he drove through Pendleton for the second time in as many days, and turned eastward, following the Columbia River. Once more he remembered the adage about safety in numbers, picking up the Merrill

brothers, Bill and Jack, for company a mile or two outside
The Dalles.

The Merrill boys were going home to Garfield, Washington, for Christmas, after months of slaving on a farm near
Dufur, Oregon. Since Ed was going east, they would gladly
ride with him as far as Pendleton.

The brothers rode in back, as if Hickman was their chauf-
feur. Ed told them he was going home for Christmas, too. In
his case, home was Salt Lake City, he said, a welcome
change of pace from his mythical collegiate studies in
Olympia, Washington. On a whim, he pulled the .45 automatic and showed it off to the brothers, with a flourish.

"He said that he carried a lot of money," Bill Merrill
recalled, "and carried the gun for protection. He handed us
the gun, told us that it was loaded and asked us to look it
over. If we had any idea then that he was Hickman, we
could have captured him without a bit of trouble, as we had
the drop on him."

They were *that* close to $65,000 in reward money but
failed to recognize their benefactor as a hunted fugitive. "He
didn't talk so very much and seemed awfully tired," Bill
Merrill said. "Then I did get a little suspicious. I thought he
might be a hijacker or rumrunner."

Close, but no cigar.

The noose was tightening that Thursday morning. In Los
Angeles, bright and early, a newsman was preparing to
spring the trap. Walter Clausen was L.A. bureau chief for
the Associated Press and a part-time captain in the U.S.
Army Reserve's military intelligence department. He didn't
know where Hickman was, exactly, but he had been up
most of the night, collating reports from Washington and
Oregon, plotting the strange, erratic progress of a phantom
in a green Hudson sedan. Now it was snowing in northern
Washington, which meant the roads and passes into Canada
would be shut down. Clausen believed the Fox might just
decide to double back instead of waiting out the storm.
Excited at the prospect of participating in the manhunt,
even from a distance, he wired all Associated Press sub-

scribers in the Pacific Northwest an urgent description of Frank Peck's stolen car, complete with license plate and engine serial numbers.

It was close to lunchtime, 11:40 A.M., when Pendleton police chief Tom Gurdane received an anxious phone call from an editor at the local newspaper, the *Eastern Oregonian*. There was something on the wire he ought to see.

Tom Gurdane was an old-fashioned lawman, his rugged visage and stern demeanor befitting a peace officer assigned to police what was once part of the old Oregon Trail. When not in uniform, he leaned toward classic Western garb, complete with cowboy boots, fringed leather jackets, and a sombrero. There were no more Indians to fight in eastern Oregon, but human nature and the federal ban on alcoholic beverages ensured that Chief Gurdane kept busy, even in a relatively quiet town like Pendleton.

Leaving his office for the short walk to the *Oregonian* offices, Gurdane met burly Buck Lieuallen of the state highway patrol, and asked him to tag along. The paper's city editor, one Parker Branin, met them in the lobby and began talking rapidly: That Hickman boy, the killer from Los Angeles, had passed another ransom bill to purchase gasoline in Arlington, some 60 miles due west of Pendleton, and he was headed eastward when he left the service station. There might still be time to head him off.

They took Lieuallen's car, Buck driving, since Gurdane had no official jurisdiction outside Pendleton. The legal niceties were not of much concern in 1928, but having Buck drive left the chief's hands free, in case he had to shoot at the rat who was described in bulletins as armed and dangerous.

They drove as far as Echo, 20 miles, before Lieuallen parked his cruiser on the soft dirt shoulder of the winding road, positioned so that they could watch the next curve up ahead. Lieuallen was filling his pipe when a car rolled into view.

"Here comes a Hudson," said Gurdane.

Lieuallen squinted for a better look. "That's not him," he replied. "It has Washington plates. *His* car has California plates."

Gurdane hunched forward in his seat. The Hudson's driver was a young man with dark hair. He wore sunglasses even though the day was overcast and gray.

"To hell with the license," Gurdane snapped. "It's a Hudson, and it's green. Get after him."

Lieuallen put his pipe away, turned the ignition key, and wheeled his cruiser through a sharp U-turn. The Hudson seemed to be accelerating now. Buck thumbed a dashboard switch to turn the siren on.

Bill Merrill tried to warn Edward. "Near Echo," he recalled, "we saw the officers and I shouted that there was a traffic cop. He [Ed] didn't seem to get excited, and when the cop blew his siren, Hickman just pulled over to the side and stopped."

What some reporters later chose to call a "breakneck chase" took all of two minutes, Hickman stopping his car a mile and a half from the point where Gurdane had first seen him. Both officers approached the Hudson with drawn pistols, Gurdane on the driver's side, Lieuallen to the right and covering the two young passengers in back.

Hickman had his window open and was smiling past the gun at Chief Gurdane. "Was I speeding?" he asked.

Gurdane ignored the question. "What's your name?"

Ed never missed a beat. There had been time, while he was driving up and down the coast, to read the Hudson's registration card. "My name is Peck," he said.

"Where are you from?" Gurdane inquired.

"Seattle," Hickman said. "I've been attending college over there, and I'm going to visit my mother."

Gurdane knew a lie when he heard one. With his free left hand, he opened up the driver's door. "Step out and over to the side," he ordered.

Hickman did as he was told, no sudden moves. A blue steel automatic pistol clattered noisily as it hit the Hudson's running board.

Gurdane drew back the hammer on his .38 revolver, ready to fire, if it came to that. "What are you doing with that gun?" he asked.

"It's customary," Hickman said, "to carry a gun when you are traveling."

"Maybe," the chief said, "but you don't need to keep it between your knees."

He braced Hickman against the car as Lieuallen unloaded the passengers on his side. A glance down past the steering wheel revealed a sawed-off shotgun lying on the floorboards, almost underneath the driver's seat. Gurdane frisked the driver, found no more weapons, but removed $65 in cash from his pockets. Buck Lieuallen, meanwhile, checked the car out and retrieved another automatic pistol.

Gurdane knew they'd hit pay dirt when Lieuallen found the stash of twenty-dollar gold certificates, more than a thousand dollars' worth.

"You're Hickman," said Gurdane. "I knew you all the time."

The hunted killer, standing with his hands against the car, did not appear surprised. "Well," he said with a shrug, "I guess it's all over."

8 ✦ "This Is Going to Be Interesting"

The city jail in Pendleton was built to house eight prisoners at any given time. Four two-man cells were situated in the middle of a Spartan room, a kind of penal Rubik's cube. Each cell had bunk beds. There was no other furniture, no view to speak of. It was not designed to be a comfort zone.

By 1:15 P.M. on Thursday, December 21, the most wanted fugitive west of the Rockies was locked up in cell number one. His hapless passengers were lodged together in another cell, booked as material witnesses until such time as Chief Gurdane received approval from Los Angeles to let them go.

The chief and Buck Lieuallen started with an inventory of the evidence removed from Hickman's car. The gold certificates came to $1,400, plus the $65.00 from Hickman's pocket. They logged the Colt .45 automatic and the sawed-off shotgun manufactured by Davis-Warner Arms, loaded with two rounds of #6 duck shot. Gurdane avoided handling the smaller pistol, a .380, leaving its disposition to LAPD. He opened a leather suitcase and saw two boxes of ammunition, one for each handgun. The weapons and ammo went into his safe.

Hickman breezed through the booking process, seeming almost cocky in captivity, as if he had been waiting for an audience. "This is going to be interesting before it is all over," he told Buck Lieuallen. "Do they only kill by hanging in California?" And then, as if uncertain where he was: "Oh, this is not California, is it?" Posing for the second mug shot of his life, he still cracked wise. "What should I look like?" he asked the officer behind the camera. "A crook?"

Ed's humor failed him on the way back to his cell. In place of wisecracks, now his lips were trembling, tears brimming in his eyes. His tone was urgent as he denied killing Marian Parker, blaming her death on an accomplice he called Andrew Cramer. "Marian and I were good friends," he insisted. "We had a good time together, and I really *liked* her. I'm sorry that she was killed."

It was all Cramer's fault, he told Lieuallen, sobbing now. The older man had strangled Marian with a wire garrote and dismembered her body. There was nothing Edward could have done to save her life.

The news of his arrest electrified Los Angeles. Reporters rushed to Perry Parker for a quote to lead their stories. "I am thankful," Parker said, on hearing the news. "I am thankful not only for myself but for the parents of all other children that such a dangerous man has been apprehended. This is too terrible a thing to talk about adequate punishments for the man."

In Kansas City, Eva Hickman was stunned by Edward's admission of even a peripheral role in the murder. "This is all so muddled," she told reporters. "It looks like I haven't a friend in the world. They are hounding my boy to death, just because they have a clue." As the full weight of Edward's predicament struck her, she burst into tears, crying out, "My God! My God! They'll kill him! They won't even give him a chance to say anything for himself. Oh, I must get to him! I must get to him some way, at once. He needs me, oh, so badly!"

Down in El Paso, Bill Hickman was also reported in tears, though his grief seemed fueled by embarrassment rather than fear for his son. "I would rather be dead," he told a local journalist, "than to think that a child of mine would commit such an atrocious crime. I love my son as much as anyone loves his child, but I want to see justice done, even though it strikes at the heart of my family, though it has never had a stain on it. I have never been in jail. I have never been arrested for anything. I know of nothing against my family in previous generations."

Eva's fears notwithstanding, Edward seemed to have no trouble speaking up for himself in the Pendleton jail. In fact, as Chief Gurdane would later testify, "He wanted to talk all the time, and I kept telling [the jailers] not to talk to him, not to question him, to leave him alone until the Los Angeles authorities got there."

The chief was a realist, though, and his ban on questions did not extend to the press. Hickman might be off-limits to locals with badges, but Parker Branin had no trouble getting in to record Ed's first public statement for the *Eastern Oregonian*, a statement that was wired to papers nationwide for the Friday morning edition.

"Where is your partner?" Branin asked, first thing.

"He said for me to meet him at the Herald Hotel in San Francisco, Sunday," Hickman answered. "But he was not there, so Tuesday morning I saw they had my name, so I got real scared, then I planned to get away myself. I thought I would get away north, because they were searching in San Francisco, as I read about it in the papers, and there was nothing I could do. After I saw him in Los Angeles, according to our appointment, I said, 'Where is the girl?' And he just kind of grinned, and I said, 'Where . . . ?' "

Ed faltered, skipping over his alleged reaction to his first sight of the mutilated corpse. "When her father met me by appointment," he went on, "he spoke and said, 'I want to see my daughter,' and I said, 'She is here.' I think I said she was asleep, and I told him to give me the money. I have had trouble with her. And then he gave me the money, right there, and I told him I would drive up there a little way and let her out, and I drove out a little way."

"Who was it cut her that way?" Branin interrupted.

"This fellow named Andrew Cramer," Hickman said. "His part . . ." Again he hesitated, shifting gears. "I ran away from home and was in California," Ed went on, the words rushing out of him, "and had been working in the First National Bank and forged checks and got paroled and went back to Kansas City with my mother, and I wanted to go back again, so I then . . . I got this coupe in Kansas City, which belonged to Dr. Mantz—I think was the doctor—and I got out here. At first, I didn't come direct out here. I went to Chicago before I came here, and I rented that apartment in Los Angeles at the Bellevue Arms. I think it was on November 23, or just before Thanksgiving, and on Thanksgiving I went down to San Diego, and when I came back the next day I picked this man and lady up. He said his name was Andrew Cramer, and the lady's name was June Dunning, I think it was. I was by myself. I didn't know anyone here. I was making my living by holdups, and I thought if I could get acquainted with some older man, we could work to better advantage and it wouldn't be as much risk and [we] could probably get away with the holdups easier.

"We just held up drugstores and places like that," he went on. "That is the reason I had all these guns. The .380 belongs to Andrew. He left it there, so it didn't make any difference. We worked several places. He wanted me to get some chloroform for him, and ether. I didn't ask him what for. So in one of our holdups I would get out and he would drive the car. He would sit in the car, and I would get the money and whatever we wanted and go out, and then he would drive away."

Hickman crafted the story to make himself seem less culpable. "I really had not intended being a crook," he told Branin, "because you will find out soon enough you will get caught, but because I wanted to go back to Kansas City and go to work and save enough money to go to college—Park College, near Kansas City—and I thought if I could get enough money to go to the school, and by working some during the day, an hour or two every day, in that way I could pay the tuition. I thought if I could save a thousand dollars, I could start next September, and no matter how I got that, I figured I would go straight from then on. And this man asked me what I thought of kidnapping someone, and I thought I would not mind doing it."

The selection of a victim, Ed conceded, had been left to him. "I happened to remember that Mr. Parker had a daughter," he said, "because in working at the bank, this girl came with him. I didn't know just what date it was. I was there in the bank several days, and I noticed especially . . . and I noticed . . . and I remember it was his daughter, because she was his favorite daughter, and he would take her down and buy her lunch, and she was around the bank like she was a big man."

Ed may have heard the bitterness creeping into his voice. In any case, he shifted gears again before Branin could speak. "I didn't think of her, however, before I thought of Mr. Hovis, who is chief teller of the First National Bank, and I think he has a very young child, and I thought of that first, and thought we would get the money from him much easier. Easier," Ed explained, "because he is a chief officer of the bank and handles hundreds of thousands of dollars, and while I was at the bank I saw all the money shipments come in and used to go around the vaults, and anyplace in the bank, and knew practically everyone in the bank."

Ed the planner. Ed the mastermind.

"Well," he continued, "in order to get this little girl, this younger girl, I was afraid it would be harder to handle her. She was a baby and would probably cry. I thought either Mr. Hovis or Parker, either one, would have sense enough to consider $1,500 an easy settlement in consideration of their own daughter. I meant no harm to either one, but I thought it would be easier to handle the older girl than a little child."

It must have occurred to Ed that he was placing his mythical accomplice in a minimal supporting role. Remembering the purpose of his statement, he went on, "So this man and I both went out, and he wanted to see her and get a look at her, and I looked in the telephone book to see where Mr. Parker lived. I went to the house to see her when she came from school, and I saw her riding around on a bicycle, but I didn't know she had a twin sister until Thursday morning. I parked by the house early so I could see her leave for school

and could see what school she went to, and it popped into
my mind that if I went for her at the school, I could get her
that way. There was no plan, but I had been thinking about
it, and it popped into my mind when I saw the girl that
morning. I did not plan out the results ahead of that, until I
saw her that morning. And that afternoon . . . you have
read in the papers how it all happened. I went and told the
teacher that her father had been in an accident, and this
other girl came over to see which one of the girls I wanted,
and I said I wanted the younger one. She looked younger,
but it turned out they were twins, but she [the teacher]
didn't question me in any way."

Hickman was on a roll, his sinister accomplice momentar-
ily forgotten. "Then," he said, "they asked what was her first
name, so I told them. I didn't think I remembered, but I told
them I worked at the bank. I didn't give my real name—I
forget the name I did give them—and they asked me which
girl I wanted, and I said the younger one, and she said,
'Marian?' And I said, 'Yes, that is the one the father was
calling for,' and one of the other teachers went and got the
girl."

Ed seemed to lose his focus for a moment. "I had been in
front of the house," he told Branin, "and I called at the
schoolhouse that morning, and I think they got on a streetcar and went to the Mount Vernon School, and when I
went up in the car I learned that the Franklin School . . .
right near a fence . . . and after we came out of the schoolhouse, we got into the car and we left, and she started asking questions about what happened and how it happened
and who hit him, and I made answers to all her questions."

After the brief lapse, Ed seemed to have found his place in
the story again. "I answered everything," he told Branin,
"and she got in, and we started back and was just having a
general conversation and talking about picture shows and
merchants and school and anything that comes up in conversation generally with people, and we got well and closely
acquainted, and I really kind of liked her. I couldn't look her
in the face when I told her she was kidnapped, as though

nothing had happened. When I told her nothing had really happened to her father, she didn't worry or scream or anything. She took it calm as could be, and I told her she could realize that if I got caught that I would have to suffer, and I would have to tie her nose and tie her mouth so she couldn't make any noise. And she said, 'Please don't do it. I will promise not to make any noise,' so I didn't tie her, and we drove around all afternoon and went to a show that night—even went to a picture show, the Rialto Theater in Alhambra—and she didn't do or say anything much."

It was time for Andrew Cramer to step in, no matter how illogical his actions sounded. "I didn't intend to do her any harm," Hickman insisted, "and this is where the other man's part of it played in. He was to have the hiding place for the girl and keep her quiet, and I was supposed to get the money. He only wanted two or three hundred dollars out of the fifteen hundred. He said he didn't want much money, anyway. He seemed to like the idea of kidnapping the girl and holding her, rather than getting the money."

Branin managed to conceal his skepticism as Edward continued.

"Thursday, that night after the show," Hickman said, "I met this man and he took the girl in charge. He took her, and the next day I saw her. That was Friday evening. Well, I kept writing all these letters and [told] her to write a letter to her father, making it seem like she was being treated bad, and I don't know . . . she didn't seem to like this man, and didn't want to go with him, and wanted to stay with me instead, but I couldn't do a thing like that. We had to go through with the plans. Anyway, she wanted to go home as soon as possible, and I thought if the father was willing to hand over the money and he had it, it was perfectly all right, and as soon as I got it over with, the better it would be for me, anyway.

"So," Edward continued, "I called up her father and he said he had the money, and we planned a meeting, and that was . . . we were to meet at a certain street. And then, after I called up his house from a drugstore between his home and the meeting place, I went up there, and I could watch him pass by. So when I went and got in the car and I sat in the car so I could watch for him, and I came back up, I saw him, and there were two cars driven clearly together, and I drove out on the side and followed him to the meeting place."

Hickman was back on solid ground now, portraying himself as the Fox. "They lived on Gramercy Street," he said, getting it wrong, "which is just one block north, and these two cars stopped, and when I saw them I was absolutely certain they were detectives and they were going to try to take the girl back and turn her over to the man again. I wrote him another letter, and this other man suggested that I [was] getting the time [for delivery] too near, but this would make it much safer, and they were making such a big search, he was afraid they would find the girl."

Ed, the cool one, was talking sense to a figment of his own imagination, laying down the law. But he could not anticipate the phantom's final desperate act.

"So Saturday," he continued, "when he came to the apartment [with] this suitcase, and when he opened it up and showed me how it was, I was sure surprised. He said, 'The police are already suspicious of the place,' and he said she was crying and he tried to stop her or something like that, and he figured that the safest way would be to go ahead and fix it that way, and for me to keep my suitcase in the car and go to this place, and if the police stopped me before I could get rid of it, they might look at the suitcase and never stop to open it. And I thought that might be all right."

That disposed of the murder, although Hickman failed to clarify how Cramer got "my" suitcase. Never mind. "He had already gone ahead and opened it anyway," Ed went on, "so in this letter I told the girl's father that if I were paid before six o'clock that night, that his daughter would still be alive. And I didn't find out [that Marian was dead] until after six o'clock, when he came up to the apartment. Even if I had written this letter after we called," Ed explained, "even if she had not been alive, I thought he wanted his daughter anyway, no matter what condition she was in, and he would rather have her, and so I went ahead and called him up and planned the meeting place.

"He was there, all right," Ed recalled of the Saturday night meeting, "and as it happened the night before, I was there before he came, and if there had been any detectives, he would [not] have gotten her back. And if this fellow had not killed her, it would have come out all right, as we had planned, because I am sure she didn't want to die. Because when she was with me, I remember she said, 'I wonder what the school kids will say when I go back to school. They will want to know what I did, and everything.' And I am terribly sorry she was killed, myself, because I sure liked her."

Ed was weeping again, the break giving Branin a chance to interject a request: "Give us the description of this fellow that you say killed her."

"He was about five feet eight or nine inches tall," Ed replied, sniffling, "and had almost black hair, and I don't remember the color of his eyes. As far as I remember, I think he had been leading an impure life. He had a sore upon his chin, but that might have been from the way he had been eating. The times I saw him, when I picked him up, he had on a kind of gray overcoat, and he just had the one suit—a kind of tan suit, or brown. He had a kind of rough face."

"How old was he?" Branin asked.

"He looked to be not much over twenty-eight," Hickman said, "but he looked older, because I think he had been leading a kind of hard life."

"Where was he staying?"

"He would not tell me that," Ed replied, "because he was to have his part in the plan, and I my part. Crooks sometimes will go back on each other, and if anyone knew what the other one did . . . and it makes everything safer and less dangerous than if we knew where each other stayed, and I don't know where he kept himself."

The answer had a built-in contradiction, since Cramer clearly knew where Ed was living, but the newsman let it pass. "He didn't stay in the same apartment with you?" Branin asked.

"No," Hickman said. "I was in that apartment by myself."

"Did this woman have anything to do with it?"

"I never saw her again," Ed replied, sidestepping the question. "Her first name was June. I think her last name was Dunning."

"How much would she weigh?" Branin asked.

"About 120 or 130 pounds, I guess. She was about twenty-five or twenty-six years of age, I guess. I know they appeared to be a well-matched couple."

"You don't know what address they had?"

Ed shook his head. "No," he said, "I never did know. You can see the condition I was in—which, being a crook any-way—when I picked him up. I had been alone quite a time, anyway. I had been to a good many places, to Chicago, and I went to New York and Pittsburgh, and Philadelphia and Washington, D.C., before I came out to the coast."

Ed was rambling, and Branin tried to bring him back on track. "Do you know where you were to meet him, or where to call him?"

"No," Hickman said, appearing confused. "We always planned to meet at places."

"You planned where you would meet again," Branin said. "You didn't have any address for any one of you?"

"No, sir."

Branin avoided the obvious question—How, in that case, had Cramer driven to Edward's apartment?—and instead asked, "When was the last time you saw him?"

"The last time I saw him was when he brought the suit-case up to the apartment," Hickman said, "and he told me when I got the money—*if* I got the money—to go up to San Francisco as soon as I could safely get away, as the police-men were awfully suspicious here, anyway. Well, one thing that did happen Sunday morning was, there were about two hundred detectives [who] came up to the apartment and looked over the apartment and started searching it. One of the fellows had the name of the apartment written on a paper, and when they came in my apartment . . . it is interesting, the way I was singing and playing the phonograph, and the detectives came in and they looked around and did not express any suspicion of me at all. And I went in the hallway and talked to seven or eight of the best detectives in Los Angeles. I asked them if there was anything I could do, and of course there was nothing I could do, and they searched the apartment."

Ed the genius, faking out L.A.'s Finest. What he failed to grasp was obvious to Branin: the detectives never would have found the Bellevue Arms to start with, if the towel recovered with Marian's body had not led them there. A towel supposedly from the residence of "Andrew Cramer" at some unknown location in Los Angeles.

"He had the girl, or part of the effects of the girl," Branin pressed, "when he came up to the apartment?"

"Yes, sir. I guess he threw the other parts away where they said they were thrown away."

"What parts did he have up there, in the suitcase?"

"He just had—she was cut right across the middle of the body, and her arms . . . he had them fixed up, and he had her dress put on her." Ed made a show of revulsion. "He had her dress, and a little sweater thrown on her face. And, of course, she was dead. But the way he had fixed the mouth, it didn't seem very deathlike. He had little threads through her eyebrows, which seemed to hold her eyes open."

"He opened the suitcase," Branin asked, "so you might see what he had there?"

"Yes, sir."

"Where were you when he did that?"

"That was in the apartment," Ed replied.

"What did you say to him when you saw that?"

"I let out a yell of surprise and wanted to know why he did a thing like that," Hickman said. "It was quite a shock to me. He was not supposed to bring her up to the apartment.

We were supposed to meet Thursday, when I got her and turned her over to him."

Another flagrant contradiction. How could Cramer deliver a dead child on Saturday, if he had never received her on Thursday?

"That is the last time you saw her living?" Branin asked, referring to the Thursday handoff.

"No," Ed corrected him. "That was the same day I got her from the school—that is, after we had gone to the show. He told me to hold her until night, so when he did take her it would not be suspicious, and no one would see us. We met, and he took her. He had a car, a Ford car. I don't remember the license number."

"What kind of car was it?" Branin prodded.

"A Ford coupe. It was a kind of old car," Hickman said. "The only time I saw a thing of it was when he took the girl, because he never did bring it around. We always used my car, which I had taken on holdup jobs and things like that. Then, the next day, he kept her all that [Thursday] night, and the next evening she came over and got in my car and sat in my car. We drove around until I called her father and planned this meeting. When it turned out a failure, we didn't meet at the same place or time. It was on Grand, way down on Grand near Washington Boulevard, when I gave her back to him. That was the last I saw of her alive."

Returning to Saturday morning, Hickman went on, "He brought the suitcase, and I wanted to know where she was. He said, 'Wait a minute,' and kind of grinned, and set the suitcase down on the sofa and opened it. I have already told you what I saw, and everything."

"You were to meet him in Frisco, in case you got away with the money?" Branin said.

"When I got the money, I was supposed to meet him there and make as quick a getaway as I could," Hickman said, "and meet him at the Herald Hotel in Frisco. I forget just where it is located."

"Had you stayed at that hotel before?"

"No," Ed answered. "He told me where it was, but I have forgotten the name of the street."

"He didn't tell you whether he had stayed there before or not, did he?"

"He said he knew where it was, and he would be around the hotel there, anyway. If I got to the hotel, he would be there."

"After you got the money," Branin said, "what did you do then? Did you go back to your apartment?"

"I got the money that night," Hickman said, "and beat it as quick as I could and left the car in a parking lot, where the police found it later. That was on Grand, and I went back to the apartment and got my things together. The next morning, as one of the policemen came up there to search it, that made me glad to get away quicker, for then I took first all of the evidence in one package, and went downstairs and checked them at a place. I left most of the stuff in the apartment—some little clothes and some other articles, a slicker and a pair of overshoes. I put the stuff all in one case and took that, and some of my other things, and took them downtown and checked them at the place and went to a show. And after the show, I went to Hollywood to get this Hudson, and I just came on back to the station and put these grips in there, and these guns, and drove right away to San Francisco."

It had not been a carefree journey, however, as Edward described it to Branin. "I was stopped three times before I got through," he recalled, "and I was questioned by policemen, and there wasn't one of them [who] suspected me at all."

The Fox reemerging, triumphant.

"You were stopped three times before you got to Frisco?" Branin asked.

"Yes, sir," Hickman said. "I was searched right out of Los Angeles, and then before I got inside Ventura and stopped by a state officer, and was stopped by two men just out of Los Angeles. In the next meeting, it was more scary than ever, because they hadn't suspicioned then, by the way they asked questions. I told them I was driving to Ventura to get my mother. That was Sunday night, and I told them my name was Peck. I had just stolen the car, but I knew it could not be reported that quick, and I had a license certificate right with me. I didn't need to show them that, for one of the fellows said, 'Let him go ahead.' And there was one state officer—I think it was just as we were pulling into Santa Barbara—he didn't stop to look. He just said, 'Hello, how are you?' and I said, 'All right.' I said, 'Are you still on that kidnapping case?' And he said, 'You bet your sweet life we are.' I said, 'I sure hope you get him,' and I said the same thing to all the rest of them. I enjoyed the conversation at first. I was not scared, but when they got me [at Echo], I knew it was all up."

Casting himself as a hapless victim of circumstance, Hickman told Branin, "There was only one thing I could do, and that was to go ahead. I knew if they stopped me and questioned me after that, they had my picture and my fingerprints, which would be positive identification. I was taking that big chance, and I thought I was sitting easy, because I thought surely I would get into Salt Lake, and from Salt Lake I was going into Kansas City to see my mother. I noticed in one of the papers that she and one of the former chiefs of police had written a letter and published it in the papers, telling me to let her know where I was, and they would help me out. I guess my mother thought the police having my fingerprints was not conclusive enough."

"Did you stop in Frisco overnight?" Branin asked.

"Yes, sir. I stopped at that hotel."

"Did you see that fellow there?"

"No," Hickman said. "I got there Monday and stayed there Monday night, and Tuesday I sat right around the hotel most of the day. Tuesday morning I went out and got a paper and saw in big headlines my own name, and that they had my fingerprints and had evidence that would convict me beyond a doubt of the crime, and I thought I was just an ace. That is all. The only thing I could do was to protect my own self and get away if I got an opportunity, so I drove to Seattle."

"Did you stop anyplace between Frisco and here?" Branin asked.

"At Davis," Ed replied. "I picked up a man, and he said there was a state road that cut off about twenty-three miles, but it was kind of rough. I was afraid if I was stopped it would be at the intersection. When this guy got out and ate a meal in the restaurant, they were talking about [the] reward, and I questioned some of them and found out as much as I could, what was going on. This man said he wanted to stop. I got in the car and drove right on to another place. I was afraid they would stop me beyond the California state line, and I left San Francisco Tuesday morning."

Yet another contradiction, after saying he had remained at the Herald Hotel "most of the day," waiting for Cramer to appear.

"I picked up two other fellows at Dunsmuir, I believe it was," he continued. "I mentioned the kidnapping to them, and they seemed to have heard a lot about it. I acted surprised. There were no more officers north of there. One of the fellows said, 'I imagine they will get us out at the state line,' and the other fellow said he was going over. I told these fellows I was going to Seattle to spend the holidays, and that I had two quarts of booze in the suitcase, in the back, and was afraid if some officers were to search, that they might find this and get me for that. I said, 'Let's wait until after midnight.' The officers generally don't sit up after midnight, and when we got up near the line it was after ten [o'clock]. We just stopped the car—it was this same Hudson all the time—and waited. We got through finally, and got to the line about fifteen minutes after twelve, and there wasn't a soul around."

His plan had not been perfect, though. "When we got into Oregon," Ed recalled, "two officers stopped the car. I was in the back seat, almost asleep, and these two fellows were in the front seat. The officers flashed a light on my companions and said, 'All right.' I don't know whether they were searching for booze or not, but there were two officers, and it was just across the line. They were not California officers. At the time I picked my companions up, they said they were going to Portland. One of them was in the merchant marine. I had his card, but have forgotten the name. When we got into Portland the next day—that was yesterday—it was around one o'clock, and that left me in the car by myself."

"I left Portland," Ed continued, "and drove toward Seattle, and picked up one other man before I got into Seattle. There was a heavy fog, but he seemed to know the road well. He happened to be a sailor, too. He had finished his enlistment in the navy and was going home. We joked for quite a bit about the kidnapping. I just listened to this man's idea of what this guy—meaning myself—was like, and what he thought of him. 'Have they found Hickman yet?' he asked me. I was sitting in the front seat with him, and I wondered if he had seen the picture of me. I know if the police in Portland had seen my pictures, they would see how foolish they were now."

The Fox, gloating.

"Going back in my story to the boys I picked up," Hickman said, "we waited on the other side of the state line until twelve o'clock. I let them drive, so I would be in the back seat." Restating his cleverness, in case Branin had missed it. "Well, I got into Seattle last night, about seven o'clock, and did not know what to do. I thought I would go to the Automobile Club and ask about the road, and the directions to Spokane. There I planned to take the Northwest Limited and work [my way] out of the country that way. Then I changed my plans and decided not to go to Spokane."

What had changed his mind? "While in Seattle that night," Ed recalled, "I went into a dry goods store and bought a suit of heavy underwear, which I am now wearing, and a pair of gloves. I gave the man a twenty-dollar bill, and he gave me back fifteen dollars. The underclothes cost two dollars, and the gloves three dollars. Then I went to the theater. I went to the window and said, 'One ticket, please,' and gave her a bill. She glanced curiously at the currency and looked straight at me. When she gave me the change, I went straight to my car and drove out of Seattle, stopping at a station between Seattle and Tacoma. I left another bill with the attendant at the filling station."

Marking his trail.

"The attendant seemed to be suspicious of the bill," Ed told Branin. "I got eighteen dollars and a few cents. I waited for the attendant to come back with the change from the bill, and then came down to Portland and got through the fog and into Portland this morning, around six o'clock. I went through Portland and out onto the highway. I was afraid someone would stop me, as I was positive the word would get out that I was in Seattle, and unless the officers thought I had gone to Canada and was not coming back to Portland, I probably would get caught."

Even so, he pushed on. The bold Fox. "I intended to circle around through Boise," Hickman said, "[on] Highway Number Eighty. I noticed it was the Columbia River highway, out of Portland. I believed this highway would follow the Columbia River, and I intended going through Boise and into Salt Lake City. Then I picked up two fellows on the highway who said they were going to get out in Pendleton. They were going to another town in Washington, and were going to catch another ride to Garfield, through Walla Walla, Washington. We passed the Pendleton officers' car east of Echo."

He was nearly finished, winding down. "One of the fellows said, 'There is a traffic officer, and there is a fellow ahead of us,'" Hickman told Branin. "I think it was the same car that came back to where the officers who made the arrest stopped me. I began studying about that car parked there, and saw the car coming behind me. They pulled in ahead of us and blew a siren. I moved over and thought I noticed the car slow down, so I did, too. I stopped, and they came up, and I knew they had me. I think they were more excited than I was."

The Fox, cool to the bitter end.

Branin came back once more to the mythical accomplice. "Did you get any word at all," he asked, "since Cramer brought the little girl to your apartment?"

"No," Hickman said. "I figure he beat it as quick as he could."

Back in Los Angeles, the Cramer story galvanized LAPD. Detectives had been chasing shadows of a second man—perhaps two other men; some said a woman—almost from the moment Marian's remains were dropped into the gutter on Manhattan Place. They had been getting nowhere, granted, but at least they had momentum going for them.

And by Thursday night they had a name.

Ironically, from that point on, the trouble wasn't finding "Andrew Cramer," but instead deciding which one made the better suspect in their case. For they had two to choose from, suddenly, and both were already locked up in jail.

In fact, the two were brothers.

At first glance, Oliver Andrew Cramer looked promising. He often used his middle name, without the "Oliver," which could have left Hickman confused. He also claimed to know a woman named June Dunning, though police could find no trace of her. She was his brother's girlfriend's sister, Cramer said. Just ask around.

More to the point, he knew the prisoner in Pendleton. No doubt about it, Cramer said, "I know Hickman." But then he added, plaintively, "I don't know why he picks on me." Cramer was innocent, and he could prove it. He had been in jail, where the detectives found him, since August 18, when he started serving a 200-day sentence for bootlegging. "It is impossible for me to have been in on that killing," he said, "as I was right here all the time. It's almost too ridiculous to talk about."

Investigators checked it out, confirmed the dates. Now what?

Suppose it was the brother? someone asked.

Frank Andrew Cramer was another hopeful prospect. Like his brother, Frank boasted a rap sheet as long as your arm, with most of the arrests recorded in L.A. He also kept company with one Rose Dunning (a.k.a. Rose Cramer, Rose Hurst), whose sister was alleged to be the woman named by Hickman in his Pendleton confession.

Once again, however, the detectives came up short. For one thing, they quickly discovered that Rose Dunning had no sister named June. In fact, her only sister—Mable—was deceased and had been for nine months. There was an outside chance that Hickman could have met her sometime early in the year, but she was clearly not in San Diego on Thanksgiving.

And neither was Frank Andrew Cramer. A phone call confirmed his arrest on August 12, six days before brother "Andrew" was sentenced, and Frank had been caged ever since.

Strike two . . . or was it three?

Reporters—and some homicide investigators—speculated that there still might be a second man involved, even a man and woman, Hickman tossing out the first names he could think of to buy his partners some time. Using real names, fingering an actual acquaintance—and one with a criminal record, at that—made the dodge more convincing.

The Fox at work.

But if the real-life Cramers both had ironclad alibis, who was the man seen helping Hickman load his car on Saturday, the seventeenth? Who was the getaway driver Harry Packer had glimpsed, albeit dimly, on December 5?

The Los Angeles County grand jury ignored those questions when it convened in special session on Thursday, at 7:30 P.M. Four witnesses were heard, with Perry Parker leading off, confirming his "ear-witness" identification of Hickman. Dr. Wagner repeated the grim evidence of wrongful death, still hoping Marian was dead before the butcher went to work, but unable to swear to it. Witness number three, Naomi Britten, had seen the kidnapper's face up close and personal, when he came for Marian at school. A fingerprint expert from LAPD put the bow on the package, definitely placing Hickman in the murder car and at the

Bellevue Arms apartment. From start to finish, the panel took a record one hour and two minutes to hear evidence and indict William Edward Hickman on two felony counts: first-degree murder and kidnapping with intent to extort money.

The second charge could put him away for ten years, but it was the murder that mattered. For that, he could hang. A bench warrant was issued for Hickman's arrest, mandating that he be held without bail.

Ed didn't know it yet, but the first contingent of California officers had taken off for Washington early that morning, hours before he was captured. Three detectives from the L.A. County district attorney's office—George Contreras, E. M. Hamren and H. G. Taylor—were airborne shortly after breakfast, mobilized by the retrieval of ransom money in Seattle and Kent. Wherever Hickman surfaced next, they meant to be hot on his trail. Now, with the Fox in a cage, urgent messages were dispatched to divert the man-hunters and reroute them to Oregon.

Hickman's offhand remark to Buck Lieuallen—"Oh, this isn't California, is it?"—raised the specter of an extradition fight, and while there was no reason to believe that Oregon authorities would shelter Hickman, it seemed better to remove all doubt. Formal extradition papers were prepared immediately after Ed's indictment in Los Angeles, flown to Sacramento for the governor's signature on Friday morning, by LAPD Inspector Dwight Longuevan. Governor Young was waiting, pen in hand, and Longuevan was airborne out of Sacramento by 3:00 P.M. on Friday, bound for an airstrip at Corning, California, 80 miles north in Tehama County. From there, the *Times* reported, he would cover the last 300 miles to Pendleton, Oregon, by car or train, whichever his superiors deemed more time- and cost-effective in the dead of winter.

At that, Longuevan was still expected to reach Pendleton ahead of Hickman's formal escort. District Attorney Asa Keyes had left Los Angeles by rail at 6:05 P.M. on Thursday, accompanied by Chief of Police James E. Davis, Chief of

Detectives Herman Cline, and three plainclothesmen for backup, in case they had to subdue their teenage prisoner—or shoot it out with lynch-happy locals—somewhere along the way. It was a lot of brass for one eighteen-year-old, but Hickman's crime had stunned shockproof Los Angeles.

And even in the 1920s, no one cared to miss a photo opportunity.

Judge Carlos Hardy, of L.A.'s Juvenile Court, was ready and waiting for Hickman by the time Keyes and Davis led their escort party to the railroad station. He explained to journalists that Hickman would be instantly arraigned upon arrival in Los Angeles. A guilty plea would streamline matters, Hardy said, but even if the lad was stubborn, conviction and sentencing might require as few as five working days. As for the technicality of extradition, it was really no problem at all. By Friday afternoon a federal grand jury had charged Hickman with violation of the Dyer Act—illegally transporting stolen cars across state lines—and Uncle Sam could take him anywhere—Los Angeles included—for trial without waiting for permission from the governor of Oregon.

As for the Cramer story, L.A. lawmen were by now prepared to shelve it as a clumsy lie. Chief Inspector Joe Taylor missed the train to Oregon, but still had plenty to tell the press on Friday, predicting that Hickman would soon change his tune when confronted by big-city cops. "It will not be necessary to use brutality," Taylor assured his audience. "Modern police methods are scientific, and by adroit questioning detectives soon get to the truth of the matter. A man lying in a case like this is sure to trip up on small details, contradict himself, and nine times out of ten, when he sees he's trapped he will start telling the truth."

At the Pendleton lockup, young Edward was having similar thoughts. When City Attorney Charles Randall stopped by for a visit, Ed asked him, "Would I have to tell . . . Could I refuse to say anything?" Randall assured Hickman that his Fifth Amendment right would be protected, whereupon Ed remarked, "Well, I have told this much now, and I might as well tell it again."

Frowning then, almost as an afterthought, he asked if his statements were being transcribed. "You know," he told Randall, "the district attorney will do everything he can to trip me up."

Ed passed a quiet night in jail on Thursday. In fact, it was too quiet for one of his keepers, the guard complaining sometime after midnight he had been watching for the past two hours straight, and Hickman had not moved or made a sound. Suppose he had committed suicide!

Two deputies unlocked Ed's cell and prodded him awake. He blinked at them, confused, as one produced a fine-toothed comb and checked the prisoner's wavy hair, searching for poison capsules fastened to his scalp. When they were satisfied that Hickman had no secret way to cheat the hangman, they retreated, grumbling, and their prisoner went back to sleep.

He woke again at half-past six, for just long enough to ask a guard the time, then slept again until a jailer brought egg sandwiches and coffee to his cell, at eight-fifteen. Throughout the evening, Chief Gurdane had fielded calls from journalists and local folk, requesting just a glimpse of the celebrity who graced their jail—and whose departure would restore the normal winter tedium. Gurdane had stubbornly refused at first, but when the calls resumed on Friday morning he experienced a change of heart. He would have to live in Pendleton after Hickman was removed, and there was no sense making needless enemies.

Besides, this could turn out to be his one and only moment in the spotlight.

Grudgingly, the chief approved a show of sorts. Hickman would be displayed, with guards on standby, at a side door of the city jail. Those who desired to see him must line up and wait their turn, pass through a narrow alley to avoid blocking the street, and keep on moving once they had their look at history.

The turnout was surprising—some might say embarrassing—with locals easily outnumbering the out-of-town journalists and cameramen. Housewives lined up with children.

Merchants and professionals alike turned out, some of the men in shirtsleeves, shivering when it began to snow. A delegation from the nearby Umatilla reservation, warm in their blankets, took their place in line like anybody else, as they came to see a white man caged for once. The crowd, described as "bellicose" in one report, appeared more suited to a sideshow than a vigilante necktie party. Flanked by uniforms, the star and freak rolled into one gave them their money's worth—or if he left them feeling less than wholly satisfied, no one complained.

The snow let up by noon and gave the heroes of the hour another chance to preen before the cameras. Gurdane was classic in his beaded buckskin jacket, chewing on a fat cigar. He and Lieuallen donned sombreros, mounted horses, cantered back and forth outside the jail while flashbulbs popped and movie cameras tracked their every move. From all appearances, the traffic cop and Pendleton's police chief might have ridden through a time warp, fresh from skirmishing with bandits from the Wild Bunch or the Dalton clan.

Inside the jail, Ed Hickman, visibly shaken by the news of Cramer's solid alibi, held court for another battery of journalists. "This is strange," he said. "It can't be. When I get to Los Angeles I want to see Cramer, and I would like to see the girl, too." Reminded that June Dunning seemed to be a phantom, Ed still clung to hope. "If you can find her," he suggested to the scribblers, "perhaps she can explain who this other man Cramer is."

As for the crime of which he stood accused, Edward repeated his assertion that the kidnapping had been conceived by Cramer. "He said he had been in a kidnapping in Denver, and he knew just how to do it," Hickman said. "I fell in with his plan because I wanted the money."

At the same time, his story was changing, acquiring new twists in the second telling. This time Ed claimed that Cramer had gone with him to the drop on Saturday, leaving the car moments before Ed approached Perry Parker. "It was necessary to put the suitcase up against the instrument board while Cramer was in the car," he explained, "and I

placed it on the seat after he left. I let him out on Alvarado
Street, after we had stopped and talked over our future
plans. Cramer said, 'I am feeling kind of funny about this
and want to get out of town just as soon as possible.' He
stated we would meet in San Francisco to settle up."

Cramer, he now suggested, must have stolen towels from
Ed's apartment at the Bellevue Arms, planting them with
Marian's body to frame Ed for the murder. His first glimpse
of the mutilated corpse had been a shock. "There is something ghastly about a dead eye," he declared. "It is even
more penetrating than a live eye."

The journalists neglected to ask how Cramer had performed these feats while he was jailed for pushing bootleg
booze. One of them *did* ask Hickman why, with his accomplice calling all the shots, he had written to Perry Parker
that he was "doing a solo" on the kidnapping.

The Fox replied by feigning ignorance of the word's definition. Did "solo" really mean *alone*? "There was no need of
me using that word," he explained. "I just thought it was
clever, like the words 'fox' and 'fate.' "

Ed clearly felt more at ease discussing his other crimes,
taking the newsmen on a verbal tour of his carjackings and
holdups from K.C. to Chicago, eastward through Ohio,
Pennsylvania, and West Virginia, and visiting New York and
Washington before he made his way out west again. It was a
string of scores to rival Jesse James, the way Ed talked it
up—he was particularly proud of the "nice write-ups" he
received in Columbus, Ohio—but he still tried to close the
recitation of freewheeling crime with a plug for his own
sturdy morals.

"I do not want people to get the idea that I am a rounder,"
he said. "I do not drink, gamble, and only smoke occasionally, and had a real conscientious desire to go to college."

A telegram came for Edward on Friday, from Kansas City:

To William Edward Hickman:
    Your mother, brothers and sister still believe in you.
Be truthful and trust in God. I long to be with you, but

"Cap" Edwards said for me to wait. I am praying he will let me come to you.

Lovingly, your mother,
Mrs. Eva Hickman

Edward had more on his mind, at the moment, than a visit from family. "I wonder," he asked one of his guards on Friday afternoon, "if I could pretend I was crazy. How does a fellow act when he's crazy?"

It was a question very much on legal minds—and in the daily press—in those days. Nathan Leopold and Richard Loeb had claimed insanity as a defense in 1924, during their Chicago trial for the murder of fourteen-year-old Bobby Franks, and while it didn't get them off, at least their lives were spared. (Like Ed, the two Chicago thrill-killers were also in their teens: another plus.) More recently, on the very day Hickman left San Francisco for Seattle, George "King of the Bootleggers" Remus of Ohio had been acquitted of murdering his wife, when Cincinnati jurors deemed him temporarily insane.

The latter case was fresh in Edward's mind that Friday afternoon. "Remus acted as his own lawyer," Ed reminded the guard, "and got acquitted, didn't he?"

A true mastermind would have kept the observation to himself, but Hickman couldn't shut up to save his own life, and his "fake insanity" ploy made the *Los Angeles Times* on Saturday morning. By that time, one psychiatrist had already examined Ed and deemed him fit for trial.

Dr. W. D. McNary lived in Pendleton, as luck would have it, and managed 1,050 inmates from his post as superintendent of the nearby Eastern Oregon Asylum for the Insane. McNary spent some time with Ed on Friday afternoon, and found reporters waiting for him when he left the jail.

"His mind seemed clear," the doctor told the journalists. "He told a straight, coherent story and never was at a loss for words. There was nothing about him to indicate insanity. He did not differ a bit from hundreds of thousands of other young men."

In response to a question about Hickman's sex drive, McNary replied, "I found no outward evidence of perversion. Of course, such perversions and inclinations are generally hidden and often difficult to detect. Many persons are afflicted with such inherited taints, but they have the willpower to control their base desires. As to whether Hickman is given to sadistic practices, I cannot tell. I observed him only casually and did not have the opportunity to make a deep study of him. I saw nothing out of the ordinary about him, nothing that would justify a defense of insanity."

More specifically, the doctor noted, "He says that he does not like girls, that he is deeply religious, and that his ambition was to become a minister. Several times he made mention of God, and in discussing his capture took the attitude that since God willed it, it had to be."

Did Hickman's dislike of girls mean he was homosexual?

"No," McNary said, "I would not say that his aversion for women is an evidence of perversion. Some men are constituted that way. Nor do I think that his religious convictions are so pronounced as to produce a hallucination that God willed that he commit this act. In our asylum we have hundreds of patients who are suffering from some delusion that they are in personal communication with Jehovah."

What should be done with Hickman and his ilk?

"It is a most difficult matter," McNary said, "for society to protect itself from degenerates. Their perversions are generally hidden. They crop out occasionally in some of the appalling crimes which fill the front pages of our newspapers. To discover, to weed out, to emasculate these people, both as a remedy and [as] protection for society, would be a most difficult matter. Young Hickman might have come to Pendleton, established himself here, gained a good reputation, and if he were afflicted with sadist desires, might have controlled them for an indefinite period. To discover these fellows before they commit their awful crime is almost impossible."

So now Ed *was* a pervert and a degenerate . . . or was he? The Reverend Mr. W. H. Robins, pastor of Pendleton's First

Baptist Church, had also visited the jail's star inmate, drawn
by published references to Ed's Baptist background, and he
came away convinced that foreigners deserved a share of
the blame—specifically, the humanistic likes of Arthur
Schopenhauer and Friedrich Nietzsche.

"He asked me if I thought God would give him a chance,"
Reverend Robins announced to the press corps. "I told him the
government of the country can punish crime but not sin,
because sin is against God. At that point, he broke down and
cried for some time, and I feel convinced that his action was not
hypocritical. I then gave a prayer of two or three minutes."

Edward had asked the minister to pass a message on,
telling his mother he was innocent of murder. "He acted as a
perfect gentleman all the time I was with him," Robins said.
"I would not definitely say that he is religious, although it is
quite evident that he has had religious training. He speaks
excellent English and is well educated in some respects,
although I would say his education is somewhat lopsided."

Could the minister be more specific?

"You must understand," said Robins, "I am not giving my
opinion as to whether or not he is guilty of murder. But I
think it's the same rotten philosophy fed to Leopold and
Loeb that is responsible for the situation. I believe also that
if any blame is to be placed, we may say that those who
gave these behavioristic teachings to this young man are
responsible."

Some within the sound of the minister's voice were less
concerned with Edward's motivation than with the price on
his head. Reward pledges had been logged in Los Angeles
up to the very moment of his capture, and while the total
remained vague, a report in the *Times* speculated that it
might run as high as $90,000. Seven or eight telephone
callers had already laid claim to shares of the loot by
Thursday afternoon, prompting Los Angeles Mayor George
Cryer to appoint a committee of thirteen civic leaders to
supervise disbursement of the cash.

The most obvious candidates to receive the reward were
Chief Gurdane and Buck Lieuallen, both of whom were

ready and willing to profit from their fifteen minutes of fame. Of course, there were limits to how much a hero should take. "I don't want the money of individuals, not the money of kids and women," Gurdane told reporters, while Lieualien stood in his shadow, nodding agreement. "But I see no reason why I should not take that which was offered by the Los Angeles banks and some of the organizations. That is legitimate reward money, legitimately earned."

The Merrill brothers, for their part, were certainly out of the running, still jailed as material witnesses. "Yep," Bill told a visiting newsman, "we might have had it, might have gone home to Ma with a lot of money. We didn't, though, and instead of being home for Christmas, here we are in jail."

The brothers could at least look forward to release sometime within the next few days. The same could not be said for Hickman, waiting in his lonely cell while press reports kept him apprised of his pursuers, drawing near. Chief Davis and the rest spent Thursday night in San Francisco, then embarked at 7:40 in the morning for the last leg of their journey. Barring blizzard or derailment, they should be in Pendleton by 8:30 A.M. on Saturday.

They would be coming for their prey on Christmas Eve.

9 ✦ "Come On, Yellow Boy"

Ed Hickman passed a restless night in jail on Friday. Prior to turning in, around 10:45 P.M., he had been heckled throughout the evening by other inmates, who told him a lynch mob would be waiting for him when he left the jail, or when he got to California. Soon after he dozed off at last, two Umatilla Indians, jailed for public drunkenness, began to fight in the adjoining cell, and deputies charged in to break it up. Hickman was up again by 5:00 A.M. for another breakfast of coffee and egg sandwiches. He was denied utensils for fear that he would cut his wrists or stab himself.

Ed's mounting restlessness had less to do with taunts from other prisoners than with the ticking clock. Each hour brought his escorts from Los Angeles a few miles closer, and he was not encouraged by reports of what the D.A. and detectives had said to journalists aboard the Portland Limited.

Chief Davis had told the newsmen, "There is little doubt that there will be a great change in Hickman's story. He has told his story to various parties, including the Pendleton police, and now he will have to prove his assertions to me and my men, who are familiar with the brutality of the Parker murder and kidnapping."

Herman Cline, for one, had already made up his mind. "The story of Hickman involving an accomplice is an absurdity," he declared. "We previously have checked every angle of his asserted accomplice and have found the story false and weak. We are after the truth of this matter, and I am convinced we shall find it when Hickman is faced with the facts by those who know the intricate details of the Parker crime."

George Home, former chief of police in L.A. who had come along for the ride, told reporters, "It is a one-man job and the evidence proves that conclusively. With Mr. Keyes and his aides preparing to question him, I believe that Hickman within a few hours will tell the world the true story of the crime."

Edward, meanwhile, seemed more concerned with portraying himself as a repentant victim of circumstance. Bright and early on Saturday morning, jailers started handing out copies of a statement Ed had dictated to City Attorney Charles Randall and signed the night before. It read:

> This affair has gained nation-wide publicity and the great reward and search by the police of the west coast show opposition of [the] American people to criminal tendencies. Kidnappings and savage murders are the worst of America's crimes and everything should be done to prevent anyone interfering in any way with the liberty and life of American citizens.
>
> Young men and college students should consider the Parker case as a typical crime of the worst that can happen when a young man gradually loses interest in family, friends and his own honesty.
>
> The young men of this country can see that I can pass as an ordinary young man as far as outward appearances go.
>
> Crime in its simplest definition is to have without work and enjoy the same place in society as other people and still show no honest effort or intention to go right.
>
> Young men, when crime has once overcome your will power to be honest and straight you are a menace to society. Take my example to illustrate this. See how I tried to get what every young man wants, but in

becoming a criminal to do so I put my own life in a mess and the way out is dark.

I hope I can do some good by giving you this warning. Think it over, see my mistake. Be honest and upright. Respect the law. If you do these things you'll be happier in the end and you will have gained much more from your life.

W. Edward Hickman

Despite his public plea, Ed was still working the angles, looking for an escape hatch. Still talking insanity. Before he was put on display that morning for the estimated 4,000 gawkers who trooped down the alley to glimpse the visiting monster, Hickman again asked one of his keepers about an insanity defense. "Do you just have to talk a little off," he wondered aloud, "or do you have to rave around?"

The prospect of a hanging clearly worried Edward. He had given up on getting off the hook; now he was simply hoping to beat the gallows, telling one fellow prisoner, "Maybe they will let me plead guilty to kidnapping and get off with a life sentence." Reminded by one officer that he had placed his own head in the noose the moment he admitted complicity in the crime, Hickman groused, "I can't help it. I have told the truth. I will feel better to go that way than to tell a lie."

It was flattering, of course, that L.A.'s police chief and district attorney would come fetch him in person, but Hickman remained apprehensive about their arrival. "I've got the worst of it ahead of me," he said. "They are trying to hang me before they get me. They won't give me a chance to tell my story and get cleared. I'm away up here and I haven't got a friend. They're right down there, where they can have everything fixed up by the time I get back."

Exhausted by 4:00 P.M. on Saturday, he wolfed down another sandwich before crawling into his bunk. Ed was already asleep when the Los Angeles detail showed up at five o'clock. Chief Gurdane shook hands all around, then led his visitors back to the cells, for a first glimpse of their quarry in the flesh.

Memories differ as to what happened next. Gurdane would later testify that Ed was on his feet when they entered the cell block, whereupon he "pulled a fit" and "throwed himself down and kicked and struck, and it took two men to hold him." Ed was forcibly restrained, the chief said, until his visitors retreated, at which point "I went back and he quieted down."

Herman Cline recalled the meeting differently. In his version, likewise offered under oath, Ed was lying on the lower bunk, apparently sleeping, when the delegation reached his cell. "We called to him to come out," Cline testified. "The door was being unlocked, and we wanted to talk to him. He did not make any response at first, and if I remember right, one of the officers—the Pendleton officers, or someone attached to the jail—went in and took him by the shoulder and kind of shook him and told him to come out, the Los Angeles officers were there. And he came out and immediately went into hysterics." According to Cline, Hickman's "body commenced to jerk, seemingly. He commenced to cry out, in a loud tone of voice, 'Marian, Marian, Marian,' and looking wildly around the room and using very violent exertions like he was trying to get at somebody, or get away from something."

Cline said that Hickman collapsed to the floor and began to kick his feet and flail his arms, shouting, "Marian, where are you? Marian, I love you!" Lunging toward Chief Davis, Ed appeared to "froth at the mouth," hissing, "I know you! I have seen those eyes before!" The scene went on for five minutes or so, Cline recalled, until his captors decided to "put the defendant back in the cell and talk to him another time."

Detective R. J. Lucas offered yet another version of events at that meeting with Edward. "He was acting as though he was in a fit," Lucas testified. "He was lying on the floor in the cell, and I spoke to him and told him to get off the floor, and he opened his eyes and looked at me, and he was mumbling, 'Oh, Marian, Marian, I love you.' And I said, 'Get up off the floor there and try to be a man.' So then we did not see him until the next day."

According to reporters who were present at the confrontation, there was more to Ed's performance—and the official response—than any of the witnesses recalled. The *L.A. Times* had Hickman crying out, "I did not kill her!" prior to rushing at the steel door of his cell and hammering his skull against the bars. A stringer for the *New York Times* reported that one unnamed officer—apparently Dick Lucas—not only advised the prisoner to "be a man" but also leaned toward Hickman, telling him, "I have a message from Marian."

At that, Edward reportedly cried out, "Man, man, where is she? Let me see her face!"

"Do you want to know what Marian said?" the officer prodded. "Sit up and I will tell you."

Hickman remained where he was, squirming on the floor, and the visitors retreated. Outside, confronted by the press, District Attorney Asa Keyes shrugged off a question as to whether Ed had lost his mind. "Of course he's not insane," Keyes said. "He is merely assuming that pose, I presume, for mercy. Tonight he will tell me the truth of the Parker killing."

But they would not get back to Ed on Christmas Eve. Instead, the L.A. delegation joined Chief Gurdane to examine the weapons, cash, and other items seized from Hickman's car on Thursday afternoon. Chief Davis gave the go-ahead for Gurdane to release the Merrill brothers, with a warning to get out of town. Departing from the jail for his hotel room, Herman Cline announced that barring "most unusual circumstances," Ed would be on his way back to Los Angeles by 11:00 A.M. on Christmas Day.

And speaking of Los Angeles, despite the statements from Chief Davis and his crew, LAPD had not entirely given up on looking for accomplices. In fact, that very Saturday, spokesmen for the department told reporters they had lifted two fingerprints of "a woman other than little Marian Parker" from a dinner plate and milk bottle found in Ed's apartment at the Bellevue Arms. (No one explained how the fingerprints of "a woman" could be distinguished from those of a man or a boy.) After ripping out the pipes, detectives also contradicted their chief's original prediction: they were certain now that Marian *was* murdered and dismembered in the flat.

In far-off New York City, educators were also feeling the heat from Marian's abduction, the expressed concerns of wealthy parents prompting Superintendent of Schools William O'Shea to issue a memo on schoolyard security. Not that there was any cause for fear, O'Shea advised the public. Marian's death was "most unfortunate," of course, but O'Shea felt confident that "there is not a principal in New York who would let a child go that way."

A curious twist on the story was added by one Milton Carlson, described as a "criminology student" and "examiner of questioned documents" in Los Angeles. In Carlson's view, the name Andrew Cramer had been lifted from reports of London's Whitechapel murders "in 1881," wherein several women were "disfigured beyond recognition." Their killer, known from press reports as Jack the Ripper, was never identified, but Carlson told reporters that a leading suspect in the case was Andrew Kramer, a Russian medical student, found drowned in the Thames seven weeks after the last Ripper slaying. "As far as I know," Carlson said, "Hickman has not yet been asked if he has ever read of the Whitechapel murder mystery, but it will be interesting to watch his reaction when the question is asked."

In fact, it never would be. Red Jack's butchery of London hookers was the last thing on anyone's mind that Christmas morning, as Ed braced himself for the trip back to L.A. Reporters got another shot at him before his escorts reached the jail on Sunday, one of them asking for Hickman's opinion on why "Cramer" killed Marian.

"Well," Ed replied, "he might have been in great danger and wanted to save his own life. It might have been that Cramer knew there were detectives coming to search his apartment and that he might serve a life sentence if he was caught with the girl. You don't know how it is when a terrible fear comes to a man. He thinks maybe they will hang him. Well, fear is a terrible thing. You don't know how a murderer feels. I guess the devil certainly must have been there when that happened. He must have been right there."

As for himself, he said, "I never would have killed Marian if I had kept her. I would have kept her alive until her father gave me the money. I could have worked it out all right."

When Chief Davis and company reached the Pendleton jail that morning, Ed was in the middle of his second suicide attempt. Plan A had been a headlong dive from the upper bunk to the floor of his cell, but Hickman only gave himself a headache and a goose egg on his scalp. Plan B was hanging, but the jailers had relieved him of his belt and shoe-strings on arrival. Thinking fast, Ed borrowed a hand-kerchief from a careless guard, tied one end around his neck, the other to the steel bars of his cell, then slumped down in a clumsy effort to throttle himself. He was twitching and gurgling when his escorts arrived and cut him down.

Sprawled on the floor again, he heard Chief of Detectives Cline say, "Listen, Hickman, are you going to be a yellow cur, or are you going to come along on this trip like a man?"

Ed groaned in answer, weeping incoherently. Disgusted, Cline turned to his men and ordered, "Take him out."

Dick Lucas and Harry Raymond hoisted Ed from his place on the floor, holding him upright between them as hand-cuffs were snapped on his wrists. They used two pairs, his left arm cuffed to Lucas and the right to Raymond. Ed was effectively immobilized, and anyone who tried to seize the prisoner would have to kill both officers, then drag their corpses after him.

Weeks later, at trial, Herman Cline described Ed's exit from the jailhouse under oath. He testified: "I walked into the jail and I told him, I says, 'Hickman,' I says, 'we are going to take you back to Los Angeles.' I says, 'You have been wanting a whole lot of newspaper notoriety, and,' I says, 'you are getting a whole lot.' I said, 'There is movie people out here, a whole lot of cameramen that are going to take your picture.' I says, 'It is up to you,' I says, 'as to how they are going to be taken.' I says, 'We are going to take you back, even if we have to take you by the heels and take you back that way, and it is going to be up to you as to how you want these pictures taken.' I says, 'Possibly they will take pictures of you all the way down the line.' I said, 'Now, suit yourself as to whether you want to walk out like a man, or whether you want us to take you out the other way and have your pictures taken that way.' Five minutes later he walked out like a man."

Cline recalled Hickman as "perfectly calm, cool, and collected," but the *Los Angeles Times* carried a different version, describing Ed as terrified by the crowd milling around outside the jail when he emerged at 10:55 A.M. His knees buckled, and he would have collapsed but for Lucas and Raymond supporting him on either side. One of them muttered, "Come on, yellow boy," as they half-carried Ed to a waiting bus.

It was a short ride to the railroad station, where 1,500 locals watched as Edward's escorts trundled him aboard a special prison car, waiting for the Portland Limited. Eyeballing the crowd as he left the bus, Hickman told his burly bookends, "If they want my blood, I suppose they will have it."

It was 12:15 P.M. before the train pulled out of Pendleton. The run to Portland took six hours, and Cline spent most of that time grilling Hickman, with Lucas and Raymond on standby. At one point, Cline showed Ed a knife retrieved from his luggage in the Hudson, and Hickman finally broke down, admitting he had murdered and dismembered Marian himself, without accomplices. It took about four hours for him to repeat his story, dropping Andrew Cramer from the script.

At that time, Cline would later testify, Ed "made the remark that he wanted to go back to Los Angeles, that he was going to plead guilty, that he thought he could get away with the Loeb and Leopold defense, and he said he wanted the judge to be acquainted with all of the facts in the case. I told him that we were just as anxious for the judge to be acquainted with all the facts in the case as he was, and that in a long statement of this kind that there was always danger of a mistake being made, and that we did not want to do him any injury, and neither did we want to do the Parker family an injury, and I thought it would be much better if he would write the whole thing out himself, just in his own language, the way it occurred, and then we would have it exact. And he stated that he would do that if I would see that the judge got a copy of what he wrote."

It was too late, by then, for Ed to start writing his statement before they reached Portland. When that train arrived at 6:10 P.M., two thousand people were waiting at the station for a glimpse of Hickman, but the officers had outfoxed Ed's public. Fearing trouble from the crowd, they had stopped at Montavilla, five miles east of Portland, and hustled Ed into a police car for a quick run to the Portland jail. Four hours later, surrounded by uniforms and guns, he boarded the Union Pacific's Cascade Limited, which rolled out of the station, headed south.

On Monday morning, after breakfasting on prunes, mush, bread, and milk, a visibly rejuvenated Hickman started working on a written statement, his latest version of the murder:

> On [Southern Pacific] train, December 26, 1927, en route to Los Angeles, from Pendleton, Oregon.
>
> My name is William Edward Hickman. I was born February 1, 1908, at West Hartford, Arkansas. I desire to make the following statement relative to the kidnapping of Marian Parker in Los Angeles, Thursday, Dec. 15, 1927.
>
> During the past six months the idea of kidnapping a young person and holding it for ransom came to me as a means of securing money for college. I had already been in touch with President Hawley of Park College, near Kansas City, Mo., and was to see him again in February following to arrange my entrance.

On November 23, 1927, I rented an apartment at the Bellevue Arms house under an assumed name of Donald Evans. At this date I had no definite plans to kidnap, but on Monday, December 12, I decided to locate Mr. Harry Hovis, Chief Teller at the First National Bank of L.A., and arrange to take his young child, but I wasn't satisfied with the situation. I then thought of Mr. P. M. Parker, because I had seen a young girl with him one day at the bank while I was employed there as a page. This was the First National Bank at 7th & Spring Sts., and since I thought that the girl with Mr. Parker was his own child, I decided to start my plans.

On Wednesday, Dec. 14, I drove out to Mr. Parker's house at 1631 South Wilton Pl. and waited to see him drive home and his daughter return from school.

On Thursday, Dec. 15, 7:30 a.m. I was again parked near the Parker residence in my car, which I had stolen in Kansas City, Mo., early in November. It had a California license plate, No. 1,677,679, which I took from a Chevrolet car in San Diego, Sunday night, about the 5th of December. About eight o'clock I saw two young girls leave the Parker home and followed them to the Mt. Vernon Jr. High School in that district. I returned to this school later from my apartment at the Bellevue Arms. I entered the attendance office at approximately 12:30 and asked for Mr. Parker's daughter, saying that her father had been in an accident and wished to see her. I gave my name as Cooper and assured the teacher that I was a friend of Mr. Parker's and worked at the First National Bank. I was asked if the girl's name was Marian Parker since it occurred that Mr. Parker had two daughters at the school. I replied in the affirmative and emphasized that it was the younger daughter for whom the father was calling. There was only a slight wait and Marian was called from her class. I told her to come with me, repeating what I had said to the teacher.

The young girl did not hesitate to come with me and we left the school immediately. I drove east on Venice Blvd. to Western Ave., north on Western to Beverly Blvd., east on Beverly Blvd., to Temple St., on Temple to Glendale Blvd., out Glendale Blvd. through the city of Glendale.

I stopped the car on a quiet street out in this vicinity and told Marian that she had been deceived. I told her that I would have to hold her for a day or two and that her father would have to give me $1500. Marian did not cry out or even attempt to fight. She pleaded with me not to blindfold or tie her and promised not to move or say anything. I believed her and took off the blindfold and the bandages from her arms and ankles. I explained to Marian just what a chance I was taking. I warned her that she would be hurt if she tried to get away and I showed her my .380 automatic revolver. Marian said she understood and that she didn't want to be shot. I started the car and we drove back to Los Angeles to the main post office where I mailed a special delivery letter to Marian's father. Marian sat right up in the seat beside me and talked in a friendly manner. It was very nice to hear her and I could see that she believed and trusted me for her safety. When I left the post office I drove out to Pasadena. Here I stopped at the Western Union office on Raynold Av., and left Marian perfectly free in the car while I sent a telegram to her father. I wanted to warn Mr. Parker not to do anything until he got my letter and told him that his daughter was safe.

Marian and I left Pasadena and drove out Foothill Blvd. beyond Azusa. We talked and had a jolly time. Marian said she liked to go driving and she went so far as to relate to me that she had had a dream just a few days before that someone called for her at the school and in reality kidnapped her. Before dark came I turned back and we stopped in Alhambra where I mailed a second telegram. At seven o'clock we went to the Rialto

Theatre in South Pasadena, and saw the picture entitled
"Fathers Don't Lie" with Esther Ralston. Marian enjoyed the picture and we both laughed very much during the vaudeville which followed the picture.

We left the theatre about ten p.m. and drove directly
to the Bellevue Arms Apts. Marian, I could see, was a
little worried and also sleepy. We sat in the car by the
side of the apartment for about thirty minutes and saw
a chance to enter without being seen. I told Marian that
my room was on the third floor and cautioned her to
follow just a few steps behind me. No one saw us go to
my apt. (No. 315) and when we were inside Marian
went to sleep immediately. She chose to sleep on the
couch and only took off her shoes and used a heavy
blanket which I gave her for cover. I placed a reading
lamp by the door and left it lighted so that it cast a dim
light over the room. I slept in the bed and retired
shortly after Marian. I stayed awake for some time to
see that the girl would not attempt to leave the apt.

Next morning Marian was awake by seven o'clock.
She was sobbing and didn't say much. I got up and prepared breakfast but she said she wasn't hungry.

After a while I began to talk to Marian and tried to
console her. I told her that she could write a letter to
her father and that I would also. So then she stopped
sobbing and wrote the note and didn't cry any more
that day (Friday). About 9:30 a.m. I left the apt. for
about thirty minutes. I went downtown where I got the
newspapers and mailed the special delivery letter
which included Marian's note. I tied Marian to a chair
while I was gone, but used cloth bandages and she was
not cut or bruised in any way. I did not blindfold or gag
her and she promised to keep quiet.

When Marian saw her pictures and name in all the
papers she felt sorry, because she didn't want her father
to give out the news of her kidnapping because I had
told her of all my plans. Later however she seemed to
like to look at her picture and kept reading the account

of her abduction. Marian didn't want to stay in the apt.
all day so I promised to go out driving again. We left the
apt. about noon and drove out through Alhambra and
San Gabriel, past the Mission Playhouse to San Gabriel
Blvd. and turned on the highway toward San Diego
near Whittier. We drove through Santa Ana and while
we were stopped there for gasoline at a Richfield station I noticed that the attendant looked at Marian very
closely. We drove on beyond San Juan Capistrano and
stopped to rest the car a while before we turned back.
We were about 70 miles out of Los Angeles and it
became dark before we got back to the city. I secured
some evening papers and Marian read to me as I drove.
About 7 o'clock I stopped the car just south of 7th
Street on Los Angeles St. and left Marian in the car
while I went to the P.E. [Pacific Electric] Station at 6th
and Main St. and called her father over the telephone. I
called twice but the line was busy each time. I told
Marian so and we then drove up Los Angeles St. to
Sunset Blvd. and out Sunset to a drug store near
Angeles Temple. I called Marian's father and talked to
him. He said he had the money and wanted me to bring
his girl back to him. He said he'd meet me anywhere
and I said I'd call him back. I called the second time
from a drug store at Pico and Wilton Sts. at about 8:30
which was about 30 minutes later than the first. I told
Mr. Parker to get in his car alone and drive north on
Wilton to 10th and turn to the right one short block to
Gramercy and park on Gramercy, just north of 10th.
Marian and I were parked on Pico between Wilton and
Gramercy and we both saw Mr. Parker drive by. There
were two other cars following his and I feared that
some detectives were planning to trap me so Marian
and I drove directly back to my apt. and didn't go by
her father. We got back inside without anyone seeing
us. Marian sobbed a little because she couldn't go home
that night but she saw everything and was content to
wait till the next morning. Marian slept the same way

Friday night as Thursday and we both were awake and up by 7:30 the next morning (Saturday).

I told Marian to write her father that he must not try to trap me or something might happen to her. She wrote the note in her own words and very willingly [the] same as in the first note, since she knew my plans as well as I did and read all of my letters. I told Marian all along that I would have to make things look worse to her father than they really were so that he would be eager to settle right away. Marian knew that I wrote her father that I would kill her if he didn't pay me but she knew that I didn't mean it and was not worried or excited about it. In fact, I promised Marian that even though her father didn't pay me the money, I would let her go back unharmed. She felt perfectly safe and the tragedy was so sudden and unexpected that I'm sure she never actually suffered during the whole affair, except for a little sobbing which she couldn't keep back for her father and mother.

I wrote my third letter to Mr. Parker and put it with Marian's note in the same envelope. I told Marian that I would go downtown again and get the newspapers and mail the special delivery letter. I said I would return in less than a half hour and then we would get in the car and meet her father somewhere that morning.

I went ahead and tied her to the chair as I did Friday morning, except that I blindfolded her this time, and made ready to leave the apt. She said to hurry and come back.

At this moment my intention to murder completely gripped me. I went to the kitchen and got out the rolling pin meaning to knock her unconscious. I hesitated for a second and changed my mind. Instead I took a dish towel and came back to where she was sitting on the chair, pushed back in a small nook in the dressing room, with her back turned to me. I gently placed the towel about her neck and explained that it might rest her head but before she had time to doubt or even say anything I suddenly pulled the towel about her throat and applied all of my strength to the move. She made no audible noise except for the struggle and heaving of her body during the period of strangulation, which continued for about two minutes.

When Marian had passed to unconsciousness and her body stopped its violent struggle I untied the bandages and laid her on the floor. I took off her stockings, her sweater and dress, and placed her in the bathtub. I got a big pocket knife which I had in the apt. and started cutting. First, I cut a place in her throat to drain blood but this was not sufficient. I then cut her arms in two at the elbows and washed and wrapped them in newspaper. I drained the blood from the tub as I cut each part so that no stain was allowed to harden. Next I cut her legs in two at the knees. I let the blood drain from them and then washed and wrapped them in newspaper also. I put the limbs in the cabinet in the kitchen and then took the remaining undergarments from the body and cut through the body at the waist. As I cut the limbs and body there were heavy issues of blood and jerks of the flesh to indicate that life had not completely left the body.

I drained the blood from the midsection and washed and wrapped this part in newspapers and placed it on a shelf in the dressing room. I washed the blood from the tub and separated some of the internal organs from the body and wrapped them in paper. Then I tied a towel about the neck and tied another towel to it and left the upper part of the body to hang until the blood had completely drained from it. I placed a towel up in the body to absorb any blood or anything which had not dried. I took this part of the body and after I had washed and dried it, wrapped the exposed ends of the arms and waist with papers and tied them so that the paper would not slip. I dressed the body and placed it in a brown suitcase. I combed back the hair, powdered the face and laid a cloth over the face when I closed the suitcase. I put the suitcase on a shelf in the dressing room and then cleaned up the bath, trying not to leave any traces of blood anywhere.

I went to the writing desk and wrote a second part to my third letter which I called the final chance terms. I opened the envelope which I had sealed and put this third part with Marian's second note and my third letter. I went downtown and mailed this letter special delivery to Mr. Parker about one o'clock. I then went to the Loew's State Theatre, but I was unable to keep my mind on the picture and wept during the performance.

I returned to my apartment about 5:30 p.m. and took all the parts of Marian's body downstairs to the car waiting by the side entrance. No one saw me and I hurried out Sunset Blvd. and turned to the right at Elysian Park where within 100 yards along the road I left all of these parts.

I was back in the apt. by 6 o'clock and took the suitcase with the upper section and drove to Sixth St. and Western Av. Here I called Mr. Parker and told him to come to Manhattan Place and park just north of 5th St. I drove around in that neighborhood to see that no police cars were coming before I met Mr. Parker and I stopped between Sixth and Fifth Sts. on Manhattan Place and took the body from the suitcase. I left the suitcase outside the car and before I got back inside I turned one number back from each end of the rear license plate. About eight o'clock I saw Mr. Parker's car where I had told him and as I approached I tied a white handkerchief about my face. I drove up to the side of his car and stopped. I had a shotgun (sawed off) in one hand and I raised it up so that Mr. Parker would see it and cautioned him to be careful. He asked for his daughter and I raised up the head of the child so that he could see its face. He asked if it was alive. I said, 'Yes, she is sleeping.' I asked for the money and he handed it right over to me. I said I'd pull up ahead of him about 50 feet and let the child out. I pulled up ahead and stopped but only leaned over and placed the body on the edge of the fender so that it rolled over onto the parked [*sic*] and then I speeded east on 4th Street and downtown where I parked the car at 9th and Grand.

Note: The knife that I used in the cutting of the child was purchased at a hardware store on South Main Street about 5th Street. I identified this knife to Chief of Detectives Cline, who now has it in his possession. He got this knife from my suitcase where I said it was.

I then went to the Leighton Cafe in the Arcade on Broadway, between 5th and 6th Sts. I passed one of my twenty dollar gold certificates when I paid for my meal.

I went back to the apt. after I left the cafeteria and retired. On Sunday morning detectives from the police dept. searched my apt. for towels but made no arrest. I took my guns and the ransom money and checked them at the P.E. Station near 6th and Main. I also checked a black handbag and a suit box at the station. I went to the Tower Theatre early in the afternoon. Shortly after five p.m. I rode out on Hollywood Blvd. on a P.E. car and got off at Western Ave. I entered a closed car parked on Hollywood Blvd. near Western and told the man sitting at the wheel to start the car. He saw my gun and obeyed. We drove several blocks away and I told him to leave the car. Before he did so I took about $15 from him in money. This occurred about six o'clock Sunday evening, and shortly after seven I had secured my packages and grip from the P.E. Station and was on my way out of Los Angeles on Ventura Blvd. I drove overnight and arrived at San Francisco Monday about one p.m. I stopped at the Herald Hotel (room No. 402), and Tuesday about 9:30 a.m. I started for Seattle, Washington. I arrived there between 6 and 7 p.m. Wednesday and left about 9:30 p.m. to go back to Portland. I passed two of the gold certificates in Seattle and another on the road about twenty miles south of Seattle. The two bills in Seattle were in the downtown district, one at a clothing store where I purchased a pair of gloves and a suit of underwear, the other was at a theatre.

Note: While at the Herald Hotel in San Francisco, room 402, I assumed the name of Edward J. King, of Seattle. I arrived in Portland early Thursday morning and started on the Columbia River Highway east. Before leaving Portland I left my California license plates and put on two Washington plates which I took from a Ford car in Olympia. On the Columbia River Highway near [T]he Dalles I picked up two boy pedestrians and drove on till within a few miles of the town of Pendleton, Oregon, where I was arrested and taken to the city jail at Pendleton. The statement that I made after arrest implicating Andrew Cramer and June Dunning was false. This is my true statement.

Note: On the highway north of San Francisco I picked up a man and left him at Redding. I picked up two fellows south of Dunsmuir who rode with me to Portland, Oregon. I might say that the names Andrew Cramer and June Dunning are merely fictitious as far as I know.

Note: In reference to Marian's body just before I delivered the portion to her father, I used a large needle which I had in my possession and some black thread to fix and hold the upper lids of her eyes open so that her father would think that she was alive when he saw the face.

The shirt with the name Gerber written on the collar which was torn and used to tie parts of the body of Marian was a shirt I had had in my possession since I left Kansas City in October, and which was given to me by my youngest brother, Alfred. The name Gerber, I believe, is one of my brother's friends with whom he has traveled, and got on the shirt when it was sent to this man's laundry.

This statement is true and made freely and voluntarily by me.

Ed signed the document and watched as his escorts did likewise, Chief Davis signing as the first witness, followed in turn by Dwight Longuevan, Harry Raymond, Dick Lucas, George Home, and D.A. Asa Keyes. The ink was barely dry on the last signature when Hickman announced his desire to write a second statement, clarifying his reasons for Marian's murder.

When he was handed more paper, he inscribed the first sheet "December 26, 1927—Motives," then scratched "Motives" out before continuing. The final statement read as follows:

My name is William Edward Hickman and this statement was made and witnessed on the S.P. Train en route to Los Angeles.

This statement regards the kidnapping and murder of Marian Parker. The time of the murder was Saturday morning December 17, 1927. The place was in room 315 of the Bellevue Arms Apts. in Los Angeles.

I wish to explain in full the motives which prompted me to commit this crime.

In the first place let me say that the only circumstances connecting my intentions of murder to Marian Parker are purely incidental. I was not prompted by revenge in the killing of Marian Parker. Only through my association with Mr. P. M. Parker at the First National Bank while I worked there as a page from January to June, 1927, made it possible for me to see Marian Parker and to know that she was P. M. Parker's daughter. This was an incidental due [sic] and I merely picked it up and followed it through. My motives in the murder of Marian Parker are as follows:

1. Fear of detection by the police and the belief that to kill and dissect the body I would be able to evade suspicion and arrest. I had warned Mr. P. M. Parker to keep the case secret and private but this he was not reasonably able to do, so that the great publicity and search which followed caused me to use what I considered the greatest precaution in protecting myself.

After successfully dodging the authorities for two days I was overcome by such fear that I did not hesitate even to murder to escape notice. I consider that this fear and precaution were the result of my instinct for self-protection in time of danger.

2. Marian had a strong confidence in me for her own safety and I considered her own wish to return to her father Saturday morning too deeply. However, my desire to secure the money and return to college were even greater. I knew that if I refused to take her back Saturday morning she might distrust me enough to give some sign which would cause my discovery. Yet I felt that if I did take her back in day light I might fall in a trap and be caught. So in order to go through with my plans enough to get the money and keep Marian from ever knowing while she lived that I would disappoint her confidence in me, I killed her so suddenly and unexpectedly, or she passed beyond consciousness so quickly and unexpectedly that she never had a fear or thought of her own death. Then in order to get her out of my apartment without notice I was prompted after she was beyond consciousness to dissect her body.

3. For several years I have had a peculiar complex. Even though my habits have always been clean and although my high school record is commendable [I] have had an uncontrollable desire to commit a great crime.

This peculiar feeling, and I believe that it borders on the edge of insanity or that it comes as a weird relief from seriousness or deep thought, found a means of expressing itself in the Parker case. I am very sensitive and have a strong sense of pride. I have not been able to find a real practical value in religion or enough satisfaction that it is based on absolute reason. My deep thought on this subject and my apparent disappointment with my conclusion have shaken my sense of morality. However, I do not believe that I am insane or crazy, yet I do think that this complex of mine should not be considered least among my motives in this crime. The fact that a young man is willing to commit crime to secure expenses through college and especially to a church school helps to explain this complex of mine. I cannot understand it myself but I do consider it a big motive in this crime.

I do not consider crime seriously enough. I think that if I want something no matter what means I have to use to secure it, I am justified in getting it. My record of crime illustrates this statement very thoroughly. Even in the murder of Marian Parker I could not realize the terrible guilt: I felt that some kind of Providence was guiding me and protecting me in this whole case. These facts, I believe, are associated with my complex.

I want to make a statement here to avoid any suspicion that during my connection with Marian Parker I took any advantage of her femininity. I can only give my word that I did not, but I give this very sincerely and truthfully. My word is substantiated by the doctor's examination of the girl's body and I feel that everyone can be assured that the girl was not molested in any way.

I would like to say that I have had no bad personal habits. I have never been drunk or taken any intoxicating drinks. I do not gamble. I have never been in any corrupt conduct with the female sex. In support of these statements reference can be made to my record in the juvenile court of Los Angeles.

In giving these motives I have been as honest as I know how. I have searched my mind and impulses under all the circumstances and this is my truthful summary.

William Edward Hickman

If Ed thought he had managed to secure himself an escape hatch from death row he was mistaken. He had, in fact, done just the opposite.

Cline had been right about one thing: at every stop along their sparsely settled route, the gawkers came from miles around to stand and watch the train—sometimes to simply watch it pass them by. Hickman enjoyed the crowds, once he was satisfied they could not reach him, and he claimed to spot familiar faces in the ranks. "I think I saw that woman in Portland," he said, at a stop farther south. "I bet she has followed me all the way down." To Carlton Williams, covering the journey for the *L.A. Times*, Hickman appeared to be "conceit exemplified."

On Sunday night, Chief Davis received a telegram from Eva Hickman, asking him to tell her son that she had hired a lawyer—Jerome Walsh, of Kansas City—to defend him. Walsh was on his way, but the journey would take time. Commercial airlines were a science-fiction writer's dream in those days, Lucky Lindy's exploits notwithstanding. Traveling from Kansas City to Los Angeles by train, Walsh hoped to meet his client sometime Thursday afternoon.

The train's passage southward was not without incident. Frigid weather below Klamath Falls froze the oil in one engine, burning out the gears, and the train was delayed for half an hour at Mount Hebron, while a new locomotive was found. The first California stop, at Dunsmuir, found 2,000 people lined up at the depot, watching for Hickman in eerie silence. Another crowd was waiting in Benicia, 160 miles farther south, on San Pablo Bay. It was a short run from there to Oakland, where Edward's car was transferred to the Padre line. Again he was delayed, leaving Oakland twenty-two minutes late, at 9:02 P.M. It would take another thirteen hours for the train to reach Los Angeles.

One more night on the rails, Ed sleeping in his little cage on wheels.

If there was going to be trouble in Los Angeles, Chief Davis and his men expected it to happen at the depot while they were unloading Hickman. They did not expect a mob to rush the train—Los Angelenos were too civilized for that, unless the prisoner was black or Mexican—but it would only take one head case with a gun to cheat the hangman and make Davis look incompetent, his men like bumbling stooges.

Leaving nothing to chance, they stopped the train downtown, at Jackson and Alameda Streets, less than a mile and a half from the spot where Hickman had left Marian's truncated corpse in the gutter ten days earlier. A caravan of squad cars waited for him, bristling with guns.

Ed left his mobile prison for the last time at 10:10 A.M., still handcuffed to Lucas and Raymond. Five minutes later they were at the L.A. County jail, press photographers jostling in the front ranks of a crowd that numbered some 4,000 souls. Patrolmen armed with riot guns and nightsticks held the curious at bay, clearing a path from curbside to the jailhouse for the boy whose crime had horrified the world.

Chief Davis led the way, as stern-faced as ever. Hickman was propelled along behind him, barely visible among the brawny coppers, ducking low as if to dodge a bullet. As they entered the jail, one of the swinging doors struck Edward in the face, presumably by accident. He cried out in surprise or pain, but the sound was cut off as he was swept inside the building, out of sight.

10 ✦ "I Have No Fear of What May Come"

Ed was surrounded by cops in the elevator, going up to the tenth floor of the jail, where he was hand-delivered to Undersheriff Eugene Biscailuz. Reporters made note of the special precautions laid on for Hickman's arrival: extra guards for the cell block, plus a ball and chain to slow him down if he should somehow manage to escape. It seemed like overkill, considering the fact that Ed was separated from the outside world by seven triple-locked steel doors, each fitted with its own alarm.

Within three-quarters of an hour after his arrival at the jail, Hickman was on the move again. Dressed in jailhouse denim, surrounded by officers armed with shotguns and tear-gas grenades, he was marched to the adjoining courthouse, minus the ball and chain, for his arraignment on charges of kidnapping and murder. As luck would have it, there was a familiar face on the bench in Department 24: Judge Carlos Hardy was scowling at the young man he had favored with probation only six months earlier.

Hickman stood alone at the defense table, Asa Keyes and his deputy, William Brayton, ready to speak for the state. Judge Hardy glanced at the slim file before him, then peered at Ed again.

"William Elwood Hickman," the judge said. "Is that your true name?"

"Edward is my name, Your Honor," Hickman answered.

"William Edward Hickman?"

"Yes."

If Hardy recognized the prisoner, he gave no sign. "Have you an attorney to represent you?" he asked.

"No, sir."

"You are entitled to an attorney before you are arraigned." Hardy swiveled in his chair to face Asa Keyes. "Mr. District Attorney?"

"The defendant and the officers who brought him from the north, together with myself, just arrived this morning," Keyes said. "On my arrival at the office I found a telegram from the mother of this defendant, in which she advised me that she has employed an attorney in Kansas City to represent this defendant; that the attorney left Kansas City this morning on the Santa Fe Chief, and that he will be here on Thursday morning next; that the attorney who is coming here has authority from the mother of this defendant to employ additional counsel when he gets here."

Keyes asked for a postponement of the hearing, and Judge Hardy readily agreed, pushing Ed's arraignment back to 2:00 P.M. on Thursday. Moments later, Ed was on his way back to the jail, where more reporters were waiting for him. His escorts hesitated, then decided there was no harm in a little media exposure. The first reporter asked about his strategy for trial.

"I'll plead guilty and stand by my confession," Ed replied, "regardless of what this attorney advises me to do."

Was he prepared to take the consequences of a guilty plea?

"Sure," Hickman said, apparently untroubled by the prospect of a hanging.

"Suppose your attorney advises you to plead not guilty and stand trial?" another reporter asked.

"I would plead guilty anyhow," Hickman said.

"You want a speedy trial?"

"Yes, I want a speedy trial." He missed a beat, frowning. "But not *too* speedy," he concluded.

What did he mean by that?

"Well," Ed replied, "I thought they were going to rush me right through the trial today."

"Would you care to see Mr. Parker?" another newsman asked.

Ed seemed to flinch at that, his face betraying emotion for the first time since arriving at the jail. "Why . . . why, yes," he stammered. "That is, if he wanted to see me."

"What would you have to say to him?"

"Well," Edward said, "I'd tell him everything in the greatest detail."

"Have you any comment to make," someone asked, "on your mother's sending an attorney here to help you?"

Ed was back on safer ground. "Nothing," he said, "except that I did not expect it. But I do not want her to send one if it will cost her money."

His jailers were treating him "just fine," Hickman said in response to another question, sounding more relaxed.

"About your confession—"

"Oh," he interrupted the reporter, "you are not going to print that are you?" Closing the barn door too late.

"You stand by that confession?" the newsman asked.

"Certainly," said Hickman. "I gave it and it is in writing, and I signed it. I'll have to stand by it."

One last question before he returned to his cell: What had Hickman done with Marian's missing shoes and stockings?

He blinked at the question, frowning again. "I threw them away," he said. No, he could not recall where.

"That's enough," one of the deputies announced, his colleagues crowding in, propelling Hickman toward the elevator for the ride upstairs.

Deprived of access to the daily papers since boarding the train at Pendleton, Ed didn't know his full confession to the murder had been front-page news from coast to coast. It made a splash in Kansas City, where his mother still clung to a slender reed of hope. "He was only a tool," Eva told the reporters who camped on her doorstep. "Oh, I know my boy couldn't have thought out such a terrible thing. He was only carrying out the scheme of some directing head."

Down in El Paso, Bill Hickman was having no truck with denial. "Since he has confessed to this awful crime,"

Hickman said of his son, "I am content to let the law have him." In case anyone missed the point, Bill said he wanted Edward "punished according to his crime."

Back in Los Angeles, meanwhile, at least one person still had doubts about the nature of the crime. Unable to determine cause of death by any scientific means, Dr. Wagner aired his feelings in an open letter, featured on the front page of the *L.A. Times:*

I understand that Hickman stated that he strangled the little Parker girl. He may have done or attempted to do what he confessed he did, but her death was not primarily due to strangulation. There were no marks of contusion or constriction about the neck, the lungs were not congested, but on the contrary were quite pale and bloodless, the whites of her eyes were not injected (or blood-shot) nor was the face bloated when I first saw the remains. There were no signs of a struggle anywhere upon the body, no contusions, lacerations or scratches upon the hands, wrists or elsewhere.

I knew Marian Parker. She was a very nervous child, and when she realized her situation she probably neither slept nor partook of food during those three terrible days, as shown by her empty, constricted stomach, and from her letters written to her parents it would appear that her captor told her he would kill her if [she was] not ransomed: therefore, when he applied the towel about her neck, she realized what was about to happen and her heart stopped as a result of fear and exhaustion.

Hickman stated that she did not struggle, in his first statement reported. There were no indications whatever that he had mistreated his victim and the chemist's [sic] reports that no poisons or anesthetics could be found in the organs I submitted to him.

A. F. Wagner

Hickman's captors were also in Los Angeles that Tuesday, dropping by Mayor Cryer's office to discuss their share of the reward. Unknown to Tom Gurdane and Buck Lieuallen, another bid for the cash had already been filed by the time they arrived in L.A., a telegram from the Seattle law firm of Hanson, Patterson and Ross pleading the case of haberdasher George Willoughby, who had received one of the ransom bills from Ed on Wednesday night, December 21. In the attorneys' view "Hickman was picked up as a direct result of the information which Willoughby gave to the Seattle Police Department" that Wednesday, inasmuch as the tip "led directly to Hickman's arrest."

Lieuallen and Gurdane were not prepared to squabble over the contested cash in public. As Lieuallen told the press that afternoon, "We haven't done so much."

"Shucks, no," Gurdane chimed in. "We are police officers and get paid for catching criminals."

"We are not used to talking to you newspaper chaps," Buck went on, "and we don't know what to say. We are so tired we are dumb."

As far as catching Hickman went, Lieuallen told the press, "He did not put up a fight because he told me that when Tom here threw his gun on him, he knew he was going to shoot. It wasn't so much. We had the description of the car and the man, and naturally when that car came by, we just drew down on it and that's all there is to it."

Well, not quite.

"We have heard from theatrical chaps," Buck admitted. "Pantages, West Coast and other agencies, but we don't know what we are going to do. There is only one thing I can do, and that is ride horses and shoot fairly straight, and Dad, here," Buck nodded toward Gurdane, "he can do the same thing, so I can't see what good we would be in a theater."

Of course, there was cash to be considered. "We came down here to Los Angeles to get the reward," Lieuallen said. "That's natural. And we are going back as soon as we can. That's natural, too."

Wednesday morning's paper brought a furious reply from Herman Cline to Dr. Wagner, blasting Wagner's contention that Marian died from fright rather than strangulation or blood loss. Parts of Hickman's statement, Cline informed reporters, had been withheld deliberately from the press and proved the doctor wrong.

"Hickman told us these facts verbally," Cline said. "He was afraid to put them down on paper. We did not allow them to become known while the train was on the way from Pendleton, Oregon, to Los Angeles for fear it would incite a lynching."

What facts, precisely?

"You can say for me," Cline told reporters, "that no penalty the law will exact is sufficient for a fiend like Hickman. Hanging is far too good for him, and anything short of hanging would be a gross miscarriage of justice."

Despite the extra-tight security, Ed had a visitor on Wednesday morning. Lionel Moise, from the *Illustrated Daily News*, talked his way past the guards for a one-on-one with Hickman, thereby scooping the more prestigious *Times*. "My chief purpose in that interview," Moise later testified, "was to find out whether Hickman had any accomplices, and whether he had made the confession that had been attributed to him."

Ed confirmed his authorship of the confession and admitted that the crime was his alone. He had abandoned any vestige of the Cramer alibi, staking his hopes instead on a defense of mental incapacity.

"I then began to question him," Moise said, "along the lines of trying to probe and go into his psychology and the motives, and to find out what had prompted this particular crime, and I asked him some questions about his life in Kansas City, and about his school life, and I talked to him on a theory—talked to him really with the idea of asking him what he had read, whether he had ever read Freud or any of the other psychological writers. And he said no, he hadn't read them, but he had heard of them. I asked him if he knew what a complex was. I asked him whether he thought he was the victim of any complexes, and he said no, he didn't think he was actually—he wasn't sure whether he was the victim of a complex or not, unless there was one particular one he had, that he thought he had a complex that a special Providence was guiding him and protecting him."

Ed was skating on thin ice here, since his second statement written on the trip from Oregon contained specific reference to "a peculiar complex" of several years' duration that "bordered on insanity," infecting him with "an uncontrollable desire to commit a great crime." Now, with Moise, he seemed to be changing his tune.

"I asked him if he still believed in this special Providence," Moise told the court, "and he said, well, he was beginning to have his doubts at the time, because if the special Providence had been on the job, he would not have found himself in the predicament he was in then. I asked him whether he considered himself insane and he said, 'I do not think so.' I went back to the question of special Providence again and asked him some more, asked him if he had any great faith in God, and he said on that subject he was a little doubtful, because he had tested it out by reason and he could not form any good basis for a reasoning belief in God, and that that had caused him a good deal of deep thought."

His sign-off on the ransom letter, warning Perry Parker to seek aid "from God, not man" had been a manifestation of Hickman's trust in Providence, Moise said. "He cited that as proof that he had this belief in the omnipotent or special Providence, the fact that he had finished these letters in that particular manner."

That explanation was weak, and Hickman must have known it. His other two visitors that day were doctors, the first arriving at his cell near 2:20 P.M. Dr. Cecil Reynolds was a London-trained physician and surgeon with special interest in mental diseases, who had toured the lunatic asylums of England and Australia prior to settling in California in 1911. Since that time, he had specialized in brain and spinal surgery, with ongoing interest in nervous and mental disorders. His first of three interviews with Hickman, conducted in the presence of Deputy D.A. Forrest Murray, consumed an hour and twenty-five minutes on Wednesday afternoon.

After introducing himself, Dr. Reynolds asked Hickman, "I suppose you know why I am here?"

"To see whether I am sane, I guess," Ed replied. "You are a specialist or expert, I suppose."

"Are you sane?" Reynolds asked.

"Yes," Ed replied, "but I don't think that question is fair. I don't know the methods. I don't think I ought to—"

"Not fair?" Reynolds interrupted him. "Not fair to whom?"

"Not fair to me, or to you."

"Why?" Reynolds pressed.

"Because you can't tell whether I'm sane or not just by what I say," Ed replied. "Isn't it a fact that insane people generally say they are sane? Insane people don't usually admit it, do they?"

Reynolds turned it around. "Oh, is that your experience?"

"I am asking you if it isn't a fact," Hickman said, sounding irritated by the doctor's artful two-step.

"Why do you ask?" said Reynolds, continuing the game. "Do you intend to plead insanity as a defense?"

"No," Hickman said. "At least, I've made my confession and I stand by that. I don't think you know much. I think you're foolish. There must be something wrong with me because I have no sense of guilt. I haven't any remorse."

"You have no sense of guilt?"

"Well, not enough," Ed qualified, "considering what I've done. I guess you want to see me hang."

"It's no affair of mine what happens to you," Reynolds told him. "The district attorney has asked me to examine you as to your health and condition. You are under no obligation to consent if you don't want it."

"The district attorney wants to hang me," Hickman said.

"What does it matter if you're hanged?" the doctor asked. "You're not much use to society, are you? Why shouldn't you be hanged?"

"I'm not afraid of death," Ed told him, sidestepping the question.

"Nor of what comes after?"

"I don't believe there is anything after," said Hickman, the matter settled in his mind.

"You have some surprises coming to you," Reynolds said, but Hickman let that pass. "Are you in good health?"

"Yes."

"Never have headaches?"

"No."

"Stomach in good order?"

"Yes."

"Never sick in your stomach?"

"No."

"Good appetite?"

"Yes."

"Did you ever have a good hard thrashing in your life?" Reynolds asked.

"Once, at school," Ed began, then changed his mind. "Not a good one."

"Not a real licking?" Reynolds probed.

"No."

"Ever had any accidents of consequence?"

"No."

"In fact," Reynolds said, "you have never suffered any great physical pain in your life?"

"No," Ed agreed.

"A sermon might be preached on that theme," Reynolds said to Forrest Murray, then turned back to Hickman. "You have been concerned in many holdups and thefts of automobiles?"

"Yes," Ed replied, in what Reynolds later described for the court as "a 'what do you expect' manner."

"You deliberately planned all these crimes?"

"I didn't exactly plan them," Hickman said. "I just did them."

"Well," Reynolds said, "you obtained a gun and went out armed with intent, didn't you?"

"Of course I had to have a gun to pull a holdup," Ed replied, his patience wearing thin.

"But you never felt any compassion for your victims?"

"No," Ed acknowledged. "I figured that what I wanted I had a right to get any way I could."

"And how long have you felt that way?"

"Since I couldn't go on with school," Hickman said. "I wanted an education."

"How old were you when you had to quit school?" Reynolds asked, apparently unaware that Hickman had in fact graduated from Central High.

"Sixteen," Ed replied, going along with the game.

"And you are now . . . twenty-what?"

"Nineteen," Ed corrected him in a tone the doctor would later call "somewhat resentful."

"Did you ever have any human feeling toward others?" the doctor inquired.

"I became completely bitter against the world at sixteen," Ed replied, "when I had to leave school."

"Do you consider yourself human?" Reynolds asked.

Hickman laughed in his face. "Of course I'm human."

"What makes you think so?"

Still laughing, Hickman spelled it out. "I walk on two legs, don't I?"

"So does a kangaroo," Reynolds shot back.

"A kangaroo has a tail," Ed reminded him. "Human beings don't."

"Some do," the doctor quipped, apparently enjoying himself as he turned to Murray and explained, "I removed a long tail from one of my friends once." Back to Edward: "Do you know of any animal that would do such a bestial act as you allege you have done?"

"What kind of act?"

"Such a bestial act," Reynolds repeated.

"I don't know much about animals," Hickman allowed.

"But you consider yourself human? What is your definition of a human being?"

Ed took his time, thinking that one over. "I wish I had an education," he said at last, "so that I could answer you properly on all this stuff. Oh, I guess you're an expert. I admit you're smarter than me."

"Indeed!" Reynolds fairly crowed. "The superegotist thinks I may have had an education!"

"Well, how do *you* know what a human being is?" asked Hickman.

"I can recognize them," Reynolds answered. "I see them here, and here," pointing to Murray and a jailer standing just outside the cage, "and also out in the cells there."

"I guess you're enjoying yourself," Hickman said.

"I am not," the doctor replied stiffly. "It is very unpleasant. I wouldn't be here if it wasn't a public duty."

"Anyway, you're being paid for it," Hickman said. "You want to see me hanged."

"Well," Reynolds asked, "what do you suggest should be done with you? Handed over to me for vivisection?"

"Would you do it?" Ed inquired.

"Without the slightest compunction," Reynolds said.

"That shows you are less human than I am," Hickman replied.

"Thanks," the doctor beamed at him. "That's just the reaction I was looking for."

Weeks later, in court, Reynolds would claim under oath that his goading of Hickman was designed to prove that the defendant "has an intellectual appreciation of accepted codes of human ethics, which are based on the feelings of the rest of humanity." In fact, a reader of the transcripts— complete with exclamation points inserted by Reynolds in his own quotations—might conclude that the doctor was indeed enjoying himself.

"Well," Hickman said, "if you could do a thing like that, you can't be any more human than I am."

"Ah!" Reynolds countered, "but I might have a little remorse toward the end, because I have feelings, but you appear to have none. I am not boasting about it, mind you. It may be simply my good fortune, and your bad fortune, that things are as they are. I am simply stating that I recognize human beings by their feelings." Shifting gears suddenly, Reynolds said, "I would like to examine your eyes."

When Hickman offered no objection, the lights were dimmed, and Reynolds leaned in close to study first one eye, then the other. In the dim light, he would later testify,

Hickman's pupils "were rather smaller than normal, indicating a low affectivity." As Reynolds told the court, "One sees the same condition of pupils in steely-nerved people."

Reynolds then asked, "Did you ever hear voices?"

"No," Ed replied, the simple answer leading Reynolds to believe the question had "evidently been asked before."

"No imaginary voices ever tell you to do things?"

"No," Ed repeated.

"Did you ever suffer from obsessions?" Reynolds asked, then added: "Oh, I suppose you don't know what that means?"

Once again, Hickman laughed in his face. "No," he replied, "I don't know what that means."

"Well," Reynolds said, ignoring the sarcasm, "take for example . . . some people who climb up a high mountain. When they get near the top, if they happen to look down, they immediately get an unnatural impulse to throw themselves down. Did you ever have any kind of impulse in that sense of the word?"

"Do you mean they had an impulse to climb the mountain?" Ed asked. Playing with him.

"No," Reynolds said. "They climbed the mountain deliberately with intent to reach the top, but when near the top, an impulse seized them to fling themselves down."

"Never," Hickman replied, "except when I killed Marian. I had an impulse to do that. I did not know what I was doing."

"You did not know what you were doing?" Reynolds echoed.

"No."

"How did you kill her?"

"Oh, that's all in my confession," Ed replied. "I guess you've . . ."

Hickman hesitated, glancing at Murray before Dr. Reynolds pushed ahead. "Yes, but the district attorney's got that," he said. "I am asking you to tell me."

"I strangled her with a towel," Hickman said.

"What kind of towel?"

"It was a kitchen towel. It was dirty."

"Was it a plain white towel," Reynolds asked, "or a green towel, or a black or yellow towel?"

"It was a white towel with a single-line red border," Ed replied.

"Where did you get it from?"

"The next room."

"What was the next room?" Reynolds asked.

"The kitchen," Ed replied, as if to ask, Where else would you go looking for a kitchen towel?

"Where was the towel in the kitchen?" Reynolds pressed, flogging the minutiae.

"Hanging on the rack."

"What rack? Above the sink?"

"No," Hickman said, "the rack nailed to the side of this dresser where the dishes were kept."

"Oh, I see." Reynolds seemed on the brink of a great revelation. "The towel rack was nailed to the side of the dresser, and this towel with the red border was hanging on that rack?"

"Yes."

"Did you walk fast or slowly to get the towel?" Reynolds asked.

"Neither," Hickman said. "Just ordinary."

"Then what did you do?"

"I came back into the room where Marian was and put the towel around her neck."

"Where was she in the room?" asked Reynolds.

"Sitting in the chair," Ed told him. "She was blindfolded."

"How was she sitting? Was she facing you?"

"No," Ed replied. "She had her back to me."

"What kind of chair was she sitting on?"

"Oh, just a chair!" Ed snapped impatiently. "I don't know what kind. Like the rest of the furniture."

"Was it a white chair?" Keeping up the steady pressure.

"No, it was a dark chair."

"Did the child seem to hear you coming?" Reynolds asked.

"She knew I was there," Ed replied.

"Then what happened?"

"I put the towel around her neck," Ed repeated.

"How? Over her head, or sling it around?"

A smile tugged at the corners of Ed's mouth. "I'll show you, if you like," he said. "I'll demonstrate on you, if you're not afraid."

"I'm not afraid," Reynolds said, "but I don't choose. Try it on that basin."

Ed picked up a piece of cloth, eyeing the sink in his cell. "I can't do it on that basin," he said at last. "Here, I'll use this pillow." Standing the pillow on end on his bunk, he flicked the towel around it with his left hand, catching it with his right and pulling it tight, raising his right knee for leverage, as if against a living victim's spine.

Dr. Reynolds would later describe how Ed "strangled" the pillow "with a vicious jerk and expression." That done, "He turned to us with the air of a showman and complete sangfroid. No sign of remorse or regret."

As an afterthought, Ed pushed the top part of the pillow forward, sagging above the garrote. "That was the way Marian's head went," he explained.

"Whilst you were doing this," Reynolds asked, "what were your feelings?"

"I didn't know what I was doing," Ed repeated, sticking to the script.

"Were your feelings pleasant or painful, or what?"

"Not pleasant," Hickman said. "I think I was a little sorry."

"You think you were a little sorry?"

"Yes. That's in my confession," Ed reminded them both, "that I wept. That shows I was human, doesn't it?"

"Not necessarily," Reynolds answered. "Weeping is sometimes an expression of human feelings. Not always. Is that your defense? That you wept?"

"No!" Ed snapped. "Here, I shall lose my meal if you keep on any longer." Pointing at the lunch tray waiting for him, Ed went on, "Look at those dishes. They'll be taken away."

Forrest Murray remarked that they should let Ed eat his lunch, but Dr. Reynolds wasn't finished yet. He completed the first examination by tapping Ed's knees, mentally recording the "moderately brisk" reaction of each leg.

"Oh, my reflexes are all right," Hickman told him, then dug into lunch "with evident good appetite, as if nothing had been done to disturb him." Taking leave of his reluctant subject, Dr. Reynolds noted that he could detect "no stigmata of degeneration, no deformities."

Five hours later, a second physician came calling. Dr. Frank Mikels was educated in Maine and spent a year with the U.S. Public Health Service before moving on, first to Harvard and then to a post as assistant pathologist at the New Jersey State Hospital for the Insane at Morris Plains. He testified at Hickman's trial that in five years at Morris Plains, he had examined some 3,000 mental patients. Since moving west and settling in Hollywood in 1915, he had been affiliated with various hospitals in Long Beach, Hollywood, and Culver City.

Dr. Mikels arrived for the first of six visits with Hickman at 8:12 P.M. on Wednesday. Unlike Dr. Reynolds before him, Mikels showed up without an escort from the prosecutor's office, but Hickman was instantly suspicious. Once burned, twice shy.

"Before I submit to this examination," Ed told Mikels, "I would prefer to consult with my attorney, who will be here in the morning. And if he does not show up, I will very gladly answer the questions. I don't see the necessity of this mental examination. I have already pled guilty, and I expect to get the extreme sentence. I expect to be hung for what I did."

Mikels would not be put off, however, and without a lawyer to advise him otherwise, Hickman relented, offering Mikels the opinion that "Society will be benefited by this whole affair."

Dr. Mikels took a different angle of attack from Reynolds, producing a printed checklist, including specific areas for observation under "Appearance and Behavior," "Emotions,"

"Ideation," and the like. As he later reported in court, he found Edward neither untidy nor slovenly, neither irritable nor agitated. "Homicidal" got a check mark, based on press reports of Edward's crime, while "Suicidal" remained open to further study. Mikels noted "a tendency to be a little surly," but Ed ranked negative on a list of other negative traits, ranging from "reticent" to "cataleptic." The prisoner was not "bombastic" or "retarded." Masturbation got a pass, until the doctor had more time to check it out.

In court, some six weeks later, Dr. Mikels seemed a bit confused about his subject's attitude toward the proceedings. First, he judged Ed reticent, because "he had a slight reticence at that time," but later he described Ed's tone as one of frank suspicion from the outset of the interview.

"Who sent you here?" Hickman demanded. "Were you sent here by the district attorney's office? If so, I don't intend to answer any questions that will incriminate me."

Hickman refused to answer any questions pertaining to his family or childhood, until Dr. Mikels told him that the interview was meant to learn if he had ever suffered mental illness. On hearing that, Mikels noted, "he became a little interested and I engaged him in conversation." In all, he spoke with Ed for barely half an hour during that first meeting, but it was enough for Dr. Mikels to conclude that "he did not show any evidence whatsoever of disturbance of the process of ideation. His replies and his objects seemed to be consistent with his emotional and his defensive attitude at the time of his examination." Furthermore, Mikels would testify, "I found his trend of ideas were logical in sequence, his association of ideas accurate and complete, his choice of terms to express ideas precise and grammatical."

Not bad, for a man with "a complex."

The visits seemed to have shaken something loose in Edward. Instead of waiting for his lawyer to arrive, he was up at 4:00 A.M. on Thursday, talking to his keepers. Jailer Frank Dewar asked Ed in passing, "Say, did you ever kill anyone else?"

"Sure," Ed responded with disarming candor. "Do you remember that druggist at Rose Hill that was shot last December?"

Dewar was unfamiliar with the case, but he knew enough to hurry when Ed asked for pencil and paper. Talking it through with Dewar as he wrote out the details, Hickman recalled the Christmas Eve holdup, the beat cop who had surprised him in the pharmacy, the blaze of gunfire as he fled with Welby Hunt. Ed hadn't known that Ivy Thoms was hit until he read it in the newspaper.

It was the first time Hunt's name had been mentioned in the case. While Ed went back to bed, apparently at ease, Dewar called the suits from Homicide and told them he had something hot. They read through Hickman's statement and secured a warrant, picking sixteen-year-old Welby up a short time later, on suspicion of murder.

In custody, Hunt admitted joining Hickman for a string of robberies that had begun in Kansas City and continued in L.A. Yes, he was present at the Rose Hill job, Hunt granted, but he never fired his gun. If anyone shot Thoms, it must have been Eddie, Hunt insisted; either that or Thoms had stopped a stray round from the cop.

Hickman, advised of Welby's comment later in the afternoon, would shrug it off. The autopsy report should tell who was responsible, he said. The guns in question were forever lost, but Hunt and Hickman both agreed that Edward had been carrying a .32 on Christmas Eve, while Welby packed a .38. In fact, before the day was out, the word came back: Thoms had, from all appearances, been killed by a .38-caliber slug.

Later that morning, the druggist's widow was brought to see Hickman in jail. There was no lineup; Ed was simply brought into the corridor, where Mrs. Thoms at first did not appear to recognize him. Only after he was steered beneath a stronger light did she cry out, "My God! That's the man!"

Hickman, for his part, seemed confused. "What's the matter with that woman?" he asked his jailers. "I never saw her before."

With the addition of Welby Hunt to the case, investigators wondered if they might have found the second man who was allegedly involved with Hickman in the Parker kidnapping. A stringer for the *New York Times* advised his readers that the sixteen-year-old thief "somewhat resembles" Hickman's oral sketch of "Andrew Cramer." It was not explained why Ed would give his partner up in one murder, yet try to shield him in another.

Welby's mother, Mrs. W. H. Wehring, had been traced to Kansas City, meanwhile, and was suddenly confronted by reporters. She echoed Eva Hickman as she told the press, "I know my son is innocent. He is a good boy, and I am certain this merely is Edward Hickman's means of retaliating. From the very first, when reports came from California that my son had given aid to the police, I was afraid of what Hickman might do. At first, I was afraid he might return to Los Angeles and kill my boy, as he killed Marian Parker. Then, when he was captured, I thought [Welby] would be safe, but I see now I was mistaken."

It was worth a shot, of course, and Mrs. Wehring may have been sincere, despite the fact that there were no reports of Welby "giving aid to the police" before his own arrest. In any case, her son's admission of participating in a four-month string of robberies torpedoed any hope she had of selling Welby as a "good boy." By the time her statement hit the newsstands, homicide detectives were already re-examining A. R. Driskell's "suicide" in Long Beach, studying the several notes that were discovered on or near his body.

By the time Ed's attorney arrived in Los Angeles, on Thursday, Hickman had already confessed to a second murder while informing two experts, hired by the prosecution, that he was sane. Another lawyer might have thrown in the towel, but Jerome Walsh was no quitter. His father, Frank Walsh, was one of Kansas City's most respected attorneys, and Jerome bid fair to eclipse the old man, having already been elected Missouri's youngest state legislator at age twenty-five. Hickman's case was a publicity gold mine, and while Walsh had no realistic prospect of seeing his client walk, he still cherished hopes, however dim, of saving Edward's life. After all, he reasoned, Clarence Darrow had done it in Chicago for Leopold and Loeb.

It was 2:00 P.M. when Hickman returned to Judge Hardy's courtroom with his phalanx of bodyguards, prepared for anything short of a cavalry charge. And for the first time since his luck ran out in Oregon, he had a lawyer at his side.

Judge Hardy called the case, with Asa Keyes and William Brayton back in their places at the prosecution table. "Are you represented by counsel, Mr. Hickman?" Hardy asked.

"Yes, Your Honor."

Asa Keyes spoke up before Walsh had a chance to answer for himself. "If Your Honor pleases, Mr. Walsh, of Kansas City, is here to represent this defendant. He has been retained by the mother of the defendant, as I advised the court a few days ago. He is here today for the purpose of arraignment, and in order that the record may be clear, I move his admission to the California bar for the purposes of this case, at least."

Judge Hardy addressed Walsh for the first time. "You are admitted to practice in the courts of Missouri, Mr. Walsh?"

"Yes, sir."

"Well, you are admitted upon motion for the purpose of this case," Hardy allowed. "You are representing this defendant?"

"Yes, Your Honor."

"Arraignment of the defendant on the indictment," Hardy announced.

"I think that the defendant will waive the reading of the indictment, Your Honor," Walsh said.

"I prefer to have the indictment read," said Hardy, whereupon the bailiff formally pronounced the charges of murder and kidnapping filed against Hickman. Asa Keyes handed a copy to Walsh, along with transcripts of the grand jury testimony.

"Are you ready to enter a plea today?" Hardy asked Walsh.

"If the court pleases," Walsh said, "as the court is probably advised, I accepted employment in this matter just fifteen hours before I took the train from Kansas City. Since that time I have consumed the time in coming to California, and I only arrived here this morning at nine o'clock. Since I have been in Los Angeles I have taken occasion to confer with the district attorney and my client, here. I am sure that the court will understand how pressed I might be to get a clear conception of this matter, knowing, as the court must understand, that the only information I can possibly have at this time about this gruesome affair is what I have read in the newspapers."

"You think you will need time to plead?" Hardy asked.

"I think so, Your Honor, that I should have a reasonable time to become familiar with this matter, especially in view of the peculiar statutes of California. Of course," Walsh added, "I am as familiar with your procedure as a member of the Missouri bar could be, but I think in fairness to my client and myself, feeling incompetent as I do to make an intelligent decision here as to in what manner this defendant should plead, I should have a reasonable time to discuss the matter and get a clear understanding, and possibly—quite probably—retain counsel in Los Angeles who are familiar with your practice and procedure."

Judge Hardy agreed to postpone for five days, until 2:00 P.M. the next Tuesday, and the hearing was adjourned. Ed shook hands with his lawyer and shuffled back to his cell, under guard.

While Jerome Walsh was testing the judicial waters in Los Angeles, police in Kansas City were busy cleaning up after Edward. That Thursday afternoon, they arrested twenty-year-old Frank Bernoudy, announcing that he had confessed to participation in some of Edward's K.C. holdups. In jail, Bernoudy recalled how Ed and Welby Hunt had enjoyed reading "murder stories" aloud to each other, evaluating the killer's technique in each case. After one such get-together, said Bernoudy, Hickman had declared, "You know, it would be worse than that to kill someone and cut him to pieces. Someday I'm going to pull a job like that."

Back in L.A. that eventful Thursday, Tom Gurdane and Buck Lieuallen reassessed their prospects in the theater and cut a deal. According to the press reports, both officers signed on for one week with a local vaudeville show, while they were waiting for Mayor Cryer to decide who would pocket the reward.

On Friday morning, after reading through the California penal code, attorney Walsh announced that he planned to defend his client on grounds of insanity. Walsh also voiced doubt that Ed Hickman had carried out the kidnapping and murder by himself. In spite of the denials issuing from county jail, Walsh thought Ed was withholding information from police that would identify the evil brains behind the crime.

Oddly, Los Angeles authorities seemed to agree with him on New Year's Eve. Investigator George Contreras, with the D.A.'s office, told the press on Saturday that he had received information from another tenant of the Bellevue Arms, indicating that an unidentified woman had called on "Donald Evans" in apartment 315 on Friday, December 16. If true, the female visitor must have seen Marian Parker, an opinion bolstered by an overheard fragment of conversation, the woman telling Hickman, "Eddie, we've got to get out of here quick!"

As for the woman's identity, the anonymous witness had managed only a glimpse of her profile. She was older than Hickman, stylishly dressed, and heavily made up. Contreras would have liked to question Hickman, but as he advised the press, Edward had finally clammed up, on orders from counsel.

Even so, despite Walsh's specific instructions, Ed was still his own worst enemy. That weekend, he contrived to pass a message to another inmate on the tier, one Dale Budlong, but it was intercepted by a guard. It read:

Listen Dale—

I believe you and believe I can trust you. Give me your advice on which one of these plans would be better. All of the depositions aren't enough to prove me insane. I've got to throw a fit in court and I intend to throw a laughing, screaming, diving act before the prosecution finishes their case—maybe in front of old man Parker himself.

Then to bewilder the jury, before the case is ended, I'll get up and ask the judge if I can say something without my attorney butting in. Then I'll get up and give all that crap about me wanting to do some good by living.

I intend to rap Mr. Keyes before the thing's over and pull some trick on him in the crazy line.

Shorty, think these things over and tell me whether it is best or not.

For God's sake tear this thing up, because it would ruin me if it got out.

See you in the morning.

> William Edward Hickman alias "The Fox"
> Ha! Ha! Ha!

P.S. You know and I know that I'm not insane however.

On Sunday, New Year's Day, the search for answers in the Parker case went on, but it had shifted to the pulpits of churches across the land. In faraway Brooklyn, the Reverend Russell Brougher of the Third Avenue Baptist Temple used his sermon to address the spreading plague of crime.

"There is a spirit of lawlessness influencing nearly everybody," Brougher told his congregation. "New York, the largest city in the world, naturally would have a very high percent of crime, and yet I believe that we have a good chief of police. He is handicapped in many ways, but I believe that he and his fellow officers are endeavoring, as best they can, to enforce the law." Judges were largely to blame, Reverend Brougher contended, "for showing too much leniency in regard to bail and probation." Likewise, fault lay with "designing lawyers and the influence of outside organizations" in defense of criminals. True Christians, he said, could do their part by paying traffic fines on time and honoring the federal ban on alcoholic beverages.

Across town, Canon William Chase took a leaf from Edward's own book, joining in a formal debate before the Ingersoll Forum on the topic "Should there be federal supervision of motion pictures?" Presenting the affirmative argument, Chase used Hickman as Exhibit A in favor of censorship. "Did you notice," he asked, "that in his account of his dreadful crime Hickman said it was his habit to see motion pictures daily?"

Ed wasn't watching any movies these days, even though he unknowingly helped sell tickets at one theater. The manager of a movie house in Belvedere, California, thought he could lure more paying customers if he displayed a gallows out in front, complete with a wax "Hickman" dummy dangling by its neck, to advertise the latest newsreel. Word got out that Hickman had been hanged in effigy, and soon a crowd gathered on the scene, some cheering his symbolic death while others jeered the crude display. Fistfights broke out, and deputies were summoned to disperse the mob with swinging billy clubs.

Ed's only source of entertainment, meanwhile, was the intermittent flow of visitors who trooped past his tenth-floor cell. Jerome Walsh made the pilgrimage on Monday, January 2, 1928, accompanied by three other men, on what the press chose to call a "mystery visit." Two of Walsh's shadows remained unidentified but were assumed to be psychiatrists working on Hickman's insanity defense. The third man was quickly recognized by local reporters as Joseph Ryan, a defector from the D.A.'s office to the ranks of private practice, his departure spiced by accusations (Ryan's) of misconduct by county prosecutors. Nothing came of the charges—L.A. was still L.A., beneath a coat of whitewash—but Ryan's flirtation with the Hickman defense team was at least a minor bombshell when it hit the papers.

On Tuesday afternoon, January 3, Hickman returned to Judge Hardy's courtroom with the usual squad of armed guards. The only member of the Parker family present was Marian's older brother, Perry Junior, seated inconspicuously at the rear of the courtroom. Despite his earlier reference to hiring local counsel, Walsh stood alone with his client at the defense table, against Bill Brayton for the state.

"People against Hickman," Judge Hardy announced from the bench. "Mr. Hickman, have you any other attorney than Mr. Walsh?"

"No, Your Honor."

"Do you wish to file some paper, Mr. Walsh?"

"I do, Your Honor," Walsh replied.

"Does this relate to the arraignment for plea?" Hardy asked.

"It does, Your Honor." Having said that, though, the lawyer from Missouri seemed to change his mind. "I would not say directly that it related to the plea, Your Honor, but it might more properly come as a matter for the plea."

"I would like to arraign the defendant for his plea at this time," Hardy said.

"If the court will indulge me for a moment," Walsh pressed on, "before I take that action I would like to preface it with some statements that I think are quite pertinent to the matter."

Hardy frowned. "Well, I doubt if they are pertinent in advance of the plea," he said.

"I might say," Walsh countered, "that they are in relation to the plea itself."

"Well, I will take the plea," Hardy allowed, "then take your explanation."

"Very good, Your Honor."

At a signal from the bench, Bill Brayton read the grand jury's indictment on charges of kidnapping and murder. "Now, William Edward Hickman," he continued, "to the charge of kidnapping contained in count one of the indictment, how do you plead, guilty or not guilty?"

"Not guilty," Ed declared, "by reason of insanity."

He had reversed himself and made nonsense of his bragging to the press. Judge Hardy betrayed no surprise, but there were still formalities requiring his attention.

"Mr. Hickman," Hardy said, "do you understand in entering the plea of not guilty by reason of insanity, under the laws of this state you admit the commission of the offense charged against you? Do you understand that?"

"Yes, Your Honor," Hickman said.

"Well, enter the plea of not guilty by reason of insanity as to the first count," Hardy said to his clerk.

Ed filed the same plea on the murder charge, again responding to the judge's query with assurances that he knew what he was doing.

"Now, Mr. Walsh," Hardy said.

"If Your Honor please," Walsh began, "I have no purpose here to hinder or delay Your Honor in the conduct of this case or in the swift and accurate process of California justice, but under this plea it is going to require grave and voluminous proof to establish, in my mind, the defense that I think can be made in this case. I am further driven to that conclusion that it is going to be a great and salutary thing for the American conscience if this boy is conclusively proven not to be a normal American boy, and in view of the fact that I am going to have to go east, and in view of all the circumstances, we should have what the court must consider a reasonable time within which to prepare this case."

The bulk of his evidence resided in Arkansas and Missouri, Walsh told the court, and he would need "some considerable time" to seek out witnesses as yet unknown to him by name. Including railroad travel back and forth, Walsh guessed that he would need thirty-five days to prepare his defense.

"I will read your affidavit," Hardy said. "Of course, you do not set up the names of any witnesses or even show what you expect to prove by any witnesses in support of the plea that has been offered. Your affidavit is very general. You just say that on the thirtieth of December last you sent a telegram to Chief Edwards of Kansas City, in which you asked for the names and addresses of persons who can give you testimony tending to establish the insanity of the defendant, and up to the present time you have not received any response to the telegram, notwithstanding the fact that you asked for information Sunday night last. So that it seems to me that the matter as to the witnesses, where they reside, who they are, what they will testify to, is very uncertain at this time."

"I understand," Walsh said.

"I feel," Hardy continued, "in view of the plea that he has entered, he is entitled to a reasonable time. But under the law of this state the court is required to set these cases for trial within thirty days, and I would not accede to such a length of time, nor do I deem it necessary. This defendant was brought into court a week ago today. He was arraigned on last Thursday, and while I recognize the fact that some holidays have intervened, nevertheless you have been here on the ground, and yourself and your associates—those that are interested in the case, it seems to me—would have an opportunity to begin to marshal their evidence. I see no reason why a time considerably short of the time of thirty-five days you have asked for would not be amply sufficient for you to produce the testimony, whatever testimony there is, that will be relevant and competent. The court feels that this should be done in two weeks ordinarily, but because of the nature of the case I am constrained, as a clear maximum, to allow you three weeks."

Hardy fixed the mandatory starting date for Hickman's trial as January 25, at 9:30 A.M. Walsh registered a pro forma objection to the decision, court was adjourned, and Hickman shuffled back to his cell without stopping to chat with the press.

In deference to fair play, the county grand jury had postponed its hearing on the Thoms murder case until Wednesday, January 4. That afternoon, while Eva Hickman and her daughter Mary were preparing for their westward journey, Edward was reported by his jailers to be "muttering and feverishly reading a Bible" in his cage. Deputy Frank Dewar, for one, was not impressed, confiding to reporters that he thought Hickman was acting strange to buttress his insanity defense. Bill Hickman, in El Paso, had experienced a change of heart, meanwhile: he now believed Ed was insane and hoped the court would spare his life.

That afternoon, Ed wrote and mailed a letter to his mother, the first direct communication since he left Kansas City in October.

Dear Mother:

I certainly appreciate your kind letter and I want you to know that I still care for you. It's so sweet of you to be willing to help, no matter what has happened—and your love is simply overwhelming. I have no fear of what may come. I have been truthful and confessed everything.

Every one has treated me nice. I have slept well and feel in perfect health. In spite of everything people can't help but sympathize with me and praise you for your strong mother love. After talking with me and being around me people can't realize my guilt, but it is so, nevertheless.

Mr. Gustav E. Briegleb, pastor of St. Paul's Presbyterian Church, gave me a Bible and I am reading it some. I like the Psalms and seem to get real comfort out of them. God bless you, Mother. May He comfort you and see the whole thing through to the end.

Your son,
Edward Hickman

Ed was wrong about one thing, of course: most people had no sympathy whatsoever for his self-inflicted dilemma. On Thursday afternoon, the grand jury indicted both Hickman and Welby Hunt for the murder of Ivy Thoms. At their arraignment a few hours later, Edward filed another insanity plea, while Hunt stood mute. At age sixteen, Welby knew he could not be hanged for any crime committed as a juvenile.

It was a different story for his sidekick, though. Ed Hickman was of "hanging age," and now the state would have two chances to kill him.

11 ✦ The Making of a Genius

On Monday morning, January 9, Jerome Walsh told the press in Kansas City that he would pursue the Leopold and Loeb insanity defense for Hickman, more specifically the claim that Edward suffered from dementia praecox (literally "premature insanity," today called schizophrenia). Walsh said that one unnamed Los Angeles psychiatrist had already confirmed Hickman's insanity. What they needed most now was testimony from teachers, classmates, and others who had known Edward as a child, before he turned to crime. Walsh planned to take depositions on Wednesday from a list of witnesses he would not name. Then he would move on to Little Rock in search of records documenting Eva Hickman's mental problems. J. P. Costello, from the D.A.'s office in Los Angeles, would be on hand to watch his every move.

Again, Walsh emphasized that he did not expect his client to go free. "All I seek to do," he told reporters, "is to find some humane and civilized solution of this thing."

Back in Los Angeles that afternoon, District Attorney Keyes appeared to have no doubts about his prospect for convicting Ed of murder in the first degree. Two eminent physicians—Cecil Reynolds and Dr. A. A. Nickels—had already studied the defendant, Keyes informed reporters, and pronounced him "absolutely sane." To cover all bases, though, Keyes said he was directing three more doctors to examine Ed before the trial convened. Guards at the county jail informed reporters that their star inmate had seemingly abandoned his efforts to "act crazy." Instead, he had immersed himself in memorizing Oscar Wilde's *The Ballad of Reading Gaol*, sent to Ed from Kansas City by an unnamed correspondent.

The parade of doctors started Tuesday morning, after breakfast. The first was Dr. J. M. Fettes, a 1904 graduate of Trinity Medical College in Toronto. He had been practicing surgery in Los Angeles since March 1927, after nearly a quarter-century of running his own clinic in Le Mars, Iowa, north of Sioux City.

Dr. Fettes was assigned to carry out a physical examination and report any evidence of trauma or disease that might have driven Hickman legally insane—that is to say, unable to distinguish right from wrong, or physically incapable of self-control. After a brief review of Edward's personal and family history, Fettes began his formal testing.

"That examination," he later told the court, "consisted of, first, general observation. The boy walked with a rather peculiar gait, in that he would take his feet up a little quickly. Nothing special about that, but I noticed it as a peculiarity." During the session, Dr. Fettes reported, Ed "cooperated fairly well in helping with the examination and answering questions, but his attitude seemed that [sic] he was a little retarded in thinking and answering."

Starting at the top, Dr. Fettes noted that Ed's hair, while nice and thick, "felt a little bit dry." His scalp was healthy, and his skin, while clear of blemishes, had a "rather soft, almost infantile feel." After Hickman stripped, the doctor said, "I noticed that where his clothes were a little tight the skin was red." It was always like that, Hickman said. "In striking this skin," Dr. Fettes went on, "it gave a very marked . . . what we call dermography. I took the blunt end of a pencil and wrote his name on his back, and it reacted bright enough so that you could have seen it a block away."

Moving on, Fettes noted that Edward's eyes, while symmetrical, had "a listless expression." His pupils "both responded to the reflex of light and distance, but they did so rather actively." Ed's face displayed "a sort of grayish pallor color." Hickman's ears and nose seemed normal, despite a complaint of difficult breathing. "He said he frequently rubbed his nose," Fettes recalled. "He said it made his head feel better if he rubbed his nose." Ed's tonsils "showed some infection. They were inflamed, rather pitted, and the narrow anterior pillars were deeply injected."

Outwardly, though Dr. Fettes found him "much undersized" at five feet four, Ed seemed to be in decent health: no tumors, no displacement or deformity of any organs, no atrophy or hypertrophy of the muscles, although "both shoulder joints and both elbows showed a fairly marked degree of arthritis." Ed's blood pressure was low, 90-something over 80, and aside from trouble breathing, he complained of brutal headaches dating back to 1925, "not every day [but] several times a week. He described it as a generalized headache, [a] full feeling, more severe at the back of his head. On exertion it would increase the headache to the extent of becoming dizzy and seeing black specks before his eyes."

Dr. Fettes also tested Edward's urine (specific gravity .11 below average), checked his blood (no trace of syphilis), and performed a spinal tap. The pressure of Ed's spinal fluid, normally measured between 16 and 30 drops per minute, was more than triple the norm, with a flow rate "considerably over 100 drops a minute." The final diagnosis: "The boy [has] infected tonsils, infection of both shoulder joints and both elbow joints, carrying a low blood pressure, low specific gravity of the urine and marked dermography, characteristic headache, with spinal fluid under increased pressure what would be known as serous meningitis." In layman's terms, Ed suffered from "an inflammation of the covering of the brain."

A short time after Dr. Fettes packed up his syringes and departed, Hickman was escorted to Frank Dewar's office, where three more doctors awaited him. Two of them, psychiatrists Paul Bowers and Victor Parkin, had prejudged the case by December 18, when they told the L.A. Times that Marian was doubtless murdered by a sexual sadist. The delegation's third member, Dr. Edward Williams, knew Bowers

from their work together on the local Lunacy Commission.
Having been acquainted with madmen since age seventeen,
when he worked part-time as an orderly at an asylum in
Independence, Iowa, Dr. Williams had been asked to join
the team by Cecil Reynolds, shortly after his antagonistic
meeting with the prisoner.

There is no reason to believe that Hickman recognized
Bowers and Parkin from their early statements to the press,
but he was still suspicious of the doctors and their motives.
As Bowers described their first meeting, "I observed him
and talked to him, as a matter of fact, about a half-hour or
forty-five minutes. At this time Mr. Hickman was not very
communicative, and I noticed his general condition of dress,
his height, general appearance, whether he was neat or tidy
or not, his general reaction to the questions that I gave him.
Most of those questions were unanswered, and finally I
elicited a statement from him that he did not care to talk to
me for two reasons: one, that he wanted to follow the
advice of his attorney; and the second one, he had made a
deliberate choice of his own that he did not care to talk. I
made a few remarks deliberately to see whether or not he
would react, and I noted his reactions to these remarks, and
he finally stated that if he had any constitutional rights that
he would like to go to his cell and not be quizzed. I told him
we had no desire to interfere with his constitutional rights.
If he did not care to talk it was perfectly all right; we would
not insist on it. And he thanked us and went back to his
cell."

While Dr. Bowers would present himself as having run
the show that afternoon, Dr. Williams hit a few licks for the
state. When Hickman arrived for their meeting, Williams
later testified, "He had in his pocket a book of Oscar Wilde's,
a poem of Oscar Wilde. Oscar Wilde is a most notorious sex
pervert. At that time, I worked it out in my mind that this
defendant was probably a sexual pervert, and I asked him
some questions, asked him if he had read this book, and he
said he had. And I gave him the information that sex perversion was not an excuse for crime, and that it would not

do him any good if he was a sexual pervert. And I understand that shortly afterwards, though he had had this copy of Oscar Wilde's poem and the Bible with him this first time, I understand that shortly afterwards he relinquished that Oscar Wilde book and kept the Bible, which is a very much better book."

Sermons aside, Dr. Williams told the court that "the incident led me to believe, in my own interpretation of it, that he was trying to give me the impression that he was a worshiper of Oscar Wilde, who was a notorious sexual pervert, and that he was in that way showing sexual perversion, and when he found that that was no excuse for crime, he turned to something else. He was obviously, at that time—obviously to me, at least—trying to feign insanity and doing it in a clumsy way, such [a] clumsy way as a person—an intelligent person who knew nothing about insanity—would attempt to do. I gave him to understand at that time that it was a very bum exhibition of a man trying to be insane."

Despite his brief examination of an uncommunicative subject, Williams assured the court that "forty-five minutes is ample time for an alienist [a psychiatrist] under ordinary circumstances to take to make up his mind rather definitely about any case." No one bothered to ask if Williams, like Bower and Parkin, had actually made up his mind before reaching the jail. Of course, he had admitted, his knowledge of Edward's physical condition had all come secondhand, from Dr. Reynolds, but he found such collusion routine, "just the same as we do not cook our own food. We have something done for us." In his opinion, Williams told the court, "Any man that could act as that man acted for forty-three minutes is not insane enough to not know right from wrong, or know the nature and quality of his acts." In fact, the doctor's judgment was infallible. "Not in this case," he proclaimed, "nor in many thousands of cases that I have examined have I had to change my mind about their insanity or sanity."

With that kind of self-confidence driving his team, Asa Keyes clearly believed he held a winning hand.

Another psychiatrist, this one employed by the defense, got his first crack at Ed on Wednesday morning. Dr. R. O. Shelton was an Iowa native with twenty-six years of medical practice behind him, the last five in Los Angeles. Before the move north, he had spent seventeen years in San Diego, all but four of them as a court-appointed medical examiner for the insane. His first session with Edward consumed three hours, interrupted at one point by the unscheduled return of Dr. Bowers, accompanied by Dr. Herman Schorr.

Shelton huddled with the prosecution's doctors and informed them that Hickman refused to be tested by anyone representing the state. His own examination, Shelton estimated, would require about three days. Jailhouse physician Dr. Benjamin Blank took exception to Shelton's attitude, declaring that if Hickman refused to meet with prosecution experts, none from the defense would be allowed to see him, either. It did not occur to Shelton that Blank lacked authority to dictate terms; instead, he folded, promising to have a talk with Edward, urge him to cooperate with Schorr and Bowers. Intimidated for the moment, Schorr spent the next few hours reading over Ed's confession and the list of motives he had written during the trip from Portland to Los Angeles.

Back with his patient, Shelton proceeded to test Edward's orientation, perception, and reasoning. The first two were normal, but in the third category he reported that Hickman "reason[ed] without emotion. His emotions are changed and he has an insane delusion, an autochthonous idea. He reasons by this. If that autochthonous idea and his emotions were correct, I think his reasoning would be good. His judgment is extremely bad, because he has an insane delusion and his emotions are disordered."

Nor was that the end of Edward's problems. "The next thing I noticed," Dr. Shelton said, "was his association of ideas, which are automatic. He has no guiding idea, and he reaches no goal. I asked him to write some things for me and they show very plainly in that. However, those things are not so bad but what would look all right, but when we get into the emotions and his reactions, they are terrible. They are absolutely terrible. . . . When I speak of the emotions I want to get clear down to the instincts. Now, the fountain for all action that we all do is based upon some instinct. . . . We have fourteen primary instincts and each one is an emotion. . . . Sometimes we have two or more of them working at the same time. That is what we call a blended emotion. Then we have another emotion which places the success of the emotion that is working. We call those derived emotions. In that we get the desire, joy, surprise. Then we have the affects—that is, the feelings—and in the affects we have three characters. First is the feeling of pain and pleasure. . . . Second, we have the feeling of tenseness or relaxation. . . . Third, we have the feeling of exaltation—happy, feeling good, great—and the feeling of depression. Then, following that, we have the sentiments, and the sentiments—the last of them . . . they concern the moral sentiments."

That was the long way around, but Dr. Shelton had a point to make. In Hickman's case, he testified, "Some of his emotions are gone, absolutely gone; he hasn't any. Some of them are diminished, some of them are exaggerated, some of them are reversed—that is negativism. In this particular case, this boy's feelings toward religion, that is probably the beginning of this insanity."

As Shelton explained his diagnosis, "When this boy was twelve years of age he lived in Arkansas, in a rural community, where they had religious revival meetings. At these revival meetings they would shout, get up, tell experiences, get emotionally greatly excited. This boy, on account of his heredity, was not able to stand it. He was 'saved.' He went home one day and prayed for an hour or two. . . . Shortly after this, he developed the autochthonous idea. He developed the idea that he was going to do something great sometime in his life. He developed the idea that he would be known in history, his name would go down in history. He didn't know what it was at that time, but he had the feeling that there was something going to happen."

In Dr. Shelton's scenario, "This autochthonous idea gradually developed. That is probably why he became such a good student. He was preparing himself, and it gradually unfolded to him, so that in the latter years of his school life—after receiving disappointments—it progressed more rapidly. It finally got to a place that he thinks that he is a divine inspiration. That is the term he used to me, that his life had been planned, that everything that he does is done in accordance with this plan of what he calls Providence. And I went into it very closely with him, and he says that Providence is for him and him alone, that nobody else ever had this Providence; nobody else ever will have this Providence, and this Providence is directing his life. And I said, 'Does it order?' 'No, it doesn't order; it tells me, and I am pleased to follow the dictates of this Providence.' This Providence—as I said, no one else ever had it, nobody else will ever have it—and if this Providence should desert him, immediately he would die."

Later that afternoon, when he was finished with the latest round of questions, Hickman got another hint that Providence was slipping through his fingers. Delivered to juvenile court at 2:00 P.M., he heard Judge Scott deny a petition filed five months earlier, in the wake of his forgery arrest, requesting that Edward be named a ward of the state. As a nineteen-year-old, Scott decreed, Ed was fit to stand trial for his crimes in superior court, where a first-degree murder conviction might send him to the gallows.

On Thursday afternoon, while Dr. Shelton spent three more hours in Edward's cell, attorney Richard Cantillon, retained to help Walsh with the defense, announced that he would seek a change of venue for the trial "because all of Los Angeles County are biased and prejudiced against the defendant." Ed's jailers, meanwhile, leaked the news that he had passed a restless night after his trip to juvenile court, first tossing on his bunk, then pacing his cell until dawn, when he finally slept, apparently exhausted.

Dr. Shelton returned once again on Friday the thirteenth, and heard more of the same from his patient. Again,

Edward harped on the theme that "his life was planned, that he was a divine inspiration, that he was . . . following the guidance of this Providence, and it didn't make any difference what he did. That was incidental. That the killing of this girl was all in the plan. He said that she was born in California, lived in California, and went to this particular school to be there at the time when he should come along and do this, and that she had dreams and knew that it was coming. He said that this Providence gave him control over her, that that was the reason he could leave her in the car and go away, that it was Providence that was doing it. It was an act of Providence that made it possible for him to handle her. He told me that this Providence had won over one of the [psychiatrists] who did not like him in the beginning. He said that if he could talk to Mr. Keyes, that in a few days that Providence would turn him over and make [Keyes] his friend."

If Ed believed *that*, he was truly insane. Keyes wanted him dead, and the sooner the better. As for the state's psychiatrists, Edward must have known, when they returned that afternoon, that none of them regarded him with anything approaching friendship or compassion.

Dr. Schorr came first on Friday afternoon, and this time Ed agreed to speak with him. Schorr asked about his family and was treated to a recitation on the Bucks—Rebecca, Paul, and Otto—with their fits and mood swings, on to Eva Hickman and her suicide attempts, her time at the asylum. Schorr listened, or pretended to, while swiftly making up his mind "that there is every scientific reason to believe that there is no hereditary insanity in the defendant, or in any of his brothers or his sister." Of course, Schorr acknowledged, "and quite apart from this case, there *is* a possibility of defective heredity to *his* offspring, should there be such; but in his generation—that is, in him and in his brothers and sisters, there is no insanity, nor is there, scientifically, any insanity possible, providing his father is normal."

It was a curious statement at best, suggesting as it does that mothers have no role, good or bad, in the genetic makeup of their children, but Dr. Schorr would stand by his opinion under oath, at Hickman's trial.

Schorr found the prisoner well oriented, conscious of his name and situation, frank in his admission of the deeds that had landed him in jail. "I noticed," Schorr would later testify, "that when he was telling me things that were absolutely true—things that he would have no reason to deny—that his expression, his facial expression, was, in a word, honest. In other words, he had the facial muscles acting as one does under natural, conversational conditions. But when a question was put to him concerning this word 'Providence' in his confession, his face got a shade whiter, his lips got a little thinner, his eyes got a little steadier. He seemed more concentrated. His entire manner was as of one on guard, and every time a question regarding Providence was put to him, the answer was practically a stereotyped one: he deviated from the exact words very little. That made me come to a very strong suspicion that this talk about Providence was feigned."

If that suggestion didn't fly, the doctor had a backup diagnosis ready. "I also had another idea which I worked on during my examination," Schorr said, "and that was this: that probably the boy was perfectly honest about his thought about Providence, and perhaps he was just using it in a way that people speak of Providence in general, or as a misnomer for something else. For instance, I felt that when he spoke of 'Providence directed me; Providence guided me,' I felt that he was referring to some mental ability that directed him, his mental ability guided him, that he spoke of his mental ability as a guiding Providence."

Schorr's second thesis seemed to cancel out the first—that Ed was shamming when he mentioned Providence at all—but once again no one saw fit to point out the contradiction or to question Schorr at trial about his waffling on the matter.

The medical team of Bowers and Parkin returned after Schorr took his leave. With passive cooperation from Hickman, Dr. Bowers made yet another physical examina-

Victim
Marian Parker
in a family
snapshot.

Newspaper photo of the Parker home, published before the ransom delivery.

One of "George Fox's" telegrams to the Parker family.

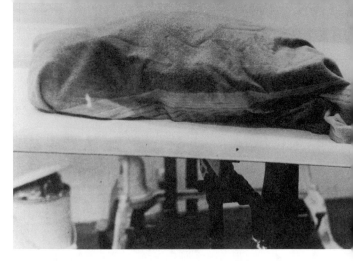

Bagged remains of Marian Parker at the
L.A. County morgue.

William
Hickman,
would-be
minister
turned
serial killer.

Three faces of "The Fox" in custody.

Hickman
broods in his
jail cell.

A 1920s criminologist tries to find evidence of
"criminal tendencies" in Hickman's face.

Hickman *(right)* with Oregon police chief
Tom Gurdane.

Hickman is delivered to a Los Angeles courtroom.

tion, evidently seeking grounds to contradict Dr. Fettes. He tapped Edward's knees, peered into his eyes, examined his tongue: all normal. Because his skin condition had suggested meningitis in the first examination, Dr. Bowers repeated the tests for himself. "I marked on his fingernail," Bowers later testified, "generally to see whether or not there was a condition present known as dermatography, which has already been mentioned here. That is a condition in which the examiner may write or draw upon the skin and, due to the fact that there is a reaction, bright red lines are left." How scratching on a fingernail would test for that condition, Bowers did not say, but he was not quite finished. "I did this with the skin of his chest," the doctor went on, "and no condition of dermatography was present."

As for the diagnosis of serous meningitis, logged by Dr. Fettes, Bowers was unimpressed. Without a spinal tap or any further tests, he told the court, "I arrived at the conclusion that there was no organic disease of the central nervous system, but the brain and spinal cord were normal and there was no departure from their normalcy."

It was Dr. Parkin's turn, and he spent the rest of that two-hour session questioning Hickman, in search of delusions or aberrant thinking. "I was unable to find anything in the man's speech or conduct," Parkin said, "that indicated that he departed from the normal in such a way as to constitute mental disease. I engaged him in conversation at great length and made the usual routine examination that one makes in a search for symptoms that might be considered abnormal—for manifestations of abnormal mental functioning—and I was unable to detect what, to my mind, were any signs or symptoms of abnormal functioning of the mind."

In regard to the murder of Marian, Dr. Parkin said, "I asked him just why he did it, how he accounted for being where he was today, and he told me. And his explanation, to my mind, was consistent with that of a sane mind. There were, to my mind, no evidences that it was the result of insanity, or there was nothing in the slightest degree to indicate that he did not know what he was doing, or the difference between right and wrong. His explanations showed that he took precautions to carry out his purpose. He knew that what he did was contrary to law, and in every way it showed, to my satisfaction, that he had within him the foundation for accountability from a moral and legal viewpoint."

Still, in Parkin's view, Edward was bent on selling the view of himself as a victim, demented and programmed for crime. "I have got all the elements that go to produce a criminal," he said at one point. "My father left my mother when I was ten years of age, my mother went insane, and I grew up without the proper parental control. I started to wander and do things very much as I wanted to. If you study me, you will find in me all the tendencies that you find in a young criminal."

It sounded like a script to Parkin, and he gave Ed's words no credence. Instead, he asked Hickman, "What seems to you to be the feature that has caused all this reaction and made all this furor?"

"Well," Ed answered him, "because I killed the little girl."

"Is that the one that strikes you as being the most awful part of it?" Parkin prodded him.

"Well," Hickman said, questioning now, "because I cut her up?"

The doctor was still unsatisfied. "Does that occur to you as the worst?"

Ed tried again. "Because I took the torso back to the father and presented it to him?"

"Well," Parkin said, "that is the one that strikes me as the reason that created the greatest furor. Does it strike you?"

"Maybe," Ed granted. "I guess it did. It was a terrible thing to do, wasn't it?"

"Didn't you have any feeling about it?" Parkin asked.

"Well," Ed replied, "at the time I was cutting the body up I did not have so very much feeling about it. I decided it had to be done, and I just did it."

On the subject of Providence, Edward told Parkin that he had been "guided" to kidnap and murder the child. "I think it is a providential act," he said, "because it will bring the attention of the public on the subject of crime."

"When did you feel that this act was the result of this guidance by Providence?" Parkin asked.

"Well," Ed replied, looking sheepish, "that just came to me yesterday."

Another nail driven into his coffin. Ed couldn't keep his mouth shut even when his life quite literally depended on it.

Dr. Reynolds and Dr. Schorr returned on Saturday morning for another abrasive session. Dr. Mikels stopped by the jailer's conference room at 11:50 A.M. to observe the grilling for some eighty minutes. "When I came into the room," Mikels later testified, "Mr. Hickman recognized me and recollected that he had met me before. He was pacing back and forth and talking very intently with Dr. Reynolds and carrying on a discussion with him, and [he] seemed to be very emphatic in his remarks, and Dr. Reynolds was the same."

Hickman was "quite annoyed," Mikels thought, by the tone and content of various "pertinent questions" from Reynolds. No examples were recorded, but we've seen that Reynolds never missed a chance to bait his captive subject. At one point, Mikels said, "Mr. Hickman made some remarks about his accomplishments in oratory and I got a chance to ask him a question, and I said, 'What have you done?' He said, 'I took a ten-dollar prize in an oratorical contest. I was only second.' I asked him was he disappointed. 'Yes. I congratulated him. I felt hurt. I still have ability to orate, to orate to the jury and to all the people of this country.' "

Mikels watched Ed tie his shoe, making a mental note that "he did that with accuracy, did it carefully, and did it diligently." That delicate operation completed, Ed began to pace his cell once more, answering questions from Reynolds. Dr. Mikels "did not catch all the remarks that he was making then," but one stood out. Mikels would later tell the court that Ed proclaimed, "If society decides that I must be hung and it will be benefited most by this method, then I am ready to stand or submit to it."

Hickman had earlier referred to Providence, and Dr. Mikels brought him back to the subject, requesting that Edward define it.

"I have felt," Hickman replied, "that some day when I die that I would be a very great—*before* I die—that I would do a very great thing for the world, that my name would live in history."

Another unrecorded question from Reynolds, and the jailer interrupted to announce that it was time for lunch. Mikels, meticulous as ever, noted that Hickman "did not refuse to go out with the jailer" for lunch, but rather that "he was ready to quit the examination and respond to his sensation, or feeling, of hunger and get his meal."

More proof of sanity, as outlined by the state: the prisoner gets hungry, so he eats.

And after lunch, more doctors. Bowers and Parkin this time, arriving at 4:30 P.M. for a two-hour session. Their first goal, as described by Dr. Bowers, was "to find out if his conversation was coherent, relevant and to the point, whether his conversation was circumstantial, whether he went around Robin Hood's barn or not in answering a question, or whether he went deliberately to the goal idea." Ed checked out A-OK in all respects, coherent and succinct, with no "flight of ideas."

Next up, an inventory of emotions through straightforward questioning. Was Edward happy? Sad? Indifferent? Did he understand his situation?

Once again, Bowers found no extremes, noting that Ed was "just about as cheerful as he could be under the circumstances, which were not very pleasant." There was, Bowers said, "no disturbance of the emotion, except of apprehension, except the worry that would come to a normal individual who was charged with a heinous crime."

Bowers decided, next, to see what Edward thought about his own state of mind. "Hickman," he said, "are you sane or insane?"

"I don't know much about insanity," the prisoner replied.

"I know that to be true," said Bowers, "but I would like to have your opinion about it, what you think about it . . . how you feel within yourself."

"Well," Hickman said, "I would not say that I was insane, but I would say that I was abnormal, because I am superior to the average person."

Bowers tried another tack, quizzing Ed about hallucinations, disembodied voices, "whether he was charged with electricity, whether there was poison in his food." Hickman denied any hallucinations, delusions, or feelings of persecution. He was coherent in discussing his childhood and correctly named the major capitals of Europe. He was quick and accurate with simple math; recognized the names of historical figures; knew the difference between a child and a dwarf, a sheep and a lamb.

"I wanted to know," Bowers testified later, "if he thought he talked with God, or if he felt that he was a great personage, that he was a great man, a great mind, or that he was a great individual. And in answer to this, he said [that] a few days before my visit he had discovered that he was an unusual individual, that he was, by some mysterious method, in connection with some kind of Providence. I asked him if it was God, and he said no, it was not God; it was a special type of Providence which he could not define particularly, but he had found out a few days before that he was under the direction of some type of Providence that assisted him in his conduct. I asked him then if this Providence directed him to kill Marian Parker. He said no, this Providence had not. I said, 'It would not have been a kind Providence if this had happened.' He said, well, this Providence sort of permitted him to do this sort of thing in order that he might be an individual who would be lifted up among people, so that he would be a lesson to the American youth. . . . I came to the conclusion, after a lengthy discussion of this Providence, that this was a newfound idea so far as this crime was concerned, and it was a deliberate effort at malingering, a deliberate intention to deceive."

One final test from Dr. Bowers, gauging Edward's ethics and priorities. What would he do, the doctor asked, if he were lost at sea in an open boat without oars and with two buckets of drinking water on board when his companion's clothes burst into flames?

"Well," Ed responded with a crooked smile, "if it was Welby Hunt, I would have thrown him overboard or let him burn."

Dr. Parkin, listening and sometimes interposing questions of his own, would later tell the court, "I have to consider him a criminal. There was much that he said to me that convinced me that [the murder] was a criminal act, rather than the act of either accident or impulse, or done under the influence of delusions or impulse of any kind."

To Parkin it seemed that Ed was trying to escape the gallows by presenting himself as a guinea pig. "I believe that the solution to crime will come out of studying me," Hickman said. "There will be no advantage to killing me now, but just study me, and then it does not matter much what becomes of it afterwards, whether they hang me or not. But study me, and you will see in me all those things that go to make up criminals. You can't find out all about me by just what has produced me, by just talking to me for an hour or two, but keep me and study me."

"By that," Parkin said, "you mean that you are just a great criminal and to know you is to know all crime?"

"Yes," said Hickman, nodding enthusiastically. He could be the nation's savior, given half a chance. "It will focus the attention of the whole world on the question of crime," he said. "The American public has been very indifferent towards crime, and this will certainly focus their attention on it."

Ed caught a break on Sunday, time to polish his act, but at 9:00 A.M. on Monday, January 16, Mikels, Schorr, and Reynolds showed up together. In his notes from that session, Dr. Reynolds wrote:

Since my last examination the prisoner has elaborated upon the former remark that a "providence" guided him, by stating that all his actions are due to an "influence" of providence in order that he might achieve some great benefit for the world. He reiterates this assertion like one who has learnt a lesson, and upon being asked, states that the first time he has ever "confided" in any human being about this "influence" was to Dr. Shelton on the 11th, 12th and 13th of this January, but he mentioned it to his mother, and also mentioned it in these words to Mr. Philip Morgan of the YMCA of Kansas in June 1926, viz: "that he intended to go to school, and really felt he was going to do something great." He further stated, in reply to [a] leading question, that the "influence" never "impelled" him to do anything, but it merely made him feel that it would finally "lead him to this great thing."

Contradicting his previous claim that he had "never been in any corrupt conduct with the female sex," Hickman now told Reynolds "that he had sexual intercourse with two little girls when he was aged ten years. He has had such intercourse with one of them on and off since, the last time in June 1917." Ed further stated that he had "masturbated during the last year only, on an average of three times weekly."

Reynolds described what happened when he asked about Welby Hunt and the Ivy Thoms murder:

[Hickman] sprang to his feet in anger, but instantly controlled himself, saying that he stood upon his constitutional rights and that if I couldn't be fair he wouldn't answer any more questions. He showed great self-control throughout. The prisoner later said, "You're prejudiced against me," to which I replied, "Can you wonder[?] Do you think there is a human being in this world, outside of a very few criminals, perhaps, who would not be prejudiced against you?["] He replied, "No." He had also complained that I was trying to trap him. When this is considered in conjunction with his statement that he knew that I was there to determine his sanity or insanity, he placed himself in the anomalous position of an alleged lunatic objecting to being made to appear sane, which is, to say the least, unusual.

Dr. Schorr used part of the session to conduct a physical examination, later reporting to the court that he "found nothing that would indicate any physical defect of any magnitude whatever, or that I would comment on in a private patient." The second part of his examination, into Hickman's mental processes, left Schorr "satisfied as to his general memory, orientation—that is, knowledge of where he was, what he was and where he was, what time it was. That was perfect." Questioned briefly on the Thoms murder, Edward "thought it was a miracle" that he had been unscathed in the exchange of point-blank gunfire.

Providence again.

But he was growing tired of the interrogation now. When Dr. Mikels started asking questions, Ed clammed up. "I asked him a lot of questions," Mikels later testified. "He did not show any disposition to answer." A dozen questions into the one-sided grilling, Mikels finally asked why Hickman wasn't talking.

"Doctor," Ed replied, "I can hear everything you say, but I don't want to answer them. I don't have the disposition to answer them."

Frustrated, Mikels moved on to his own physical examination of the prisoner. He found Ed's color "white," then curiously noted that "his complexion would throw him into that class of what we call the brunette type." Ed's lips were "rather small," but Dr. Mikels "did not find anything pathological" in the shape of his nose or ears. He noted Edward's high forehead, indicating "a large force of brain," found no "evidence of dullness" in his chest, no trace of "arca senilus, which is a hazy line around the iris of the eye."

While examining Ed's throat, Mikels said, "I pushed the thyroid gland towards the right [and] he evidently got a sensation which enabled him to use his imagination, and he said to me when this was being palpated, 'That is where the rope goes around, isn't it, Doctor?' "

At that point, Mikels was distracted by a rapping on the office door. He later testified that it was Dr. Shelton, the defense psychiatrist, inquiring after "some paper that Mr. Hickman promised to give him." Ed took a coin from his pocket, telling Shelton, "I will flip this to see whether I give you those papers or not," but the toss went against the doctor, and Hickman refused to hand over the papers.

Shelton left, but returned moments later, knocking on the door again. "This interruption was rather embarrassing to me," Mikels said, "and I went out of the room to see who the doctor was that was making the inquiry, and to find out what he wanted." In the outer hallway, Dr. Shelton introduced himself and offered his view of the subject's mental state, but Mikels later testified, "I did not get it very clearly at that time, what he said the diagnosis was."

No matter. Nothing Shelton could have said or done would have swayed the prosecution team from their determination that the prisoner was sane and fit to hang.

Returning to the office, Dr. Mikels found Hickman dressed, pacing for warmth in the chilly room. "He refused to submit to any further physical examination then," Mikels said, "and then we carried on a little conversation, an informal conversation." The talk turned to pugilism, Dr. Mikels remarking that he wished they had some boxing gloves. Ed agreed, "in a jovial, jocular way," that he wouldn't mind boxing with Mikels to warm himself up.

The doctor tried again for Ed's permission to complete the physical exam, but Hickman insisted on another coin toss. "So he flipped the coin," Mikels recalled, "and said it came up tails, and there would not be any further examination today."

Tomorrow morning, then?

Ed flipped the coin again. It came up heads this time, and he agreed to meet with Dr. Mikels after breakfast.

Monday's run of doctors was not finished yet, however. A new player, Dr. Thomas Orbison, arrived that Monday afternoon to have a look at Hickman. In his thirty years of practice, Dr. Orbison had served in the Spanish-American War and, as an army psychiatrist, in World War I. A colleague of Williams and Bowers on the L.A. Lunacy Commission, Orbison missed the military and lamented the soft handling of "rotten eggs" in civilian life. "In the army," he liked to say, "we could get rid of those people, put them out of circulation right away. Unfortunately, in private life you can't do it quite as summarily as you can in the army."

Before the first of four visits to Hickman in jail, Orbison had taken time to read the statements Ed had written on the train ride back from Oregon. If he prejudged the case, however, Orbison took pains to hide the fact during his testimony in court:

> I can make it very brief. I might just say that my approach to the case was a little different from the other alienists. In other words, I have certain privileges they did not have. I did not go into the case, in the first place—in fact, I did not have in my mind at all the idea of taking any side. I was not asked at all to take any side in the matter. I simply went up at the request of two professors of psychology at a local educational institution, and was introduced to Mr. Hickman by his own counsel, Mr. Cantillon, and it was a very great courtesy and kindness for him to do that. But he did not—I was not introduced to him as being an alienist for either side.

Not that it mattered, on the first approach. When he was introduced to Hickman, Ed informed him, "I don't want to talk today. I don't feel like it. Some days I feel like talking, and some days I don't feel like talking."

"All right," Dr. Orbison replied, "we won't talk today. I'm very busy. I don't care particularly to talk to you. I have no particular interest in talking to you. I will take my coat now and go."

The reverse psychology unsettled Edward. Digging in his pocket, he produced the coin and offered Orbison a toss, to see if he should stay or leave. "No," Orbison replied, "I am not going to stay at all. I will not talk to you."

Defeated, Hickman almost pleaded, "I would like to talk to you."

The doctor thought about it, finally asking, "When should I return?"

Ed brightened, still the Fox. "I'll talk to you tomorrow," he replied.

But first, he would have to deal with Dr. Mikels, who came back again that Tuesday morning at 9:15 for an exam that would consume three hours. When a pair of reporters trailed Mikels into the office, Hickman bristled at the sight of their cameras. "There will be no pictures taken this morning," he said. "Did you bring these men in?"

"They came in incidentally," Mikels replied.

"Well, let them go out incidentally," Ed sneered.

The doctor saw an opening to test for delusions of grandeur. "This is an opportunity," he told Edward, "for you to become famous, go down in history, by having your pictures in the papers."

Ed's reply was scornful. "I have had enough pictures made of me," he said. "Out with them."

His attitude convinced the doctor that Hickman had no "sense of personal superiority nor of exalted ego." They discussed Ed's schooling and experience on the debating team, but Hickman started hedging when the topic shifted to religion. He acknowledged going to church "once or twice" in Kansas City, glossing over his years in the Hi-Y Club and his expressed desire to join the clergy.

"My mother was religious," Ed told Dr. Mikels. "I don't remember my father. He left when I was about ten years old. I felt that I was just as religious as anyone else, and that I did not have to go to church to be religious. I had a pride, and was selfish, thought myself better than others. I never did boast much."

Mikels started quizzing Edward on the Ten Commandments. What was his interpretation of the first injunction, "Thou shalt have no other gods before me?"

"When I first converted," Hickman said, "I thought I believed in God until I went to the large city and there were so many different kinds of churches, then I began to feel independent about religion, one God and one church for all. That is what the Bible intended us to have."

What about the second commandment's ban on idols?

"It seems to me," Ed answered, "that the heathens have a better method, because they have something to represent their god. The Providence which I have is the same as the God that other people believe in and guides them in their actions."

"Did it ever guide you to do wrong and contrary to your own will?" Mikels asked.

"No," Hickman said. "It always directs me to do great good."

What about the third commandment and taking the Lord's name in vain?

"Whenever I swear or take the name of God in vain," said Hickman, "I do not give it much concern, because it is so commonly done."

Remember the Sabbath day to keep it holy?

"I have been to church about twenty times," Ed estimated, "since I was fourteen or fifteen years old. I attended of my own accord. Most always went with someone, or to please someone else. When I was younger, I went so I could get a chance to go home with the girls after church."

"I have done the same thing," Mikels told him. "Now, 'Honor thy father and thy mother.' This is the fifth commandment. What is your interpretation of it?"

Frowning, Hickman said, "I have hated and cursed both my parents, my father because he deserted my mother and left us when I was about nine or ten years old. I resented it so much at times that I felt I could kill him for it, but never made any attempt."

And his mother?

"I blame my mother lots of times," he said, "for splitting up the family. I can't help but feel, though, that she was the better one of the two. When I was back in Kansas City in

September 1927, I wanted to get away by myself, and they—the folks—objected. They thought if I went out by myself that I would go crooked again, and I told my mother and the rest of them if they interfered with me . . . I told Mother that I would shoot her if she interfered with me."

Which brought Mikels to the sixth commandment: "Thou shalt not kill."

"Evidently I did not have any respect for it," Hickman said. "If Marian Parker was killed and cut to pieces, it was meant to do so [sic]. I expect to die someday. Seeing so many killed by accident and murders or executions, life don't seem to have much value today. I have always felt that in committing a murder, a person is surely violating the law. I also felt that the execution for committing murder is also a murder."

" 'Thou shalt not do any wrong act,'" Mikels prompted, misquoting the seventh commandment. "What is your interpretation of it?"

"I always thought that I wanted to do something that was right," Ed replied. "Everything that I did, I think was right. I did not try to distinguish between right and wrong, because in the custom of various nations, things that were considered right once are now considered wrong. If doing a thing serves my purpose, then it is right, just as it is with a nation."

" 'Thou shalt not steal'?"

Hickman admitted periodic thefts, beginning in a Hartford watermelon patch and running through his stickups in Los Angeles. "I have pulled about twenty or twenty-five of these holdups," he told Mikels, sometimes with accomplices. "Discord in the home, breaking up of our homes by our parents, seemed to bring us fellows together. I think that the breaking up of the family is a factor causing boys to go wrong."

" 'Thou shalt not lie,' " the doctor prompted.

Hickman shrugged. "It is as easy for me to lie as it is to tell the truth. For example, I lied about others being involved in the kidnapping."

"Why did you do it?" Mikels asked.

"I think I did it to complicate the situation, I guess," Ed replied. "I made up the names and—a funny thing—they happened to be real people with whom I was not acquainted."

" 'Thou shalt not covet,' " Mikels finished off the list. "What is your interpretation of it?"

"I wanted $1,500," Ed replied. "I wanted to get it in the easiest and best way for me. Why work a year for $1,500 when I could get it in a few days? I did not think of the Ten Commandments. I did know it was against the law, but I did not care."

Sealing his fate, as surely as if he had aimed a pistol at his head.

Was he afraid of being captured for the kidnapping?

"I had an apprehension," Ed responded, "that I might get caught." As for the penalty, "I was not thinking of this, then."

Was he afraid of punishment?

"I did not fear it," Hickman said, "but I would rather not be hung."

"What emotional state were you in just before you killed Marian Parker?" Mikels asked.

"I was not . . ." Ed faltered, frowning. "I don't know," he said at last. "What do you want me to do, answer this question so the prosecution will have a better case against me?"

Mikels tried again. "What emotional state were you in immediately *after* you realized that you killed her?"

"I was indifferent," Ed replied.

There was no coin-tossing when Dr. Orbison returned on Tuesday afternoon. A physical exam convinced Orbison that Hickman's parents were lying about his having been dead at birth, since Edward was not "spastic" or "simple-minded." Psychologically, Orbison found Ed's religious conversion at twelve years of age "rather precocious," yet commonplace for a son of evangelical parents. ("I went through that myself," Orbison later told the court. "I know what I am talking about.") In terms of sex, Orbison decided that Ed "had an ordinary sex life, perfectly ordinary, no suppressions or complexes of any kind of that nature." Likewise, Edward's achievements in school had been well above average.

How, then, to explain his violent crimes? "Well," Orbison would tell the court, "he has developed crooked. He was not sick. He was not insane. But he has developed along crooked lines. We call them crooked."

Discarding any pretense of psychological analysis, Dr. Orbison felt qualified to judge his subject in moral terms. "There was a conflict," he explained, "an early conflict between his religion and his criminal instincts, and he chose the criminal side of it. He says so himself. There is no reticence about it; he does not hesitate about it. The last won out, won out in the struggle."

For those who questioned the scientific basis of his judgment, Orbison went on explain that Hickman had suffered from a "character defect right along. You can't keep doing one line of business and not acquire certain characteristics in that business. There were repeated trials and failures. Now, I mean by that that he tried many jobs that were straight, going straight. Well, it was just too irksome; he just didn't want to hold them; he gave them up from time to time. That is in the record. He found crime easier." Over time, Orbison said, Hickman had "developed a certain systematized set of concepts and ideas regarding crime as a business."

Edward repeated his story of wanting the ransom money for tuition at Park College, but Dr. Orbison was skeptical. "If you looked back on your life," he said, "do you think you would spend four years plugging at college like that?"

Ed considered the question for a moment, then laughed and said, "I guess I wouldn't."

Asked about his use of the Greek letter delta on various ransom notes, Ed admitted to near total ignorance of Greece, though he had heard of Socrates.

"What did you think of Socrates?" asked Orbison.

"I considered him a great philosopher, Ed replied.

To Orbison, the response was arrogance personified. "Well, there was a nineteen-year-old boy," he scornfully told the court, "passing judgment on a great philosopher."

"What do you think about these other alienists you talked to?" Orbison asked.

"I rather enjoyed them," said Hickman. He recalled Dr. Reynolds, blustering and threatening vivisection, and said, "You know, he was just about as bad as I was, wasn't he?"

Orbison noted the stack of mail in Ed's cell. "All these letters I get," Hickman said, "those people are just like I was, only they are worse. They are gone off half-cocked."

Orbison was inclined to agree on that point. "He gets scores of letters," the psychiatrist testified, "nuts, all kinds of people all over the country write him letters."

Ed was tiring of the game, becoming uncommunicative, but Orbison still had more questions to ask. It was agreed that they should meet again in two days' time.

Meanwhile, more doctors. Dr. Mikels showed up for another three-hour session on Wednesday morning, arriving at 9:20. After a few preliminary questions from Mikels, who wanted to satisfy himself that Ed was still rational, Hickman had one for the doctor.

"How," he wondered, "can a fellow be a cold-blooded monster and at the same time be sane?"

Mikels explained the figure of speech, using it as a bridge to resume his exploration of Hickman's feelings after he killed Marian.

"The first time I felt sad or had remorse," Edward said, "was when I was in the Loew State Theatre. I broke down and cried while I was watching the picture. The title of the show was *Forbidden Women*. I remember the picture."

Dr. Mikels saw his chance to test Ed's mental process with a series of "suggestive" questions. "The kidnapping and the attempt to get the $1,500 was a distinct and separate piece of business?" he asked.

Ed nodded. "Yes."

"You were using Mr. Parker as a means toward a definite end?"

"Yes."

"You were using his daughter as a means to a definite end? The object was to get $1,500, wasn't it?"

"Yes," Ed agreed.

"You understood that this kidnapping was a crime and was punishable by imprisonment?"

"The idea in my mind," said Hickman, "was more that I was violating the law, and I told the girl if I got caught I would go to the penitentiary."

"When you were there Friday night and found that the father failed to keep his word, did you get peeved over it?" Mikels asked.

"Yes," Ed replied. "It kind of disgusted me."

"Did the impulse to kill the girl come to you before or after writing the letters?"

"That came to me after I was in bed," Hickman answered. "Then it went out of my mind again before I went to sleep. It was a thought of the simplest kind of an idea at first."

Or maybe not so simple. He had just confessed premeditation.

"When you went to sleep, were you disturbed by any dreams?" asked Mikels.

"No."

Moments later, Ed "assumed a rather arrogant attitude" and balked at describing his reasons for dismembering Marian's body. "If I answer these questions the way you want me to," he said, "it will be used to build up the case of the prosecution. I can say I don't know."

When Ed "persisted in this defensive evasion and negation," Dr. Mikels switched subjects, veering toward "a discussion of his excessive indulgences, vicious practices, idiosyncrasies, hobbies, diversions, love affairs, sexual experiences and family history."

"I never indulged in smoking excessively," Ed told Mikels. "I never drank intoxicating liquors. When about ten years of age I played around with other boys and mostly girls, and it was about this time that I got my first sexual impressions. The first time that I masturbated was about two years ago,

shortly after I left high school. The first time I had intercourse was about thirteen years of age. The girl was about
twelve. I did this several times while I was at Kansas City."

"Did your mother ever get wise to what you were doing?"
Mikels asked.

"No, she did not."

When Mikels asked about the risk of pregnancy, Hickman
explained that "the girl always pushed him away from her,
did not let him complete the act." The doctor's next question was an apparent non sequitur, producing an even
stranger response.

"Why did you do this to this girl?" asked Mikels.

"Well," Ed replied, "I did it so I would not get a dose of
clap. I don't have any use for whores. Whenever I see a
whore, I feel like choking her."

Letting the strange statement pass, Mikels asked, "Have
you any idiosyncrasies?"

"I can't recall any peculiar stunts or funny things that I
did while I was alone or with other people," Hickman said.
"I can't say I have any idiosyncrasies."

"How did you and your mother get along together?"

"Like a cat and dog," Ed replied.

"Was there any insanity in your family?"

"I don't know of any insanity," Hickman said. "There is no
insanity in our whole damned family, I think. I don't think
Mother was insane. I think she was discouraged and dis-
tressed because of [our] family troubles."

Dr. Bowers followed Mikels for another brief visit, but the
dialogue added nothing to his view of Edward as a malingering fraud. Dr. Fettes was next, insisting on another spinal
tap. He made a rough job of it, taking several jabs to pene-
trate the cord, while Edward gasped and writhed in pain. He
was still hurting from the ordeal when Dr. Mikels returned
at 9:20 on Thursday morning.

"He said when he woke up in the morning his back hurt
him on lying down," Mikels recalled, "and when he stood
up his head began to ache. I asked him what kind of
headache it was, and he said it was a dull ache in the fore-

head and over his eyes. Then he remarked, 'No one will ever give me another one of those spinal punctures.' "

Mikels, in fact, had been planning a similar test, but he crossed it off his list in the face of Ed's reaction. There was a barber's chair in the office, and Mikels directed Ed to sit down, cranking the chair back until his intracranial pressure was stabilized and the headache disappeared. Relieved and grateful, Ed agreed to continue the interrogation.

Why, Mikels asked, had Ed dropped out of junior college, given his desire for higher education?

"I didn't get the studies that I wanted," Ed replied, "so I quit. If I could have gone to college, I would have studied for the ministry or some teaching position. I didn't want to study to be a lawyer or doctor."

While working at the public library, Ed explained, he met Welby Hunt and Frank Bernoudy. "Both of these boys had been to California and they wanted to go back there again, and they suggested it to me. I was ready to go. We planned to pull some big job, such as stealing cars and large amounts of money."

Mikels returned to the subject of "vicious habits," eliciting more denials from Edward on liquor and drugs. "I have smoked cigarettes," he admitted, "but never inhaled them." Then he asked, "Do you regard arsenic as a drug?"

Dr. Mikels replied that arsenic was a poison, and Edward launched into a story from his senior year at Central High. "The teacher in chemistry showed us some arsenic powder," he said, "and told us a tiny bit the size of a pin head would kill a person instantly. I became interested, because the stuff seemed so deadly. I had a notion to put some in some candy in a drugstore, or put it in one of those Life-Saver tablets, and let somebody buy it and then get poisoned."

"I asked him if he ever did it," Mikels later testified, "and he said no, he never had distinct reason or motive, but just a notion that he would like to do it."

Dr. Reynolds arrived for another belligerent visit at 12:30, some fifteen minutes after Mikels left the jail. Observing Hickman in the corridor, Reynolds noted that his stride was "jaunty and careless," yet somehow simultaneously "like a panther, stealthy." Ed's eyes were greenish gray, further evidence of sanity in Reynolds's expert opinion, since in "dementia praecox cases that I have observed, the majority have had pale blue eyes." The doctor's notes reveal a typically pugnacious approach to his subject.

> He complained of headache and pain in the back, from the spinal puncture, and made some fuss about getting comfortable in the chair. His headache, he said, was the worst pain he had ever had (but it did not prevent him from being talkative and facetious). . . . Upon being asked if he thought Marian Parker suffered any pain at his hands, he said she might have a little when she was strangled and added "no conscious pain." . . . He went on to say that he supposed I wanted him to say that he "got a fiendish pleasure out of cutting her up, but he didn't." Upon being asked why he cut her up, he replied that he didn't know. Upon being asked if it was not to enable him to put the trunk in the suitcase, he said that if that was the reason he wouldn't have cut her to pieces. Upon it being pointed out that he only cut her in such a manner [so] that the trunk could be fitted into the suitcase, he laughed. Upon being asked why he laughed, he replied that my expressions were so amusing. . . . Upon being asked how he was treated in jail, he replied that he was treated "fine," in fact he would rather be in jail than outside. He then said that the law was a murderer for executing Mrs. [Ruth] Snyder, and that he would say, "Forgive them, Lord, they know not what they do." Upon being told that that was merely a cheap blasphemy by a very objectionable murderess, he laughed. He then said he guessed he was headed for the electric chair but at all events it didn't hurt much. The questioner remarked that hanging was the penalty in California, to which he replied with the question, "[Does] that hurt?" The questioner then said that he

would not wish to try it, but that he did not worry much about what happened to the prisoner on this earth, but he did feel a little sorry for him when he thought of what he had to face in the ages to come. The prisoner then asked, "Do you think there is any hereafter?" to which the questioner replied that he would suggest that the prisoner get in touch with some broad-minded priest.

The session ended on a typical sarcastic note: "The questioner then said that he might bring a prominent dramatist to see him next time. Prisoner said that if this Mr. ——— would condescend to come and see him he would be very honored."

Dr. Orbison returned to visit Ed a short time after Reynolds left, but found his subject prostrate with a headache. After giving Ed some aspirin, Orbison left him with the promise to return another day.

Dr. Mikels showed up for a "supplemental examination" on Friday morning, January 20, but Ed was fighting a fever and still complaining of headache, so Dr. Mikels left ten minutes later. The architect of Ed's discomfort, Dr. Fettes, paid another call on Saturday, but lingered only briefly.

Dr. Shelton, still collecting evidence for the defense, met a surprise roadblock when he checked in that afternoon. Upon arriving at the county jail, Shelton was told, "You can't come in." When asked the reason, one of Hickman's guards produced an order from the sheriff, barring Dr. Shelton from the jail "on the recommendation of the district attorney." (Challenged on the point in court, when told that Dr. Shelton was unable to complete his tests on Hickman, Asa Keyes simply shrugged and said, "You have been misinformed.") In any case, Shelton had seen the last of his patient.

Dr. Orbison met no such obstacles when he visited Ed the third and last time, on Tuesday, January 24. Hickman's trial was scheduled to begin the next morning, and the D.A.'s team was still gathering proof of his sanity.

"What do you mean by Providence?" Dr. Orbison asked, seeking the key to Hickman's crimes.

"There is a Providence that shapes our ends," Ed told him.

"You mean to say that *you* were Providence?"

"Oh, no."

"Do you mean to say that you heard this Providence telling you and directing you what to do?" Orbison asked.

"No, no, not at all," Ed replied. "It is not like that at all."

"You claim to be insane," Orbison said. "How do you mean you are insane?"

"Well, no," Hickman said, "I don't think I am insane. It was claimed for me."

Edward produced a sheaf of papers, the first page headed "Solution of Crime," and asked the doctor to read it. Orbison thumbed through the pages, then bent to the task:

Is the abolition of crime worthy of deep consideration? Is it worth more than one life? Is it of such a wide spread or inconsiderable [*sic*] nature that to check its progress is believe[d] impossible or undesirable by the American people? Do the American people really understand crime? Can a criminal help himself? Do prisons help sufficiently to cure criminals? Do modern criminal prevention methods avail the people of the U.S. of sufficient protection or reasonable security? Has crime diminished or is it increasing? Are murders and atrocities becoming more ordinary and less repulsive to the American people or is crime blotting out itself or is it not? Do the American people think they have satisfactory protection and control of their properties and lives? Are these questions of vital importance to every American citizen? Do their answers determine the welfare of American society? Will the American people listen to me? Will you members of the jury and court reason with me?

Crime cost[s] the U.S. much money and many lives each year. Crime threatens society. Crime hinders efficient government. Crime disturbs the peace, property rights, lives, welfare, even the destiny of the American people. Crime is increasing in the U.S. Crime has become astounding in the U.S. Crime [is] radically improper. Crime must be studied more carefully and checked. If the U.S. wants to continue, if the American people want a satisfactory solution to this grave situation they must reason most thoroughly with young criminals.

I want to appeal to your complete justice, to your soundest reason[,] to every feeling and sense that you possess. I want to do a great good for you. I want this case solved with the greatest and most beneficial results to society. I love the American people. I respect the people of California. I forgive the members of the prosecution and admit that they do have a good cause to prosecute me. I want to help you in a way that no one else has ever helped you. A great Providence is urging me to do this. Don't look at Edward Hickman and think only E.H. Don't look at murder and say only death. Don't look at crime and say only terrible. Think first of the welfare of your homes, your community, your city, your state, your nation. Think of the safety of your lives and properties. Think of peace and prosperity. Think of adjustment. Think of understanding. Think of your future and your city's future, your success and your city's success. Think of destiny and forget fate. Believe in yourselves and your fellow citizens for good. Consider society.

I want Los Angeles, California, and the United States to benefit from this case. I want society to see my example and derive a great benefit. In me has originated the tendency toward crime and there is a possibility in me for adjustment. Crime has been generated in me. Young criminality has been demonstrated in me. Now which is better, that I hang by the neck until dead and let public opinion gradually go back to normalcy until the next disastrous atrocity or would it be more fitting to place me on a shelf for life in a penitentiary adding me to the list of Loebs and Leopolds? I say that either of these courses is very inconsistent with the proper reaction to the case. What does my life matter to the American people? What does my death matter to the American people? Can't you see that it only confuses the average mind to try to discern in this matter[?] If I hang[,] some people will be gratified and some disappointed. If I receive life imprisonment[,] some people will protest while some will agree. In [either] case would the proper solution be found[?] Would the law be completely fulfilled; have modern criminal methods been sufficient then in making your lives and properties more secure and in diminishing crime? Crime will not stop with my trial. This case is not the finis of crime. Loeb and Leopold were sentenced to life imprisonment. [Judd] Snyder and [Ruth] Gray were sentenced to death for the killing of Gray's husband. [Wife killer George] Remus was sentenced to the asylum. Has there been a noticeable reaction for the prevention and demolition of crime throughout the U.S. as a result of these notable cases? They represent each important phase of the modern system of court justice and criminal law procedure. Are they separately or collectively sufficient to the modern demands for the protection and security of human rights and properties? Are homes, families, cities and states any safer or less involved in crime? To be frank and honest with you in my own belief, I think not so.

You do want to save your own lives, do you not? You do want your own rights and your own liberties to [be] secured and safeguarded, do you not? You do want to check crime, I know you do. Well, if you kill me, you will not be doing any more than has already been done[,] while crime will keep up just the same as before. If you sentence me to life imprisonment, you will not be doing any more than has already been done[,] while your rights and lives will be in the same and increasing danger as before. If you send me to the

asylum for life, you will be following an example hith-
erto tried but which has not benefited you[,] while
crime continue[s] just the same as before and is even
increasing and ever threatening you more and more as
each day passes by.

I am not being selfish when I beg and plead with you
to save your own lives and properties[;] do you think I
am? I am not being prompted by personal insight when
I try to bring about a great public benefit to you and the
whole of American society. If you think so and if you
do not think so, let me make at this time, a complete
and open statement to the court.

It matters no[t], as far as I am concerned, whether I
live or die, only as it regards your own welfare. I have
already pleaded guilty to this crime, but before I die I
want to do a great good for my country and for humanity. I give myself completely over to the jurisdiction of
this court and to the judgment of you jurymen. I ask
that you will allow me to explain the great calling of
Providence, a great Providence which [I] profoundly
believe has brought me into this world[,] which has
guided and directed my every action throughout my
entire life[,] and which will take me away from this life
at the appointed time.

Allow me to stand here like a man and explain the
whole truth and honesty of my life and to offer you the
plea which this great Providence has given me to utter.
From the time of my youth, I have felt the presence of a
great guiding power. This power has manifested itself in
me and has made me feel that I would become great. It
has made me feel that I would become widely known
and that my name would live in history. It has made
me feel that I would live to an old age and accomplish a
great good for my fellow countrymen and the world.
This great presence[,] and you may call it God if you
wish, but I shall call it a Providence which has been
with me since the age of twelve. I have felt it and
known all these great secrets from this early age, and I

can prove to you that it is real and that there is a likelihood of this fulfillment of this great work, if you will listen and hear my explanations.

In my life, there has already been a great range of activity. Environments, subjections, manifestations and accomplishments, all of which have been in a definite pursuit of the guidance and protection of this great Providence. My experiences have been such that I have been made susceptible to crime, and they are the same experiences which have occurred in the lives of other young men, who also have been made susceptible to crime and who have turned away from society. In plain words, my life was intended by Providence to exemplify the tendency in modern youth to generate criminality, and the terrible atrocity of my last deed with the subsequent wide [report] of this case, are only steps in the plan of Providence to bring me before the world so that I could do the great good which has been confided in me by this same Providence, for the benefit of society and especially the safety and security of human rights and liberties here in the United States of America. Let me explain.

I was born in Arkansas state and before I was ten years of age my father deserted the family and my mother was placed in the custody of an insane asylum at Little Rock, Arkansas. I had a broken home, so you can see, but before I left the country I tried to accept God, and it then being my twelfth year, I received the first calling and feeling of Providence. I came to the city with my remnant family and while there I got discouraged with religion and the church. Religion in the city didn't seem serious enough and I began to disbelieve in it and God somewhat. I attended high school and graduated with second highest honors and scholarship in Kansas City['s] largest high school. There was always quarreling and fighting in my family. We were poor and I didn't have money to go to college and I didn't try hard to get it honestly. I had discouragements and thought I would get a job and work and not go back to school. I tried several jobs and couldn't remain with any of them. I became dissatisfied. My family could not understand me. I was disgusted and felt hurt unjustly. I met two boys who wanted to leave home and be crooks. I was perfectly willing to do this because no one cared for me. I was disappointed. I wouldn't work, so I left home and took to crime. I always felt apart from society. I didn't actually know of one real friend. I even threatened to kill my own mother. I hated my father because he left me and married another woman and had other children. In spite of the circumstances, I always felt the presen[ce] of this Providence. I believe I had the makings of a genius. My shaken morality always brought me back to the idea of college and preparation for this great thing I felt I was surely intended to do before I die.

A companion and I came to California in a stolen car and committed burglaries on the way. On Christmas Eve night, 1926, we entered a pharmacy in Los Angeles and in a shooting battle an innocent man was killed. Here I received a positive manifestation of Providence. An officer of the law within three feet of me and with his revolver directly aimed at my conspicuous body fired three shots and touched me not even once. This was a miracle. This great Providence had saved me and proved itself to me. We continued in crime for a while longer and then decided to go straight. I got a job and stayed with it a few months and fell to the lot of forging checks. I was caught and jailed for a short time on this felonious charge but received probation and went back to Kansas City, Missouri. I got another job and tried to go straight again but only stayed with it several weeks and was led back to crime again. This was only the work of this Providence. I was only doing what many other boys had done whenever [they] got a right start in life susceptible to crime and unaccountable for their criminal deeds. I thought that the end justified the means. I didn't recognize right and wrong. I wanted to be alone in my next crimes and get enough money to go back to college. I roamed over the East in stolen cars, and then Providence led me to come to California and Los Angeles in particular on Thanksgiving Day of last year.

On December 15 last I abducted a little girl by the name of Marian Parker from the Mount Vernon School and held her for a ransom of $1,500, to be used to defray my college expenses at Park College at Parksville [*sic*], Missouri. Here I thought Providence made a great manifestation to me. [F]rom the lips of Marian Parker herself, I received this amazing and positive proof of the presence of a great Providence which was using me for a great work. Marion [*sic*] Parker told me from her own lips and with the same honesty that I confess my crimes before this court, I will speak the true words of this little girl. Marian Parker told me that in the very week that preceded her kidnaping that she had dreamed of a strange man coming to the Mount Vernon School and taking her away in a car. Marian Parker further related that in dreams she had many times been kidnaped and that she always felt that some day she would be taken away from her home and family, in this way. Even the little girl freely told me that she believed the whole thing was intended and if there is a God in heaven, I ask that he will strike me down at this instant if I am in the least particular diverging from the absolute truth and honesty not only in this matter but in everything that I say here.

These matters are of great significance. There is a great Providence prompting me to reach each word of this declaration and this same power brought this declaration from my own mind and I believe it has brought me to live and do all these things.

The murder of Marian Parker and the horrible, terrible, simply awful mutilation of Marian Parker's helpless body, a separate deed from the kidnaping of Marian

Parker, a distinct crime done in blood with a knife by
my own hands on the morning of December 17, 1927,
in the bathtub in Apartment No. 315 at the Bellevue
Arms Apartments of Los Angeles, California, was not
meant by me, Edward Hickman, but through me under
the guidance and protection of, and as a duty to this
great Providence for the great work which it had been
calling me since the age of twelve to perform for the
safety and security of human rights and liberties in the
United States of America. Please listen to me further.

Gentlemen, [I] cannot assign any other possible
motives for my crime. I felt it my duty to perform for
my Providence and the hideousness of the affair and its
widespread publicity were not intended by me for my
own benefit or satisfaction, but were the works of the
powers of destiny. My escape from California, my positive identification through valuable clues which a criminal seldom leaves behind, my detection and arrest in
far off Pendleton, Oregon, and the publicity surrounding my capture were all steps in this mighty plan. They
only served to bring the incident before the nation and
to foreign nations. The entire U.S. is aroused and interested in this affair. It is meant by Providence for you,
the people of this court and the people of Los Angeles
City and [C]ounty to listen and reason with me and act
in a way that will satisfy California and America that
the best solution of criminal law and punishment in
this case will be made possible. The American nation is
even beginning to expect that out of this case will arise
some great solution. The United States is ready for the
example of California. In California's hands lies the
opportunity and right to bring a sufficient verdict in this
case. Now, members of this jury and court, and I wish
that the entire population of this state and nation could
hear me at this time, listen to my greatest reason. Listen
to my inspired logic.

Here I stand before you. You see that I am here and
you recognize me as William Edward Hickman, who

calls himself the Fox. You hear my speech and in your minds only can you reason for yourself. I am on trial for kidnaping and murder. I have pleaded guilty by reason of insanity. The question for you to decide is whether I am sane or insane. I believe that I am best able to speak for myself and judge my own mind and to say and feel of my own true condition. A human being always reserves the right and ability, I believe, to feel and express the true condition of his soul and mind, and knows his innermost parts better than his coexistat [*sic*]. Your duty is to judge me, concerning a condition [of] which only I know the true status. Yet, only in your own minds can you judge me for yourself and American society.

I only say that, if I was insane or an insane [*sic*] at this moment, I believe it not and say that it is a marvelous genius straining to keep itself alive, a mighty genius striving under Providence.

Whatever I may be, I judge it not of myself alone but from the power in me and over me of this great Providence. Listen to me now for your own cause and feel securely in your own reasoning that my greatest desire is for your good and not of any consideration for my own life or death. The acts of crime which were done by my own hands cannot be held accountable in my own mind but were intended for me by another presence to show that in adverse [or] abnormal American social environments today, there is a tendency for certain unfortunate American youth to become enemies of their own society and to be classified as criminals only because society does not understand them and they do not understand society. These disappointed, dissatisfied, careless young men are the most dangerous faction in the United States today. This army of young criminals is steadily increasing. It is the product of society's own degeneration and weaknesses and, unless the American people take certain precautions, or undertake new preventions, personal rights, liberties and properties here in this country will be greatly endangered. This affair strikes at the very heart of the nation. It is of fundamental importance and should be of your deepest concern.

The entire nation is looking on and waiting for the outcome of this trial. I am in your hands and you can do with me whatever you wish. I ask it of you to make such a study and observation of me before you kill me which will help in a new definite way to combat the spread of crime in the United States. I plead with you to do this for the benefit it may be to California and America, or even humanity. I ask that you will allow me to cooperate with you fully because I feel destined to help you in this great cause. I am just an example of your own reckless modern youth, but I have the greatest vision that in this example you will be better able to search out the tendency for crime and find a new prevention which will be of great value to American society. I have always loved my country and it thrills my heart to hear the Star Spangled Banner, or to witness the stars and stripes in parade. I have always felt that before I died I would do some great good and Providence tells me that this is about the time.

I place my body in your hands. You can sentence me to hang if you think it will pacify those who crave my blood. Is there not too much blood shed already in this country without having more? Are not the American people beginning to have the same bloodthirsty impulses that the young desperadoes and criminals themselves have? What terrible end will there be to society if these savage tendencies are allowed to continue? Public opinion never has expressed the true sentiments of the American people. The American press is responsible for many grave errors in this case alone. The American press tries to educate the mob in riot and bloodshed. The American people should, and will, resent these dreadful policies.

Let me make my final plea for the welfare and peace of the peoples of California and America. It is eviden[t] to you that your rights and safety are of first importance to you. I ask to help in the preservation and continuance of these rights. Please take me and work with me and let this great Providence work in me for your good. Robberies and murders and public atrocities are steadily increasing, not only here in Los Angeles but everywhere throughout this country. I plead with you to take me and try to discover the means of staying the hands of young American criminals.

Why America! America! My country and your country will always live. Nothing will bring the downfall of this great republic. There will always be a great mass of the people who understand and keep peace and prosperity among us. Don't think this plea will be easily forgotten. It concerns the preservation of the very fundamentals of manhood, which are the foundation of our republic. It is inevitable that the people will understand and appreciate this reasoning, because I am not reasoning out of my own mind alone but I have been inspired and guided by a great supernatural power in bringing this message to you. Because I am not pleading for myself[,] for my own life[,] but for the American people and for the protection of their own property and lives. Because, in my own confinement, will the greatest benefit come to my country through me. If I live, everything in me of Providence will be exerted for your good. If I die, I hope that some day my country will hear from another youth who is destined and guided by Providence unto the same great work that I have wished to accomplish.

For your consideration, and to your interest, may this message and plea be dedicated. I trust that you will bear me out so that the great power over me can exert itself for this great good for the American people and humanity.

William Edward Hickman

Dr. Orbison finished reading the speech—Central High's star debater in rare form—and for some reason asked Ed to write "death" across the bottom, near his signature. Hickman cheerfully complied, telling Orbison, "I think this would be a very good address before the judge and jury. What do you think about it? Don't you think that would help me out?"

Instead of answering, Orbison pointed to the small Bible in Hickman's pocket and asked if he was reading it.

"Oh," Ed replied, "I carry it with me, but I don't read much of it. I used to think on religious subjects at times, but I am beginning to doubt."

With good reason.

By that time the next day, he would be in court before Judge Hardy, on trial for his life.

12 ✦ "We Looked upon Him as Brilliant"

Reporters and the simply curious turned out early on Wednesday, January 25, to jostle for seats in superior court. Death threats against the morning's star performer had bailiffs on edge, patting men down for weapons and opening women's handbags as spectators filed into the courtroom. Hickman himself was on hand for their pleasure, seated with his attorneys at 8:30 A.M., an hour before the trial was scheduled to begin.

In fact, attorneys Walsh and Cantillon had made up their minds that the trial would not proceed that day. Defeated in their motion for a change of venue, they had framed an affidavit charging Judge Hardy with prejudice against their client, seeking his replacement by another jurist prior to trial. Among other accusations, Walsh and Cantillon alleged that Hardy had described their search for witnesses in Arkansas and Kansas City as "a fishing trip"; that as presiding judge, given his history with Hickman, Hardy should have chosen someone else to hear the case; and that he had, in fact, resigned his ranking post with the specific understanding that the jurist who replaced him would assign him to the Hickman case.

The court was gaveled to order at 9:30 A.M., and Walsh presented his motion as the first order of business. Asa Keyes objected after skimming briefly through the document, contending that it failed to satisfy requirements of state law by spelling out specific acts or statements that suggested prejudice. Judge Hardy, likewise, argued that there was no rule of law requiring him, as the presiding judge, to pass on hearing any given case.

"The only portion of the affidavit, I feel," he went on, "that calls for any statement on my part is the statement that I am biased against the defendant, and that he could not have a fair and impartial trial before me." Hardy flatly denied any bias, then recessed the court until 2:00 P.M., while he took the plea under advisement.

Asa Keyes met with the press outside, calling Walsh's motion "the most ridiculous thing I ever heard of." He clearly expected the motion to be denied, but Judge Hardy surprised him when court reconvened that afternoon.

Reading his own affidavit to the court, Hardy declared that "while I do not admit—but do deny—that I am in any way biased or prejudiced against the defendant and his said cause, yet, in the interest of public justice and the speedy prosecution of the cause, and to avoid the delay that may be occasioned by a protracted hearing with reference to my qualifications as such judge . . . [I] do hereby consent that the cause should be heard before another judge."

The district attorney seemed shaken. His reading of the state's new penal code suggested that prosecutors and defense counsel might now be called to confer and agree on the choice of Judge Hardy's replacement, but Keyes was having none of it.

"In view of the fact," he proclaimed, "that this affidavit has not set up one single fact, if the court please, which shows or tends to show the least bias on the part of this court, I want to announce now that so far as the people are concerned— and I am speaking here for the people of the state of California—we are not now and never will be willing or ready to meet counsel on the other side on the proposition of selecting a judge of our own choosing. Neither the defendant nor the people has a right to any particular judge to try this case, any more than we have a right to any particular juror to sit upon the jury, or any particular jury to try the issue. Therefore, at this time I want to announce to this court that so far as the people are concerned, speaking through me, we will ask that this matter of the selection of a judge be left to the chairman of the judicial council, as the law provides."

Walsh, having won his victory, agreed with the D.A.'s suggestion. Court was adjourned once again and scheduled to resume at 10:00 A.M. on Thursday. It had been a wasted day for those spectators who had come expecting fireworks or some morbid details of the case, but most of them would try again the next morning.

At five o'clock that afternoon, Ed had another visitor in jail. Dr. A. L. Skoog was a psychiatrist from Kansas City, hired by the defense to pick up where Dr. Shelton had left off. Skoog made the first of six visits to Hickman on Wednesday afternoon, remaining with the prisoner for ninety minutes. Like the others before him, Skoog began with a physical examination of his subject, but with rather different results. He found Ed "rather pale," his neuromuscular reactions "probably a little brisker than that which we find in the normal" subject. Reflexes of the upper extremities were "somewhat exaggerated," while abdominal reflexes were "rather extensively brisk." By stroking the sole of Ed's foot, watching the big toe rise "instead of coming down quickly, as in a normal state," Dr. Skoog diagnosed a disease of the spinal cord, including nerve damage. Examining Ed's eyes, he found the retinas "had more blood in them than we find in a strictly normal individual, and possibly there was a little exudate."

Switching to a verbal exam, Skoog asked Hickman, "Do you consider yourself a Christian?"

"No," Ed replied.

"What are you, then?"

"I have no religion, because I have a power over me that is equal and which is more than God to anybody, but that no one feels," Hickman said. "They have something over them and they are satisfied, and I am satisfied."

Was his governing power a god?

"No," Ed answered, "it is something superior to a god, different."

Did anyone else share his power?

"No," Hickman replied, "no one else does, can or will have contact with this Providence."

"Can't this Providence help you?" Skoog asked.

"I do not think it will," said Hickman. "It might direct me. I do not think I know what it will do. I do not try to study what it will do."

Had Hickman received any messages from Marian since he killed her?

"No," he replied, "but I do think Marian knows what is going on."

"How do you know?" Skoog asked.

"I just feel that she knows and can see just what is going on."

"Is she angry with you?"

"No, sir. She is not mad at anyone."

"Why?" the doctor pressed.

"She has no reason, does not want to be," Ed told him. "Her life was taken away. I took her life, but did I?"

"I am asking you the question," Skoog replied.

"I murdered her, yes," Ed acknowledged. "I do not think I took her life away."

"Was that right, that you murdered her?"

"Yes, it was."

"Explain that," Skoog demanded.

"I think," Ed replied, "she actually was born and lived for this very thing. It is true that she never knew about it, [but] she was prepared and brought into the world for this very thing, and her spirit is now seeing that this is done."

Ed repeated his tale of Marian's kidnapping dreams. "It was about five or six—she told me then, just voluntarily—she said she had several dreams concerning this. She said her mother always warned her about strange men and getting into accidents, but she never did think it was so bad to be kidnapped. She dreamed of it and thought perhaps some day she might, but did not think she would be afraid, did not think it was as bad as it would seem."

In terms of robbery and murder, Skoog inquired, "How do you justify that with your religion and your conscience?"

"My conscience—I don't feel that I have a conscience," Ed replied.

"How long have you been minus a conscience?"

"What I mean by conscience," Hickman tried to explain, "is by speaking."

"By direction?"

"Yes," Ed agreed. "I feel some power over me. I feel it is for the good. With the aid of this power I would become great by doing some great thing. I never stop to study or figure it out. If I feel it was something to do, I was ready to do it. I always looked forward to the great end but did not have much consideration . . . never gave any attempt on my own part . . . did not think I should try it."

Ed insisted that the "power" was greater than he was. He "wanted to be humble and passive. I never did like to be reluctant." He hoped that Providence might someday speak to him directly. "I think it will come ahead," he told Skoog. "A man has to be so very broad-minded, and I think this power gives me a visionary conception. It makes my mind so broad that I can even forgive whatever they do, the fact that they cannot help what they do. I feel no blame on anyone."

Dr. Skoog left that meeting convinced that Hickman was insane. Nothing he heard or saw in his next five visits would alter that judgment.

Late Wednesday night, Presiding Judge Victor McLucas—Hardy's replacement in the top slot of Superior Court—chose Judge J. J. Trabucco to hear Hickman's case. A visiting jurist from Maricopa County with thirty years on the bench, Trabucco was on loan to help clear the L.A. court's congested calendar. Now, without warning, he found himself handling the trial of the decade.

That trial began in earnest, more of less, on Thursday, January 26. The court convened at 10:00 A.M., Judge Hardy showing up just long enough introduce Trabucco and surrender his position on the bench. It was apparent from the start that Judge Trabucco took a firm, no-nonsense view of the proceedings, overruling Walsh's opening objection to the seating of a judge not chosen by agreement of the prosecution and defense. That done, a number of prospective jurors, having been transferred from Department 25, were ushered into the courtroom and asked to fill the empty seats.

Dick Cantillon began his examination of the first venireman: "Have you at any time contributed any sum of money to a reward for the apprehension and conviction of the person who slew Marian Parker?"

"No, sir."

Trabucco interrupted at that point. "It seems to me," he said, "that question can be asked collectively of all the jurors."

"If Your Honor will make the order," Cantillon replied, "or is [it] a suggestion?"

"I will make the order," Judge Trabucco said.

"We object to the order of the court to the asking of the question in this manner," Cantillon replied.

"Objection overruled."

Clearly, the new judge was determined to avoid the kind of marathon proceedings that would be routine for L.A. courts half a century later. Under protest, Cantillon began to quiz the panel at large with a list of fifty-six questions: Were any potential jurors related to or acquainted with the Parker family? Were they friends or relatives of any lawyers, law enforcement officers, or witnesses involved in Hickman's case? Did they belong to any church or club that had expressed opinions on the case? How much reported information on the case had they absorbed, and from what sources? Had they talked about the case with relatives or friends? If so, how often? Were their minds made up about the suspect's guilt or sanity? If so, could any evidence presented to the court revise those views?

While the veniremen were being questioned, Dr. Mikels sat in court and studied Hickman, jotting down notes about his every move. ("Once he brushed the left side of the back of his neck with his right hand," "His coat collar seems to ride up when he sits down," etc.) When court adjourned for lunch, Ed saw the doctor watching him and said hello. "I have got down there 'Joy.' " Mikels later testified. "Maybe he was joyful or not, but he appeared to be pleased."

When court resumed at 2:00 P.M., Cantillon voiced his wish to question five prospective jurors individually. Again, Judge Trabucco refused, overruling the defense objection. Once again, Cantillon worked his way through the list of questions, noting each person's response. When he was finished, still without a challenge, court adjourned for the day, Judge Trabucco warning members of the panel not to talk about the case with anyone.

That order didn't stop Hickman from talking, though, and while reporters traded quips about Trabucco's evident dislike of Jerome Walsh, the star of the proceedings held another press conference. Ed planned to testify, he said, no matter how his lawyers felt about it. Asked for a response, Walsh told reporters, "We do not want Hickman to take the witness stand, in view of the insanity defense, and we have told him so. Of course, if he is determined to talk, we cannot stop him, but such a move will seriously injure defense plans."

On Friday morning one potential juror was excused at the request of the defense. That afternoon, Jerome Walsh passed on any further challenges, while Asa Keyes was suddenly uncertain of the panel, asking for postponement of his final challenge until Monday morning. Judge Trabucco readily agreed and warned the veniremen one more time against discussing any aspect of the case. "I particularly admonish you," he said, "should any person talk to you or attempt to talk to you or in your presence or hearing about this case, tell them that you are jurors, and that they must not speak to you, under the orders of the court. And if they persist in speaking to you, report that matter to the court, and they will be dealt with according to law."

On Saturday, January 28, a rumor started circulating that Hickman had recanted his confession. The source was said to be impeccable: Attorney Walsh himself. Reporters tracked him down and Walsh denied the rumor. There had been no recantation, nor had Walsh discussed the case with anyone. In short, whoever spread the story had been lying through his teeth.

Before the prosecution had a chance to challenge any jurors on Monday morning, Jerome Walsh asked the court to seek the appointment of three new psychiatrists, chosen from across the country by leaders of the American Psychiatric Association, to review Hickman's case. His purpose, Walsh declared, was to obtain expert opinions from analysts who "could in nowise be a subject of local influence or the hysteria that seems to have gripped this community." Asa Keyes objected to the slur on California, and Trabucco denied the motion on grounds that "it might mean the delay of the trial of this case." Walsh objected to that rationale, suggesting that the trial would take at least a week in any case, but he was overruled.

Walsh then took the unusual step of having himself sworn in as a witness, to "make a showing in the record" that his client was impoverished and thus prohibited from seeking out the best experts available for his defense. Under questioning from Keyes, Walsh acknowledged that a battery of doctors representing both sides of the case had already examined Edward, and that two of the defense physicians would be called as witnesses. With that, the motion for a fresh examination was again denied.

That settled, the prospective jurors were recalled, with four excused on prosecution challenges because they opposed capital punishment. The final jury consisted of nine men and three women; nearly half—five of the twelve—had admitted prejudging the case, based on newspaper coverage, but all swore they could judge Hickman impartially, based on the evidence. Dick Cantillon filed notice of dissatisfaction with the jury and was overruled before the lunch break.

Coming back at 2:00 P.M., the jurors were informed that they would be sequestered in the custody of sheriff's deputies for the duration of the trial. A bailiff would arrange for any necessary personal effects to be delivered. Once a protest from the jury was disposed of, Judge Trabucco ordered any scheduled witnesses to leave the courtroom. Asa Keyes requested that the state's psychiatrists be allowed to stay, and Trabucco granted the motion, overruling yet another defense objection.

The opening statements were brief, adding barely one page to the transcript. Hickman had already confessed to kidnapping, killing, and dismembering Marian Parker; the only point at issue was his state of mind—sane or mad—at the time he performed those deeds. The state meant to prove him sane, while the defense planned to "establish the taint of insanity in the family of this defendant back to the third generation."

Jerome Walsh had forty-nine witnesses on tap, but only sixteen of them would testify in person. The rest had supplied depositions in Kansas City and Arkansas, which Walsh now intended to read for the jury. It seems a curious approach today, but in those days of tighter budgets, before commercial air travel, the transportation of thirty-odd witnesses halfway across the country was an impossible burden. The first phase of the trial, then, would consist of a recitation that challenged the most ardent juror to stay awake and pay attention while Walsh read through the affidavits, one by one.

First up was Benjamin Bailey, a brother-in-law of the late Otto Buck, from Hartford, Arkansas. He knew little about Eva Hickman, but described her cousin Otto as "insane to some extent," subject to "pretty frequent" seizures. Under cross-examination, Bailey granted that Otto "would work all right" between seizures, and that "he had a peculiar look. Most everybody noticed his looks."

Eva's brother-in-law, Thomas Lewis, had provided the next deposition. He had testified that Rebecca Buck's mind was "awfully weak," while grandson Otto was even worse: "From a boy on up he had some kind of fits. I don't know what you call them." As for Eva herself, Lewis said, her married life "was a hard one." Her husband "let women get the upper hand of him, taking up with other women," finally leaving Hartford with another man's wife. Eva "never would tell us much of her troubles," but they clearly preyed on her mind. Asked his opinion of her mental state, Lewis replied, "Well, I would think she was insane." In fact, he said on cross-examination, Eva's strange behavior while she lived in Hartford had convinced him that she "didn't know the difference between right and wrong."

A Hartford neighbor of the Bucks, Irvin Harris, agreed in his deposition that Rebecca was "an awful nervous person," given to fits of weeping and paranoid delusions of persecution. Grandson Otto, meanwhile, was subject to "pretty frequent" seizures in which he "was liable to kill himself," and was incapable of carrying on a rational conversation at the best of times.

The first medical witness, Dr. W. J. Hunt, had lived in Hartford for twelve years, before relocating to Oklahoma. During eight of those years, he had treated Eva Hickman's family "off and on." Following her suicide attempt with the carbolic acid, Hunt had diagnosed Eva as suffering from "a form of insanity, but the cause, I don't know." After her release from the asylum, Eva "seemed to be" normal, but only "for a while." She still "imagined things," including sundry nonexistent illnesses, and often wept inexplicably "for half an hour at a time."

Dr. William Grigsby, still in Hartford, agreed with Dr. Hunt, although he wasn't sure if Eva was insane. "That would depend," he said, "on what it takes to constitute insanity. I wouldn't consider her absolutely sound [of] mind. She was slightly subnormal, mentally." On top of that, she was "very emotional" and imagined frequent illnesses, but the only one Grigsby could ever document was chronic constipation. "I wouldn't want to say she was sane," he concluded. "She had the appearance of ordinary intelligence, unless you observed her closely. . . . I thought at the time, and think yet, that her intellect was slightly impaired."

Sarah Slankard had known Eva Hickman for a quarter-century, pronouncing her "a little bit queer," although she was "always nicely behaved." Eva's personality "was kind of

funny turned," a fact which Slankard blamed upon her
German ancestry. Sarah saw less of her friend after the 1912
suicide attempt, but still concluded that she was insane. On
cross, the prosecution won a grudging admission that Eva
"knew what she was doing" in daily life: "Sure, she knew
she was sweeping, and those things."

Sister-in-law Ida Hickman agreed with the earlier witnesses that Eva had long been "a strange acting woman"
who lapsed into melancholy moods for days at a time. Even
before she was married, Eva "didn't act just like other people," but pregnancy exacerbated the problem, Ida said,
making her "greatly worried and upset." She hedged a bit
on cross-examination, admitting that Eva "got along pretty
well" until Bill started womanizing, but stood firm on her
opinion that "at times"—especially while pregnant with
Edward—Eva had been so far gone she couldn't tell right
from wrong.

Bill Hickman's sister, Mrs. Artie Smith, who had known
Eva from childhood, said she was "a little high strung and
nervous" from their earliest acquaintance. There were problems with Mrs. Smith as a witness, though: she thought Bill
and Eva had been married "about thirty years," when in fact
it was less than seventeen, and she denied any knowledge
of Bill's flagrant adultery, saying, "I wasn't living here much
of [Eva's] married life." In fact, Mrs. Smith concluded, Eva
"hasn't been insane all the time" and seemed rational
enough the last time they met.

Neighbor Mae Forrester had a clear memory of Bill
Hickman's transgressions, which left Eva "the most despondent woman I ever saw." Concerning the suicide attempt,
she concluded that Eva "was insane at that time, for no one
would want to kill themselves if they were sane." After her
release from the asylum, Mae said, Eva remained "sullen,"
though she still qualified as "a good housekeeper and a
devoted mother." On cross-examination, Mae allowed that
Eva "always knew the difference between right and wrong,
but still at the same time she was always a nervous
woman."

Judge Trabucco interrupted Walsh's reading of the Forrester affidavit, and court was adjourned until Tuesday morning. Dr. Mikels, watching Edward from the gallery, had more incisive observations for the state: "He walked in steadily and sat down without preliminarily adjusting his clothes on this day. He seemed to feel comfortable and got accustomed to the clothes he had on and the seat that he was in, and it did not annoy him." On the other hand, Mikels noted a "kind of fixed stare in his eye," while "a gloomy expression came over his face, and I noticed he was probably reflecting or recollecting."

Dr. Skoog and Dr. Shelton called on Ed in his cell that evening between 5:30 and 6:30. They left with diametrically opposed conclusions, Skoog determining that Ed was rational, while Shelton viewed him as incurably insane.

Tuesday morning found Walsh completing the deposition, in which Mae Forrester tried to explain why she thought Eva Hickman didn't know the difference between right and wrong. It finally boiled down, in Mae's mind, to the suicide attempt: "She didn't do right when she took the medicine."

Elderly Spence Lane, another Hartford resident, provided a comic touch to the proceedings with his deposition, describing Otto Buck as "a fitified kind of fellow," known to acquaintances as "a nutty guy, just an idiot." Asked for specifics, Lane replied, "He would slobber like a mad dog and grind his teeth." The transcript indicates that Lane performed a demonstration, but Walsh made no attempt to mimic the display. On cross, the D.A. tried to win a concession that Buck was "all right" between seizures, but Lane stood fast. At the best of times, he testified, Otto "would wallow around over his wife, lay over into her lap, and act like a foolish child."

Next up, Walsh read the statement Bill Hickman had signed in 1912, on committing his wife to the Little Rock asylum. That brief document was followed by the deposition of Stella Smith, formerly a nurse at the institution where Eva was confined. She recalled knowing Eva "for about a month," and had immediately recognized her name when the story of Marian's murder broke in the newspapers. While confined, Smith testified, Eva "was in a state of melancholia, a deeply depressed state, most of the time."

Dr. L. R. Brown confirmed that diagnosis in his deposition and provided various hospital records to document Eva's treatment in 1913. Brown recalled that Eva Hickman "seemed to have periods when she was more or less normal, but was at other times very melancholy and worried about things that did not amount to anything." He described her condition "as among the curable types of insanity," then admitted that depression did not fit the legal definition of insanity.

Dr. H. P. Routh had moved from Hartford to Tulsa, Oklahoma, but Walsh had tracked him down and secured a deposition that included firsthand observations of Bill Hickman's infidelity. Of Eva, Routh testified, "I would say that she was insane—I would have to—as compared to normal." Specifically, Routh and Eva's regular physician "pronounced it a case of dementia praecox of the melancholia type." Cross-examination pointed out that Dr. Routh did not specialize in psychiatry, furthermore that Eva had seemed "perfectly normal" in various casual encounters. She was not, in other words, "a raving lunatic that would run up and down the streets throwing her arms and body about and clawing at the air and so forth." Still, Routh insisted, "She was insane. From a medical standpoint she was insane all the time."

Shifting from Eva to Edward, Walsh next read the deposition of former classmate Don Johnstone, filled with praise for Ed as a student who ranked "nearly at the head of the class" at Central High. Ed's downfall came, in Johnstone's view, when he became "completely wrapped up" in oratorical contests, losing the main prize two years in a row. In defeat, he said, Hickman "seemed to gradually acquire a feeling that people were against him, that because he had lost this, that people couldn't like him any more." By the time Hickman enrolled in junior college, Johnstone thought he was insane, but he filed no report with the administration, since he "didn't consider it as [a] dangerous form of insanity at that time."

Another former classmate, Baylor Sutton, was the next to testify for Hickman in absentia. His deposition rehashed much of what Don Johnstone had said, concerning Ed's achievements in the first three years of high school and his sudden shift in personality after his junior year. Unlike Johnstone, though, when asked if he considered Hickman crazy back in 1926, Sutton first said he "didn't give it a thought," then reversed himself to allow that Ed "was a little off" prior to graduation. It was in the summer of 1926, Sutton explained, when he noted "startling inconsistencies" in Edward's behavior, concluding that his friend had slipped beyond the pale of sanity.

Joe Tiffany's deposition was next, yet another take on Ed's decline from a bright, fun-loving youth into obsessive melancholy. Still, despite the shift in attitude, the abandonment of friends and extracurricular activities, it "never occurred" to Tiffany that Edward was insane until he heard that Marian Parker had been slain in Los Angeles. Without the murder, he acknowledged on cross, "it would never have dawned on [him]" that Hickman was mentally ill.

Howard Hibbs was apparently more perceptive, noting a dramatic shift in Edward's mind-set between June and September of 1925. "I believe he was abnormal at times during his senior year," Hibbs testified, "and probably something was affecting him at that time, which was noticeable, and which grew larger all the time, and probably developed into what his crime record shows he has done already."

Yet another former classmate from Central, John Proudfit, agreed with the rest that Edward's change in personality sprang from his losses in the *Star* oratorical contests, but he refused to pass judgment on Hickman's sanity. "I would say," he hedged, "with the occurrences—since the last time I saw him, in general—that he is, in my opinion, not the same boy that I knew."

C. M. McFarland's brief deposition claimed that he knew Ed from Central High, where they were classmates, and "talked with him every day," describing Hickman's personality as "steady throughout all four years." It seemed curious, then, that he judged Ed insane. Pressed for an explanation, McFarland ascribed his opinion to "the fact that his actions of the last few weeks have been inconsistent with my previous association with him."

Teacher Alfred Richmond, the first Central High staff member deposed by Walsh, elaborated on the change in Hickman's personality during his senior year. "I did not think at that time that he was insane," Richmond said, "but there was a decided change." He regarded Edward's falling grades and later false starts at the junior college as atypical of honor students he had known.

Principal Otto Dubach, in his deposition, recited Ed's grades for his years at Central High. "We looked upon him as brilliant," Dubach testified, "but not as steady as, for example, his older brother." Ed was "rather sensitive," but Dubach had no knowledge of any indulgence in drugs. Where after-school jobs were concerned, Dubach said, "My understanding is that he would make good at his work, but that he wouldn't stay."

Vice principal J. L. Laughlin, who followed Dubach, described his close relationship with Hickman at Central. Walsh read through the portion of Laughlin's deposition that described his role in getting Ed a job with the Kiger Jewelry Company, but it was running late, and Judge Trabucco interrupted him again, adjourning for the day.

Dr. Mikels, in the audience, had more keen observations for the D.A.'s team. "After walking into the courtroom," Mikels noted, "[Hickman] paused for a moment and gazed at the spectators and looked them all over, and then continued to his seat. He did not arrange his coat but dropped his hands across his lap and directed his attention forward. He maintained vigilant attention and followed the recitation of the depositions. He had an expression of curiosity about what those depositions were going to bring about."

When court resumed the next morning, Ed would be an older man. Wednesday, February 1, was his twentieth birthday, and now he had reason to doubt he would make twenty-one.

13 ✦ "An Average American Youth"

Court convened a few minutes later than usual on Wednesday, at 9:45 A.M. Dr. Mikels was staked out in the gallery, observing Hickman as he entered with his escort, jotting down observations that would later form the basis for his testimony. On that birthday morning, Mikels noted that Edward "walked briskly to his seat. He did not arrange his clothes. He used his handkerchief, which he took from his right hip pocket, and in doing this his coordination of purposive motivation was accurate and unimpaired. He resumed his attentive attitude and braced his feet against the chair in front. He maintained a very attentive attitude during this entire session. I have a notation of 'joy,' which comes down in here."

Jerome Walsh picked up that morning where he had left off the day before, reading J. L. Laughlin's deposition to the jury. Central High's vice principal believed Edward was insane when he killed Marian. His reason? "He was respected and honored by the best class of students that we ever had," Laughlin replied, "and by the entire faculty. I can't conceive of a boy like he was committing an act of this sort unless he was insane." On cross-examination, Laughlin grudgingly admitted that he based his opinion on "the horribleness of the crime and what [I] have heard or read in the newspapers."

Rebecca Tomlin, who had coached Ed for the *Star* oratorical contests in 1925 and 1926, described him in her deposition as "a very serious, constant worker." He did have "some very peculiar little habits," and on balance Tomlin concluded that he was "too high-strung to be a good orator." The latter part of Edward's senior year was marked by a "noticeable change" in his demeanor, and Tomlin firmly believed he was insane throughout the kidnapping and murder. Why? "Because of such a boy, as I knew Edward Hickman to be, ever being accused of it."

Grace Hudson's deposition was the shortest yet, only ten questions, confirming Edward's part-time job at the Kansas City Public Library in 1926, while he was "supposed to be going to junior college."

The next long-distance witness, Mrs. Charles Edwards, would not get off so easily. She had known Edward "very intimately," and noted a striking change in his behavior following his first oratorical trouncing. Overnight, it seemed, Ed was transformed from "a very sweet tempered boy" into one who "would get real angry and flare up" over nothing. As for his mental competency, Mrs. Edwards testified, "I think he has been insane for a long time." Pressed for specifics, she reckoned Ed had lost his mind "about the time he graduated from high school."

Charles Harper's deposition was another quickie, establishing that Edward worked for the Schmelzer Company the summer after graduation. Leslie Smith recalled working with Ed on the Central High yearbook and noted his "brilliant turn of mind." Another brief deposition, from Edward Bainter, described Ed's departure from junior college after two weeks, but he had never met the defendant, nor had he prepared the records himself. Indeed, he admitted, the transcripts might belong to "some other Edward Hickman for all [I] know."

And the recitation in absentia went on. Marion Huscher described Hickman's excellent performance in freshman mechanical drawing class. Grocer James Parker noted Ed's refusal to kill chickens, and recalled him as "an awful good boy, about the best boy I ever had." Mrs. M. E. Doran remembered Hickman visiting her son as Vincent lay dying from tuberculosis. None of the witnesses thought Edward was insane, but their combined impression of a bright, soft-hearted boy was strikingly at odds with Hickman's behavior in Los Angeles. Reading between the lines, their message was clear: anyone who changed so radically, in such a short span of time, was clearly deranged.

Walsh saved his biggest gun for last, with the deposition of Charles Edwards. As a former police chief, Edwards could hardly be described as soft on crime; at the same time, however, he knew Edward intimately—indeed, had been the closest thing to a father figure in young Hickman's life—and Walsh hoped that his opinions would sway the jurors, imbue them with at least a hint of sympathy for the defendant.

Like other witnesses, Edwards dated the change in Hickman's demeanor from his first oratorical-contest defeat, in 1925. His near daily visits to the Edwards home had dwindled after that, until the chief saw Edward only "six to eight times" in 1926. When Hickman did drop by that year, he always seemed "restless," worried about his future, asking for advice and for introductions at Park College. Chief Edwards did what he could, but Hickman never followed through, dropping one job after another. Edwards balked at voicing an opinion on the boy's sanity, four times refusing to answer the question, but Walsh kept at him. As far as the murder of Marian Parker was concerned, Edwards admitted, "I can't help but believe that he must have been in a state of mind bordering on insanity." Moments later he was more emphatic: "Personally, I believe that that boy, when he committed that murder, was insane. That I am positive of. . . . My personal opinion is that he is suffering from some form of insanity, which I know nothing about."

Judge Trabucco ordered a five-minute recess after the last deposition was read, permitting bailiffs to track down the trial's first live witness. Detective Lieutenant Richard Lucas had ducked out during the monotonous recital, but he soon returned and was sworn in, ironically, as a witness for the defense.

Jurors and spectators alike knew Lucas from daily press reports as a member of the team that had retrieved Hickman from Oregon. He had been quoted in the *Times* and was among those who had witnessed Hickman's statements on December 26. Soft-spoken to a fault—the judge admonished him four times to "talk up loud"—Lucas began with his first view of Hickman, in the jail at Pendleton, and continued through the trip back to Los Angeles.

When he had first seen Hickman, Lucas testified, the prisoner "was acting as though he was in a fit," thrashing about on the floor of his cell and calling for Marian Parker. His antics had precluded any questioning on Christmas Eve, but Lucas had seen through the charade.

"I asked him why he was acting this way," Lucas told the court, "and why he was pulling this fit stuff. I said, 'Now, you will go back to Los Angeles, and you can go back any way you like. We will take you back like a man, or,' I said, 'if you want to have a lot of fits around here it won't be very comfortable, and you won't go back as easy as you will if you don't have any more fits.' So he said, in the conversation he said, 'Well, what kind of fit do you think I made up there?' I said, 'You may have fooled the people in Pendleton, but you certainly were not fooling me.' "

In their initial questioning, Lucas recalled, "Chief Cline was lecturing him," and Hickman had repeated his original story of handing Marian off to an accomplice. Lucas and company were not deceived. When they pressed him for the truth, Hickman came clean and confessed he had acted alone. Lucas paraphrased Edward's confession, inserting quotes for dramatic effect without referring to his notes. The female jurors wept as he described the dissection of Marian Parker. Eva Hickman was weeping, too, in the audience, while Lucas reported her son's description of the body twitching under his knife.

When Lucas finished, taking Hickman to the point of his arrest in Oregon, Walsh introduced a copy of his client's confession and read it. Ed's second statement, headed "Motives," was introduced next, and Walsh read that to the jury as well, giving jurors their first glimpse of Hickman's apparent obsession with "Providence."

On cross-examination, Asa Keyes was quick to emphasize the bogus nature of Hickman's "fits" in Pendleton. "At the time you went in there on that Christmas Day morning," Keyes asked Lucas, "did the defendant continue his actions?"

"Yes," Lucas replied.

"Went into a fit, did he?"

"Yes. He was doing another one, he said."

Keyes jumped on that. "He *said*?"

"He said he was having another fit," Lucas confirmed.

"Did he say that at the time?"

"No, he said that after we got on the train. He asked me, 'What kind of fit do you think I made up there?' I said I thought it was a very poor one."

"In other words," Keyes pressed, "after you had gotten on the train and gotten to talking to the defendant, he indicated to you by his words and actions that he had been trying to pull a stall on you up there, to use the vernacular, the language of the street?"

"That is what he said, yes," Lucas replied. "He said—he asked us what kind of a fit he pulled."

"Did he laugh about it?"

"Yes."

"You told him at that time," Keyes said, "he might have fooled some of the people up in Pendleton, but he did not fool the officers from the South, didn't you?"

"I did," said Lucas.

"What did he say about that?"

"Well, he said if they—he said, 'I will pull one right in front of the judge,' he said. 'When I get down there, if he sentences me to be hung,' he said, 'I will pull one right in front of the judge.' "

Once again, Hickman seemed intent on burying himself.

After leading Lucas through a description of Hickman's midwestern crime spree, Keyes returned to the defendant's state of mind. "You had a chance to observe him during all of that time, did you?" he asked.

"I did," Lucas agreed.

"During all of that time while you observed him, state whether or not he appeared to you to be rational and [in] the full possession of his faculties."

"He absolutely did," said Lucas. "He talked to us regarding all about it. He asked all about the jury system, about how they selected the jurors, about the procedure in court, and about how insane people acted, and whether their pulse was normal or their temperature was normal, and all about that stuff. And as we were getting into Los Angeles, he said that he had made up his mind to go into court and plead guilty."

"Did he display any emotion on that trip down, Mr. Lucas? Isn't it a fact," Keyes asked, "that on many occasions on the trip he did display considerable emotion?"

"Oh, yes, sure," Lucas replied. "He would see people as we were coming along, see the people along the track. They would be down to the depots to meet us, and lots of them would—one fellow especially, I remember, he pulled his hand up to his throat this way, you know"—Lucas mimicked a hanged man—"and Hickman laughed about that a great deal. He said, 'Well, just turn me loose out here and these people would fix me up right now.' "

"He laughed, did he?"

"Yes."

The only time Hickman wept, Lucas said, "was when he broke and started to telling the story" of Marian's murder. By that time, Edward had abandoned any mention of accomplices.

"That was after you had told him that a man named Cramer was in jail here, wasn't it?" Keyes asked.

"Was doing time," Lucas agreed, "and he was in jail at the time that this kidnapping occurred. He was doing six months, a man by the name of Cramer, but [Hickman] did not know Cramer."

"He told you," Keyes went on, "that he just made this name of Cramer up out of thin air?"

"He spoke about that," Lucas replied. "He said, 'I understand that they have found a man by the name of Cramer, and June Dunning also.' We told him that they had, and that they had known one another. He said, 'That is a funny thing,' that he should pick up a couple's name that were really people by that name, that had been here in this town, in Los Angeles."

As Lucas left the witness stand, Judge Trabucco adjourned for the day. There was, however, one more bit of drama to be acted out before the courtroom cleared. Moving toward the exit, Jerome Walsh found his way blocked by the widow of Ivy Thoms, her features contorted with rage. "I hate you for helping that murderer!" she sobbed. "Oh, how I hate you!"

Defense psychiatrist A. L. Skoog paid a final visit to Hickman in jail that afternoon, between 5:30 and 6:15, and while he took a stenographer along, the examination yielded no surprises. Dr. Skoog already had his diagnosis ready for the witness stand. He was convinced that Edward was insane within the legal definition of the word.

Walsh continued with his case on Thursday morning, but the first two witnesses he called—Chief of Detectives Herman Cline and LAPD Chief James Davis, both under subpoena from the defense—were running late and had not reached the courthouse. Visibly irritated, Walsh called Naomi Britten, the secretary from the Mount Vernon School, and confirmed her identification of Hickman as the "quiet and courteous" man who had abducted Marian Parker. On cross-examination, Asa Keyes scored points by eliciting her description of the kidnapper.

"He seemed to be very composed and in full possession of his faculties, so far as you could observe, didn't he?" the D.A. asked.

"Yes, sir."

"Talked rationally and intelligently?"

"Yes, sir."

Mary Holt was next on the stand, grim-faced as she described her role in handing Marian over to her murderer. Once again, Walsh stressed his client's demeanor at the time: "Was he quiet and peaceful, or did he appear nervous, or how?"

"Very calm, courteous," Holt replied.

"Mrs. Holt, you had no reason to doubt his good faith, did you?"

"Not in the least," she agreed, welcoming absolution.

Keyes was satisfied to play the same tune for the jury. "Now, he was well dressed on that occasion?" he asked.

"Very well groomed," Holt agreed.

"Seemed to be very neat in appearance?"

"Very neat in appearance," she echoed.

"There was nothing in his appearance at that time to excite any suspicion in you?"

"Not in the least."

"He seemed to be in full possession of his faculties, and intelligent?"

"Absolutely."

By the time Holt finished, Herman Cline had finally arrived in court, and he replaced her on the witness stand. It was a curious reversal of procedure, having homicide investigators called to testify for the defense, but Walsh's client had already confessed to murder. All that remained for the defense was to try to cast doubt on his state of mind.

Walsh could expect no willing help from Cline in that regard. Cline readily identified the statements signed by Hickman and confirmed that there had been no promises of leniency before he wrote his story down. Walsh did not bother asking whether Cline believed that Edward was insane.

On cross from Asa Keyes, Cline described how he had broken Hickman down and convinced him to give up the "Cramer" charade. "I told him, I says, 'Hickman,' I says, 'you have acknowledged the fact that you did kidnap this girl.' I says, 'It does not matter, really, in the eyes of the law who she was murdered by.' I said, 'The very fact that you kidnapped her and was working with someone else, in case the girl was murdered, would make you just as guilty as if you had actually murdered her.' I says, 'There has been evidence found in the Bellevue Arms Apartments that leads us to believe that the crime was committed right in the Bellevue Arms Apartments, and while we do not exactly believe that you intentionally killed the little girl, we do believe that possibly you gave her an overdose of some kind of an opiate, and that that was the cause of her death, and that later, then, you cut the body up the way you did in order to get rid of it.' He said, 'No,' he said, 'the girl did not receive any opiate.' He says, 'She was strangled.' "

In Cline's view, diverging substantially from the language of Edward's confession, police believed that Hickman "realized that she was getting beyond his control; in other words, he said that he did not think he could keep her quiet much longer, that she was making too much noise, and that he feared she was going to make sufficient noise that someone would find out that she was in the apartment."

In fact, Hickman's various statements said just the opposite, that Marian had been quiet and cooperative, that she "was not worried or excited," and that she "felt perfectly safe." Still, Cline's revision of events passed without objection from Walsh, leaving the jury with one more impression of a logical, clearheaded killer.

Keyes returned once more to Hickman's state of mind. "Now, Mr. Cline," he said, "during all the time you were conversing with the defendant on the train there, on this Sunday and on the next day, Monday, at all times when you were with him he appeared to you to be perfectly sane and rational, didn't he?"

"He did," Cline confirmed.

"And he appeared to be intelligent and in full possession of his faculties?"

"He did."

Inspector Dwight Longuevan followed Cline to the stand but added nothing new for the defense. He confirmed that Hickman's statements on the southbound train were voluntary, untainted by threats or promises. And once again, on cross-examination, Asa Keyes affirmed his portrait of a calm and levelheaded criminal.

"During all the time you were with the defendant, Mr. Longuevan," Keyes said, "from the time you first saw him until you delivered him here to Los Angeles, he appeared to be perfectly sane and rational, didn't he?"

The inspector, having missed Hickman's "fits" in the Pendleton jail, replied simply, "He did."

Judge Trabucco granted a ten-minute recess while Walsh's next witness was summoned. Coming down from the jail, Welby Hunt was a change from the parade of burly policemen. At sight of his one-time accomplice, Dr. Mikels noted "a little smile" on Hickman's face, "one of those smirks of disdain."

Walsh led Welby through a brief recap of his acquaintance with Hickman, from their meeting at the Kansas City library until they left for California.

"Now, during that time," Walsh said, "I will ask you to state whether or not the defendant ever expressed a desire to you to commit a murder."

"He did make one statement, yes."

"Will you state to the jury the general substance of the conversation?"

"I don't know the conversation," Hunt replied, "how it came up. But he made the statement one time that it was his wish to get someone and chop them up all in little pieces, he said, and throw them along the highway, I believe was the words he used."

"Those were the words he used?"

"Yes."

Keyes came back to the point on cross-examination. "Do you know where you were when he made that statement?" the D.A. asked.

"I could not tell you exactly," Hunt replied, "because I didn't think of it to any great extent at that time."

"You considered it more in the way of a joke that he was trying to pull, didn't you?"

"Somewhat, yes. I didn't think seriously about it at the time at all."

"Well, was there any discussion right at that time," Keyes asked, "about killing any particular person?"

"No, sir."

On redirect, Walsh tried to repair the damage. "I will ask you to state, Mr. Hunt, whether or not you recall that Hickman expressed the same desire in Kansas City to you and to Frank Bernoudy, that he would like to kill somebody and dismember their body and sprinkle the parts along the highway?"

"No, sir," Hunt replied. "To my knowledge he never made such a statement."

"As you recall it," Walsh prodded, "it was when you were on your way out here to Los Angeles?"

"Yes, sir. Just one time."

Herman Cline was briefly recalled to the stand after Welby stepped down. Having retrieved a large pocketknife from the evidence locker, the chief of detectives now introduced it as the knife found in Hickman's possession when he was arrested. According to Cline, Hickman had admitted using the knife to dismember Marian Parker.

"I asked the defendant which blade in this knife he used," Cline testified, "and opened both blades and showed them to him, and he stated it was the blade with the sharper point."

"The larger blade?" asked Asa Keyes.

"Larger blade," Cline agreed, then reconsidered. "They are both about the same size, but this blade here, with the sharper point."

"All right."

"I asked him where he procured the knife," Cline went on, "and he said he bought the knife on Main Street about two weeks before [the murder]. I asked him what the idea was in buying such a knife, and he stated that he was out committing robberies, and he was liable to get in a close place where he couldn't use a gun, and he might have to cut his way out."

Assistant probation officer A. L. Mathews followed Cline on the stand for a brief appearance, authenticating correspondence between himself and Chief Edwards that Walsh introduced into evidence. Next up, Frank Peck described the Sunday night when Hickman stole his car at gunpoint on

Hollywood Boulevard. They had been together some twenty or twenty-five minutes, Peck testified, and he recognized Hickman in court. On cross-examination, Asa Keyes returned inevitably to the killer's state of mind.

"As far as you could observe, Mr. Peck, he seemed to be perfectly sane, didn't he? Rational?" Keyes asked.

"Absolutely," Peck replied.

"Absolutely? He knew what he was doing?"

"Yes, sir. I will say that he did."

As for his mood, Keyes asked, "Did the defendant smile when he talked to you or appear to be jovial, or was he serious?"

"Well," Peck replied, "he was rather serious. I don't know that he was jovial."

"Look at his face now," Keyes directed, turning toward Hickman. "He has a sort of smile on his face now. Did he appear to be that way?"

"Very similar," Peck agreed.

In the audience, Dr. Mikels was hanging on every word. His notes on the exchange read: "He displayed more emotional reactions this A.M. He was amused when Mr. Peck related about his being held up and having his Hudson car taken away, and when Mr. Peck said, 'He sure did know his business,' that seemed to bring a reaction. His countenance beamed."

Perhaps, but since the witness made no such comment, we are at liberty to question the doctor's assessment of Hickman's reaction.

The next witness was reporter Lionel Moise, from the *Illustrated Daily News*, called to describe his jailhouse interview with Edward on December 28. Moise recalled his effort to determine whether Ed was familiar with Freud or knew the psychiatric definition of "complex." As far as divine guidance went, Moise said, Hickman cited his tag line on the ransom letters—"If you want aid against me ask God, not man"—as evidence of his belief in omnipotent "Providence."

Another newsman, photographer George Watson, was next on the stand. He identified pictures he had taken at the morgue and which Walsh now introduced as evidence for the defense. It was a gamble, Walsh hoping that anyone who glimpsed Marian's mutilated corpse would think her killer insane. It could backfire, of course, perhaps hardening the jurors' hearts, but Walsh knew Asa Keyes would introduce the photographs if they were not produced by the defense. This way, at least, Walsh had a chance—however slim—of staging a preemptive strike.

Hickman may have felt the moment turn against him, as the photos passed from hand to hand. Dr. Mikels, watching from the audience, observed that "an expression of suppressed anxiety came over his face when the jury was reviewing the photographs." When everyone had seen the gruesome black-and-whites, George Watson was excused and Judge Trabucco called the noon recess. The jurors filed out silently, a number of them pale and shaken, clearly having lost their appetite for lunch.

When court resumed at 2:00 P.M., Ed's brother Alfred took the witness stand. Cantillon used Alfred's testimony to buttress the Arkansas depositions, providing firsthand descriptions of the odd behavior that marked the Buck family. Grandpa Paul emerged as a religious zealot whose profane, violent outbursts suggested a disintegrating mind. "He would slap his hands," Alfred testified, "and his facial expressions were not what the ordinary person['s] would be in a case of that sort." As for Grandma Rebecca, Alfred could only say that "she was always ill."

Alfred went on to describe his father's desertion of the family, his mother's black moods. "At times," he told the court, "I would think she was insane." Edward's slide into mental illness was traceable to his junior year at Central, as evidenced by falling grades, resignation from once-beloved clubs, and the new, inexplicable distance between Ed and Alfred. By the fall of 1927, Alfred said, when Edward returned from Los Angeles, "the changes I noticed were such that caused me to be very worried." At that, he didn't know the worst of it. Alfred had no idea his younger brother was a murderer.

On cross-examination, Forrest Murray tried to minimize the Buck strain of weirdness. Alfred admitted that his grandfather had never been arrested and had never physically assaulted strangers.

"Did you think that he knew the difference between right and wrong?" Murray asked.

"At times," Alfred said, "I imagine, yes."

"Do you think there was any time when he *did not* know the difference between right and wrong, that you remember of?"

"If he would act like that," Alfred replied, "he evidently didn't know the difference between right and wrong."

"Well," Murray prodded, "what did he ever do that you thought was not right?"

"Well, to treat anyone like that—demean his relatives like that—fall into swearing spells, beat animals."

As for his brother, Murray noted, "You think, in your opinion, that Edward is insane to such a degree that he does not appreciate the difference between right and wrong?"

"I don't think he knows the difference between right and wrong, no."

"You don't think he does," Murray replied, "and you base that opinion on what you have related to us today, of what you observed of him after he was in his senior year, and after he came back from out here in California?"

"Yes," Alfred said, "and on other things I could relate to you, if you so desire."

The last thing Murray wanted was further examples. "When did you first become of the opinion," he asked, "that Edward did not know the difference between right and wrong?"

"I cannot say just exactly when," Alfred answered. "I noticed right at the end—or during his senior year in high school, and all the other times in which I have seen him—I noticed he was very different, and I noticed—a man who would be so irritable to his friends and showing so much change in his nature in a very short time, there was something wrong with him. And when he would come and tell me, as he has, some things he has done which we consider wrong, and he did not think it was wrong, I perhaps made up my mind he did not know what was right or wrong."

Above all else, Alfred was convinced that his brother had been crazy when he murdered Marian Parker. Apparent rationality and obvious premeditation did nothing to change Alfred's mind on that score. "I think as long as he wanted to do that," Alfred said, "he did not think it was wrong, because he did it."

"You think," Murray challenged him, "if there had been a policeman there in the car with him and went up to the school with him, do you think he would have done the same thing?"

"Probably not in the presence of a policeman," Alfred admitted, "and then, he might have. I don't know."

"You know the difference, do you not," Murray pressed on, "the difference of *knowing* what is right and wrong and the difference of *caring* what is right and wrong? Are you sure you do not mean he did not *care* whether it was right or wrong or not, instead of *knowing* whether it was right or wrong or not?"

"Everything he did," Alfred said, "he made up in his own mind that he was doing it—"

Murray cut him off. "Read the question to him, Mr. Reporter."

Once the question was repeated, Alfred tried again. "I do not think there was any great difference between [knowing and caring about right or wrong]," he said. "They are both the result of a man's own thinking."

"You think they are just the same, whether a man *cares* whether it is right or wrong, or whether he *knows* whether it is right or wrong? You think they are just the same?"

"Not identically, no," Alfred conceded. "They are not exactly the same."

"Do you think Edward *cared* whether it was right or wrong, or whether he *knew* it was right or wrong?" Murray demanded.

Alfred tried to explain. "I think he knew that—that is, I do not think he knew whether he was doing right or wrong and, of course, it did not make any difference what he was doing, as far as caring was concerned."

"There is no doubt in your mind he did not care whether it was right or wrong?" Murray asked, twisting Alfred's reply.

"As long as he did not *know* whether it was right or wrong," Alfred insisted, "it did not make any difference whether he cared or not."

"You do not think he did care whether it was right or wrong, do you?"

"He must not have," Alfred acknowledged, "if he did not think it was wrong."

The jury was well acquainted with Bill Hickman by the time he followed his son to the witness stand that Thursday morning. Ostensibly called to help Edward, the elder Hickman often seemed more intent on defending himself. Rebecca Buck had been insane, he testified, while her husband "was rational, although he was very peculiar in some ways."

Richard Cantillon wanted details. "When you state that he was very peculiar in some ways—"

"Any little thing go wrong," Hickman interrupted, "he was awfully nervous and excitable, and he would feel mad and just have what we always called mad fits. I have seen him throw down his hat, jump on it and stomp it, pull his hair, and fight the stock around the place something awful. And different occasions I have seen him—one time I remember, he was working on a plow out on the farm. He could not get the plow set just to suit him, and he throwed it down and jumped on it with his feet and stomped it and swore, and just had what we always termed mad fits."

Paul suffered those "mad fits" twice a month, on average, Hickman said, depending on "whatever came up to bother the old man's mind." Paul had been "pretty well fixed in his young days," Bill testified, until an uncle cheated him out of some $30,000 and fled with the money to Germany. In Hickman's view, "He never did seem to get over that entirely." In fact, it was "about all he talked about. He would express himself very much about the hardships, you know, and how the work was so hard and how if the uncle had not done that way he would probably have had an easier life."

Eva was also insane, Bill told the court. "Just shortly after we were married, she began [acting] just like her mother." Eva "always had a horror of children, giving birth to children, and married relations—such as sexual relations—she always had a horror of that. That was her one great fault that she always had to me, that I wasn't of the same nature she was. Of course," Hickman added, "I was just like any other man."

As Eva's condition degenerated, Bill said, she would often threaten him or the children. "I had her stand up many, many times, stand up and look me in the face and tell me she [would] just rejoice to see me cut to pieces. It seemed like that was all she ever had on her mind, is to cut somebody up."

Having Eva committed to the Little Rock asylum wasn't *his* idea, Bill swore. Rather, local doctors had confronted him "during one of her worst spells," and insisted on committing her, over Bill's objections. On his third visit to the hospital, he explained, Eva had "begged so hard to go home, and made all kinds of promises what she would do," that Hickman had reluctantly agreed to her release. Things went from bad to worse after that, despite constant surveillance. Eva seemed fine with the children while Bill was at work, "but just as soon as I came home, why she would start throwing things at them and swearing [that] she was going to kill them and going to kill me, and all that kind of stuff." At last, Bill said, his family insisted that he move away for the good of the children and Hickman agreed, bailing out with the clothes on his back and $125 skimmed from the family's $400 bank account.

Eva's pregnancy with Edward, Bill recalled, was "the worst of her whole life. . . . She was worse during that nine months than she ever had been previous, or after that, although from then on, at different times after that, she was awfully bad—that is, in the way of keeping me uneasy all the time about her unusual threats, and during the time of his conception [*sic*] was the worst of all. I will never forget it."

Asa Keyes was ready for Hickman on cross-examination. "How long after you left home," the D.A. asked, "did you continue to support any of your family?"

Bill thought about it. "Well," he replied, "I guess it was about two months, or a month and a half."

"When did you first notice any symptoms of insanity in your wife?" Keyes inquired.

"Well, I knew there was something wrong with her all the time," Bill said, "but I could not get it in my head that she was insane up until we had been living together—up until after our second child was born."

"When was that?"

"Well, I would say about six years."

It seemed that Bill had a problem with dates. As Keyes brought out through questioning, Bill and Eva had been married in 1900; their first child was born in 1901 and the second in 1903.

Keyes tried again. "Now, how soon after your marriage was it that you commenced to notice that Mrs. Hickman was afflicted, as you have described it to us?"

"Just about a month and a half or two months after we were married," Bill answered, changing his story again.

"That condition apparently grew worse, did it not?"

"When she found out that she was conceived [*sic*]," Hickman said.

"And that condition apparently grew worse," Keyes repeated, "did it not?"

"It grew worse right along, all the time," Bill agreed.

"From year to year?"

"Yes, sir."

It was time to drop the bomb. "Well, now, Mr. Hickman," Keyes said, "you at one time had her placed in an institution back there, didn't you?"

"Yes, sir."

"That was in 1913?"

"Yes."

"And do you remember making a statement . . . concerning her condition when you got the warrant for her arrest on this charge?"

"I did not get no warrant for her arrest," Hickman said. "I did not make any statement. The doctors did all that."

"Well," Keyes suggested, "didn't you make a statement at the time these insanity papers were taken out?"

"No, sir."

"You made no statement at all?"

"No, sir, never made any statement," Bill insisted. "The doctors came to me and told me she would have to go. She was too dangerous to leave her there."

Keyes sprang the trap, producing a copy of Defendant's Exhibit D, titled "Statement by: W. T. Hickman, husband," from 1913, in which Bill swore that his "first indication" of Eva's mental problems "was about two months ago."

"I don't remember," Hickman groused. "I might have told the doctors that. They knew it as well as I did, though, because they had all had a round at her."

"It was shortly after you were married, within a year, or two years at least," Keyes said, "that you made up your mind that Mrs. Hickman was wrong mentally. Is that true?"

"No, I did not say that." Contradicting himself once more.

"What *did* you say?" asked Keyes.

"I said she acted queer," Bill answered, "but I did not think there was anything wrong with her mind. I just thought it was—I did not suspicion that her mind was wrong until she started to threaten to kill me and make the attempts to kill me."

He had thrust his head into the second noose.

"Well, isn't it a fact, Mr. Hickman," Keyes said, "that you simply thought that it was the natural worrying of a woman who was being treated by a husband as you treated her?"

"I always treated her the best I could," Bill said.

"Have you read these depositions that have been given in evidence here?" Keyes asked.

"No, sir, and I don't care nothing about the depositions. I know how I treated her."

"Now, didn't you consider, Mr. Hickman, that your wife's condition and her actions were the natural response to the treatment which you accorded her?" Keyes asked, tightening the noose.

"No, sir."

"You did not?"

"No, sir! I always treated her the best I could," Bill insisted. "I supported her and stayed with her and done the best I could with her."

"You know, don't you," Keyes challenged, "that it was the common repute around the neighborhood where you were living, there, that you were running around with other women and neglecting your wife and children?"

"Well, I can't help that," Bill said.

"Well, isn't it a fact that you know that it was common repute, that you were doing that?"

"No, I don't know that it was."

"You don't know whether it was common repute or not, but it was a fact—"

"No," Bill interrupted, "I was just an average man."

"Wait until I ask the question," Keyes instructed. "It is a fact, isn't it, Mr. Hickman, that during all your married life with Mrs. Eva Hickman, and during the time she was conceiving and rearing these children for you, that you were neglecting her and chasing around with other women?"

"No, sir."

"You deny that?"

"I will explain that, if you will give me a chance."

"All right, explain it," Keyes said. "I have no objection to you explaining it."

"That was her condition," Bill said, "the state of mind she was in. She was all the time running around amongst the other neighbors, the other women, telling them the great things about me, but I was just like any other man. I done the best I could. I do not say that I was an angel. I was just like anybody else, but I did not neglect her. The neighborhood women was all good to us. They all seemed like they was sorry for me and sorry for us, and every one of them, every neighbor, expressed a little sympathy, in a way, for me, and she got hold of it and she started to raving and would say I was running after that woman. It was a little country town, and you know how it is around these little country towns: if you even say 'How do you do?' to a woman and treat her kind, someone else sees it and they go running and talk about you. It is not like it is in a place like this. That is about the sum and substance of it. I did the best I could for the family, and anybody who directly knows the circumstances will have to tell you the same."

"You think," Keyes said, "you were doing the best you could for her and for the family when you packed up and left Hartford, Arkansas, and moved down to New Mexico?"

"I do, for a fact," Bill fired back, "and it has proven since that I did, because after I left her she did fairly well for the children, and she was a lot better after that than she was when I was with them."

Another trap. "Right after you left she became sane, didn't she," Keyes asked, "and was all right in her mental condition?"

"No, sir," Bill reversed himself again. "She is not all right yet."

"She is not all right today?"

"Only just at times."

"Do you want to tell this jury, Mr. Hickman, that you deserted that insane woman with five children?"

Cantillon objected to that "as being a degrading question," but Judge Trabucco overruled him.

"I didn't desert her," Bill whined, as if two months of child support in eleven years constituted a great sacrifice.

Dr. Mikels, scribbling in the audience, wrote down: "Disgust. [Hickman] appeared concerned when his father testified. He stared at him and then suppressed an expression of disgust at his father's pseudo-pathetic recitation of his marital infidelity." Mikels did not explain how he was able to detect "suppressed" expressions.

Eva Hickman's testimony, following her ex-husband's, was relatively brief, almost anticlimactic. Discussion of her family was limited to a single question about Otto Buck's epilepsy. Her protracted labor with Edward, culminating in his stillbirth, was disposed of in three short questions from Richard Cantillon. As far as mental illness was concerned, Eva professed to have no memory of "anything" before she was committed to the Little Rock asylum. In response to other questions, though, it seemed some memories of Bill and their tumultuous marriage had survived.

"Now, at the time prior to Edward's birth," Cantillon said, "from the time of conception up to the time of his birth, how did you and Mr. Hickman get along then?"

"We didn't get along at all," Eva replied. "We very frequently quarreled, and I didn't—I took a great dislike against him. The fact of the business [is], I really hated him."

"And did that condition continue, Mrs. Hickman?"

"Yes, sir."

"For how long a period of time?"

"Oh, mostly all the time when he was present."

Unlike the other witnesses before her, Eva said she had first noted that Edward was "different" in the summer of 1927, after he returned from Los Angeles on probation. At that time, she told the court, Ed "didn't seem to care for me like he always had, and he was restless. He never seemed to know what he wanted to do."

Asa Keyes had no questions for the witness, and she was excused. Dr. Mikels watched Ed's face and wrote: "Sorrow. When his mother appeared on the witness stand his upper eyelids drooped. A mask of gloom and [profound] dejection and depression covered his face. This expression of profound sorrow and chagrin continued for the rest of the afternoon. His lips quivered and then became set for the rest of the session. When his mother said, 'He is my son[,]' his upper lids drooped, and this is one of the emotional reactions to sorrow, grief. The upper lids drooped and the face has the expression of grief and sorrow. If you have ever seen one of these faces you can't forget it. . . . He was almost overwhelmed by the ordeal."

Dr. J. M. Fettes followed Eva to the stand, reciting his credentials for Richard Cantillon before they got down to cases. Fettes had found Edward "a little retarded in thinking and answering," but still managed to elicit his family history. Ed's face was "expressionless," and he complained of severe headaches dating back to 1925. Fettes had finally diagnosed Edward as suffering from serous meningitis.

Forrest Murray opened his cross-examination with a motion to strike the doctor's testimony as "incompetent, irrelevant and immaterial, having no bearing on the issues of this case," but Judge Trabucco denied the motion. Forging ahead, Murray tried to cast doubt on the doctor's professional competency.

"How many people have you examined professionally, Doctor," he asked, "in the course of your profession, that have been suffering from mental diseases—that is, insane people?" Before Fettes could answer, Murray told the bench, "We will withdraw the question."

"Question withdrawn," the judge echoed.

But Murray was not finished yet. "The doctor has not stated on direct examination, Mr. Keyes says, that he examined *anybody* that was troubled with mental disease, so I will withdraw the question."

Richard Cantillon bristled at Murray's remark to the jury. "I don't think the doctor heard your question, Mr. Murray," he said.

Murray shrugged it off. "Well, we will withdraw the question."

Fettes had moved to Los Angeles from a small town in Iowa in early 1927. "What has your practice been devoted to since you have been out here?" Murray asked him.

"I have not been doing very much of anything," Fettes said. "I am a stranger here. I came out here with a purpose in mind, and I have been waiting to see if I could get to do what I wanted to do." He had an office on South Western Avenue, but no patients. Murray challenged his meningitis diagnosis, but the jurors seemed lost amid references to dermascopic examinations, epigastric reflexes, and Koernic signs. It was a visible relief to all concerned when Dr. Fettes was excused.

Thursday's last witness was Dr. R. O. Shelton. After yet another recitation of credentials, Walsh cut to the chase. Shelton had examined the defendant five times. "Did you," Walsh asked, "as a result of those examinations and observations that you made, come to any opinion with reference to his mental condition?"

"I did," Shelton replied.

"Will you kindly state to the jury, Doctor, what that opinion is?"

"He is suffering from dementia praecox," Shelton said, "one of the worst types of insanity. He has one of the worst forms of this type. It is the paranoia type with delusions of grandeur. It is technically known as megalomania. He is a megalomaniac."

It was "a little hard" to explain Ed's condition, Shelton told the court, but he tried his best, walking the jury through definitions of dementia, catatonia, paranoia, and schizophrenia. His monologue had filled eight transcript pages by the time Judge Trabucco interrupted to ask, "Are you practically through, Doctor?"

"No," Shelton replied.

"He is just getting a good start, Your Honor," Asa Keyes chimed in.

"It will take me three hours to get through," Shelton told the judge.

Trabucco seemed incredulous. "You mean to say it will take you three hours?"

"At least three hours to get through this explanation," Shelton said. "Two hours, at least."

"Three or four hours," Keyes suggested from the prosecution table.

"This is a very difficult subject," Shelton said.

It was too much for Trabucco, and court was adjourned for the day. Shelton would have another chance to educate the jury on Friday morning.

The psychiatric testimony seemed to trouble Hickman, at least from the viewpoint of his constant observer in the gallery. On Friday, Dr. Mikels wrote: "The evidence of the alienists [psychiatrists] is giving him great concern. An expression of anxiety. A few casual glances at him reveal a face pallid and motionless, as if his mind is preoccupied by his reactions to fright. He appears scared to death."

The jurors, meanwhile, seemed more in danger of being bored to death, as Dr. Shelton resumed his lecture on catatonia, automatism ("it is unexplainable"), stereotypy, and negativism, slowly working his way back around to dementia praecox. In cases like Hickman's, the doctor declared, victims of "premature" dementia believe themselves controlled and directed by some outside force or intellect. "They will seize upon the silliest facts to boost up their argument," he advised, "and they will resent the soundness of argument which is against their belief."

He did not mean to say, however, that demented persons always *looked* crazy. "Even when the emotions appear gone, perverted down to their lowest ebb," Shelton said, "sometimes they will retain intellectual faculties." In fact, he told the court, "The ordinary people talk to them and thinks they are queer, cranks, but they ordinarily talk—if you keep them off their delusions—the people generally, their associates, think that they are all right." It was not explained how a person could appear "all right" while simultaneously acting "queer."

After droning through more definitions—of "orientation," "emotion," and "reaction"—Dr. Shelton raised the subject of Edward's statement on "Providence," which he had written in jail. Walsh sought to introduce the rambling diatribe as evidence, but Keyes instantly objected.

"I don't want to take up the time to read it all, Your Honor," Keyes said, "but I have read the first page and I object to it on the ground that it is incompetent, self-serving."

Walsh replied, "It is a statement and declaration of the defendant, Your Honor."

"Well, it can't be admitted in evidence," Keyes fired back, "if the court please, a statement of that kind, any more than he can get up and tell this jury that he is insane."

"It is as competent to introduce in evidence as the confession, Mr. Keyes," Walsh replied.

"Well, we will leave that to the court," the D.A. said. "A man hasn't any right, after he is accused of a crime or after he has been incarcerated in jail for a few days or weeks, to come in and write down a lot of tommyrot for the benefit of the jury."

"He wrote down the confession," Walsh reminded Keyes.

A rap of the gavel ended their exchange. "No argument, gentlemen," Judge Trabucco ordered. "Objection sustained."

Frustrated, Walsh walked Dr. Shelton through his conversations with Hickman, picking out questions and answers that alluded to Ed's guiding "Providence." At one point, Shelton noted, "He said that if he could talk to Mr. Keyes, that in a few days that Providence would turn him over and make him his friend."

Keyes glanced up from his notes. "What was that?"

"He said if he could talk with you for a few days," Dr. Shelton repeated, "that you would be his friend."

"Well," Keyes replied, "that is the first sign of delusion you have given us."

On cross-examination, Keyes hammered away at Dr. Shelton's diagnosis, quoting psychiatric texts to contradict his report, but Shelton stood fast. "This boy is incurable," he told the court.

"He is incurable?"

"Incurable," Shelton confirmed. "No chance to get well. Deteriorated now."

"How is that?" Keyes asked.

"Deteriorated now," Dr. Shelton repeated.

"Do you think, Doctor, if this boy had appeared before you and you were sitting on a lunacy board, that you would have diagnosed his case as you have before this jury and recommended that he be confined in an institution?"

"I would have sent him up in the first thirty minutes," Shelton said.

"Isn't it true," Keyes asked, "that [in] all cases of dementia praecox the patient is rather silly and childish?"

"No, it is not true."

"You were in the jail there and talked with the defendant for the purpose of trying to help him out of his trouble, weren't you?" Keyes challenged.

"No, sir," Shelton replied. "I was in the jail to make a diagnosis, and I aided the doctor—or tried to aid your alienist. I got them in and introduced them, or one of them. No, sir."

"Isn't it true you stated a moment ago," Keyes said, "in your opinion this defendant developed this form of insanity when he was about twelve years of age?"

"That was the beginning of it," Shelton said. "I don't know whether he was actually insane. That was the beginning of that autochthonous idea."

"What do you mean, Doctor, by the term 'malingering'? How do you define the term?" Keyes asked.

"Malingering?"

"Yes."

"Pretending," Shelton said.

"Pretending?"

"Simulation."

"Do you think," Keyes asked, "that a patient who was malingering could deceive you?"

"Well," Shelton replied, "I do not believe a case of dementia praecox could. I would not say that I am infallible. I do not want— We are all fallible. I don't *know* that I am in this court, but I *believe* I am here."

Keyes looked incredulous. "You don't know that you are here?"

"No," Shelton said. "I *believe* I am in this courtroom, but I may be mistaken."

"Is that so?"

"Yes."

"Well," Keyes said, "that is somewhat of a delusion, isn't it?"

"It might be," Shelton agreed.

"You have delusions yourself?" the D.A. asked.

"It might be that is a delusion," Shelton said. "I do not believe it is. I think I am perfectly sane."

Keyes saw his opening and took it. "Don't you believe, Doctor, that you might have had some delusions with reference to your statement that this man has dementia praecox?"

"I do not believe so, but that is my opinion," Shelton said. "That is my honest opinion after a close, careful examination."

"In line with your reasoning," Keyes said, "you might be mistaken about that. You believe it, but it might not be true?"

"I might be mistaken about anything," Shelton said.

"*What?*" Too good to be true.

"I might be mistaken about anything," the doctor repeated.

Keyes could not suppress a smile. "Oh, I suppose, Doctor," he pressed on, "I might question you here for two or three days, which I am not going to do, and you would still hold the same opinion that you believe this defendant to be suffering from dementia praecox, but you might be mistaken. That is true, isn't it?"

"Well, that is my opinion now," Shelton replied. "I don't know what it would be three days from now."

"You don't know what your opinion would be three days from now?"

"No."

"Well, I guess that's all," Keyes told him, looking satisfied.

It was a less than stellar performance, and Walsh hoped to repair some of the damage when he called Dr. Skoog to the stand. The witness was well into his description of Edward's "very definite delusional idea" of divine guidance when Walsh noticed Dr. Reynolds and Dr. Mikels chuckling in the audience.

"If Your Honor please," Walsh interrupted Skoog, "just a minute, Doctor. I regret to have to state to the court what I have to state now, Your Honor. I think the conduct of certain doctors in this courtroom is both reprehensible and unprofessional, and I ask Your Honor, if they still persist in these smirks and laughs, that they be excluded from this courtroom."

Indignantly, Keyes replied, "I have not noticed anything of that kind, Your Honor, on the part of anyone, and I think that remark of counsel is entirely uncalled for and was made for effect."

"If there is anything of that kind going on," Judge Trabucco said, "it will not be permitted."

"I have not seen anything of that kind," Keyes insisted.

Wrapping up his diagnosis moments later, Dr. Skoog told the court that "in addition to [an] abnormal ego and this almost perfectly systematized delusion which I have indicated, we also have definite evidence of a split personality. We psychiatrists use the term schizophrenia, or the adjective schizophrenic."

"Doctor," Walsh said, "is this disease an inherited one?"

"Yes," Skoog answered. "Decidedly."

"Decidedly so?"

"Yes. We can find definite heredity in at least eighty or ninety percent of the cases, if we search thoroughly and our diagnosis is correct."

"Generally, from what type of parent may this disease be traced, Doctor?"

"Where mental disorders have been in evidence among the ancestors, and closer ancestors," Skoog replied, "you will more likely find feeblemindedness and manic depressive psychosis. I believe that they are more often found in the mother, and more likely to express themselves as dementia praecox in the offspring—and especially in the male offspring."

Dr. Skoog had just drawn a perfect word sketch of Ed's family. Over time, he went on, such afflicted male offspring predictably suffered a declining intelligence and general dissolution of personality.

There was an instant spark of antagonism between Dr. Skoog and Asa Keyes on cross-examination. "Doctor,"

Keyes began, "you have testified in a great many criminal cases, haven't you, on matters concerning the mental condition of defendants?"

"'A great many' is not a very accurate term," Skoog replied.

"Well, on a few, then?"

"Probably *quite* a few," Skoog said, as if that were somehow more precise.

"Did you have your mind made up before you got here that this man was insane?" Keyes asked.

"No," Skoog said, "not positively."

"But you had some ideas about the subject?"

"I had some conception."

"And you got those ideas from what you had read in the papers concerning this case, didn't you?"

"No, sir," Skoog replied.

"From what you had heard from others?"

"From what I had heard from Mr. Walsh," the doctor said, "my interrogation of the mother in Kansas City before she came out here, and from a certain picture that I saw."

"That is the picture of the body of the deceased girl?" Keyes asked.

"Yes, sir. Mr. Walsh showed me that."

Skoog agreed with Walsh that brutal murderers were "not necessarily" insane, but still believed the mutilation of Marian Parker "most likely . . . was the product or the results or conduct coming from an abnormal mind." Such dissection *might* have been committed in an effort to conceal the corpse, Skoog granted, but the willful scattering of body parts suggested that the killer was "more likely insane."

"Are you familiar with [German psychiatrist Emil] Kraepelin?" Keyes asked.

"Yes, sir," Skoog replied. "I met and talked to Kraepelin, and I have his original textbook, written in the German language."

"Well," Keyes said, "that wouldn't do me any good, because I can't read German."

"It does me," Skoog said. "I would rather read the original than the translation."

"You are very fortunate," Keyes said, before switching abruptly to the subject of Hickman's "fixed delusion" of his own supernatural abilities. Skoog believed Edward's statement that his every action, up to and including the murder of Marian Parker had been carried out at the direction of his guiding "Providence," whereas his early claim of kidnapping for cash had been a lie.

"He said he lied originally?" Keyes challenged.

"Some," Skoog said, "yes, sir."

"Well, you chose to believe, then, that he did lie originally, did you, and that he was telling you the truth when he told you that he committed this crime in response to a divine command?"

"Yes, sir."

"Well, didn't you think he might have been lying to you at that time?"

"I considered that seriously," Skoog replied, "but I do not believe he was."

"You know that people do malinger?" Keyes challenged.

"They do," Skoog agreed.

"Don't you think it is a strange fact, Doctor, that these people who are afflicted with paranoia—or who claim to be afflicted with paranoia, in the paranoid type, or any other type—are never caught, never found, until after they have committed some crime? Isn't that a rather peculiar thing, in your judgment?"

"Well," Skoog said, "that seems to me a rather absurd question."

"It does, huh?"

"Yes."

"Well, let's see if you can give an absurd answer to it," Keyes sneered.

"I refuse to give an absurd answer," Skoog replied. "I do not think I am sworn to do that."

"Well, what is there absurd about this question?" Keyes demanded.

"In the first place," Skoog said, "they must commit crime to be under the suspicion of the law and are caught for the crime. Therefore, they *must* commit the crime. That is the absurdity of the question."

"Don't you think, Doctor, and isn't it your belief, that if this man Hickman had not come out here and committed this crime and been caught, that he could have gone along all his life and never been suspected, even of having dementia praecox or any other form of insanity?"

"No, I believe not," the doctor replied. "I believe sooner or later some other crime would have involved him with the law, so that he would have been under the same suspicion, and the diagnosis made sooner or later."

When Keyes began to read from yet another psychiatric text, Skoog challenged his pronunciation. "You used a term there, earlier: 'catonic.' I am not acquainted with that," he said.

"Catatonic," Keyes corrected.

"Catatonic?"

"Yes."

"It is stated there—you said 'catonic,' I believe," Skoog chided him.

"*Catatonic*," Keyes insisted. "You may not have heard the second syllable, but I pronounced it 'catatonic.' "

Fairly steaming, the D.A. asked Skoog, "Now, did it ever strike you, Doctor, that while you were examining the defendant in the county jail he might be malingering?"

"Yes, I considered that," Skoog said.

"But you came to the conclusion that he was not?"

"That is correct."

"Well, I suppose if the defendant had told you—if you had asked him what he thought the moon was made of and he had answered he thought it was made of green cheese, you would have put that down as an evidence of insanity, wouldn't you?"

"No," Skoog insisted, "I would not."

"You would have thought he was malingering and trying to fool you?"

"No, not necessarily."

"Well, what reaction *would* you have got to such an answer to such a question?"

"Well, possibly that he was trying to spoof me."

"You were absolutely sold to the idea that this defendant was acting fairly with you?" Keyes said.

"No, I wasn't sold," Skoog replied.

"Well, you believe it?"

"I believe it."

The defense rested with Dr. Skoog's testimony, and following a fifteen-minute recess, Forrest Murray called handwriting expert J. Clark Sellers as the prosecution's first witness. Through Sellers, the various ransom letters were introduced and read to the jury, Jerome Walsh stipulating for the defense that his client had indeed penned the letters.

Next up for the state, still smarting from Walsh's verbal wristslap, Dr. Cecil Reynolds took the witness stand. His credentials, Reynolds told the court, included twenty-nine published articles and operations performed on "hundreds" of brains.

"Doctor," Asa Keyes began, "I wish you would state to the court and the jury, from the examinations that you have made of this defendant, whether or not in your opinion this defendant is sane or insane."

"Sane," Reynolds replied. More to the point, he said, Ed had been sane on December 17, when he murdered Marian Parker. Clearly a religious man, the doctor could not seem to resist explaining Hickman's crime in biblical terms.

"It has been suggested," he said, "in the depositions particularly, that the fiendish nature of the crime is to be considered by itself suggestive of insanity. Well, now, what is the fiendish nature of this crime? It is exaggerated conduct in an infamous direction. And if exaggerated conduct in an infamous direction is a sign of insanity, then exaggerated conduct in an altruistic direction also must be a sign of insanity. So Jesus Christ, who died for the world upon the cross, must necessarily have been insane, and that is certainly not the belief of the vast majority of people in the United States, at all events."

It was a unique approach—if Jesus was sane, so must be Edward Hickman—but the doctor wasn't finished yet. He also had a warning for the jury. "If to make a crime horrible is to make it excusable," he cautioned, "then all you have got to do is to make crimes more and more horrible, to escape punishment, and what would be the state of society under those conditions?"

The sermonette complete, Reynolds began reading at length from his interview notes—a tactic forbidden on Judge Trabucco's orders to the two defense psychiatrists while they were testifying—careful to include his gibes about vivisection and Hickman's evident lack of humanity. As for his physical examination of the subject, Reynolds found "all responses unusually snappy." Ed displayed no fatigue or stress and seemed to possess "an intelligence above the average of adult patients." Overall, Reynolds concluded, Hickman's "brain is evidently of very tough fiber." At one point in their dialogue, Reynolds alleged, he had apologized to Edward for planning to testify against him—a display of sympathy at odds with every other statement Reynolds made, unless it was intended as a form of mockery. According to the doctor, Hickman had replied, "I don't blame you a bit. I'm as sane as you are. You are quite right to do as you are doing." Moments later, Reynolds claimed, Hickman added, "I can't figure out why I have no remorse." The statement prompted Reynolds to jot down another note: "Cry of a lost soul."

On cross-examination by Jerome Walsh, Dr. Reynolds grudgingly admitted that he had asked Ed no questions about his family background, preferring to skim the defense depositions after his examination of the patient was concluded. Reynolds had dismissed reports of Eva Hickman's confinement to an asylum as "mere hearsay" and "absolutely immaterial" to Edward's case. No background investigation was needed, Reynolds told Walsh, since Hickman's sanity "is obvious from the patient himself," while heredity was merely "a slight, indefinite element" in diagnosing dementia praecox.

Producing an article that Reynolds himself had written for the *Southern California Practitioner*, Walsh asked, "Do you remember what you said about dementia praecox in there, Doctor?"

"No," Reynolds answered, "I haven't the least idea."

"Then, if this statement is in there, you did not make it, I take it: 'I believe that dementia praecox is an atavistic disease.'"

"Yes," Reynolds said.

"You made that statement?"

"Yes."

"Now, just exactly explain to us what you mean by atavistic," Walsh said.

"Atavistic disease? Oh, stocks degenerating," Reynolds said.

"Stocks degenerating?"

"Yes."

"Doctor, if you made that statement at this time, don't you think that you should have made some investigation of this defendant's heredity before you came to any conclusion with reference to him?"

"I did," Dr. Reynolds replied.

"You did?"

"Yes, sir."

"Which did you do, Doctor? Did you or did you not make two conflicting statements?"

"No, sir. I told you I had evidence before, from Mr. Murray."

"First you stated that you did not want to take hearsay; then you state you spoke to Mr. Murray about it, and then you did make an investigation. Just explain to the jury what you *did* do."

"I have said—and I have not contradicted myself once—that I got as much valuable history from Mr. Murray as there was."

"The first time that you went to examine this patient, Doctor, you had your mind pretty well made up as to what you were going to find, didn't you?"

"I did not," Reynolds insisted.

"Well, I refer to your own questions and answers, then. They showed that you were making notes. They were certainly used to bear out some theory that you had when you started."

"You say so?" Reynolds challenged.

"I think I can show you, Doctor," Walsh said, "if I may see your notes."

"Well, I am afraid the reporter has taken them," Reynolds said, with a helpless gesture.

"Well, you can bring them tomorrow," Walsh told him. "I don't suppose we will be through, Doctor."

As Walsh began to quiz Reynolds on the published symptoms of dementia praecox, the doctor balked at giving any answer, dismissing the questions as "meaningless" and "a jumble of nonsense."

"Well, Doctor," Walsh challenged, "isn't the symptomology of this disease quite apparent to an intellectual medical man?"

"Oh, yes. I think he—"

"Well, will you answer my question, then?"

"Which question?"

"The question I just propounded to you."

"I say it is a jumble of nonsense. It was simply words, and meant nothing."

"Then if I should put that question to you—"

"In plain language," Reynolds requested.

"—as Mr. Rosanoff puts it in his book, would you still maintain it was a jumble of nonsense?"

"I would," Reynolds sneered. "I have heard Rosanoff talk nonsense before now."

"Well, Doctor, then, would this be a symptom of dementia praecox: 'Delayed appearance of intellectual disorders proper and their less marked intensity.' Is that meaningless, Doctor?"

"Yes," Reynolds said. "It has no constellation."

"That is absolutely and utterly meaningless to you, is that right?"

"There is no reference, no context," Reynolds said, "in relation to what it is—a dog, or a cat, or what."

"You know perfectly well we are talking about a human being here, don't you?"

"No, I don't," Reynolds stubbornly insisted. "You did not say so."

"Well, what are you, a veterinar[ian] or a doctor?" Walsh fumed.

"I beg your pardon?"

Walsh ordered the question read back.

"I think that remark is uncalled for," Reynolds said, stiffly.

"Well, you asked me if I meant an animal, Doctor. You know as well as I do that we are talking about the human beings."

"The difficulty," Reynolds said, "was that you pick out a sentence there without any context, and therefore it could not have any reference or any meaning."

"I am picking out the symptoms of dementia praecox, Doctor."

Judge Trabucco had heard enough for one day. His gavel fell, interrupting the verbal brawl, and court was adjourned.

Reynolds was back for round two on Saturday morning, looking rested after his first skirmish with Walsh. In the audience, his colleague Dr. Mikels was still jotting down notes. That morning, he found Edward "very pallid. The nerve strain of the trial and the confinement in jail is telling on him. He has the characteristic prison pallor."

Walsh resumed where he had left off on Friday, reading symptoms of dementia praecox from the Rosanoff text and soliciting judgments from Reynolds as the doctor kept on ducking and weaving: "That question cannot be answered in its present form." "I can't answer that." "I can say nothing about that."

On another tack, Reynolds claimed he had "paid attention" to Edward's statements about Providence, but dismissed them as lies. At times, the increasingly bitter exchange took on elements of an Abbott and Costello routine:

> Q: Can you state there once where you discussed the defendant's alleged delusion with him?

A: It was not an alleged delusion.

Q: Well, can you show me there where you discussed it, whether it be an alleged delusion or not, with him?

A: Discussed what?

Q: His so-called delusion.

A: I did not call it a delusion.

Q: What did you call it?

A: Call what?

And so it went, Dr. Reynolds balanced on a tightrope between professional acumen and a pose of ignorance, Walsh striving in vain to elicit straight answers. He had dismissed the notion of Providence, Reynolds said, "tentatively at all events, after my first examination, but when he started talking about it deliberately in the second examination, when I was there, it was all humbug." Reynolds himself would never raise the subject, of course, because "suggestion is the worst way of getting at the truth."

Likewise on epilepsy: Reynolds considered the very name "an antique, obsolete term which was used in the days of profound ignorance of the cause of convulsions." Ed's convulsions in jail meant nothing to Reynolds, since "a great many of them froth at the mouth; in fact, most of them do."

"Have you ever seen a case where they fell to the ground and flopped around like a dead chicken?" Walsh asked.

Smiling, Reynolds answered, "Oh, they always fall to the ground whenever there is a loss of consciousness."

Did Otto Buck's convulsions sound like epilepsy?

"I cannot discuss a term that has absolutely no meaning to me," Reynolds replied.

"The term 'epilepsy' means nothing to you?"

"It means nothing to me, no."

Questioning Reynolds was a futile exercise. Even granting that dementia praecox represented atavistic regression "right back to the monkey," Dr. Reynolds still saw nothing in Hickman's background to suggest hereditary mental illness—assuming he agreed to recognize the term.

Dr. Paul Bowers was less pugnacious than Reynolds when he took the witness stand but no less committed to the state's case against Hickman. Based on four meetings with Edward, their conversation, and his physical examination of the subject, Bowers had no doubt the prisoner was sane. Ed's admission to Bowers that the notion of a guiding Providence "just came to me yesterday" wounded the defense, and it was left to Richard Cantillon to try to repair the damage on cross-examination.

Cantillon opened with another shot at Dr. Reynolds, quoting his definition of "mind"—"thought, experience, knowledge, will, as evidenced by conduct"—and asking if Bowers agreed. In response, Bowers hedged, first telling Cantillon, "I cannot say I understand that exactly," yet refusing to suggest that his colleague might be wrong.

"No, I would not say that," Bowers hastened to explain, "but from where I sat over there, with an occasional noise here in the courtroom—Dr. Reynolds talks quite rapidly. My memory may have failed me, and all. I cannot say that I can disagree or agree with it exactly. I don't know exactly what he said." When the original statement was repeated, Bowers grudgingly admitted, "No, that is not my definition of 'mind'; that is his definition."

Cantillon repeated the question: Was the definition of "mind" offered by Reynolds right or wrong? Bowers seemed flustered, demanding, "Well, now, say it again. You talk loudly, and there was a car went by. Give me a chance to think." By the fourth reading of the Reynolds definition, Bowers finally decided that "on the whole that is all right."

What about hereditary insanity?

"If the statements given in this case are correct and true," Bowers allowed, "I will say the young man is burdened with an unfortunate heredity." The doctor was even willing to admit a possible predisposition to insanity in Edward's case, although he staked his reputation on a finding that the threat had not been realized.

Quoting statistics on dementia praecox from the doctor's own published work, referring to a "hypothetical" youth whose life mirrored Hickman's in every detail, Cantillon won admissions from Bowers that insanity "might" be passed down to a child or grandchild . . . but not in Hickman's case. The boy was sane.

"Now, Doctor," Cantillon said, "at the time you made your diagnosis of this particular case, what was the date of that?"

"I made my diagnosis . . ." Bowers hesitated, perhaps sensing a trap. "Well, I did not make my diagnosis until after my examinations," he said. "In fact, until about yesterday I came to my conclusion. I made no report to the district attorney's office as to what I thought about it. They have never asked me, and I made no comment."

"So up until yesterday you had never made a diagnosis in this case?"

"No," Bowers said, "just thinking the thing over, mulling it around in my mind, trying to consider the whole situation."

"Now, Doctor," Cantillon said, "as a matter of fact, didn't you make a diagnosis of this case before you had ever seen the defendant?"

"I did not."

"Didn't you state in an interview to the newspapers that this was a sadistic murder?"

Bowers replied that he had been asked a "hypothetical question" by some unknown newsman and had responded accordingly. "Whether he quoted me accurately or not, I do not know." Cantillon was trying to elicit details of the question when Keyes intervened with an objection, noting that the newspaper interview had not been mentioned in direct examination, and was therefore out of bounds. Judge Trabucco agreed.

Moving on, Cantillon elicited admissions that Dr. Bowers had made no personal investigation of Edward's background, beyond a briefing by Deputy D.A. Forrest Murray. No spinal tap had been requested, Bowers said, because he found no evidence of physical disease. In terms of the much-discussed "skin writing," Bowers had found no evidence of dermatography at all.

Cantillon decided to repeat the experiment for the jury, securing permission for Edward to strip off his jacket and shirt. In the audience, Dr. Mikels watched and wrote: "Elation. When requested to strip off his clothes to have the dermatographia test made: Here was a situation when something was going to be put across that was going to make a favorable impression for him. He was elated. . . . The muscual [*sic*] actions and coordination in removing the clothes and walking did not evince any impairment of a brain functioning. Joy: He was slightly amused and elated by the performance. . . . His accurate cooperation is another manifestation of his defensive mechanisms or defensive action."

Approaching Hickman as he stood before the jury box, Dr. Bowers scratched a large *H* on his chest and another on his back. The marks flushed pink and were still visible three minutes later, though starting to fade. Rather than true dermatography, Bowers said, Hickman displayed "diffused erythema" (inflammation of the skin). "I say that is not a typical dermatography," Bowers told the court. "There is *some* dermatography, but it is not marked."

Looking for any concession at all, Cantillon said, "Now, in your testimony prior to this you said he had none, did you not?"

"Yes," Bowers replied.

"So you were mistaken?"

"No, sir. I will not admit that. You may have erythema one day, and the next day you may not. I have myself sometimes been subject to hives." On his first examination, Bowers insisted, Edward had displayed no such symptoms at all.

Sidestepping to Dr. Shelton's earlier detailed listing of primary and secondary emotions, Cantillon said, "Now, Doctor, will you enumerate the emotions, as you know them? State them for me."

"Emotions?"

"Yes, emotions."

"Well," Bowers said, sounding confused, "hate, anger."

"What kind of an emotion is that, Doctor?"

"Love." Missing the question altogether.

"Primary, secondary, or what?" Cantillon asked.

"Love, fear," Bowers said. "You sometimes use the words 'primary' and 'secondary.' I don't know what you mean by that."

"Would you say that self-preservation was not a primary emotion?" Cantillon asked.

"I don't say that," Bowers replied.

"Is it, or is it not?"

"Well, it is one of them," the doctor said, apparently deciding that he *did* understand the term, after all.

"Is it a primary emotion?"

"Why, certainly it is. I just got through saying it was!"

Wouldn't Hickman's apparent indifference to death constitute a deadening of primary emotions, then?

Not at all, in the learned doctor's view. "Some of them feel that they want to get it over with," he said. "Others feel that they are facing a new experience."

"Now, Doctor," Cantillon said, "a boy who would kill and horribly mutilate the body of a twelve-year-old girl—that exhibits some impairment of the emotions, doesn't it, Doctor?"

"Probably indicates a defect in the social sense," Bowers said, "malignity, depravity, or it might indicate disease."

Even quoting from the witness's own published work, Cantillon had trouble pinning Bowers down on the symptoms of dementia praecox. Symptoms "generally" found or "many times" noted in victims of the disease meant nothing when noted in Hickman's specific case, the doctor maintained. Each might be significant, Bowers allowed, "if it is considered with a lot of other symptoms," but no matter how many Cantillon listed, the diagnosis remained unshaken: Edward Hickman was sane and had been sane the day he killed Marian Parker.

The jurors seemed relieved when Judge Trabucco adjourned for the weekend, but Bowers was back on the stand Monday morning, for further examination. The doctor had regained his composure since Saturday, serene and unflappable in his insistence that, while Hickman displayed certain symptoms that *might* suggest dementia praecox in *another* patient, his "overall picture" was that of a sane, albeit depraved, individual.

The next prosecution expert's testimony was mercifully brief. Dr. Herman Schorr had examined Edward three times in private and had watched him every day in court. "I say he is sane," Schorr told the jury, "because there are no symptoms which an impartial observer could say belong to an insane individual." Despite concession of mental illness in both maternal grandparents, his mother, and a maternal cousin, Schorr maintained, "there is every scientific reason to believe that there is no hereditary insanity in the defendant, or in any of his brothers or his sister." Edward's children might turn out to be insane, of course, but Keyes and company were standing by to make sure that hypothesis was never tested. The defense, surprisingly, had no questions for Dr. Schorr.

It would be another story, though, when Victor Parkin took the stand. Here was another psychiatrist who had prejudged Ed's case in the papers before he was even identified, now testifying for the state that Hickman was sane and responsible for his actions. Throughout private examinations and public observation, Parkin testified, "I was unable to find anything in the man's speech or conduct that indicated that he departed from the normal in such a way as to constitute mental disease." The allusions to Providence were a transparent afterthought, proof positive of Hickman's malingering.

On cross-examination from Cantillon, Dr. Parkin acknowledged that Edward might well suffer from "psychopathic inferiority, but that does not mean that he is insane, by any means." In fact, on second thought, Parkin believed "it would be quite a stretch to bring him into that group." Ed's decision to kidnap, murder and dismember a child in pursuit of the tuition to divinity school "is sane," Parkin said, "inasmuch as the conclusion was logically arrived at, no matter how faulty the judgment might have been."

Still gunning for Dr. Reynolds, Cantillon harked back to the earlier witness's testimony. "Doctor," he asked Parkin, "do you agree with Dr. Reynolds that there is no such thing as epilepsy?"

"It depends on a man's conception of epilepsy," Parkin replied. "I don't quite get your question."

"Well, does the term 'epileptic' mean anything to you?"

"Yes, the term 'epileptic' means something to me."

"Dr. Reynolds, I believe, stated that the term 'epileptic' did not mean anything to him, was an obsolete term. Now, do you agree with that statement of Dr. Reynolds?"

An objection from Keyes spared Parkin from having to contradict his colleague.

One last shot: "You don't think that kidnapping and killing a little girl, a twelve-year-old little girl, to get $1,500 to study to become a minister is the act of an insane person? Is that right, Doctor? Is that your opinion?"

Parkin was cool in his response. "Well, I don't know whether he was going to use the money to study for the ministry or not. They may be just as false as many of the other statements that he made."

Frank Mikels had been making detailed notes from his first meeting with Edward, on December 28, up to the moment he was called to testify, and he read them in laborious detail, minute by minute, consuming a hundred transcript pages and the rest of Monday's session. Walsh objected to the reading, and Judge Trabucco sustained him, while granting Mikels the right to "refresh his memory" in tedious detail. Despite repeated objections and reminders from the bench, it was clear in the doctor's stilted tone that he was reading the notes verbatim: "Fear and awe was noticed on this day. No morbid fears [or] phobias. I did not get them in any of my examinations of him. In my questionnaires did I get any evidence of any reactions here of what we call morbid fears."

And so forth. Those jurors who remained awake through that testimony deserved congratulations on their stamina; how much they understood was anybody's guess. The gist of it was found, at long last, in the final exchange between Mikels and Walsh, on cross-examination.

"I want you to tell me whether you found all of the emotions and reactions of this boy healthy, active, and normal," Walsh demanded.

"I did," Mikels said, "so far as I could evaluate them and determine from my observations and examinations."

With thinly veiled sarcasm, Walsh replied, "He is just, in other words, an average, normal, sane American youth of nineteen?"

"I should say that he is," Mikels said.

Dr. Thomas Orbison led off for the state on Tuesday, February 7, confirming the judgment of the five preceding expert witnesses that Hickman was sane and responsible for his actions. His military background echoed in his stark contempt for civilian "rotten eggs" and the judicial process that would not let him "put them out of action right away." His bottom-line judgment of Hickman? "Why, he is sane," Orbison told the court. "He *was* sane. He *is* sane, in my opinion, both medically and legally." Edward's crimes sprang from the fact that "he has developed crooked. He was not sick. He was not insane. But he developed along crooked lines." There was no mystery to it, in Orbison's view. Edward simply abandoned the old-time religion of his forebears and "chose the criminal side of it." Indeed, Dr. Orbison was almost as contemptuous of Frank Mikels and his detailed observations as he was of the defendant. "As for all his little attitudes, whether he crosses his leg on his left side or right," Orbison scoffed, "I am not going into that at all."

He *would* go into Edward's rambling "Solution to Crime," however, and Orbison's introduction of the subject finally gave Walsh and Cantillon their opportunity to put the diatribe on record. Before they reached that point, however, Cantillon and the jury were treated to Orbison's view of the American judicial system. "It is perfectly ridiculous," he said, "to have a man claim a defense of committing a preconceived murder on the ground of insanity and have all this turmoil and all this expense and all this time, and have all this pomp and ceremony of a great long trial, when we have at our disposal a place where we can send all the ordinary people that are alleged insane, namely, where we can put them in the psychopathic ward and have them examined there, and if we find out that they are insane we can treat them accordingly. . . . The only thing that is extraordinary about this case is the emotions aroused in the people as a whole at the kind of murder that was committed. That is all."

After reading Hickman's long-winded address "to the American people," Orbison reduced the document to one sentence: "He is attempting to try to get out of the predicament." There was no "mental confusion," certainly no evidence of dementia praecox. Keyes proved the point on redirect examination, having Orbison read from Edward's jailhouse letter to fellow prisoner Dale Budlong, including his plan to "get up and give all that crap about me wanting to do some good by living."

Dr. Edward Williams followed Orbison on Tuesday afternoon. He offered to state his credentials "just as briefly as I can," then launched into a recitation of his life beginning at age seventeen. Eight transcript pages later he reached the point where Cecil Reynolds had invited him to study Hickman, and Williams noted that Edward had arrived for their first session carrying a book written by Oscar Wilde, "a most notorious sex pervert." The doctor viewed it as a dodge, some lame attempt on Hickman's part to make himself seem homosexual, and Williams was proud to say that Hickman had later switched to reading the Bible, "which is a very much better book." The bottom line for Dr. Williams, once the literary criticism was deleted: "He is not insane."

On cross-examination, Walsh produced a psychiatric textbook coauthored by Williams and Dr. Ernest Hoag, quoting a passage that referred to yet another Los Angeles defendant, this one diagnosed by the authors as suffering from dementia praecox, who had appeared in court as "a distinctly good looking, clean-cut, and somewhat dapper appearing young man." Williams balked at applying the same diagnosis to Hickman, sparking his first angry exchange with Walsh.

"You helped write it?" Walsh asked.

"Not that particular part," Williams said.

"Your name is on the book, though," Walsh reminded him. "When you subscribed your name to this here, you embraced everything that was within the covers here."

"Most assuredly I did not," Williams answered. "I was writing another book in the name of Williams and Hoag, and I think he did not show me most of the manuscript."

"Did you file an injunction to suppress it, then?" Walsh asked.

An objection from Keyes to the "frivolous" question was sustained, but Walsh kept after Williams. Why would the doctor contradict his own work?

"I have not disputed it," Williams insisted.

"You were disparaging it for the moment," Walsh said, "weren't you?"

Williams forced a smile. "If anybody has a right to disparage his book, I have, haven't I?" he said. "It is my own book."

"You certainly would not write anything that was false in here, would you?" Walsh asked.

"I did not take the oath before I wrote it," Williams answered stiffly. "And I think Hoag wrote that at the time."

"Your name is signed to it?"

"Thank you," Williams said. "Yes, sir, it is."

"You will have to stand upon what is in it?"

"I will stand upon anything in my book," the doctor said, contradicting himself once again.

On they went, through the list of symptoms for dementia praecox. All applied "in some cases," but none, apparently, if the patient's name was Hickman.

"I was hoping, Doctor, you would overlook the patient that you now have in hand," Walsh said, "and try to agree with me on [that] which you attempted to write for the benefit of mankind—the young medical students, what they could study to learn about dementia praecox."

"May I ask," Williams replied, "what leads you to think that this is written for the benefit of mankind?"

"I assume you did not waste your time in just sitting down and writing ramblingly, did you, Doctor?"

"No," Williams said. "That was written, as I understand, so as to be published, not for the benefit of mankind, but for the benefit of the men that wrote it. That is all [such books] are written for."

Apparently satisfied with the doctor's self-inflicted wound, Walsh returned to the controversial subject of epilepsy. "Will you state what it means?" he asked Williams.

"Epilepsy," Williams said, "is an old and obsolescent—that is, going out of use—term. It means very little to the scientific psychiatrist or surgeon at the present time. It is a disagreeable term."

"Has the cause from which epilepsy originated become obsolete, too?" Walsh asked.

"Yes," Williams said, then rushed to qualify his answer. "It has changed—not obsolete, but the causes have changed pretty much."

One thing that had not changed was Dr. Williams's opinion of Ed Hickman. The defendant was sane and responsible for his actions, Williams told the court again. The pose of insanity was a malingering sham.

Dr. Williams was the last psychiatrist called to testify. The D.A.'s next witness was inmate Dale Budlong, from the jail upstairs, called to identify the note Hickman had written on his plan to "throw a laughing, screaming, diving act" in court. The note was passed to him while playing cards with Hickman, Budlong said. On cross-examination, Walsh determined that the card game was a onetime event, but he failed to elicit an admission that Budlong was planted in jail to incriminate Edward.

Welby Hunt was recalled by the state after Budlong testified. Keyes recapped Hunt's first meeting with Hickman, noting that they were close friends for eight months, before Hickman was jailed for forging checks.

"You got to know him pretty well, did you?" Keyes asked.

"Yes, sir."

"State, in your opinion, whether or not during that period the defendant was sane or insane," Keyes directed.

"Perfectly sane," Hunt replied, "to my knowledge."

More witnesses followed in swift succession. Walter Rappold, assistant chief clerk at First National Bank, told the jury that Hickman "always conducted himself in a very normal and sane manner" on the job. Three other bank employees—Mark Trauggot, L. S. Gilhousen, and Edward Brewster—agreed. Percy Beck had met Hickman while Ed was living with the Driskells, recalling that "all of his acts were perfectly sane." Hale Parks knew Edward "in a passing way" at Central High and found him "apparently sane," though he never saw Ed outside of class and could not recall specifics of a single conversation they had ever had. Another Central High graduate, Solomon Laykin, pronounced Edward "perfectly sane," but admitted on cross-examination that he never socialized or shared a class with Hickman. Carroll Hakes recognized Hickman from his visits to a grocery store where Hakes worked, in Alhambra, and while they had barely spoken, Hakes thought he was sane. Grocer M. K. Wadley concurred, as did Birch Street neighbor Frank Thompson and Walter Price, from the neighborhood gas station. Detective E. M. Hamren had arrested Hickman in June 1927 and found him rational.

Defense objections to all of these amateur psychoanalysts were overruled by Judge Trabucco, and court was adjourned after Helen Seelye, a telegraph operator for Western Union, fingered Edward as the man who had sent a wire to Perry Parker's house at 6:20 P.M. on Thursday, December 15.

Chief Tom Gurdane, from Pendleton, was Wednesday's first witness. He described Hickman's arrest on December 22 and the inventory of his personal effects made at the city jail. He described how Edward "pulled a fit" when he greeted his escorts from Los Angeles on Christmas Eve, and while his memory of the performance differed in some respects from that of Dick Lucas and Herman Cline, their stories were essentially the same.

Walsh had no questions for the witness or for any of those who followed. Buck Lieuallen replaced Gurdane on the stand, confirming the inventory of Hickman's belongings, and LAPD's Dwight Longuevan agreed with the list of items received in Pendleton. Dr. A. F. Wagner described the condition of Marian's remains upon arrival at the morgue, while Perry Parker related his family's ordeal from the arrival of the first telegram on December 15, to the delivery of Marian's mutilated corpse two days later. George Contreras, from the LAPD, was the final witness. Prosecutors rested their case after he described his first view of the partial body propped up on the seat of Perry Parker's car.

It was a grim finish to the people's case. Keyes had left the worst for last, deliberately, to keep the butchered victim fresh in the jurors' minds as they retired for lunch. Closing arguments would begin when court resumed at 2:00 P.M.

14 ✦ "The Touchstone of Common Sense"

Forrest Murray led off for the state when court reconvened after lunch. There would be a series of closing arguments, four in all, and Asa Keyes was saving himself for the sprint to the finish line. It was Murray's job to warm up the jurors, some of them drowsy from lunch, all chafing at the continued sequestration.

"I don't know whether there is anything I can say to help to analyze the details of these proceedings of the last two weeks or not," Murray began. "There are a few observations, as we went along, that I would like to call your attention to."

First and foremost, he reminded them, they would not be expected to determine Hickman's guilt or innocence—that much had been decided by his choice of a guilty plea—but they would be called upon to judge his sanity. In such a case, Murray explained, the normal burden of proof was reversed: as the law presumed a man innocent until proven guilty, so it presumed he was sane until proven otherwise.

"Now, can we, after a crime has been committed, determine the intent, determine this one issue that you are here to decide from all the evidence, whether on these respective dates he had the intent to do wrong; he knew that it was wrong; he knew that he was violating the laws of both God and man?" Murray asked. "How do we determine that question?"

By examining the evidence in stages, Murray replied to himself. And the first stage involved a review of "the things that cluster around this man's conduct, these little things that we all know from human experience, whether a man is odd or peculiar, or whether he is sane."

Hickman had demonstrated clarity of mind, the prosecutor said, by scouting the home of an alternative kidnap victim four days prior to his abduction of Marian. He had weighed the pros and cons of snatching a twelve-year-old versus an infant. Hickman had been sane enough to trail the Parker girls to school on Thursday, December 15, the first of several ransom notes already written out and waiting in his pocket. "Doesn't that show some intellect?" Murray challenged the panel. "Doesn't that show power enough to plan and scheme?

"Now he comes in here and, through counsel, tells you that that mind and that brain of his was diseased and so deranged that he is incapable of knowing what a crime is." Murray's tone was scornful. "Apply the touchstone of common sense," he suggested. Why had Hickman driven Marian to "a lonely road the other side of Glendale" before stopping to bind and gag her, if he did not know the act was criminal? Why had his Saturday ransom note chastised Perry Parker for "all this publicity," unless Hickman sought to avoid capture? Premeditation of murder was found, Murray said, in the first letter Hickman had written on Saturday, December 17—the one that said he would not accept payment for "a lifeless mass of flesh." Murray reminded the jurors that Hickman, in his written confession, admitted killing Marian to protect himself and to minimize the risk of capture.

"Yet these learned alienists that the defense put on," Murray scoffed, "say that he has no feelings, that he has no emotions. Well, that is partially true, as far as the outside world is concerned. As far as society is concerned he has very little emotions. But as far as he himself is concerned, his emotions are very keen. He has the keen characteristics of a hardened criminal. One of the distinguishing features of a man who has been schooled in crime is the keen appreciation of his own rights and his utter disregard for the rights of everyone else."

Hickman viewed crime as his profession, Murray said, and like any other professional, he had started out at the bottom. Petty theft was followed by stolen cars, forged checks, armed robbery and shootouts with police, culminating in the cold-blooded kidnapping and murder of a helpless child. Wherever he went, Hickman was armed to the teeth. "There was his guiding Providence," Murray said. "There was the Providence that he relied upon when he himself was concerned. That is the guiding hand for him."

As for Hickman's willingness to kill, Murray told the jury, "I say this is not a mental disease. This is a callousness of feeling, just like any other hardened, cruel, and calculating criminal." Just as employees in a slaughterhouse were indifferent to the blood and suffering of livestock, Murray said, "that is the way this defendant has become. His feelings are so callused, his greed is so great, he has such an utter disregard for the rights of others, that he will even take a life if anyone opposes him in what he desires to do."

Ed's flight from Los Angeles provided further evidence that he was rational and acting in the interest of self-preservation. When police had visited the Bellevue Arms, on Sunday, December 18, Hickman expressed his hope that they would catch the "fiend" responsible for killing Marian. "How did he know it was a crime," Murray demanded, "he whose mind is so diseased and so deranged that he could not tell the difference between right and wrong?" Why had he packed his things and hurried out to steal another car, if he was not afraid of the authorities? Why had he left Los Angeles at all?

"Now, where do we next see him," Murray asked, "he who is so anxious to attract attention, he who has such a big message for the youth of America? Where do we next see him?" Hiding out in San Francisco under an alias, moving on from there to Seattle, then doubling back in an admitted bid to confuse his pursuers. Driving with a pistol in his lap, prepared to shoot if necessary, at the time of his arrest.

"What does he say about Providence committing this crime?" Murray asked the jury. "What does he say about this guiding influence of committing this crime?" Instead of trumpeting his holy mission, taking credit for his actions, Hickman tried to lay the crime off on a mythical accomplice. "He does not say anything about Providence," Murray went on. "He does not say anything about the great message that he has for the youth of America. What emotions does that indicate to your mind? What is he trying to do when he says that Cramer was the one that actually killed the little girl? The same old keen instinct of every criminal: self-preservation, self-greed, and desire."

Hickman's belated reference to Providence, seen for the first time in his written confession, was a clumsy dodge in Murray's opinion, a last-ditch attempt to save himself "after he had pulled these two insanity fits" at the Pendleton jail. "And he tells you now, through his counsel and through his defense in this case, that on account of that guiding Providence he jumped one stage farther until he became the right-hand man of God, making it a little bit more severe. He tells you that on account of that Providence, his mind was diseased. And then, finally, he tells you how this Providence is going to do the great good."

But Hickman had betrayed himself again, Murray said, in his long recitation of murders committed by other defendants like Remus and Snyder, Leopold and Loeb. "How does he know they are crimes?" Murray asked. "How does he know those people had done wrong?

"And then," Murray said, "to cap the thing—which I think insults the intelligence of the ordinary individual—he tells you, sitting there with the dripping blood of two victims on his hands and the noose around his neck, he says, 'There is too much bloodshed. There has been too much bloodshed already. Let us do away with bloodshed.' And then his own expert says he hasn't any emotions. He doesn't know; his feelings do not respond; he doesn't know the difference between right and wrong."

In fact, Murray agreed with Hickman that there was too much bloodshed in society. "No doubt about that," he told the jury. "But *he* wants to abolish it when it comes to *him*. Does that indicate whether his emotions are warped or not, that they are dulled, and he does not know the difference between right and wrong, that he has no emotions? What would that indicate to your mind?"

As far as the question of inherited mental illness went, Murray granted that "I don't know any more about heredity, probably, than you people do." Eva Hickman had suffered from "family troubles, even though Mr. Hickman himself says that he was a dutiful husband." Murray claimed no expertise on the impact of marital discord on children, but he told the jurors, "We have all had disappointments. We have all had grief. We have all had sorrow." Alfred Hickman, he maintained, was living evidence that Bill and Eva Hickman had not spawned hopeless maniacs. The main difference between Alfred and Edward, in Murray's view? Al Hickman "did not have his diploma, he did not have his schooling in this life of crime. He did not have his finer sensibilities so warped and deadened that he did not care about the feelings of anyone else."

Fixing his sights on the two defense psychiatrists, Murray declared that Dr. Shelton "finally wound up admitting that he was not oriented to the place himself, that he didn't know whether he was in the courtroom or not, for sure." Shelton's diagnosis of Edward was written on the wind, subject to change every two or three days. This from "a man called here under his oath to testify, to give you—who have an obligation and a responsibility to perform—the benefit of his opinion. What kind of advice, what kind of help is that? I leave it to you."

Dr. Skoog, by contrast, "appeared as a very nice, high-class man," in Murray's opinion, but he had arrived in Los Angeles too late to make any valid diagnosis of Hickman. "This boy was jail-wise already," Murray reminded the jurors, "but he became more jail-wise after he had had the benefit of all the examinations of the other doctors." He had been ready for Skoog, serving up all the right symptoms and answers on cue, running a game on the doctor.

As far as Hickman's defense was concerned, Murray told the court, "I myself have no sympathy with a plea of insanity when it would be impossible, if a man was *not* charged with a crime, to put him away in an asylum. How could you put that man away in a California asylum? Four of the distinguished members of the lunacy commission have testified here under oath that he was sane, that if that man came over there to their commission to determine whether or not he should be confined in an institution, they would dismiss the case. Think that over. That is why [when] counsel knew the facts of this case, he knew that this insanity [plea] was the only chance he had, some chance of confusing, throwing out a smoke screen, and probably getting a favorable response from one mind or so in a body of twelve."

The jurors should not be confused, said Murray. They should focus on their duty and perform it to the best of their ability, applying plain old common sense. He proclaimed that "this defense is a sham, and is as ridiculous as if this defendant had entered a plea of self-defense. There is not one place in the bucket that holds a drop of water. Not one."

Judge Trabucco called for a ten-minute recess before the defense summations began. Defense attorney Jerome Walsh, unlike D.A. Keyes, had decided that the leader should speak first for his team. He began on a solemn note, making it plain to the jury that had no plan to whitewash Hickman's crime.

"For the murderer, William Edward Hickman, ladies and gentlemen," Walsh proclaimed, "I hold no brief, nor do I come here possessed of any commission to speak for him. But for the madman, ladies and gentlemen it is my right and my solemn and bounden duty to try and convince you what I feel in my heart are the circumstances that surroun· this madman."

Of course, Walsh acknowledged, Hickman was bound by the ancient commandment "Thou shalt not kill"—an injunction that Walsh suggested, with no apparent irony, had been "handed to us by Divine Providence." The jurors should remember, though, that they too were bound by the same injunction. "If any of you ladies and gentlemen sitting in this jury box have come in here with your mind surcharged with a gross prejudice," Walsh intoned, "or with a bias that you have been unable to place or eject from your mind when you solemnly raised your hand before your living God and swore that you would do that, then if you have sworn to sit here as unbiased and unprejudiced jurors and have failed to eject that prejudice or that bias and, as a result of your verdict, that youth goes to his doom, then, ladies and gentlemen, *you* violated that divine injunction."

District Attorney Asa Keyes was likewise guilty, Walsh suggested, if he had "through any ill-timed jest, or in his earnestness, deliberately injected any prejudice" into any juror's mind. Even Walsh was potentially at fault, he admitted, "if I have done anything here in my earnestness that might prejudice you." It was a broad definition of "prejudice," to be sure—apparently including any effort by the prosecution to convict Walsh's client—but once he had finished spreading the blame around, Walsh finally got to the meat of his argument.

He understood his problem going in, and Walsh launched into his recitation on insanity by reading from one of the psychiatric textbooks he had cited throughout the trial: "The reader should bear in mind that frequently there is nothing in the patient's appearance, at least to casual observation, that would suggest a mental abnormality." Granted, Edward Hickman was a handsome, even dapper, specimen who seemed completely rational, but how could any normal youth commit a crime Walsh described as "probably the most dastardly thing that human hand has ever accomplished in the whole history of the world"?

Granted, kidnapping for ransom was a fairly common crime in those days—an epidemic, in fact, according to press reports—and Walsh acknowledged that such deeds were often planned by sane, if not precisely normal, minds. Marian's motiveless murder, though, was in Walsh's view "the first act of the madman," followed closely by "the most outrageously horrible thing that can possibly be conceived of," as Edward dissected her. "I say such conduct is so incomprehensible, ladies and gentlemen," Walsh declared, "that no normal mind attempting to view it without prejudice or bias could possibly say that it was the act of a normal, well-regulated mind."

The last straw, of course, was Hickman's delivery of the truncated corpse to Perry Parker. "How outrageous!" Walsh thundered. "Can you think of that? Can you think a human could do such a thing? Yes, a human could not, but a *fiend* could do it, a completely disordered mind, one whose normal emotions were completely driven from his body could do it."

The prosecution had described Ed's flight from California in a stolen car as the logical action of an habitual criminal trying to evade capture. In fact, Walsh claimed, every move Hickman made between the daring auto theft on Sunday night and his arrest in Oregon four days later was fraught with irrational risk. "If every act that this boy did," Walsh told the jury, "from the time he took this little girl until he was apprehended in Pendleton, Oregon, is not a complete abandonment of the first instinct of life, each and every act, then I have lost all semblance of the intelligence that I should have." Proof positive of Hickman's insanity, to Walsh, was the fact that Edward "traveled the highways" in his flight from L.A.—but jurors were already asking themselves how else he could have gone.

Exactly how and when had Hickman gone insane? Walsh traced it back to his roots in "this little godforsaken community" of Hartford, Arkansas, spawned by a family of lunatics and imbeciles. Walsh warned the jury that "to say, after the testimony in this case, that this boy is the normal product of American education . . . is to indict every high school and every high school student in this country." If Hickman was sane, Walsh challenged the panel, "then I say the system is a failure."

Comparing expert witnesses, Walsh referred to Dr. Skoog's "evident sincerity just leaping from that box into yours." The D.A.'s leading expert, Cecil Reynolds, had by contrast "chanted his hymn of hate and venom in such an unusual manner that it completely strips everything that he said of scientific value. I have never heard a more venomous witness on a witness stand in my life," Walsh said, "when he was trying to advise a jury of scientific facts." Walsh then dismissed Bowers, Schorr, Parkin, Mikels, and "old Dr. Williams" as "too insignificant when we come down to the point of what we really have to consider here." He advised the jurors that their ultimate decision was a choice between the views of Dr. Orbison and Dr. Skoog, both "outstanding men in their profession." Even Dr. Orbison's diagnosis was suspect, however, because he had to "stop and ponder" the question of whether Hickman was "a normal, average American youth. . . . Did you notice the pause that came before the answer?" Walsh asked. Dr. Orbison had finally pronounced Hickman sane, Walsh acknowledged, but it [the decision on Hickman's sanity] had "charged the very largest stretch of his honest conviction and imagination and probity that could possibly have been put to him."

Even Edward's jailhouse letter detailing his plan for a bogus insanity defense was "another and more conclusive symptom of his insanity," in Walsh's opinion. "If he is the normal, calculating type that is attempting to beat the process of the law here by a plea of insanity," Walsh said, "and his mind is orderly, working along all lines to befuddle and fool you, ladies and gentlemen, do you think that he would not have the intelligence and foresight enough to at least keep his ideas about this case out of writing, especially the writing of his own hand?"

Finally, Walsh's defense of Hickman came down to a defense of society itself. "That is the question that I am going to put to each and every one of you ladies and gentlemen," he said. "Do you want to send the word, broadcast to the world, that William Edward Hickman is the normal, average nineteen-year-old American youth? If you do, you indict every boy graduate of a high school in this country and tell him he is no better than this boy is."

The defense was not finished when Walsh sat down, however. Following a brief recess, Richard Cantillon rose to make his appeal for Hickman's life. Like Walsh before him, Cantillon began with a discourse on the perils of prejudice—"the child of animus"—beseeching the jurors to "deliberate calmly, coolly and collectedly." Judgment of sanity was "the acid test" for every juror in the land, "an extremely difficult matter to adjudicate upon." Insanity was "a strange, a peculiar thing," Cantillon cautioned. "There is a fine hairline between an orderly mind and a deranged mind," he said. "One faculty out of order, ladies and gentlemen of the jury, may destroy and may disturb every other part of the mind, so that a man—while he would have the remainder of his faculties intact—would be so deranged that he could not and would not, because of this controlling delusion, understand the difference between right and wrong."

Such was the case with Edward Hickman, Cantillon maintained, but a glance at the clock showed him that he was running out of time to make his case. Judge Trabucco adjourned for the day, and Cantillon resumed on Thursday morning, citing one of the state's own experts to make his case. Dr. Bowers had agreed, on cross-examination, that some three-fourths of all dementia praecox patients were "the offspring of psychopathic or neuropathic stock." It was also "quite true," according to Bowers, that Edward's mother and maternal grandparents fit the definition. Rebecca Buck was "absolutely insane," in Cantillon's view, and had apparently passed the taint on to grandson Otto. Why not Edward as well? An Arkansas judge had ruled Eva Hickman insane in 1913, and fifteen years later her testimony on the witness stand was "sufficient in itself," Cantillon judged, to prove her "definitely feebleminded."

Where Walsh had dismissed Dr. Bowers as "insignificant," Cantillon found him "a very fine witness for the state and for the defense," because he had published a book on dementia praecox in 1924. Recapping the list of recognized symptoms, Cantillon claimed to see every one reflected in Edward's recent life, but the sudden change in his personality was most striking. "You can't tell me," Cantillon said, "that a boy who wanted to take a course and be a minister—and working in school the way this boy did, in one of the largest high schools in Kansas City—you can't tell me when a boy like that suddenly changes and absolutely starts in the opposite direction, you can't tell me that there isn't some derangement of his mind. There isn't any doctor—Dr. Orbison, Williams, or anybody else—that can sit up there and testify to that honestly."

It was "almost an insult to your intelligence," Cantillon suggested, that eminent psychiatrists would "try to explain to you how this boy is such a hardened criminal and became so within a period of a year and a half, suddenly branches into this career of crime, and they try to tell you that in a year and a half he became the most hardened criminal." Heredity was to blame, Cantillon said, "and they have not brought one scintilla of evidence—nor could they bring a scintilla of evidence—to disprove that the grandmother was insane, the cousin was an epileptic, and the mother was insane, and the grandfather was neuropathic."

In short, Edward was doomed from day one. He was delusional, Cantillon said, and while Dr. Reynolds "had the temerity" to suggest that Hickman "has been coached into these delusions," Cantillon flatly denied any such conspiracy. "We did not coach the mother when she drank carbolic acid fifteen years ago," he said. "I will say that we did not coach the grandmother. She was dead, I guess, before I was born. . . . And speaking for myself, I know that I would not know how to coach anyone upon the subject of insanity."

Finally, Cantillon told the jury, broad denials from the D.A.'s expert witnesses did nothing to refute the diagnosis of serous meningitis made by Dr. Fettes in the wake of Edward's first spinal tap. That diagnosis explained Hickman's headaches dating back to 1925, demonstrating "that this boy's brain is inflamed. What more would you expect? What other symptom could you find that would be stronger evidence than that, or that could more conclusively establish this condition of disease of the defendant in this case? You have the heredity, the physical condition that you have, the history of the boy himself, the mental stress, all going to establish it."

But first, of course, the jury had to grant that all those "facts" *were* facts, and Asa Keyes was eager to challenge that assumption when he rose to present the trial's final argument. Speaking last was a distinct advantage for the state, assuming that Keyes could do it well enough to banish any reasonable doubt concerning Hickman's sanity.

Justice was blind, Keyes told the court, but it was "neither deaf nor dumb." He spoke for justice, for the people of the Golden State, to guarantee that every criminal was fairly tried and punished for his crimes. "I am not going to go into the horrible details of this crime," Keyes said, "as counsel indicated to you that I might. I have no wish or desire to do that. When we started out to try this case, during the course of the trial, I anticipated that it would be necessary for me, and I expected to have to prove to you and display before you some of the gruesome details. Counsel for the defendant has anticipated my move and beat me to the punch, as they say in the street, and proved those things himself.

"Why?" Keyes asked rhetorically. "He didn't fool me. I don't believe he fooled you. He wanted to prove to you that this crime was so horrible and so gruesome that it might cause you to believe that no man in his sane mind could have committed it. Now those gruesome details are in the past."

It would be un-American, Keyes said, for him to play off base emotions and revulsion in pursuit of a guilty verdict. Harking back to his own witness, Dr. Orbison, Keyes said, "We have been criticized for giving this man a trial at all, by certain people. Oh, no! Not in America! Not in America is the law administered that way." The Constitution guaranteed every man a fair trial, Keyes declared, and Hickman had been ably represented by lawyers from two separate states. His guilt was not at issue; Edward himself had conceded that. The sole issue remaining was his sanity, as narrowly defined by law.

Keyes bristled at the alleged suggestion of anonymous critics that he had somehow been unfair to Hickman. "I am going to be fair with this man," he proclaimed, "although I loathe the ground he walks on." As proof of that fairness, the D.A. referred vaguely to "several occasions" when he had "stopped trials in the middle and . . . said, 'I will not prosecute this man further. Let us put him where he belongs,' and he has gone to the insane asylum." If none present could recall such a case, it hardly mattered; Keyes had made his point.

There would be no such surprises in the present case, however. "From the time I first set eyes on that man up in the jail in Pendleton, Oregon," Keyes said, "I did not believe, and I do not believe now, that that man was insane at the time he committed that kidnapping and murder, or that he is any more insane at this present moment than anyone else in this room."

He would cast no aspersions on defense expert witnesses, Keyes promised. "I know nothing about either one of them," he said; he had never heard of Skoog and Shelton before they signed on to testify for Hickman. "But I have the right, ladies and gentlemen," he went on, "to direct your attention to one or two things as I have observed them from the witness stand."

As Keyes recalled it, "Dr. Shelton, in his anxiety to prove to you that this defendant is insane and was insane at the time he committed this murder, took two-thirds of a whole afternoon in telling you the things that this defendant did not have"—specifically emotions, empathy, the whole broad range of human feelings. Dr. Skoog, meanwhile, had only arrived in Los Angeles on January 25, and had met Edward for the first time a day later, while Hickman had been refining "his insanity dodge" for over a month. "And I call it his insanity dodge advisedly," Keyes said, "because I am convinced from this evidence that it was nothing more or less than a dodge on the part of this man, in an effort to dodge the law."

Hickman had done "everything that he could do to try to fool the doctors," Keyes advised the jury, and had bragged about his plan repeatedly—at least once in writing. If the defense description of his "controlling delusion" was accurate, Keyes said, Hickman would have surrendered as soon as he killed and dismembered his victim, thereby calling world attention to himself and his message from "Providence." Instead, he planned out an escape, which—unlike the chain of hopeless blunders sketched by defense counsel—had very nearly succeeded, carrying him hundreds of miles from the scene of his crime.

Where was Providence, Keyes wondered aloud, in the years prior to Hickman's arrest in Oregon? Where was any mention of divine guidance in the string of robberies Ed pulled with Welby Hunt? Where was any hint of Providence in the shootout that killed Ivy Thoms? In the Pendleton lockup? At any point in Hickman's life before he left Oregon in chains? Why, if Hickman felt himself embarked on a great mission for mankind, did he fail to express that mission publicly?

Hickman had been truthful, Keyes allowed, when he wrote down the first and foremost of his motives for killing Marian Parker: "Fear of detection by the police and the belief that to kill and dissect the body I would be able to evade suspicion and arrest." The rest was a transparent sham designed, by Hickman's own admission, to deceive a judge and jury. It was the same motive that compelled Ed to disguise his handwriting on the ransom notes, to fit his stolen cars with stolen license plates, and to travel under cover of night.

"You ladies and gentlemen have been chosen by both sides in this case to decide this issue," Keyes concluded, "because we believe you to be fair and honest, because we believe you to be men and women of judgment. I am going to submit this matter to you at this time, with this hope: that it does not go out across the wires to the Atlantic seaboard, across there to Europe, the other way to Asia and the countries of the world that Los Angeles County and the state of California are not able to adequately cope with the criminal, because criminal this man is, and not insane."

The court broke for lunch as Keyes sat down, resuming at 2:00 P.M. It was Judge Trabucco's turn to address the jury, reminding them of the specific charges filed against Hickman and the fact that they were not charged with determining his guilt or innocence. They simply had to decide if Hickman was sane when he abducted Marian Parker on December 15, and again when he killed her two days later.

"It is not every kind or degree of insanity which renders a person incapable of committing crime," Trabucco said. "Before you can find that the defendant was insane at the times charged in the indictment as of the dates of said offenses, you must find not only that he at those times suffered from insanity, but that the insanity was of that kind and degree which constitutes a defense to a criminal charge and which is more fully explained in the following instructions.

"All persons are presumed to be sane," Trabucco went on, and the burden of proving otherwise lay with the defendant claiming insanity as a defense against criminal charges. Specifically, that meant "such a diseased and deranged condition of the mental faculties as to render the person incapable of knowing the nature and quality of the act or of distinguishing between right and wrong in relation to the act with which he is charged." If the defendant understood his act would violate another's rights, he was responsible under law for that action. California statutes recognized no "irresistible impulse" as relieving a defendant of responsibility; neither did it recognize "moral insanity . . . if such a state exists." It mattered not "how perverted the feelings, conscience, affections, and sentiments of a defendant may be," Trabucco said. If Hickman understood the concept of right and wrong *as defined by society*, then he was legally sane. Likewise, "partial insanity"—a particular delusion or hallucination which did not affect his understanding of the law—would not be an acceptable excuse. "Temporary insanity," on the other hand, was a perfectly acceptable defense, as long as it met the standards of the legal definition and overwhelmed a defendant "at the precise time of the commission of the acts as alleged in the indictment."

Insanity must be proved by a "preponderance of evidence," carefully distinguished by Trabucco from a mere head count of witnesses, pro and con. Assessment of the defendant's own statements or writings should be made in light of all the evidence concerning his physical and mental condition. Nor, in fact, did it matter if Hickman was crazy *now*, unless he had been crazy *then*. "You are to determine what the condition of the defendant's mind was at the precise time of the commission of the acts charged in the indictment," Trabucco repeated. "Its condition before or afterward is only to be considered by you for the purpose of throwing light upon its state at the time of the commission of said acts."

Finally, Trabucco told the jurors, they should perform their duty "uninfluenced by pity or sympathy for the defendant, or by passion or prejudice on account of the nature of the charge against him." Jury members were "the sole and exclusive judges" of any particular witness's credibility. Every witness was presumed to speak the truth, but that presumption "may be repelled by the manner in which the witness testified, by the character of his testimony, by testimony affecting his motives, or by contradictory evidence."

The charge took twenty minutes, the panel retiring at 2:20 P.M. Forty-three minutes later, the jury was back in court, prepared to deliver its verdict. By unanimous vote—and in time that would be nothing short of dazzling, by today's standards—Hickman was judged to be sane and legally responsible on the dates of both confessed crimes. Judge Trabucco scheduled sentencing on the charges for ten o'clock Saturday morning and gaveled the session to a close.

Jerome Walsh used what time he had to whip up a delaying tactic. Come Saturday morning, Judge Trabucco asked Hickman "if you have legal cause to show why the judgment of the law and the sentence of the court should not be pronounced upon you." Walsh replied in the affirmative.

In fact, Walsh had twenty reasons why—in his opinion—Hickman's sentencing should be deferred. The four-page list of grievances constituted Walsh's motion for a whole new trial. His roster of complaints included unspecified "errors of law occurring at the trial"; Trabucco's alleged misdirection of jurors on matters of law; allegations that the jury's verdict was both "contrary to law" and "contrary to evidence"; a claim that said verdict was reached by some unspecified means "other than a fair expression of opinion on the part of all the jurors"; allegations that various defense objections and motions were improperly denied at trial; sundry assertions that Hickman had been "legally deprived of the rights of due process" under state and federal law, including the right to a jury trial; that introduction of his several statements and letters somehow violated Edward's Fifth Amendment rights; and that the defense had discovered unspecified "new evidence" since court adjourned on Friday afternoon.

The list was a showstopper, and Judge Trabucco adjourned until Tuesday morning—Saint Valentine's Day—to consider the motion. Walsh had to know his chances of a favorable ruling in Superior Court were slim to none, but he was buying time, stretching out Hickman's life before its days were officially numbered.

The other weekend news of Ed's case came from faraway Ada, Oklahoma, where the mayor and the PTA joined forces to seek an injunction barring the local theater from showing newsreels that included pictures of Hickman. It was all "for the good of our children," the plaintiffs insisted, and Pontotoc County District Judge Orel Busby agreed, making the ban official. An appeal to the Oklahoma Supreme Court was rejected on Saturday, that august body leaving Busby's ban in place.

On Monday, February 13, Edward was handed his second judicial defeat, when Asa Keyes formally rejected the defense bid for a plea bargain on the Ivy Thoms case. Walsh and Hickman hoped to swap a guilty plea for life imprisonment, but Keyes would not budge. He had an airtight case and intended to seek the death penalty against Hickman. Reporters dourly predicted "a long and tedious review of the insanity defense" at yet another trial. Judge Carlos Hardy was scheduled to hear the case, and Walsh immediately filed the paperwork required by law to make Hardy step aside. Ever the optimist, Keyes told reporters "there was a possibility" that Hickman would hang for killing Ivy Thoms before his appeal in the Parker case was decided.

Keyes was dreaming, but he moved a step closer to the cherished goal of Hickman's death on Tuesday morning. Expecting the worst, Walsh kicked off the session with a nine-point motion in arrest of judgment (denied), followed by formal submission of the new-trial motion (denied), and a nine-point list of objections challenging the court's jurisdiction (overruled). One final objection was raised against the court accepting any further testimony prior to sentencing (overruled).

Asa Keyes had only two witnesses standing by for the penalty phase of Ed's trial. The first, Dr. A. F. Wagner, briefly recapped the condition of Marian's body as found on December 17 and December 18, once again reviewing morgue photos introduced during trial. Chief of Detectives Herman Cline condensed a five-day manhunt into three pages of testimony, then summarized Hickman's written confessions. Walsh had no questions for the witnesses, but rather moved to have their testimony stricken from the record.

Motion denied.

Judge Trabucco did not retire to consider his verdict after Cline stepped down from the stand. His mind had been made up going in; the rest of it was ritual, a courtly dance required by law to validate the end result.

"The court now determines and finds," Trabucco said, "that the degree of crime in count two of the indictment is murder of the first degree without extenuating or mitigating circumstances. William Edward Hickman, stand up."

Reporters in the audience watched Hickman rise "without a quiver and gaze straight into the venerable judge's eyes," prepared to meet his fate.

"It is the judgment and sentence of this court," Trabucco said, "that for the crime of kidnapping, the offense described in count one of the indictment, that you, William Edward Hickman, be confined in the state prison of the state of California, at San Quentin, for the term prescribed by law, which term will be fixed by the Board of Prison Directors."

Hickman stood, impassive, waiting for the other shoe to drop.

"Testimony was received by the court," Trabucco went on, "for the purpose of ascertaining and determining the degree of the crime charged in count two of the indictment—to wit, murder. The court, after due consideration, determines and finds that the degree of the crime in count two of the indictment is murder of the first degree without extenuating or mitigating circumstances, and that for the crime of murder, the offense described in count two of the indictment, you shall suffer the penalty of death. Therefore, it is the judgment and sentence of this court, William Edward Hickman, that for the crime of which you have been convicted—to wit, murder in the first degree—that you be delivered by the sheriff of Los Angeles County to the warden of the state prison of the state of California at San Quentin, to be by him executed and put to death on Friday, the twenty-seventh day of April, nineteen hundred and twenty-eight, in the manner provided by the laws of the state of California. And may God have mercy on your soul."

Walsh took a wild, hopeless shot with a request that the death sentence be revoked, on grounds that Judge Trabucco had no legal jurisdiction in the case.

Trabucco saved the last word for himself: "The motion is denied."

Of course, no one anticipated or believed that Edward would be hanged in ten weeks' time. California justice was relatively swift in those days, but it was not *that* swift. All present understood that there would be appeals and delays, but the law required the court to set an execution date before the process could begin.

And in the meantime, Hickman faced another murder trial.

Jury selection in the case of Ivy Thoms began on Wednesday, February 15, with Judge Elliott Craig presiding, and continued through Friday. (Judge Hardy had recused himself once more, but flatly rejected a defense bid to postpone the trial.) Attorneys Walsh and Cantillon were once again defending Hickman, while lawyer A. Gray Gilmer represented codefendant Welby Hunt. This time around, the D.A.'s case would be presented first, and jurors would be required to decide the guilt or innocence of both defendants in addition to judging Hickman's sanity at the time of the shooting.

On Friday, after four and a half hours of grilling prospective jurors, Walsh filed written notice of his intent to appeal the Parker verdict. The next twenty-five days, by law, would be spent producing and editing the 1,612-page transcript of Edward's trial. Another thirty days were then allowed for both sides in the case to file additional briefs. It would thus be April 18 before Hickman's appeal reached the state supreme court, and postponement of his hanging would be automatic while that body reviewed the case.

The Thoms murder trial was an instant replay of the Parker case, in many respects. Both defendants had confessed participation in the robbery, thus making them equally guilty of any resultant deaths, under California's felony murder rule—though Welby Hunt still denied having fired any shots in the drugstore. Ballistics evidence was against him on that point, although the .38-caliber revolver he admitted carrying that Christmas Eve was never found by police. Hunt made no claim that he was crazy when the crime occurred, but Walsh and Keyes repeated their parade of expert witnesses, grappling once more over the issue of whether or not Ed Hickman suffered from dementia praecox. No one in court appeared surprised when, after sixteen days of testimony, both defendants were convicted, with Hickman deemed sane, on Saturday, March 10.

There *was* a surprise on Monday, March 12, however. Judge Craig had scheduled sentencing for Tuesday morning, but word had come to him over the weekend that Walsh and Hickman wanted to speed things up. Instead of raising multiple objections, Walsh now told the court, "The defendant Hickman moves Your Honor to sentence him at this time in conformity with the verdict of the jury."

Walsh's seeming eagerness was based on news that Craig would not sentence Hickman to death. Triggerman Welby Hunt was barred from the gallows by his age at the time of the murder, and Craig saw no justice in hanging a relatively "innocent" accomplice simply because he was older. It was the best judgment Walsh could hope for, and he wanted it formalized, on record, at the earliest possible moment.

"Is there any legal reason why the judgment of the court should not now be pronounced?" Judge Craig asked Walsh.

"There is none, Your Honor," Walsh replied.

"You have never been in a state prison before, have you?" Craig asked Hickman.

"No, Your Honor."

"It is the judgment and sentence of this court, William Edward Hickman, that you be confined in the state prison at San Quentin, California, for the period prescribed by law— to wit, for the term of your natural life."

Welby Hunt, in no hurry, would wait to hear his life sentence pronounced on Tuesday morning, as scheduled. He had nothing left but time, and nowhere else to go.

For Walsh, the easy part was over. Now he had to come up with some desperate last-ditch tactic that would save his client's life.

15 ✦ "A Contrite and
Humble Sinner"

Escorted by sheriff's deputies from Los Angeles, Hickman and Welby Hunt were delivered to San Quentin Prison on the afternoon of Saturday, March 17. They were shackled together, despite Welby's anger at the friend who had "sold him out" to the authorities. The massive gates of "Q" had barely closed behind them when their escorts started talking to the press. According to the deputies, Hickman had made yet another confession, this time naming himself as the shooter who killed Ivy Thoms. "I killed that man Thoms," he supposedly said. "Welby Hunt didn't do it. I did it myself."

That claim—assuming Hickman ever made it at all—flatly contradicted the known evidence. Hunt and Hickman both agreed that Welby had been carrying a .38 the night Thoms died, while Edward packed a .32-caliber pistol. According to ballistics experts, Thoms had been killed by a .38 slug, meaning he was shot by Welby Hunt or by the patrolman who had foiled their stickup. Furthermore, Ed's claim would not free Hunt in any case, since Welby had confessed his role in the aborted robbery, thus sealing his fate under California's felony murder law.

Assuming Ed did make the statement, what motive would have prompted him? Not sympathy for Hunt, since he had fingered Welby in the first place and would later reject an eleventh-hour plea to exonerate his accomplice. He may have craved more notoriety, but his murder of

Marian Parker already ranked as L.A.'s most sensational crime of the decade; the rest was anticlimax, seedy window dressing.

There is, however, at least one other possible motive for Hickman's alleged confession. It is commonly believed—though it's not always true, by any means—that rapists and killers of children who do hard time in prison are constantly harassed, assaulted, and even murdered by convicts doing time for "normal" crimes. There is a possibility, however slim, that Hickman may have claimed the druggist's murder for himself in an attempt to boost his status in the joint—to prove, in effect, that he was more than a demented child-killer, someone to be reckoned with, a genuine tough guy who had shot it out with the cops and didn't care who died in the crossfire.

If so, the effort was too little too late.

Hickman was registered at San Quentin as inmate Number 45041, photographed, weighed, and measured. His occupation was listed as "student," but it made no difference; his job-hunting days were over.

As part of the induction process, Hickman was examined by San Quentin's chief surgeon, Dr. Leo Stanley. Stripped down for the exam, Edward displayed no reticence, rather seeming proud of his five-foot-four physique. "Pretty good shape, huh?" he said, beaming at Stanley. "And look at those muscles." Dr. Stanley later noted that official scrutiny, however intimate and intrusive, "seemed to make Hickman feel important." That day, and in subsequent interviews, Edward spoke freely of his crimes to Dr. Stanley, displaying no remorse.

In fact, by Ed's reckoning, Perry Parker was responsible for his own daughter's death. "The little girl's father made the mistake," he told Stanley. "He trusted me. That was silly of him. He should have telephoned the police the minute he knew she was kidnapped, in spite of my note warning him not to, because no crook plays fair, and I am a master crook."

Why had he murdered the child? Stanley asked.

"It was this dual force, I think," Hickman answered, "the impulse to harm anyone I cared for, and the desire to execute a master crime, that made me kill her."

Was he sorry, at least, for Marian's parents?

"No," Ed replied, "I felt no pity for the father. I felt no remorse at all. I just felt I was executing a master stroke. As for the little girl, she's better off than I am. At least she's out of this world of turmoil and strife. I no longer believe in a heaven or hell, but I know we shall have everlasting life."

Concerning crime in general, Ed told the doctor, "Any man has the right to hold up another man if he wants to. Even if the holdup results in murder, it is all right." He still hedged his bets, though, seeming to deny conscious pursuit of a criminal career. "Everything is foreordained," he told Dr. Stanley. "Our lives are mapped out for us from the beginning. Yours has been laid out for you. What I have done was my destiny, and I could not help it."

Hickman and Hunt entered San Quentin as "fish"—first-time convicts unfamiliar with the system, inexperienced at prison life, without connections to a gang or inmate "boss" who could protect them from the veteran predators inside. Young, handsome cons are always in demand, sought out by prison "wolves" for sex, and those with headline-grabbing reputations in the free world are doubly at risk from any inmate seeking to enhance his own status by maiming or killing a "star." In that respect, Hickman was fortunate that he had been condemned to hang. Confinement on death row provided more security than housing in the general population, where Welby Hunt was placed. The gallows might be waiting for Edward, but at least the other prisoners would not rape him in the shower room.

Back in Los Angeles, Tom Gurdane and Buck Lieuallen were running out of patience in their pursuit of the Hickman reward fund. Initially reported in the neighborhood of $90,000, the fund was "reevaluated" and determined to contain no more than $55,000. Even that wasn't right, though. The L.A. City Council soon discovered that it had no legal authority to post rewards, so that $10,000 offer was deleted from the fund. Other donors took the clue, reneging on their pledges, until the *Morning Oregonian* reported that Lieuallen went home with "only a few thousands of the pledged money." (No mention was made of Gurdane.) Lieuallen stopped short of calling the reward scheme fraudulent, but told reporters that "there appeared to be a disposition to let none of the money get out of Los Angeles."

Attorneys Walsh and Cantillon, meanwhile, were hard at work on their appeal of Hickman's conviction and sentence. Their effort included a frontal assault on California's year-old statute governing insanity defenses. Prior to 1927, Golden State defendants who pled insanity were not required to warn the prosecution prior to trial, nor did the plea include admission of involvement in the acts charged against them. The new law required advance notice of intent to plead insanity, thus granting prosecutors time to call in experts of their own; it also provided for separate hearings on guilt and sanity, provided a defendant pled not guilty *and* not guilty by reason of insanity. Presumably, if he was acquitted in the guilt phase of his trial, a defendant would then skip the sanity hearing. Hickman, of course, had confessed his crimes and moved directly to the sanity phase—an obstacle his lawyers could never surmount, no matter how they tried.

On May 18, Governor Young received a letter from attorney Walter Tuller in Los Angeles, announcing that the California Supreme Court had granted permission for Tuller to submit an amicus curiae brief in Hickman's case, defending the new sanity statute. A copy of said brief was enclosed for the governor's perusal. The twenty-one-page document contained no startling revelations or insights, but it helped drive home the prosecution's case.

At this point it may be as well to consider the claim that the defendant was deprived of some right to show some sort of mental condition which he concedes was not insanity but which he asserts might have affected the degree of the crime. There are several answers to this claim. The first answer and a complete answer is that the defendant is in no position to raise the point. He voluntarily and purposely refrained from pleading "not guilty." Therefore, he cannot claim that if he had pleaded "not guilty" he would have been entitled to introduce certain kinds of evidence. He elected to make but one plea, that of "not guilty by reason of insanity." The law particularly stated and he was particularly advised by the court that this plea raised only one issue, namely whether he was insane within the contemplation of the law at the time the offense was committed. Thus it is clear that the defendant himself and not the law restricted the issues in this case to the one question of whether the defendant was legally sane or insane at the time of the offense. It is idle, therefore, for him to claim that the law or the court deprived him of the right to submit evidence on some other issue or evidence which he concedes would not have shown legal insanity. He had a right to plead "not guilty" and also "not guilty by reason of insanity." If he had done so, every issue would have been raised that ever could be raised in a criminal case, and he could have put in any evidence that fairly bore on any issue. But the defendant himself voluntarily elected and chose to limit the case to the one sole and only issue of whether he was legally insane at the time of the offense. He cannot now complain because the court confined the evidence to the one issue which he himself elected to make the only issue in the case.

Nor was it true, Tuller went on, that the California legislature had effectively eliminated the insanity defense, as claimed by Hickman's defenders in their appeal. "It must be remembered," he wrote, "that this legislation *has not taken away the defense of insanity*. The Legislature might have taken it away without violating any provision of the Constitution— but it has not chosen to do so. The only change that has been made is that where a defendant pleads 'not guilty' and also pleads 'not guilty by reason of insanity,' the issue under the plea 'not guilty' is tried and after that is determined, if determined adversely to the defendant, then the issue of sanity is tried. It simply *fixes the time in the case* when the alleged defense shall be heard and determined" (emphasis in the original).

Jerome Walsh emphatically disagreed with Tuller's assessment of the law. Filing his final brief with the court on Wednesday, May 30, he argued that the 1927 legislation violated fair-trial rules of both the state and federal constitutions. By law, the court had ninety days in which to rule on his appeal.

While Keyes, Tuller, and Walsh were writing their briefs about Hickman and fine points of constitutional law, hundreds of persons across the country were also taking pens in hand to write about the case, bombarding California governor C. C. Young with hundreds of letters. Predictably, those who cared enough to write held strong opinions on the case—or on capital punishment—and were not shy in making those opinions known. Their messages ranged from crude threats to eloquent appeals—and some of them were downright weird.

Curiously, given the angry temper of those times, letters seeking clemency for Hickman outnumbered pieces of hate mail by a margin of five to one. Among the first received was a note from Eva Hickman herself.

Dear Gov. Young:
   If you can understand the feeling of a heart-broken mother please have mercy on my poor son Edward and not let them kill him. This is breaking my heart[,] to see my boy killed[,] for he was not himself. Won't you open your heart to my plea and give him life in prison[?] If you will only show mercy[,] only God will know the appreciation of my humble and broken heart. My only prayer is please don't kill my boy[,] but give him life.
                                   Edward's Mother
                              Mrs. Eva M. Hickman

Most of the others who wrote in favor of clemency based their arguments on religious precepts or the belief that Hickman was insane, a more fitting object for study than for execution. Others opposed capital punishment in principle, regardless of the crime. Still others, like attorney William Herron of San Francisco, were convinced that an accomplice in the Parker slaying remained at large and would escape his just deserts if Hickman was hanged. "I am thoroughly convinced," Herron wrote, "from the press reports of the case, which are matters of common knowledge and the accuracy of which has never been challenged, that Hickman had an accomplice in the murder, who has been shielded by the authorities in return for a so-called 'tip-off'—information given to the police."

Another correspondent, M. V. Wardell, wrote from Petoskey, Michigan, to warn Governor Young of a bizarre conspiracy in the Hickman case. His letter read like something from *The X-Files*:

Dear Sir:

Am writing in regards to the Hickman case of Los Angeles, and wish to say that Hickman was handled by a psychologist, and also given the powers of psychology. Now I am not writing this to save Hickman's life, because there is no doubt to me that he is guilty, but I do think he should be spared until this psychologist is caught.

I am the only one that can clear up this mystery, but I cannot be in California until sometime this winter.

This crime was predicted to me in 1920 by the psychologist that handled Hickman. He told me how Hickman would be able to watch the policemen as they were trying to catch him, told me how he would be able to hear them & know their movements.

This man also pridicted [*sic*] that there would be a lot of ex[-]football players committing crimes, said that they would all have scars on their heads & blame their crimes on the injury to their heads. I see Los Angeles has one case already.

These men will all be handled by this psychologist, as Hickman and Hawkins were.

I hold the key to the solution of these crimes & would like to do all I can to help capture this man, as he is very dangerous & a fiend.

There followed a list of persons allegedly "handled" by the nameless malefactor, including schoolteacher Mary Holt ("ask her if she knew the thoughts she had of Hickman to be her own, and if she wasn't urged to give the girl to Hickman"); "Policeman Jacobson of Los Angeles," who apparently had "the entire underworld of Los Angeles at his feet"; and one Johnnie Hawkins, driven to crime by the mad doctor's advice "that the pains in his head were caused by him not getting enough excitement." The nameless fiend "is a hypnotist," Wardell wrote, and "can squeeze your brain to a subconscious condition and hypnotize you on any subject he wants." Worse yet, "He has tried to hold people alive in their graves, and will continue to do so until he is captured." Wardell would face instant death if he returned to California, he said, but he assured Governor Young that "I am not afraid and am coming back and do what I can to clear up this thing, even though I am being watched."

D. C. Fretz, a private detective in Wichita Falls, Texas, wrote Governor Young to request "a short reprieve which will enable me to conduct an investigation of the rumor" that Hickman had one or more accomplices in the crime. An anonymous letter, postmarked from Los Angeles, accused Marian Parker's half brother "and the surgeons son, also a surgeon," of molesting both sisters, then accidentally killing Marian during a botched abortion; Hickman, the author claimed, "agreed to take the blame, because he wished money very much and was promised a get-away, and that now he is being 'double-crossed,' naturally, to satisfy public opinion and incidentally to free the others from suspicion." Elizabeth Everett, in Berkeley, told a similar story, claiming "that Marian Parker . . . was fourteen, not twelve, that she was sub-normal and had already had a criminal operation.

That she died as a result of a second criminal operation. That Hickman had been employed, with the knowledge of her father but not of her mother, to take the body, so no suspicion would fall on the physician or any scandal upon the family."

The conspiracy theories went downhill from there. Alexis Dumas wrote from Denver, suggesting a supernatural solution to the case supported by "new facts":

> In 1900, 1904 to be exact, there occurred a Precession of the Equinoxes, resulting in our earth being moved from the Picean sign to the Aquarian sign, changing mens minds; the change taking place because the belts of earth were broken, and inhabitants of the unseen world began stalking thru earth searching for bodies thru which they might again function to work out their redemption. A thoro study of this situation will explain crime waves, and why men are so obsessed by Evil. . . .
>
> Hickman is what we call an inhabited being. His mind and body being occupied by a demon. . . .
>
> In Rome this demons pleasure was to cut out the viscera of his victims, wrap them in beautiful packages, and send them as gifts to the victims relatives. . . . In England he used feather mattresses to smother little children. In Germany, he was a high official putting countless thousands to death without reason.

Dumas went on to explain that the demon's purpose—its "redemption"—hinged on the necessity of committing a crime so sensational that it would knock Charles Lindbergh off the front page of the *Times*. For reasons not coherently explained, "If Lindberg[h] had been kept on the front page of the press until his 'good will' had been accomplished, CALIFORNIA WOULD HAVE BEEN DESTROYED."

When it came to sheer obscurity, though, the prize went to Emory Lacy, who wrote to Governor Young from a veterans' home in Dayton, Ohio:

Inclosed find a copy of a letter written by myself to Mr. J. Green, Lansing, Michigan, Feb. 7th 1928.

Will this help you in deciding about the capital punishment question and about the Hickman case? Can it be that the Hickman case is for the purpose of giving attention to Los Angeles and to divulge or make opposition to a more serious condition existing in the U.S.

Are these two persons in Los Angeles Mr. Harrison Gray Otis, if still alive, and Mr. MacAdoo who are associated with an international question, and so bring either the persons into more consideration or the question and to give an idea of the hunousness of the condition has the alleged crime been committed? The question is that of the defense of the posterity of the Human race.

Each correspondent—including several who wanted Hickman hanged on their birthday as a special present from the governor—received a courteous response from Young's secretary. None of them, predictably, had any impact whatsoever on the governor's opinion of the case.

Ironically, while M. V. Wardell's rambling letter on the "powers of psychology" had warned against lodging Hickman in a cell "with any pugilist or any violent tempered man," Ed's cellmate was in fact a former boxer, Joseph Troche, condemned to hang for murdering a girl in San Francisco. On the afternoon of July 1, Edward trounced his roomie four games straight at dominoes, and Troche got rowdy, spoiling for a fight. The battle was finished by the time guards on the tier responded to the racket; they found Troche sprawled on the floor, "beaten and scratched," while Ed stood over him, apparently unscathed—the Fox triumphant, even in a cage.

His cell-block victory was forgotten four days later, when the state supreme court landed its own knockout punch, rejecting Hickman's appeal and ordering the trial court to set a new execution date. Jerome Walsh, back at home in Kansas City, took the news in stride and told reporters that his next appeal would go directly to the U.S. Supreme Court, citing alleged violations of the "due process" and "equal protection" clauses of the Fourteenth Amendment. Walsh had to know it was a long shot, but he wore a mask of cautious optimism, as if looking forward to the last-ditch fight.

The last ditch got a little deeper on August 9, when Judge Douglas Edmonds, in Los Angeles, overruled nine defense objections and scheduled Edward's date with the hangman. Barring intervention from Washington or Governor Young, Hickman would die on October 19, 1928.

Looking backward from a time when California trials routinely take a year or more, and death-sentence appeals go on for decades, Hickman's case seems to have sped from arrest through trial and on to execution at the speed of light. It did not feel that way to some observers at the time, however, and the *New York Times* expressed its royal impatience on August 19, in an editorial titled "Hickman Case Drags On." The paper complained that Edward was "still in jail eight months after his arrest, and with no apparent prospect of being hanged for many months—if at all." As viewed from the *Times* editorial office, "The source of the large sums of money necessary to take this case through the courts to the highest tribunal has caused no little speculation and has never been explained satisfactorily." Jerome Walsh—"the scion of a famous Middle West criminal lawyer"—was primarily to blame, the *Times* implied, although it lacked the nerve to print his name. Overall, the editorial declared, Hickman's case had "produced a 'what's the use' attitude on the part of the public, that has had its reaction in the ranks of the police and other peace protecting organizations." What that grave reaction was, the *Times* did not explain.

Four days after that editorial ran in the *Times*, Hickman's death warrant from L.A.'s superior court was delivered to Warden James Holohan at San Quentin. Unless some higher power intervened, Holohan was ordered to hang Edward on Friday, October 19.

On September 20, Walsh was still working on Hickman's final appeal, telling reporters that he planned to file it with the U.S. Supreme Court "next week." His argument: California's new law on insanity pleas was a direct unconstitutional "infringement upon the right of a defendant to trial by jury." California's highest court had already rejected the argument, but Walsh was hoping for better luck in Washington.

It didn't work.

On October 9, ten days before Edward was scheduled to hang, U.S. Supreme Court Justices Pierce Butler and Oliver Wendell Holmes refused to hear Hickman's appeal. Back at San Quentin, where rumors had Hickman on the verge of suicide, he told reporters, "I am not going that way. I have made up my mind to take my medicine." Lately converted to Roman Catholicism, Edward issued a statement of gratitude "that the Supreme Court has given me time to prepare for death. Please ask the people in the name of God to pray for us condemned men here at San Quentin Prison."

He also had a more personal message for the widow of Ivy Thoms, mailed from prison on October 5:

Mrs. Ivy C. Toms [sic],
Dear friend:
I do not wish to hurt your feelings at this time and I am most sorry for having caused you any past grief. You know that I am facing death. I am a wretched sinner but I believe in the salvation of Jesus Christ, our Lord. I want to try to reconcile any differences between myself and others in so far as I am able. Please do not be bitter against me. You trust in God and he will bless you if you do not hate anyone. Of course, you have a very good cause to be indignant against crime. However, I hope you will not hinder your harmony with God by bitterness.

I am writing this letter from a purely Christian standpoint. I do not hold anything against anybody. I wish you joy and happiness and I wish Mr. [LAPD Patrolman

D. J.] Oliver the same. God loves us all. I have opened my heart to him. I repent and praise Jesus for my deliverance. I hope everybody will love and serve God so that all violence and injury will cease. I do not ask any favor for my own self. I ask you to pray for us condemned men here at San Quentin for the glory and in the name of our Lord. Please ask Mr. Oliver to do the same.

I believe Mr. Toms is living in the spirit of Christ and you can meet him in Heaven. Life is eternal through the Son of God.

A contrite and humble sinner

W. E. Hickman

Whatever the depth or sincerity of his newfound conversion, any payoff would be waiting for him in the afterlife. By October 11, when Edward made his public plea for prayers, he had only eight days to live.

16 ✦ "I Hope We Can Forget"

On the same day Hickman expressed a resolve to "take his medicine," Governor Young issued a statement from Sacramento, dashing any hope for executive clemency.

"I will treat the Hickman case as any other that might come before me," Young told reporters. "I take the position in all matters such as this that the judge and jury and other officials who were in charge of the trial are in a better position to judge what action be taken than I, and as my duty to the state dictates I will always sustain them unless some unforeseen circumstance arises to prove an innocent man is to be punished. Unless something new that would tend to establish the innocence of Hickman can be produced, I will not consider executive clemency. It is my fixed policy to presume that the courts and juries have ample means of determining the guilt or innocence of accused persons. The notoriety of the Hickman case does not differentiate it from any other case."

At the same time, Governor Young—through his executive assistant, Keith Carlin—granted Jerome Walsh an audience at the state capitol. They would meet at 9:30 A.M. on Tuesday, October 16. For all the good it would do, Walsh had one last opportunity to plead his client's case.

Around the country, meanwhile, arguments concerning Hickman's sanity had long since lost their fascination. Halfway across the continent, in Indianapolis, the Reverend T. J. Simpson told his congregation at the West Washington

Street Presbyterian Church, "Hickman should die, sane or insane." The pastor was particularly angry at those sob sisters who cited the Sixth Commandment in pursuit of mercy for condemned killers. Simpson told his congregation:

> It seems to be the common opinion that the Bible, and especially the Sixth Commandment, "Thou shalt not kill," teaches that the state as well as the individual should not take life. But we should understand that the Sixth Commandment does not declare against capital punishment, for throughout the laws of Moses the death penalty is repeatedly prescribed for murder.
>
> The Sixth Commandment was broken by William Hickman, but it will not be broken by the state of California if it takes his life.
>
> We may have opinions against capital punishment, but we should not quote the scripture to support our views, for the Bible sanctions it. The Old Testament clearly teaches it, and the New Testament does not abrogate it in any way. The law of the Bible in this matter is the law of retaliation: a life for a life.

The *Miami Herald* was more concerned with practical matters than with Scripture when it addressed Hickman's case in a fiery editorial:

> It would be a disgrace to permit the law to fail. Why preserve the life of such a creature? What is it worth— sane or insane? To let him live would encourage further crimes and also mob rule, the mob seeking justice that the government will not afford. "He was not himself." Naturally. A person who kills seldom is at that moment. Hickman admits his guilt. Then why all the palaver?

If nothing else, the *Herald*'s editors were experts of a sort on the subject of mob rule. Four months before that editorial was written, a black prisoner accused of scuffling with police had been taken from jail and lynched at Lake City, Florida. A year before that, almost to the day, four Tampa residents were killed and thirty-three injured in a three-day riot, after National Guardsmen foiled the lynching of a black murder suspect.

Through all the furor, Ed Hickman did nothing to help his own case. In fact, he was busy writing more confessions, mailing them off to police chiefs around the country, adopting tell-all mode as "the Christian thing to do." While passing through Texas in December 1926, Hickman said, he had robbed a Fort Worth café and a pharmacy in San Antonio. In San Francisco, Ed wrote, he had paticipated in "five robberies and the theft of several automobiles" in December 1926 and January 1927. He had stolen and wrecked a car in Ottawa, Kansas, Ed recalled. He had also robbed a restaurant in Muskogee, Oklahoma. There were four holdups to his credit in Columbus, Ohio, and three more in Saint Louis, Missouri. By admitting those crimes—and confessing once again to the murder of Marian Parker—Hickman hoped he would "get right with God."

His efforts were rewarded, after a fashion, on Sunday afternoon, October 14, when death row inmates were marched to San Quentin's athletic field and allowed to watch a baseball game between two convict teams. A journalist observing Hickman from the sidelines noted that he "took less interest in the game than in gazing at the sun and the brilliant blue sky and fleecy clouds overhead."

Jerome Walsh was in Sacramento on Monday, October 15, when he learned that his scheduled meeting with Governor Young would be a waste of time. Some unnamed legal scholar had belatedly discovered that Young lacked any power to grant clemency in Edward's case, even if he chose to. Specifically, an old state law required a majority vote of the State Supreme Court before any convict twice convicted of a felony, as Hickman had been, could even *ask* for commutation of his sentence. Blocked or not, Walsh prepared a letter to the governor and had it hand-delivered on Tuesday morning.

My dear Governor Young:

On behalf of my client, Mrs. Eva M. Hickman, of Kansas City, Missouri, mother of William Edward Hickman, who is under sentence to be executed in the State Penitentiary, at San Quentin, California, upon Friday, October 19, 1928, I desire to respectfully petition you as follows:

I. As Governor of the State of California, I ask you to command your great prerogative of executive clemency invested in you by the law of the State of California, and commute the death sentence heretofore imposed upon William Edward Hickman, to that of a sentence for the balance of his natural life, in the State's Prison at San Quentin.

II. If you will not accede to that request, I then beseech you upon the broad grounds of human justice to take the necessary steps to appoint a board or commission, of your own choosing, from the ranks of the medical profession in the State of California, or elsewhere, of persons learned in the science and practices of psychiatry, to immediately inquire and make investigation into the mental condition of William Edward Hickman, and report to you before you as Governor of the State of California, permit the forfeiture of the life of this unfortunate lad.

In this connection, regardless of the judgment of the courts of California, I positively assert to you that William Edward Hickman is an insane person. Too, that he was for a long period prior to the time that he so justly outraged the public conscience of California by his wholly incomprehensible deed, afflicted with that, the greatest of scourges known to the human family. He is unquestionably possessed of an insanity that is progressive in nature and one that all of the medical authorities agree proceeds in an insidious manner to a complete ravaging of the mental facilities, and finally to a total dementia. No unprejudiced person conversant with the facts surrounding this demented boy can say that he is the type of person contemplated to be the victim of the capital punishment laws of the State of California.

Your Excellency will not gainsay the proposition that no insane person should be hanged. No intelligent person with a genuine appreciation of the real moral values of human life would advocate such a procedure. I, therefore, consider that it will highly become your Excellency, as it will comport with the great dignity of your high office, to adopt this request to make certain that a great stigma will not become fastened upon the fair name of California, that in the exaction of the supreme penalty from William Edward Hickman, will grow in the succeeding years to be an abhorrent and malodorous crime.

This boy is but twenty years of age—an age at which the great State of California, by its law, holds a person incapable of contract, or of disposing of their property, and many other kindred acts, and yet incongruously enough that very same law will impute to this boy sufficient mental capacity (conceding for the moment that he be perfectly rational) to admit of him performing acts that will work a forfeiture of his liberty, aye, even of his life.

Your Excellency is not without precedent in making a humane disposition of this case. In the great Commonwealth of Illinois, a case of monstrous circumstances involving boys of tender years was disposed of in a humane and righteous manner because of their youth, questionable mental capacity, and because of other circumstances. I make bold to assert that if William Edward Hickman is permitted to die, at your hand, in the face of the record and disposition of that case, it will in no uncertain measure be tantamount to both a state and a national disgrace.

In conclusion, permit me to indulge the ardent hope that Your Excellency may be guided by an all-wise and provident God, in the discharge of this the most sacred of your duties.

Respectfully submitted,
Jerome Walsh

Young predictably denied the request for clemency, but he left Walsh one slender ray of hope, however dim. Warden Holohan, at San Quentin, himself possessed the power to delay Hickman's execution if he thought Ed was insane. In that case, Holohan could instruct the Marin County district attorney to appoint a panel of physicians to examine Edward once again.

Hickman, meanwhile, seemed bent on throwing every obstacle that he could think of in his lawyer's path. While Walsh was en route to a last-minute meeting with Warden Holohan, Ed told reporters he regretted that he had not "stood up like a man and made my peace with God the way I should have done. I am really sorry that I pleaded not guilty by reason of insanity.

"I want no young men to study my crimes," he went on. "My life has been deplorable. I think the publicity given to crooks and crime has a bad influence. It should be given to men and women of high purpose who deserve it."

That said, he delivered a written statement to the press, ensuring even more attention to the same "deplorable" subject:

Crime and other evils are signs of ignorance and death. All criminals and unrighteous men are struggling in the clutch of Satanic error. By willful disobedience to God's law they become ignorant of the laws of truth and life. All creation is based upon positive force. Such is the will of God. However, the devil is exerting his influence upon the minds of men in order to tear down the work of God. By the defeat of Satan crime and violence have come into the world. Men who willfully reject Jesus Christ and deny the grace of God have ultimate damnation and torment. . . .

The reason that I became such a horrible criminal was because I allowed a demon of hell to lead me on. I praise God for lifting me up out of the pit of darkness and corruption. I was most ignorant. . . .

I beg young people to keep a close watch over their morals. Cling to the Christian faith and practice. Then you will have a solid foundation upon which to build a good life. . . .

Jesus Christ is the only way, truth and life. Let all evil-doers think on this. Do not let the devil deceive you any longer. May God bless the people of the United States.

If nothing else, Edward had finally found the pulpit he craved. That was his last sermon, but at least he had been able to deliver it before a national audience.

Repeated confessions notwithstanding, some people still believed Hickman to be innocent—or, if not entirely blameless, at least the dupe of a larger conspiracy. Two days before his scheduled hanging, some of them were meeting in Los Angeles to publicize their "evidence":

OCT. 17TH   WEDNESDAY   8 P.M.
THE TRUTH ABOUT THE HICKMAN CASE
MUSIC ARTS HALL
233 SO. BROADWAY
(OPPOSITE OLD CITY HALL)

A story has been widely circulated in Los Angeles to the effect that two other young men were implicated with Hickman in the kidnapping and killing of Marion Parker; that these two, though equally guilty, have been sent to a place of safety, while Hickman is to hang.

To find out the real truth—and make public—to right an injustice, if one is being done—is the purpose of this meeting.

The two young men are invited to be present. WILL
THEY BE THERE? . . . Come and See.

Speaker

Eunice McMullin Martin

Admission Free Good Music

The meeting was not entirely unopposed, however, as Ms.
Martin told Governor Young in a letter dated October 17:

Dear Sir:

Last night three lieutenants of the Los Angeles Police
Dept. visited me and "personally requested" me to call
off the meeting. And to say, by way of excuse, that I
had changed my mind and was convinced of the
absolute innocence of these other young men. I told
them that I would not say that I had changed my opinion when I had not—and that I would only agree to
cancel the meeting if the Police Dept. officially requested this to be done. They said they had no right to
officially request the canceling of the meeting; that they
did not want the public to know that they were interested—but that they would stop the meeting in some
way because they thought it should not be held *just
now*. They are to confer with the Chief of Police and the
District Attorney this morning, and said they would
take me to interview these two men [Police Chief
Davis] and [District Attorney Keyes] today.

Whether they will go so far as to arrest me and lock
me up until after Friday, I do not know. Protest meetings, of every kind, being such a common thing in this
country of ours—their intense interest, coupled with
their lack of willingness to openly shoulder the responsibility for any interference, their statements that "a little later" it might be alright to have a meeting of this
kind, but that *now* isn't the proper time, looks bad.

I am writing this statement to you today so that you
may be kept informed. If I am arrested or if I disappear
today, my friends will at once notify you of that fact.

There are about 2,500 people, in two organizations (both incorporated under the laws of the State of California) who are interested in knowing what the attitude of the State Government is in this matter.

If—three people are equally guilty of a crime—and if there is a conspiracy (in which our public officials play a part) being carried out—to prevent any investigation until after the lips of the *one* witness from whom evidence to help convict the others might come, has been silenced by the noose—then the people have a right to know that fact. And you, as Governor of this State, have a right to be informed and to take any action, that in your opinion, should be taken to clear up the situation. *If* there is any truth to the story that has been circulated—and Hickman is hanged without a thorough investigation being made, then one of the greatest acts of injustice that has ever been performed in this State will have been done.

Later today, if circumstances permit, I shall write a detailed account of the "story" so that you may be informed.

Sincerely
Eunice McMullin Martin

There is no record of a second letter from Martin to Governor Young, but it would have been a wasted effort in any case. Young did not subscribe to the conspiracy theory and he was not prepared to delay execution while alternate suspects were investigated.

If Perry Parker was aware of the rumors surrounding his family, he gave no sign. Interviewed for the L.A. *Illustrated News* the week of Hickman's scheduled hanging, Parker denied any plans to watch Edward swing. "Certainly I'll not attend," he declared. "Such reports are absurd. That is furthest removed from my mind.

"The execution means nothing to us," he explained, "except that the law is taking its course. We have no desire to be present; none whatever. In the execution we recognize only one more link in that inevitable chain of events that must be welded before we can forget. Since the trial we have had only one desire: to have it all over with, so that we can begin healing over our wounds and forgetting our loss. Removal of this man is necessary to that end. When he is gone, when he is dead, there will be that much less left to bring back to us the memory of what we have lost and what we have suffered."

Overall, Parker told the newsmen, his family was "getting back pretty well to a normal life again. Sometimes, you know, to those of us who await the flour, the 'mills of the gods' do grind exceedingly slow. Sometimes, it has seemed to us that justice has moved with leaden wings in this case. But the fact remains that justice is being meted out and that this man must pay for the sorrow and grief he has given."

"Probably, after he is dead," Parker concluded, "we can forget easier. I hope we can."

As that day came closer, Hickman seemed altogether comfortable with the notion that he had "found Jesus," and he seized every opportunity to share religious messages with anyone who would listen. Twelve years later, in his memoirs, Leo Stanley, the prison doctor, would write that "Such a killer as Hickman is the worst type in the world. His kind excuse their crimes with self-pity, conceit, and bravado—and then pray for their victim's souls."

Warden Holohan had scheduled Hickman's transfer to the death house—two Spartan cells adjoining the execution chamber—for Wednesday afternoon, October 17, but he delayed the move upon receiving word that Eva Hickman was en route to see her son. In fact, she never left Kansas City, but Ed's father, William Senior, made a surprise appearance at San Quentin on Wednesday and was allowed to speak in private with his son for several minutes, in the watch captain's office.

Bill emerged from the meeting in tears. "The boy is very brave," he told reporters waiting on the street outside. "I thought I'd console him, but he consoled me, instead. He told me to live a Christian life and he'd see me in a little while. He gave me a message to his mother. I'll give it to her, and to nobody else."

Another visitor for Ed that afternoon was Welby Hunt. His old friend had not come to say good-bye, however, but to beg for favors. "Eddie," he said, "I wonder if you'd do something for me now?"

Hickman, who knew what was coming, shook his head. "No, Welby," he replied, slamming the door on any last-minute exoneration for the Thoms killing. "I thought you did it then, and I still think so. If I can help you without lying, I will. Otherwise, I'm afraid I can't do anything for you."

Hunt, grim-faced, was turning to leave, when Hickman added, "You have my forgiveness for squealing on me, Welby. But let my fate be a lesson to you. Turn from a life of sin and embrace God, then nothing can touch you."

Scheduled for his last recreation period between 12:30 and 2:00 P.M., Ed met with his lawyers, Jerome Walsh and Richard Cantillon, instead to draw up his will. According to Walsh, Hickman was calm in the face of death. He reportedly told his attorneys, "What is going to happen to me on the nineteenth is an incident to something, the accomplishment of which I have long desired. It marks the end of my physical life and the beginning of my spiritual life." By the time Edward mounted the gallows, Walsh told reporters afterward, he would have "fortified himself with a religious fervor bordering on fanaticism."

Eva Hickman still had not arrived by 9:00 P.M., when the prison bugler blew Taps, and Warden Holohan proceeded with Ed's transfer to the death house. His home for the next thirty-seven hours was a narrow wooden-barred cage situated on the third floor of the prison's old shop building. The amenities were limited to a mattress and two blankets, a plain table and chair, a battered old phonograph, and a small stack of records provided by special request. Hickman played them incessantly, alternately staring at the turntable or scribbling farewell messages, ignoring the two guards who were assigned to watch his every move, around the clock.

Walsh and Cantillon made their last hopeless bid for Hickman's life on Thursday morning, presenting Warden Holohan with a sworn affidavit from Dr. C. C. McFall, a faculty member at the University of Virginia. Dr. McFall, who had examined Edward on fourteen occasions over the past eight months, had concluded that Hickman suffered from the "mixed type" of dementia praecox. He predicted that periodic recurrence of his "excitement periods" would reduce Edward to raving lunacy within two years. It hardly mattered, though, since he didn't even have two days. Holohan conferred briefly with Mark Noon, secretary of the prison board, and then returned the affidavit to Walsh. Across the bottom, Holohan had written, "The petition is denied for the reason that I believe William Edward Hickman is sane."

Leaving the prison, a dejected Walsh told reporters, "It's all over now. The only possible thing that could save him is voluntary clemency on the part of the governor, and that will take a miracle."

Hickman, for his part, seemed cheerful enough. He polished off a breakfast of scrambled eggs, fruit, rolls, and coffee—journalists would later squabble over whether that was a "light" or a "hearty" meal. Lunch was peaches and cream and bread and butter. Between meals, Ed played the phonograph and wrote more letters. One of them, to Chief Gurdane in Pendleton, included an apology: "I am most sorry to have pretended insanity in your jail. That was as great a sin as killing the little child, for which I am also heartily sorry."

On Thursday night, Ed spent three hours with Father William Fleming, priest of Saint Raphael's Church in nearby San Rafael. Father Fleming had already given communion to Edward on Wednesday, and they spent the time from 6:00 to 9:00 P.M. discussing his salvation, trust in Jesus, and his funeral plans. Hickman would not be going home to

Kansas City, where his mother waited in seclusion for the news of his death.

Sleep was elusive on his final night. Ed had the phonograph to keep him company—reports would vary, afterward, on whether his favorite tune was "Humoresque" or "In a Monastery Garden"—and he kept writing letters, interspersed with fervent, mumbling prayers. At some point, he also penned a note to no one in particular: "I have no fear of death for I have tried to atone for my wrongs. I believe I shall have everlasting life."

Around 2:30 A.M. on Friday, Hickman called out to one of his guards, Charles Alston, "I'd like to talk to you."

Alston approached the cage, waiting for Hickman to speak. Finally, Edward said, "Is there anything you want to ask me, just to start the conversation?"

"Why did you kill Marian Parker?" Alston asked.

"Because I got tired of finding her in the room where I kept her while I was trying to get the ransom money," Ed replied. "It got so that the sight of her face drove me into a frenzy, and I began figuring out that I was a fool to be annoyed."

Alston frowned. "If you wanted to get rid of her, why didn't you take her out on a side street or into the country and leave her?"

"That's where I used bad judgment," Ed allowed. "I used bad judgment all the way through. I guess it was the most terrible crime in the history of the world, and if ever a mortal deserved to be hanged, I do."

Despite his inflated opinion of the murder and his evident remorse, Ed forged ahead in an almost jocular tone, describing the murder for Alston, explaining that he got "a kick" out of dissecting Marian's corpse.

"I wasn't crazy when I killed the Parker girl," he admitted. "I remember when I was young that I wanted to go for a religious life. Then my ambitions changed and I went just the opposite way. I would have killed my best friend to get what I wanted."

And speaking of friends, Edward continued to embellish the tales of his nonexistent relationship with Perry Parker.

"Mr. Parker was one of the best friends I had, I thought," he told Alston. "I remember how he got me out of trouble once, when I got in a forgery jam. If you read the last three verses of the Epistle of Paul to the Romans, you may figure out why I killed Marian."

Alston had no Bible handy. What did Hickman mean?

"It was because I was a scoffer at God, I guess," Ed explained. "Talk about bad judgment! Why, instead of kidnapping and killing her, I could have robbed a bank, got ten times that much money, and would have suffered far less serious consequences when captured."

However typical of Hickman, it seemed a curious observation for a newly "born-again" Christian. Despite all the sermonizing, with less than eight hours to live, Hickman could only think in terms of comparing one crime to another, weighing the relative risks and rewards.

Shortly before 10:00 A.M. on Friday, Father Fleming returned to the death house, accompanied by Warden James Holohan. The warden had barely slept, fielding crank calls through the night, including twenty-five from women pleading with him to spare Hickman's life. Edward seemed calm as he walked "the last mile"—in reality some 40 feet, and passed into the execution chamber. Twelve official witnesses and sundry journalists were waiting for him, ranged around the gallows platform, when he entered.

Wearing the new black suit he would be buried in, Hickman mounted the thirteen steps to the platform. He faltered around the eighth step, his legs turning to rubber, and a pair of burly guards half-carried him the rest of the way. His responses to Father Fleming's reading of the Litany of the Dying, clearly audible as they entered the chamber, now trailed away to a whisper.

The guards held him upright as Hickman stepped onto the trap, supporting him as his arms were strapped to his sides and his ankles tightly bound. He had no last words to offer before the black hood slipped over his head. A moment later, when the noose was placed around his neck and tightened, its thick knot behind his left ear, his legs buckled as Hickman swooned.

The hangman did not hesitate. He sprang the trap as Edward slumped into a faint at 10:10 A.M. Ed slithered into empty space, his body twitching as the rope went taut. He may have been unconscious, but that was a mixed blessing in the end. Instead of dropping clean, with his neck snapped for an instant death, he dangled, quivering, lungs starved for oxygen. Three of the spectators fainted, toppling from their wooden chairs, before Dr. Ralph Blecker stepped forward and pronounced Edward dead at 10:25.

There would be arguments, in days to come, about exactly how Ed Hickman had died. Dr. Blecker told the press that only an autopsy could determine the exact cause of death, and since the Hickman family had requested that no postmortem be performed, the question would remain unanswered.

There was a mystery as well concerning the disposition of Ed's corpse. The *L.A. Times* reported on page one that he was buried on Friday afternoon, around 1:30, at Holy Cross Cemetery in Lawndale, in San Mateo County. One page later, though, the same paper told its readers that Ed's father was taking his body back to Hartford, Arkansas, for burial near his birthplace. In the end, it hardly mattered. Either way, he could expect few visitors to stop and pay their respects.

With Hickman safely underground, wherever his grave might be, state psychiatrist Edward Williams saw his chance to have the last word in the case, firing back at his critics, proclaiming that Edward's collapse on the gallows was proof positive of his sanity.

"If Hickman were a victim of dementia praecox," Williams told reporters, "the indifference that was characteristic of him during his trial would have stayed with him until his death. Of course, whether he was sane or insane means nothing legally now, but various articles have appeared in medical journals throughout the country, pointing to

Hickman's indifference as a sign of his insanity. His reported last-minute collapse is, to my mind, of scientific value to mental specialists."

In truth, though, no one really cared. A monster had been laid to rest.

The next one would be coming soon enough.

Epilogue

It is a fact of modern life that headline-grabbing crimes evoke a call for action from the public, angry voters turning to their government with protests that "there oughta be a law." It scarcely matters that in almost every case there *is* a law, which criminals stubbornly ignore. Outrage demands release, and politicians being what they are, the promise of a quick fix is the next best thing to a real solution—especially in an election year. From Prohibition to today's "war on drugs," one piece of crime-busting legislation has been heaped upon another to create a veritable Everest of good intentions.

All in vain.

The Volstead Act of 1919 backfired on its authors in the most dramatic way imaginable. Far from drying up America, the law that was supposed to bury Demon Rum increased the number of saloons tenfold and spawned a national crime syndicate unprecedented in human history. A federal ban on switchblade knives, in 1958, had no discernible impact on juvenile crime. A similar ban on so-called assault weapons, thirty-six years later, has done nothing to curb the violence of drug lords and disgruntled postmen. Still, the knee-jerk urge to regulate and legislate lives on. In 1998, a school yard massacre in Jonesboro, Arkansas, prompted cries for a new ban on rifles, while the president interrupted a tour of Africa to consider filing federal charges against the adolescent shooters.

It is all the more remarkable, therefore, that the William Hickman case did not produce a grassroots movement to "protect our children" with new statutes in the Golden State. There were complaints about his appeal "dragging on" for eight months—a mere blink of an eye by today's standards, when some trials in L.A. exceed two years in length, with appeals stretching over a decade—but most Californians clearly agreed that justice had been served, and there was no agitation to increase the state's existing penalty of ten years to life for ransom kidnapping.

It should not be presumed that Hickman was forgotten, though. In 1929, a Hawaiian junkie was executed for the ransom abduction and murder of a Honolulu banker's ten-year-old son. In custody, the kidnapper admitted having done his homework by studying Hickman's crime, then poring over a list of bank vice presidents before selecting the parents of young Gill Jamieson. When asked why he had killed the child after receiving the ransom, the defendant calmly explained that "kidnapping never works unless you do."

Another echo of the Hickman case was heard in early 1932. Police in New Jersey were already scrambling to find the Lindbergh kidnappers when eleven-year-old James DeJute, the son of a wealthy contractor, was abducted in Niles, Ohio. The ransom note, demanding $10,000 in cash, bore a grim warning printed across the top of the page: "Remember Marian Parker."

By that time the legal juggernaut was in motion. A *New York Times* editorial branded ransom kidnapping "a new crime" on March 3, 1932, and the next day's edition carried a headline that proclaimed, "Kidnapping Wave Sweeps Nation." Editorial writers for the *Newark News*, the *Washington Post*, and the *Washington Star* chimed in with demands for a federal death penalty in ransom abductions. Within weeks of the Lindbergh tragedy, capital kidnapping statutes were introduced in New Jersey, New York, Mississippi, Louisiana, and Virginia. Even states that had banned execution, like Massachusetts and Rhode Island, felt compelled to do something, so they increased their penalty for kidnapping to life imprisonment.

Uncle Sam joined the fight on June 2, 1932, when President Herbert Hoover signed a new federal law imposing a penalty of twenty years in prison and a $5,000 fine on anyone using the mail to demand or extort money with threats of bodily harm. Three weeks later, Hoover signed the "Lindbergh Law," making the interstate transportation of kidnap victims a federal crime. No death penalty was provided, but FBI agents were empowered to investigate any kidnapping after seven days, on the presumption of interstate flight.

The ink was barely dry on President Hoover's signature, before critics assailed the Lindbergh Law as "too soft" on kidnappers. Amendments were called for, imposing the death penalty in cases where victims were harmed by their abductors, but it took another rash of ransom kidnappings in 1933—most of them involving wealthy businessmen snatched by organized racketeers and released unharmed upon payment of ransom—to produce further action from Congress. California, meanwhile, had belatedly climbed aboard the bandwagon in the summer of 1933, with a "Little Lindbergh" law mandating life imprisonment or death in cases of kidnapping with bodily harm. Washington caught up to the national trend in May 1934, when President Franklin Roosevelt signed a package of five new anticrime bills, one of them amending the Lindbergh Law to provide for execution in cases where kidnapping victims were injured or killed.

The revised Lindbergh Law got its first workout in May 1934 when petty criminal Arthur Gooch and an accomplice were stopped by police for routine questioning in Paradise, Texas. After a scuffle, two policemen were kidnapped at gunpoint and driven across the state line into Oklahoma. Federal agents working near Okemah on another case were summoned to assist in the manhunt, and the kidnappers were quickly run to ground. Gooch's sidekick was killed in an exchange of gunfire with lawmen. Swiftly convicted and sentenced to die, Gooch appealed his death sentence on grounds that no ransom demand had been made and no victims were killed. The U.S. Supreme Court rejected his argument in February 1936, finding that abduction of a police officer fulfilled the letter of the law concerning kidnap "for ransom, reward, or otherwise." Gooch was hanged four months later, on June 19, 1936.

California, meanwhile, had an opportunity to test its Little Lindbergh law in the same month Art Gooch was arrested. Retired oil millionaire William Gettle was abducted from his home in Arcadia, on May 9, 1934, and a telephone demand was made for $80,000 ransom. Police traced the call, Gettle's three abductors were swiftly arrested, and their victim was recovered alive. Gettle had accidentally injured his ribs, however, which left his kidnappers liable to execution under the revised statute. Fearing death, the trio struck a plea bargain within twenty-four hours of capture, all three pleading guilty in return for life terms in San Quentin.

By the time California witnessed its most notorious kidnapping—that of Patty Hearst, in 1974—a full century had passed since the abduction of little Charley Ross, and ransom kidnapping was largely relegated to political terrorists. Indeed, private abductions for ransom have become so rare in latter-day America that the discovery of an apparent ransom note at the JonBenét Ramsey murder scene in Colorado in December 1996, convinced detectives that the slaying was an inside job and that the note was designed to throw investigators off the killer's track. When children—some three hundred each year, according to an FBI estimate released in 1995—are kidnapped by strangers in America today, the abductors are predominantly pedophiles, compulsive killers, or unbalanced would-be parents seeking to achieve by force what nature has denied them. Compared to the mercenary kidnappers of yesteryear, the modern crop is simultaneously more numerous and more frightening. Their madness has no price tag; they do not negotiate.

If kidnapping for ransom has become almost passé in the United States, the same cannot be said for controversy over the insanity defense. Nothing was solved at William Hickman's trial, much less on the October morning when he met his death. In fact, four months before he was hanged, another case was in the making, from the far side of the continent. Another twelve-year-old girl, Grace Budd, was missing from her home in White Plains, New York. She had vanished on June 3, 1928, while en route to a birthday party. Her middle-aged escort, a brief acquaintance known to her family as Mr. Howard, was likewise missing and presumed to be responsible for the abduction.

In the Budd case, no ransom was demanded, and six years elapsed before the family received a letter from Grace's abductor, relating grisly details of her death, including references to cannibalism. Distinctive stationery led detectives to the author of the note—one Albert Howard Fish, age sixty-four—and Grace's parents recognized him as the "Mr. Howard" who had stolen their daughter away. In custody, Fish readily confessed his crime and tacked on other homicides, including those of children killed in 1919, 1927, and 1934. Authorities disagreed on the final body count, although a justice of New York's Supreme Court later claimed he was "reliably informed" of Fish's guilt in fifteen murders.

Fish, then, was clearly a killer . . . but was he sane? A background check on his "respectable" family, in Washington, D.C., disclosed seven recent ancestors with severe mental disorders, including two who died in asylums. Fish himself had been institutionalized in 1930, discharged after two months' observation with this diagnosis: "Not insane; psychopathic personality; sexual type." A year later, found with torture instruments after his arrest for mailing obscene letters, he spent two more weeks in a psychiatric ward and was again released. Facing trial for murder in 1935, he was described by court-appointed psychiatrists as leading a life of "unparalleled perversity." Authorities compiled a list of eighteen sexual perversions practiced by Fish on a regular basis, including coprophagia, the consumption of human excrement—in Fish's case, his own, with salad on the side.

It looked like a no-brainer, going in. Fish was demonstrably as crazy as the proverbial outhouse rat, but the state of New York was determined to see him fry. So determined, in fact, that a battery of doctors told the court, presumably straight-faced, that "[c]oprophagia is a common sort of thing. We don't call people who do that mentally sick. A man who does that is socially perfectly all right. As far as his social status is concerned, he is supposed to be normal, because the State of New York Mental Hygiene Department also approves of that." With Fish's rambling, obscene confession in hand, the jury bought it, finding him sane and guilty of premeditated murder. Sentenced to die for the murder of Grace Budd, Fish was electrocuted at Sing Sing Prison on January 16, 1936.

Two decades passed before another Gothic case made headlines in America, with the arrest of fifty-one-year-old Edward Gein at Plainfield, Wisconsin. A mild-mannered handyman and sometime hunting guide, Gein was regarded by his neighbors as a kind, if somewhat simple-minded, man. Then again, they didn't know about his hobbies, which included robbing graves of the remains of female corpses that he used to fashion household decorations, also stitching ghoulish costumes out of human flesh which Gein put on to dance around his yard, by moonlight. When the cemetery raids became too strenuous, Gein turned to murder in his search for fresh materials. The deputies who searched his farmhouse in November 1957 found the headless, gutted corpse of a woman suspended by the heels in Gein's smokehouse, which was cluttered with skulls, skinned faces, and other grim objets trouvé—enough nightmare fodder, in fact, to inspire such horror films as *Psycho*, *The Texas Chainsaw Massacre*, and *The Silence of the Lambs*.

Like Albert Fish, Gein readily confessed his crimes—the parts he could remember, anyway—and he recalled two murders, one in 1954, the other on the day of his arrest. The outcome in Ed's case was radically different, however. On January 16, 1958, a judge found Gein incompetent for trial and packed him off to Central State Hospital at

Waupun, Wisconsin. Ten years later, when Ed was finally deemed competent to face a murder charge, the proceedings were held in mid-November 1968. Judge Robert Gollmar found him innocent by reason of insanity, and Gein returned to Waupun, where he died in 1984.

Edmund Emil Kemper III was fourteen years old in August 1963, when he murdered his grandparents on a rural California ranch, but his aberrant behavior dated back to early childhood, including mutilation and live burial of family pets at age ten. In the wake of his first double murder, Kemper was pronounced insane and confined to the state's maximum-security hospital at Atascadero, where he remained until his twenty-first birthday. Released into the custody of his abusive mother, he claimed eight more victims over the next two years, mostly young women abducted while hitchhiking around Santa Cruz. Kemper finally surrendered to authorities after killing his mother, feeding her larynx into the garbage disposal, and using her severed head as a dartboard. Deemed sane by state psychiatrists, he was convicted on eight counts of murder and sentenced to life imprisonment, with the theoretical possibility of parole.

A contemporary of Kemper's, twenty-five-year-old Herbert Mullin, was stalking the citizens of Santa Cruz around the same time. He slaughtered thirteen victims between October 1972 and early February 1973. The dead included a Catholic priest and two young boys, all sacrificed—as Mullin later told psychiatrists—in a bizarre effort to forestall catastrophic earthquakes. Like William Hickman before him, Mullin had been a star in high school, voted "most likely to succeed," but his mind had gone adrift after graduation, resulting in hospitalization with a diagnosis of paranoid schizophrenia. Returned to the streets after Governor Ronald Reagan slashed funding to state asylums, Mullin subsequently launched his murder spree at the behest of voices that only he could hear. At trial, a jury found him sane and convicted him on ten murder counts, resulting in a sentence of life imprisonment. He will be eligible for parole in A.D. 2020.

While Kemper and Mullin were prowling the West Coast, New Yorkers were confronted with a predator of their own—a child-killer whose sexual mutilation of young boys earned him the nickname "Charley Chopoff." Three boys were dead, a fourth gravely injured, before mental patient Erno Soto was arrested in May 1974, following a bungled effort to abduct a nine-year-old. In custody, he confessed to one of the "Chopoff" murders, and while physicians offered a tentative alibi, claiming Soto had been in their custody on the day in question, they later admitted that he sometimes slipped away from the facility, unnoticed. Ruled incompetent for trial on murder charges, Soto was returned to the hospital, presumably under closer watch, and the "unsolved" murder series ended.

Manhattan was the scene of yet another test case on insanity in 1981, when the blade-wielding "Midtown Slasher" killed two men and wounded twelve others in a series of random, unprovoked attacks. The ten-day reign of terror ended on July 6, when police captured thirty-two-year-old Charles Sears near the scene of the latest assault, the bloody razor still in his pocket. Sears initially struck a plea bargain, on August 25, for two counts of attempted murder, then changed his mind two months later, claiming he was high on drugs when he confessed. The argument was academic, as psychiatrists found him incompetent for trial in March of 1982, and Sears was confined to a hospital for the criminally insane.

By that time, the insanity defense had been propelled into national headlines by would-be assassin John W. Hinckley Jr., after his 1981 attempt to kill President Ronald Reagan. That shooting, Hinckley said, was inspired by the film *Taxi Driver*, as a bid to impress actress Jodie Foster. Jurors found him innocent by reason of insanity, and Hinckley was committed to a mental institution. His subsequent applications for early release were sabotaged by revelation of his ongoing correspondence with killers Charles Manson and Theodore Bundy.

In the wake of the controversial Hinckley verdict, there were calls to limit—or eliminate entirely—the insanity defense. It was presumed, by many stunned and furious Americans, to be a loophole utilized by countless felons, a handy get-out-of-jail-free card in a system already widely despised for revolving-door justice. Vote-hungry politicians were quick to inveigh against juries and judges who coddled brutal killers.

In fact, the truth of the insanity defense is rather different. In any given year, fewer than 2 percent of America's felony defendants plead insanity at trial, with something less than one in three of those being acquitted. Serial killers, for all their outlandish behavior, fare no better in that regard than do other criminals. In this century, fewer than a dozen American serial killers have been found incompetent for trial on mental grounds, and while several have feigned insanity in bids to avoid punishment, juries err more often on the side of caution, dismissing most insanity pleas out of fear that crazed killers will soon be released from confinement as "cured."

Perhaps the best solution to the problem is that adopted by a handful of American states and several foreign countries, which permits a compromise verdict of "guilty but mentally ill." In those jurisdictions, criminals judged mentally defective may receive both punishment and psychiatric treatment, with an eye toward rehabilitation—or at least toward understanding of their crimes. Interestingly, the truly mad often refuse to plead insanity, insulted by the very notion that they may not be "right in the head," and thus, like William Edward Hickman, they finally collaborate with those who would imprison them or send them to their death.

Notes

Preface

p. xi: The Ross kidnappers were shot on December 14, 1874, while burglarizing a home on Long Island, New York. William Mosher was killed outright; accomplice Joseph Douglass lived long enough to confess the abduction, but died without revealing the child's whereabouts. Young Charley's father died in 1897, his mother in 1912, still clinging vainly to the hope that they would someday find their son alive.

1. The Drop

p. 1: The sequence of events in this chapter and Perry Parker's reactions are reconstructed from his testimony at the trial of William Edward Hickman (Transcript Vol. 3, pp. 1426–36) and from contemporary press reports. Various telegrams and letters received by the Parker family between December 15 and December 17 are also quoted from the trial transcript (Vol. 2, pp. 586–98, 895–902; Vol. 3, pp. 1388–90, 1427–30).

p. 4: The history of California ransom kidnappings is drawn from Ernest Alix, *Ransom Kidnapping in America: The Creation of a Capital Crime*, Southern Illinois University Press, Carbondale, Ill. (1978).

p. 9: William J. Burns was arguably America's most famous—and most controversial—detective, founder of the private investigative agency that still bears his name. In 1921, after a long career in the private sector, he was appointed to lead the U.S. Justice Department's Bureau of Investigation (later FBI), but he quickly bogged down in the rampant corruption of President Warren Harding's Ohio Gang and the Teapot Dome scandal. In 1924, Burns resigned in disgrace, replaced by a young J. Edgar Hoover. Three years later, once again in private practice, Burns was accused of jury tampering on behalf of Teapot Dome defendant Henry Sinclair, but avoided serving prison time. He died in 1932 at age sixty-four.

p. 10: Perry Parker testified in court to his "impression" that the final telephone call was received around 8:00 P.M., but he also, quite naturally, admitted to being "a little bit confused," (Transcript Vol. 3, pp. 1433–34). The times cited here are drawn from a reconstruction of Saturday night's events as published in the *Los Angeles Times*, based on police reports.

2. Born Dead

p. 13: Alfred Hickman is quoted from his testimony at his brother's murder trial in 1928 (Transcript Vol. 2, pp. 670–703).

p. 14: Irvin Harris is quoted from a sworn deposition read into the record at William Edward Hickman's murder trial (Transcript Vol. 1, pp. 86–102).

p. 15: Thomas Lewis's remarks are drawn from a deposition read at William Hickman's trial in Los Angeles (Transcript Vol. 1, pp. 61–86).

p. 15: Benjamin Harrison Bailey is quoted from his deposition in the Hickman murder case (Transcript Vol. 1, pp. 53–60).

p. 16: Ida Hickman's remarks come from a 1928 deposition in the Hickman-Parker murder case (Transcript Vol. 1, pp. 117–23).

p. 16: Mrs. Artie Smith is quoted from her deposition in the L.A. murder case (Transcript Vol. 1, pp. 124–34).

p. 17: Dr. A. L. Skoog is quoted from his testimony at trial (Transcript Vol. 2, p. 875).

p. 17: Dr. W. J. Hunt's remarks come from his deposition, secured by the defense in William Hickman's murder trial (Transcript Vol. 1, pp. 92–102).

p. 17: Dr. H. P. Routh is quoted from his deposition in the Hickman murder case (Transcript Vol. 1, pp. 191–220).

p. 18: If we accept Bill Hickman's self-serving version of events, delivered more than twenty years after the fact, the butcher knife episode was not an isolated incident. In fact, he testified in 1928 that Eva terrorized him throughout the latter half of their marriage, prompting him to sleep in a separate room, with the door locked and barricaded, to prevent her from slaughtering him in the night (Transcript Vol. 2, p. 714).

p. 18: Mae Forrester's deposition in the Hickman murder case is found in Transcript Vol. 1, pp. 133–48.

p. 18: Hickman's comments on Eva's attitude toward sex and childbirth are quoted from his 1928 trial testimony (Transcript Vol. 2, p. 714).

p. 19: Dr. Routh, deposed in 1928, could not recall the date when he examined Eva Hickman, since his records had been lost. He placed it vaguely in the period between 1907 and 1910, indicating that it might have followed the birth of Alfred, William, or Mary.

p. 19: Alfred Hickman's observations on his mother are quoted from Transcript Vol. 2, pp. 675–76.

p. 20: Dr. A. L. Skoog described Eva's symptoms during pregnancy in his 1928 summation at William's murder trial (Transcript Vol. 2, pp. 875–76).

p. 20: Ida Hickman's observation on Eva's fourth pregnancy is found in Transcript Vol. 1, p. 119.

p. 20: Eva described Edward's birth in testimony at his trial (Transcript Vol. 2, p. 736). Bill Hickman's description is found in Transcript Vol. 2, p. 720. Dr. A. L. Skoog noted the chloroform sedation and "unusual means" of resuscitation in his 1928 testimony (Vol. 2, p. 873). Twenty years after the fact, based on the absence of evident brain damage or physical disabilities, an expert witness for the prosecution disputed the story of Edward's stillbirth. (Vol. 3, pp. 1212–13), but no records have survived to settle the question.

p. 21: The hatchet incident is described in Dr. A. L. Skoog's testimony (Transcript Vol. 2, p. 876).

p. 21: Mae Forrester recalled Eva's discussions of suicide in her 1928 deposition (Transcript Vol. 1, pp. 135–36).

p. 22: Sarah Slankard recounted her visit with Eva, following the suicide attempt, in her 1928 deposition (Transcript Vol. 1, pp. 112, 115, 116–17).

p. 22: Mrs. Smith's observations are contained in her 1928 deposition (Transcript Vol. 1, pp. 129–30).

p. 22: The recollections of Eva's neighbors and physicians were confused regarding the time lapse between her suicide attempt and her commitment to the Arkansas state hospital. Sarah Slankard recalled Eva being sent to the asylum "two or three months" after she tried to kill herself (Transcript Vol. 1, pp. 112–13), and Dr. W. J. Hunt further confounded the problem. According to his deposition (Transcript Vol. 1, pp. 93–95), he examined Eva for the first time in 1912, having been summoned by two other physicians "before she was taken away" to the state hospital. As Hunt recalled the occasion, "She had taken some carbolic acid, and I went out, before sending her away." This statement contradicts hospital records for July 1913 and Dr. Hunt's own interrogatory, attached to those records, which placed Eva's suicide attempt two years before her commitment to the asylum. I have accepted the hospital records as accurate in this instance.

p. 22: The report on Eva's arrival at the Arkansas state hospital is quoted from Transcript Vol. 1, pp. 180–81.

p. 23: Judge Hester's commitment order is found in Transcript Vol. 1, pp. 175–77.

p. 24: The statements of William T. Hickman and Dr. Chambers are found in Transcript Vol. 1, pp. 183–84. Some fifteen years later, testifying at his son's murder trial in Los Angeles, Hickman claimed that he had first noted aberrant behavior by his wife within a month or two of their marriage— that is, twelve years before she went to the asylum. Challenged on the contradiction, Hickman first replied that he "never made any statement" at the time of Eva's commitment; then he backpedaled to claim he "didn't remember" his written statement, insisting that his later testimony was accurate (Transcript Vol. 2, pp. 722, 725–26). We know his memory was faulty in other respects, if not deliberately selective, since he incorrectly described his wife as an only child and flatly denied any acts of adultery while they were married, claiming, "I always treated her the best I could" (Transcript Vol. 2, pp. 705–6, 727–29).

p. 24: Dr. Murphy's report is quoted from Transcript Vol. 1, pp. 184–86.

p. 26: Minutes of the July 22 staff meeting are quoted from Transcript Vol. 1, pp. 186–87.

p. 27: The interrogatory responses of Dr. Chambers are found in Transcript Vol. 1, pp. 170–71; the identical replies of Dr. Routh are found on p. 174.

p. 27: Stella Mann's deposition (under her married name, Mrs. Marshall Smith) is quoted from Transcript Vol. 1, pp. 156–57.

p. 29: Bill Hickman's application for Eva's parole is quoted from Transcript Vol. 1, pp. 167–68. Fifteen years later Hickman would once again contradict his own statements and those of attending physicians. There was no improvement in Eva's demeanor at Little Rock, he swore under oath. Rather, Bill insisted, Eva had "begged so hard to go home," making "all kinds of rash promises," that the psychiatric staff virtually forced him to sign for her release (Transcript Vol. 2, pp. 716–17). That story is, to say the least, suspect.

p. 29: Sarah Slankard's observation is quoted from Transcript Vol. 1, p. 113.

p. 29: Dr. Hunt's remarks are found in Transcript Vol. 1, pp. 97–98.

p. 29: Mable Bright's remarks are quoted in the *Los Angeles Times*, December 24, 1927.

p. 30: References to Hickman's abuse of animals are found in the *L.A. Times*, December 24, 1927.

p. 30: Psychiatrist A. L. Skoog described Edward's religious zeal in his 1928 trial testimony (Transcript Vol. 2, p. 885).

p. 31: Bill Hickman's excuses for leaving his family are quoted from Transcript Vol. 2, p. 717.

p. 31: Alfred Hickman's comments about his mother are found in Transcript Vol. 2, pp. 694–95.

p. 31: Dr. Grigsby is quoted from Transcript Vol. 1, pp. 103–4.

p. 32: Hickman described his early thefts in statements to police following his 1927 arrest (Transcript Vol. 2, pp. 1150–51; Vol. 3, p. 1214).

3. *"An Unusually Kind, Good Boy"*

p. 33: Mrs. M. E. Doran is quoted from her deposition in the case of William Edward Hickman (Transcript Vol. 1, pp. 461–62).

p. 34: Don Johnstone's remarks are found in his 1928 deposition (Transcript Vol. 1, p. 236).

p. 34: Changing times have caused confusion in regard to Hickman's progress through the Kansas City school system. At his trial in 1928, various teachers and administrators testified that Central Junior High consisted of "seventh grade and the freshman grade," with high school spanning another three years (Transcript Vol. 1, pp. 360, 456). The freshman year of high school, however, is normally the ninth grade. A February 1998 report from the Kansas City School Board indicates that Hickman paid his first visit to a K.C. classroom when he "entered eighth grade," in September 1921, followed by four years of high school. Regardless of terminology, it is clear from surviving records that he spent a total of five years in school while residing in Kansas City.

p. 34: Don Johnstone is quoted from his 1928 deposition (Transcript Vol. 1, p. 223).

p. 34: Baylor Sutton's remarks are drawn from his sworn deposition (Transcript Vol. 1, p. 264).

p. 34: John Proudfit is quoted from Transcript Vol. 1, pp. 322–24.

p. 34: Howard Lee Hibbs is quoted from his 1928 deposition (Transcript Vol. 1, p. 316).

p. 34: Joe Tiffany is quoted from Transcript Vol. 1, p. 292.

p. 34: C. M. McFarland's remarks come from his sworn deposition (Transcript Vol. 1, p. 339).

p. 35: Marion Huscher is quoted from his 1928 deposition (Transcript Vol. 1, p. 457).

p. 35: Hickman's sophomore grades are from Kansas City school records and the testimony of Otto Dubach (Transcript Vol. 1, p. 366). No record is available of which class resulted in the slip in his GPA.

p. 35: Alfred Hickman is quoted from Transcript Vol. 1, p. 680.

p. 35: Joe Tiffany is quoted from Transcript Vol. 1, p. 293. Alfred Hickman described the Central Webster Club as "a literary organization" (Transcript Vol. 2, p. 680).

p. 36: James O. Parker is quoted from Transcript Vol. 1, pp. 459–60.

p. 36: Howard Hibbs is quoted from his 1928 deposition (Transcript Vol. 1, p. 316).

p. 36: Thirteen years later, Principal Otto Dubach noted that Edward finished his junior year with an M (for "moderate") in two classes and a P ("passing") in one. On Central's scale, the M was equal to a C, while P was equivalent to a D.

p. 36: Otto Dubach is quoted from Transcript Vol. 1, pp. 371–72.

p. 37: Central High's yearbook for 1926, the *Centralian*, identifies Hickman as a member of the Negative Debate Team. The name is ironic and oddly appropriate, in view of its impact on Hickman.

p. 37: Chief Edwards's involvement with the Central High debate squad is described in Transcript Vol. 1, p. 467.

p. 37: Although a matter of some debate among witnesses in 1928, Edward's victory in the 1925 intramural debating contest seems well established by Transcript Vol. 1, pp. 246–47.

p. 37: Don Johnstone is quoted from Transcript Vol. 1, p. 225.

p. 37: Howard Hibbs is quoted from his sworn deposition (Transcript Vol. 1, p. 314).

p. 37: John Proudfit's contradiction of Hibbs is quoted from Transcript Vol. 1, p. 325.

p. 38: Hickman's remarks were quoted by Rebecca Tomlin in 1928 (Transcript Vol. 1, p. 398).

p. 38: Rebecca Tomlin is quoted from Transcript Vol. 1, pp. 399, 401.

p. 38: Mrs. Charles Edwards is quoted from Transcript Vol. 1, p. 421.

p. 38: Alfred Hickman is quoted from Transcript Vol. 2, p. 679.

p. 38: Don Johnstone's deposition is quoted from Transcript Vol. 1, pp. 235, 249–50.

p. 39: Mrs. Edwards is quoted from Transcript Vol. 1, pp. 421–22.

p. 39: Alfred Hickman's testimony is quoted from Transcript Vol. 2, p. 682.

p. 39: Howard Hibbs is quoted from Transcript Vol. 1, p. 314.

p. 39: Hickman's 1925 summer job is described in Transcript Vol. 1, p. 250.

p. 40: G. Leslie Smith is quoted from Transcript Vol. 1, p. 450.

p. 40: Hickman's break with the football team is described in Transcript Vol. 1, p. 289.

p. 40: Don Johnstone is quoted from Transcript Vol. 1, pp. 229–30.

p. 41: Howard Hibbs is quoted from his 1928 deposition (Transcript Vol. 1, pp. 317–18).

p. 41: C. S. Matthews is quoted from Transcript Vol. 1, pp. 333–35.

p. 41: Joe Tiffany is quoted from Transcript Vol. 1, p. 293.

p. 42: Howard Hibbs is quoted from Transcript Vol. 1, pp. 316–17.

p. 42: Baylor Sutton is quoted on Hickman's relationship with girls from Transcript Vol. 1, p. 288. Principal Otto Dubach's comments are found in Transcript Vol. 1, pp. 369–70. Howard Hibbs is quoted on the same subject from Transcript Vol. 1, p. 317.

p. 42: Hickman's written statement to police is quoted in Transcript Vol. 1, p. 570.

p. 42: Dr. Victor Parkin quotes Edward's comment in Transcript Vol. 2, p. 1163.

p. 42: Dr. Thomas Orbison is quoted from Transcript Vol. 3, p. 1213.

p. 43: Mrs. M. E. Doran is quoted from Transcript Vol. 1, p. 464.

p. 43: Alfred Richmond is quoted from Transcript Vol. 1, p. 348.

p. 43: Joe Tiffany is quoted from Transcript Vol. 1, p. 294.

p. 44: Don Johnstone is quoted from Transcript Vol. 1, pp. 228, 251. Johnstone quotes Hickman in Transcript Vol. 1, p. 251.

p. 44: Howard Hibbs is quoted from Transcript Vol. 1, p. 315.

p. 44: John Proudfit is quoted from Transcript Vol. 1, p. 328.

p. 44: Howard Hibbs is quoted from Transcript Vol. 1, p. 315.

p. 44: Joe Tiffany is quoted from Transcript Vol. 1, p. 298.

p. 44: Don Johnstone is quoted from Transcript Vol. 1, pp. 229–30.

p. 45: Baylor Sutton is quoted from Transcript Vol. 1, pp. 266, 275–77.

p. 45: Rebecca Tomlin is quoted from Transcript Vol. 1, p. 401.

p. 45: Baylor Sutton is quoted from Transcript Vol. 1, pp. 264, 279. Hickman's attendance record from Central High shows a total of nine days absent and two tardies in four years.

p. 45: John Proudfit is quoted from Transcript Vol. 1, p. 324.

p. 45: Joe Tiffany is quoted from Transcript Vol. 1, p. 296.

p. 45: Alfred Richmond is quoted from Transcript Vol. 1, p. 350.

p. 46: Rebecca Tomlin is quoted from Transcript Vol. 1, p. 404.

p. 46: Hickman's grades are taken from his high school records. The Best Boy Orator award is recorded in the 1926 *Centralian*.

p. 46: Chief Edwards is quoted from Transcript Vol. 1, p. 470.

p. 46: Park College is described in Transcript Vol. 1, p. 470, and Vol. 1, p. 696.

p. 46: Chief Edwards's letter is found in Transcript Vol. 1, p. 473; the response from Dean Sanders is quoted from p. 474. Mrs. Edwards mistakenly testified that the correspondence occurred in July 1926 (Transcript Vol. 1, p. 436), but the dated letters prove her wrong.

p. 47: Chief Edwards is quoted on Edward's increasing unreliability from Transcript Vol. 1, pp. 470–71, 475.

p. 48: Baylor Sutton's observation on Ed's interest in the ministry is quoted from Transcript Vol. 1, p. 288. Don Johnstone is quoted on the same subject from Vol. 1, p. 233.

p. 48: M. Stipp's letter to Chief Edwards is quoted from Transcript Vol. 1, p. 476; the reply is found on p. 477.

p. 49: Charles Harper's testimony on the dates of Edward's employment at Schmelzer are quoted from Transcript Vol. 1, p. 446.

p. 49: Chief Edwards described Hickman's changing jobs in Transcript Vol. 1, p. 478.

p. 49: Edward's brief tenure was described at trial, in 1928, by his brother Alfred and by Dr. A. L. Skoog, quoted here from Transcript Vol. 2, p. 886.

p. 49: Don Johnstone recalls Ed selling cars, in Transcript Vol. 1, p. 235. Baylor Sutton's observations are quoted from pp. 286–87 of the same volume.

p. 49: Alfred Richmond is quoted from Transcript Vol. 1, pp. 352–54.

p. 50: President Edward Bainter offered the dates of Hickman's attendance at Junior College in Transcript Vol. 1, p. 452. Dr. A. L. Skoog later misstated Ed's date of enrollment as September 3, 1926, and erroneously claimed that Hickman started work at Schmelzer's on the same date (Transcript Vol. 2, p. 886).

p. 50: Charles Harper gives the dates for Edward's second stint at Schmelzer's in Transcript Vol. 1, p. 446.

p. 50: Baylor Sutton is quoted from Transcript Vol. 1, p. 269.

p. 50: Grace Hudson is quoted from Transcript Vol. 1, p. 418.

p. 50: J. S. Laughlin is quoted from Transcript Vol. 1, pp. 381–82.

p. 51: Edward's meeting with Welby Hunt is noted in Transcript Vol. 2, p. 635, although Hunt erroneously placed it in November 1926 (Vol. 3, p. 1350). Alfred Hickman is quoted on his brief encounter with Hunt from Transcript Vol. 2, p. 698.

p. 51: Thomas Lewis is quoted from Transcript Vol. 1, pp. 79–80, 82.

p. 52: Hickman's confession to the Kansas City robbery is quoted from Transcript Vol. 2, p. 1151.

p. 52: The exact date of Hickman's and Hunt's departure from Kansas City is unknown. Eva Hickman placed it "along about the seventh of December" (Transcript Vol. 2, p. 142), while Dr. A. L. Skoog pegged the date as December 1 (Vol. 2, p. 887). Welby Hunt, always vague on dates, recalled only that they left town in the "first part of December" 1926 (Vol. 2, p. 637). Ed Hickman himself never suggested a date.

4. Easy Money

p. 53: The references to L.A. as the "white spot" of America is from Carey McWilliams, *Southern California Country: An Island on the Land* (New York: Duell, Sloan & Pearce, 1946), p. 293.

p. 54: William Wright is quoted from McWilliams, p. 158.

p. 54: Mayor Porter is quoted by Joe Domanick, in *To Protect and Serve* (New York: Pocket Books, 1995), p. 32.

p. 54: Welby Hunt is quoted from Transcript Vol. 2, pp. 635–36. He was clearly mistaken about the duration of the trip to California, since he left Kansas City with Hickman in the first week of December 1926 and arrived in L.A. before Christmas Eve.

p. 55: The Driskells are described in Transcript Vol. 3, pp. 1351, 1371, and in the *New York Times,* December 30, 1927, and January 2, 1928.

p. 55: Eva Hickman referred to Edward's correspondence from California in Transcript Vol. 2, p. 743.

p. 55: Hickman's description of the L.A. holdup and shooting is quoted from the *New York Times,* December 30, 1927.

p. 57: M. K. Wadley's comments on Hickman are found in Transcript Vol. 3, p. 1374. Walter Price's testimony is in Vol. 3, pp. 1378–80. Frank Thompson is quoted from Vol. 3, p. 1377. Percy Beck is quoted from Vol. 3, p. 1364.

p. 57: The date of Hickman's employment at First National Bank was cited by Walter Rappold in his trial testimony (Transcript Vol. 3, p. 1353).

p. 57: The Nern-Edwards correspondence is described, but not quoted, in Transcript Vol. 1, pp. 479–82.

p. 57: Mark Traugott is quoted from Transcript Vol. 3, pp. 1355–56. Edward Brewster's remarks are found in Vol. 3, pp. 1361–62. L. S. Gilhousen is quoted from Vol. 3, pp. 1359–60. Walter Rappold is quoted from Vol. 3, pp. 1353–54.

p. 58: Information about Perry Parker's background is derived from his sworn testimony at trial (Transcript Vol. 3, p. 1426).

p. 58: The Driskell "suicide" was described in the *New York Times*, December 30, 1927, and January 2, 1928.

p. 59: Hickman's firearms purchases were described in the *Los Angeles Times*, December 23, 1927.

p. 59: Ed's arrest was described in the *New York Times*, December 21, 1927. Detective Hamren is quoted from his testimony at trial (Transcript Vol. 3, pp. 1381–83).

p. 59: Eva Hickman told the court that she went to California in April 1927, "when Edward got in trouble at the bank" (Transcript Vol. 2, p. 743), but she was clearly mistaken on the date.

p. 59: A juvenile forgery case rated no coverage in the L.A. daily press. Judge Hardy is identified, and his verdict noted, in Transcript Vol. 1, p. 574.

p. 59: Edward's rejection at First National was reported in the *New York Times*, December 21, 1927.

p. 59: The letter from A. L. Mathews to Chief Edwards is quoted from Transcript Vol. 1, p. 484. The chief's reply is found on pp. 486–7.

p. 60: The Reverend Dr. Lash is quoted from the *New York Times*, December 29, 1927.

p. 61: Eva Hickman is quoted from Transcript Vol. 2, p. 743.

p. 61: J. L. Laughlin is quoted from Transcript Vol. 1, pp. 379–80.

p. 61: The second letter written by A. L. Mathews is found in Transcript Vol. 1, pp. 493–94.

p. 61: The date of Ed's employment at the Linwood Theatre was offered by Dr. A. L. Skoog in his 1928 sworn testimony (Transcript Vol. 3, p. 887). It should be regarded with skepticism, since Skoog was demonstrably inaccurate on other dates (see note to p. 50, above), and published reports suggest he may have been off by as much as ten days on the date of Ed's leaving the job in question.

p. 62: Don Johnstone is quoted from Transcript Vol. 1, pp. 258–9.

p. 62: Eva Hickman is quoted from Transcript Vol. 2, pp. 743–44.

p. 62: Alfred Hickman is quoted from Transcript Vol. 2, p. 695.

p. 62: Mrs. Edwards is quoted from Transcript Vol. 1, p. 438.

p. 62: Howard Hibbs is quoted from Transcript Vol. 1, pp. 319, 328.

p. 63: J. L. Laughlin is quoted from Transcript Vol. 1, pp. 380, 387–88.

5. "I Mean Business"

p. 65: John Proudfit is quoted from Transcript Vol. 1, p. 329. Don Johnstone's remarks are found in Vol. 1, pp. 241–42.

p. 65: Edward Bainter's summation of Hickman's college career is found in Transcript Vol. 1, p. 453.

p. 65: No one was ever prosecuted for the murder at Cottonwood Falls. Details of the crime were gleaned from reports published in the *New York Times* and the *Los Angeles Times* on December 28, 1927.

p. 66: Don Johnstone is quoted from Transcript Vol. 1, p. 242. Dr. Skoog, frequently mistaken on specific dates, is quoted from Vol. 3, p. 887.

p. 66: Alfred Hickman is quoted from Transcript Vol. 2, p. 688.

p. 66: Edward's crimes in Kansas City are described in the *New York Times*, December 24, 1927, and the *Los Angeles Times*, December 28, 1927.

p. 67: Hickman's apparent lie about driving straight from Kansas City to Chicago is quoted from the *New York Times*, December 24, 1927.

p. 67: The Milwaukee murder case is described in a *New York Times* report, dated December 29, 1927. There was no follow-up, and a search of Milwaukee's two daily papers failed to turn up any reference to the case.

p. 68: Morgan Armstrong is quoted from the *New York Times*, December 21, 1927. Edward's holdups in Chicago are described in the *New York Times*, December 24, 1927, and the *Los Angeles Times*, December 28, 1927.

p. 68: Hickman's alleged visit to the Weiss Employment Agency was reported as fact in the *Los Angeles Times*, December 22, 1927. At the time, no inconsistency was noted between that story and Hickman's known movements in the eastern United States.

p. 69: Hickman is quoted from the *New York Times*, December 24, 1927. Private Connell's version of the trip is found in the *Los Angeles Times*, December 25, 1927. Both men had imperfect memories of their brief encounter, Hickman recalling his passenger's name as "O'Connell or O'Donnell," their destination as "Queensburg." He believed the officer "had left his horse behind" while working on a case and thus required a lift. Connell, for his part, mistakenly believed the meeting had occurred in July 1927 rather than October.

p. 69: The Claire murder at Chester, Pennsylvania, is described in the *New York Times*, December 31, 1927. The case remains officially unsolved.

p. 70: Details of Hickman's itinerary are drawn from his statement published in the *New York Times*, December 24, 1927.

p. 70: Hickman's robberies in Columbus are described from reports of November 2, 1927, published in the *Columbus Dispatch*, the *Columbus Citizen Journal*, and the *Ohio State Journal*. The papers disagreed on details of the robberies, one article referring to Morris Helman as "Norris," while Arthur Mayo is variously identified as a customer and an assistant druggist at Buck's pharmacy. The reports also disagree on whether the victims at Buck's were lined up against a wall or forced to lie down behind the counter. One article says Joseph Grant spent "a cold five minutes" in the freezer at his grocery, while another has him locked in for half an hour. The latter version also has the bandit looting Grant's home while the grocer was trapped in his store. Reports on the amount stolen from Grant's grocery range from $15.00 to $42.00.

p. 71: Hickman is quoted from the *New York Times*, December 24, 1927.

p. 71: The description of Edward's appearance and demeanor are quoted from the *Columbus Dispatch*, November 2, 1927.

p. 71: Edward's holdup in Saint Louis is described in the *Los Angeles Times*, December 25, 1927.

p. 71: The abandonment of James Cook's Chrysler is described in the *New York Times*, December 24, 1927, and in the *Los Angeles Times*, December 25, 1927. No specific date is given for the car's recovery, but the *L.A. Times* report of December 28, 1927, is clearly wrong in stating that he returned to Kansas City on November 1.

p. 72: Ed's encounter with Dr. Mantz is described, complete with dialogue from the doctor's recollection published in the *Los Angeles Times*, December 20, 1927.

p. 72: Hickman's second trip west is described in the *New York Times*, December 24, 1927, and the *Los Angeles Times*, December 28, 1927. His comment on the price of gasoline in Phoenix is quoted from the *New York Times* report.

p. 73: Hickman's arrival in L.A. and his first holdup there are described in the *Los Angeles Times*, December 28, 1927.

p. 73: Edward described the trombone theft in his statement to LAPD, quoted from Transcript Vol. 1, p. 575.

p. 73: Hickman's registration at the Bellevue Arms is described in his statement to police, Transcript Vol. 1, p. 550, with additional details from reports published in the *Chicago Tribune*, December 21, 1927, and the *New York Times*, December 24, 1927.

p. 74: The Thanksgiving trip to San Diego is described, and Edward's remarks on meeting Andrew Cramer are quoted from the *New York Times*, December 24, 1927.

p. 74: The Jackson robbery is reported in the *Los Angeles Times*, December 21, 1927.

p. 74: Edward is quoted on the genesis of his kidnap plan from Transcript Vol. 1, p. 550. He later blamed the plot on Andrew Cramer, but his candid statement to police reveals that he had hatched the plan in Kansas City, months before returning to L.A.

p. 74: The December 5 robberies are described from a *Los Angeles Times* report, December 21, 1927. Hickman claimed that Cramer was the driver for all his L.A. robberies, but only Packer actually saw a second man, and the driver—if he existed—was never identified or charged.

p. 74: The Sunset Boulevard snafu is described in the *Los Angeles Times*, December 28, 1927. In San Diego, an abandoned car was found, sans license plates, after use in a local robbery. Hickman admitted stealing the tags, but never confessed to participating in the holdup.

p. 75: Hickman's comments on the early kidnap plan are quoted from his statement to police (Transcript Vol. 1, p. 550) and from statements reported in the *Chicago Tribune*, December 23, 1927.

p. 75: Ed's dry run at the Parker home is described in his statement to LAPD (Transcript Vol. 1, p. 550).

6. Stolen Away

p. 77: Lorna Littlejohn's sighting was reported in the *Los Angeles Times*, December 17, 1927.

p. 77: Detective Lucas is quoted from Transcript Vol. 1, p. 527.

p. 77: Marjorie Parker's statement is quoted from the *Los Angeles Times*, December 17, 1927.

p. 78: Lucile Greene's sighting of Hickman in Alhambra was reported in the *L.A. Times*, December 21, 1927.

p. 78: Hickman's first-person account of the kidnapping is quoted from his statement to authorities, reproduced in Transcript Vol. 1, pp. 551–60.

p. 78: Naomi Britten is quoted from Transcript Vol. 1, pp. 588–90. Mary Holt's remarks are found in Vol. 1, p. 595.

p. 80: Helen Seelye's identification of Hickman is recorded in Transcript Vol. 3, p. 1384. Dorothy Snyder's ID was reported in the *Los Angeles Times*, December 21, 1927.

p. 80: The check-passing incidents in Long Beach are described in the *Los Angeles Times*, December 21, 1927. Witnesses identified Ed from published photographs, and handwriting analysis confirmed his authorship of the rubber checks, although he was never prosecuted for the petty thefts. His transaction at the Culver City garage was reported in the *New York Times*, December 22, 1927.

p. 80: Reports of the missing children in Los Angeles and of the clothing found in San Dimas were published in the *Los*

Angeles Times, December 17, 1927. No follow-up reports are available from L.A. papers on any of the cases cited.

p. 84: Hickman's version of the abortive Friday drop contradicts an early police report carried by the *New York Times*, December 20, 1927. Officers believed their trap had been observed from the second-floor windows of an abandoned garage, overlooking Tenth Street, that had been vacated by an unnamed "Greek letter fraternity" in November 1927. Owner James Dolan reported finding fresh tire tracks in the garage on Saturday morning, December 17, while a window shade in the upstairs apartment—pulled down on Friday afternoon—was raised when he arrived on Saturday. The fraternity connection also meshed with Edward's use of the Greek letter delta on the ransom notes, but the theory falls flat if we accept his story of watching Perry Parker and his police escort from the Chrysler coupe parked on Pico.

p. 80: In his statement to LAPD (Transcript Vol. 1, p. 554), Hickman mistakenly described the publication of news reports about the kidnapping on Friday, December 16. A review of the *Los Angeles Times* and other local papers confirms that no such stories appeared before Saturday morning.

p. 87: Edward was wrong about the time he mailed his last letter to Perry Parker. The postmark on the envelope shows it was mailed at 2:00 P.M., from Arcade Station in Los Angeles (Transcript Vol. 2, p. 898).

p. 87: Detective Lucas is quoted throughout from his sworn testimony in court (Transcript Vol. 1, pp. 532–40).

p. 88: Hickman may have been wrong about no one observing his disposal of the body parts. On December 22, the *New York Times* carried a report of an unidentified neighbor who allegedly watched Hickman *and a second man* carry several paper-wrapped parcels and a suitcase to a car parked behind the Bellevue Arms sometime "early Saturday night." Two obvious problems with the story are (a) Hickman's final admission that he committed the crime alone, and (b) his statement that the suitcase containing Marian's upper body remained in the Bellevue Arms apartment while he drove to Elysian Park.

p. 89: Dr. A. F. Wagner is quoted from his testimony in Transcript Vol. 3, p. 1423.

p. 90: Hickman never explained why he claimed Marian was asleep, after taking the trouble to sew her eyelids open. It made no difference, in any case, since Perry Parker had no clear view of his daughter's face at the time.

p. 90: Perry Parker is quoted from Transcript Vol. 3, p. 1436.

p. 90: Detective Contreras is quoted from Transcript Vol. 3, pp. 1438–41.

p. 91: Dr. Wagner's findings are quoted from Transcript Vol. 3, pp. 1422–23. It is fairly common for so-called soft, or gentle, strangulation, using some object like a folded towel, to produce unconsciousness or death without the obvious signs of trauma found in strangulation with bare hands or a narrow ligature.

p. 92: The "Gerber" shirt discovery was reported in the *Los Angeles Times*, December 22, 1927.

p. 92: A report in the *New York Times* (December 19, 1927) placed the parking lot at Ninth and "Figuero," presumably a garbled reference to Figueroa Street, some three blocks northwest of Grant. Either location would have placed Hickman within a short walk of the café where he dined, at Fifth and Broadway.

7. Fox and Hounds

p. 93: Hickman's description of his movements prior to arrest are quoted from Transcript Vol. 1, pp. 560–62. Comments from Detective Lucas are drawn from his trial testimony (Vol. 1, pp. 540–43).

p. 94: The discovery of missing body parts and the discarded suitcase was described in both the *Los Angeles Times* and the *New York Times*, December 19, 1927.

p. 95: Dr. Wagner is quoted from Transcript Vol. 3, p. 1424.

p. 95: Doctors Bowers, Parkin and Catton are quoted from the *Los Angeles Times*, December 19, 1927.

p. 96: S. A. Nemeth's red herring was reported in the *New York Times*, December 19, 1927.

p. 96: The detention of various suspects on Sunday is described in the *Los Angeles Times* and the *New York Times*, December 19, 1927.

p. 97: The wire from Pitts to Governor Young is quoted from the *Los Angeles Times*, December 19, 1927.

p. 98: Frank Peck described the carjacking in sworn testimony at Hickman's trial, and the dialogue is quoted from his account (Transcript Vol. 2, pp. 650–56).

p. 101: The curious train trip between nonexistent destinations is reported in the *Los Angeles Times*, December 19, 1927. Chief Matheson's remarks are from the same edition.

p. 102: Ironically, the front-page reports of the ongoing manhunt ran beside a column written by aviator Charles Lindbergh, still some four years away from his own kidnapping tragedy, describing a bullfight he'd seen in Mexico City.

p. 102: The *Times* editorial is quoted from page one of the December 20, 1927 issue.

p. 103: Testimony at the coroner's inquest is quoted from the *Los Angeles Times*, December 20, 1927.

p. 103: Superintendent Dorsey's statement is quoted from the *Los Angeles Times*, December 20, 1927.

p. 104: Early suspects are described and their statements are quoted from the *Los Angeles Times*, December 20, 1927.

p. 106: Rose Neritue's disappearance was reported in the *Los Angeles Times*, December 20, 1927. There was no followup report, but it is safe to assume that any further homicides of children would have received blanket coverage in the press.

p. 106: Adeline Howard's story, reported in the *Los Angeles Times*, December 20, 1927, was almost certainly a publicity stunt. No report of the alleged kidnapping attempt was made to police at the time it occurred, in September 1927, and Hickman was in Kansas City at the time. The notion of a separate, independent kidnapper stalking Marian Parker three months before her death is simply too implausible to accept.

p. 106: The Prescott-Edwards telegrams and Chief Edwards's statement are quoted from Transcript Vol. 1, pp. 490–92.

p. 107: Hickman later told police that he first saw his name in the papers on Monday afternoon, when he reached San Francisco (Transcript Vol. 1, p. 580), but he was clearly in error, since the first reports of his identification were published on Wednesday morning, December 22, recounting statements made on Tuesday.

p. 107: Eva Hickman is quoted from the *Los Angeles Times*, December 21, 1927. Her ex-husband is quoted from Transcript Vol. 2, pp. 732–33.

p. 108: Charles Downing and Perry Parker are quoted from the *Los Angeles Times*, December 21, 1927.

p. 109: Unless otherwise noted, alleged Hickman citings on December 20, 1927, were reported in the *Los Angeles Times*, December 21.

p. 109: Homer Mays is quoted from the *Los Angeles Times*, December 22, 1927.

p. 111: Hickman's movements are described from coverage in the *Los Angeles Times* and the *New York Times*, December 23, 1927, including excerpts from his statements to police and statements of various witnesses.

p. 111: The scattered "sightings" are summarized from reports published in the *Los Angeles Times* and the *New York Times*, December 22, 1927.

p. 115: The Missouri telephone conversations are quoted from the *Los Angeles Times*, December 22, 1927.

p. 114: Various California leads and red herrings are described from reports in the *Los Angeles Times*, December 22, 1927.

p. 115: Judge Allen is quoted from the *Los Angeles Times*, December 22, 1927.

p. 115: The appeal from Chief Edwards appeared on December 22, 1927, in the *Los Angeles Times*, the *New York Times*, and other daily newspapers.

p. 117: Hickman's comments from Seattle were quoted by Detective Lucas in Transcript Vol. 1, p. 545.

p. 118: A *Los Angeles Times* report, December 24, 1927, quoted the Merrill brothers as saying they rode with Hickman "from Pendleton to Echo," Oregon, but the statement is clearly in error, since Pendleton lies *east* of Echo, and Hickman was stopped by police before they traveled that far.

p. 118: Bill Merrill is quoted from the *Los Angeles Times*, December 24, 1927.

p. 118: The Associated Press alert and Parker Branin's call to Chief Gurdane are reported in the *Los Angeles Times*, December 23, 1927, and in the *New York Times*, December 24, 1927.

p. 119: Chief Gurdane's conversation with Buck Lieuallen is quoted from the *Los Angeles Times*, December 23, 1927. Bill Merrill's warning to Hickman is described in the *Los Angeles Times* of December 24. Gurdane's exchange with Hickman is reconstructed from the *Los Angeles Times*, December 23, and from Gurdane's subsequent courtroom testimony, recorded in Transcript Vol. 3, pp. 1394–98.

8. "This Is Going to Be Interesting"

p. 123: Hickman's comments in jail and Perry Parker's reaction are quoted from the *Los Angeles Times*, December 23, 1927.

p. 123: Ed's parents are quoted from separate reports in the *New York Times*, December 23, 1927.

p. 124: Chief Gurdane is quoted from Transcript Vol. 3, p. 1404.

p. 124: Hickman's statement to Parker Branin was published verbatim in both the *Los Angeles Times* and the *New York Times*, December 23, 1927.

p. 131: Despite Ed's claim to Branin, LAPD denied searching his apartment at the Bellevue Arms on December 18.

p. 135: Once again, Hickman is mistaken about seeing his name in the papers on Tuesday. While police had already identified his fingerprints and telegraphed Charles Edwards in Kansas City, the first newspaper mention of his name occurred on Wednesday, December 21.

p. 135: Perhaps understandably, no officers ever came forward to admit stopping Hickman in California or Oregon, prior to his arrest by Chief Gurdane.

p. 138: Hickman would later revise his account of the Seattle theater visit, telling LAPD that he went in and watched the show, emerging later to find police cruising the street outside.

p. 138: Ed's description of the patrol car stopping "ahead of us" contradicts the stories told by Chief Gurdane, Buck Lieuallen, and the Merrill brothers.

p. 139: Oliver Cramer is quoted from the *New York Times*, December 24, 1927. He never explained how he met Edward Hickman, but the most logical answer seems to be a jailhouse encounter in June or July, before Ed was released on probation and before Cramer received his 200-day bootlegging sentence.

p. 142: Judge Hardy and Chief Inspector Taylor are both quoted from the *New York Times*, December 24, 1927.

p. 142: Hickman's conversation with Charles Randall is quoted from the *Los Angeles Times*, December 23, 1927.

p. 143: The bizarre search of Hickman's scalp is described in a *New York Times* report, December 24, 1927.

p. 144: Hickman's comments to the press on Cramer are quoted from the *Los Angeles Times*, December 24, 1927.

p. 145: Eva Hickman's plaintive telegram is reproduced from the *New York Times*, December 24, 1927.

p. 146: Edward's comments to his guard, concerning plans for an insanity defense, are quoted from the *Los Angeles Times*, December 24, 1927.

p. 146: Dr. McNary's remarks are quoted from the *Los Angeles Times*, December 24, 1927.

p. 148: Rev. Robins aired his opinions of Hickman and behaviorism in the *Los Angeles Times*, December 24, 1927.

p. 149: Chief Gurdane's comment on the reward money and Bill Merrill's lament for loss of same are both quoted from the *Los Angeles Times*, December 24, 1927.

9. *"Come On, Yellow Boy"*

p. 150: The lynching threat was serious. Six years later, in 1933, a mob stormed the jail in San Jose, California, and hanged two kidnappers in the town square, before 10,000 cheering spectators. The next morning, Governor James Rolph Jr. praised the mob's action as a "fine lesson" for criminals.

p. 150: The press reported that Hickman requested a meat-free diet while lodged in the Pendleton jail, hence the steady menu of eggs.

p. 150: Chief Davis, Herman Cline, and George Home are all quoted from the *Los Angeles Times*, December 25, 1927.

p. 151: Hickman's appeal to the youth of America is quoted from the December 25 edition of the *Los Angeles Times*.

p. 152: Ed's remarks in jail are quoted from the *New York Times*, December 25, 1927.

p. 153: The sometimes contradictory reports of Hickman's first encounter with Los Angeles authorities are drawn from various sources. Chief Gurdane's version is found in Transcript Vol. 3, pp. 1405–6; Herman Cline's testimony is quoted from Vol. 2, pp. 622–25; Detective Lucas's recollection is found in Vol. 1, p. 524, with his comments amplified from reports in the *Los Angeles Times* and the *New York Times*, December 25, 1927. District Attorney Keyes is quoted from the same edition of the *L.A. Times*.

p. 153: Cline's statement to the press is drawn from the *New York Times*, December 25, 1927.

p. 154: The new evidence found in Los Angeles was reported in the *Los Angeles Times* and the *New York Times*, December 25, 1927.

p. 155: Milton Carlson's theory linking Hickman's alibi to Jack the Ripper was reported in the *Los Angeles Times*, December 26, 1927. For a "criminology student," Carlson's knowledge of the Whitechapel case is nothing less than shockingly inaccurate. The Ripper crimes occurred in 1888, not 1881; none of the victims in that case were unidentified; only one victim was mutilated "beyond recognition," and she was readily identified, having been found dead in her home. More to the point, there was no suspect in the case at any time named Andrew Kramer. The lone Russian suspect, believed by some Ripperologists to be a mythical figure, was called Michael Ostrog. The closest name to "Andrew Kramer" in the case was that of Aaron Kosminski, a Jewish hairdresser from Poland. The corpse found in the Thames in December 1888 was that of Montague John Druitt, a British barrister who apparently committed suicide. One can only hope that Carlson was more accurate in his reports on "questioned documents" than in his reading of the famous case.

p. 155: Ed's comments to the press on Christmas morning are quoted from the *Los Angeles Times*, December 26, 1927.

p. 156: Hickman's suicide attempts are described in the *Los Angeles Times* and the *New York Times*, December 26, 1927.

p. 156: Herman Cline's testimony is quoted from Transcript Vol. 2, pp. 626–27. The media version of Ed's departure from the Pendleton jail is drawn from the *Los Angeles Times*, December 26, 1927.

p. 157: Hickman's remark upon boarding the train is quoted from the *New York Times*, December 26, 1927.

p. 157: Herman Cline is quoted from Transcript Vol. 2, pp. 617–18.

p. 158: Edward's first written statement is found in Transcript Vol. 1, pp. 549–62.

p. 161: Hickman is once again mistaken in saying that Los Angeles newspapers reported the kidnapping, with photos of Marian, on Friday morning, December 16. The first reports came a day later.

p. 165: Ed was apparently wrong about not being seen while he loaded the Chrysler outside the Bellevue Arms on Saturday night. The witness, never publicly identified, insisted that a second unknown man helped carry parcels to the car.

p. 167: Hickman's reference to the "fictitious" names of Cramer and Dunning fails to explain his earlier admission—and that of Oliver Cramer—that the two men did, in fact, know each another. Nor does it account for Frank Cramer's jailhouse reference to June Dunning as a sister of his brother's girlfriend.

p. 168: Ed's second written statement of December 26 is found in Transcript Vol. 1, pp. 567–70.

p. 171: Hickman's remark on the woman in the crowd, with Carlton Williams's reply, is quoted from the *Los Angeles Times*, December 26, 1927.

10. *"I Have No Fear of What May Come"*

p. 173: Comments at Hickman's arraignment are quoted from Transcript Vol. 1, pp. 2–3.

p. 174: Ed's remarks to the press are taken from the *New York Times*, December 28, 1927.

p. 175: Hickman's parents, Dr. Wagner's open letter, the Seattle telegram, and comments from the Oregon lawmen are all quoted from reports in the *New York Times*, December 28, 1927.

p. 178: Herman Cline's response to Dr. Wagner is taken from the *New York Times*, December 29, 1927.

p. 178: Lionel Moise is quoted from Transcript Vol. 2, pp. 658–60.

p. 180: Remarks from Dr. Reynolds and his interview with Hickman are quoted from Transcript Vol. 2, pp. 912–19.

p. 187: Dr. Mikels is quoted, and his examination of Hickman is reconstructed, from Transcript Vol. 2, pp. 1114–31.

p. 188: Ed's conversation with Frank Dewar is quoted from the *New York Times*, December 30, 1927.

p. 189: There is no record of ballistics tests designed to learn if Ivy Thoms may have been killed by a bullet from the anonymous patrolman's .38-caliber revolver, but it would have made no legal difference in the case. Under California's felony murder rule, all participants in a crime (such as armed robbery) are legally responsible for any deaths resulting, even if those deaths are caused by the authorities. Although the rule is never carried to its logical extreme, one robber could theoretically be convicted of murdering an accomplice shot dead by police while resisting arrest.

p. 189: Ed's confrontation with Mrs. Thoms and the reaction of Welby Hunt's mother are quoted from the *New York Times*, December 30, 1927.

p. 190: No charges were ever filed in the Driskell "suicide."

p. 192: Hickman's abortive arraignment is reconstructed from Transcript Vol. 1, pp. 4–6.

p. 192: Frank Bernoudy is quoted from the *New York Times*, December 30, 1927.

p. 193: George Contreras's pursuit of the "other woman" at the Bellevue Arms is taken from the *New York Times*, December 31, 1927.

p. 193: Hickman's jailhouse note is quoted from Transcript Vol. 2, pp. 892–93.

p. 194: Reverend Brougher and Canon Chase are quoted from the *New York Times*, January 1, 1928.

p. 197: Remarks at Hickman's arraignment are quoted from Transcript Vol. 1, pp. 7–12.

p. 199: Ed's letter to his mother is quoted from the *New York Times*, January 9, 1928.

11. The Making of a Genius

p. 201: Jerome Walsh is quoted from the *New York Times*, January 10, 1928.

p. 202: Dr. Fettes is quoted from Transcript Vol. 2, pp. 747–52, 755–58.

p. 204: Dr. Bowers is quoted from Transcript Vol. 2, pp. 991–92.

p. 204: Dr. Williams is quoted from Transcript Vol. 3, pp. 1307–9, 1321–22, 1340–42.

p. 206: Dr. Shelton is quoted from Transcript Vol. 2, pp. 776–82.

p. 209: Dr. Schorr is quoted from Transcript Vol. 2, pp. 1071–74.

p. 211: Dr. Bowers is quoted from Transcript Vol. 2, pp. 993–95.

p. 211: Dr. Parkin's exchange with Ed is quoted from Transcript Vol. 2, pp. 1080–88.

p. 213: Dr. Mikels is quoted from Transcript Vol. 2, pp. 1132–35.

p. 214: Dr. Bowers is quoted from Transcript Vol. 2, pp. 995–1003.

p. 216: Dr. Parkin is quoted from Transcript Vol. 2, pp. 1083–88.

p. 217: Dr. Reynolds is quoted from Transcript Vol. 2, pp. 922–25.

p. 218: Dr. Schorr is quoted from Transcript Vol. 2, pp. 1073–77.

p. 218: Dr. Mikels is quoted from Transcript Vol. 2, pp. 1135–44.

p. 220: Dr. Orbison is quoted from Transcript Vol. 3, pp. 1206, 1211–12, 1291–92.

p. 221: Dr. Mikels is quoted from Transcript Vol. 2, pp. 1144–57.

p. 223: Again, Hickman denies the acquaintance with Cramer that both men had earlier admitted.

p. 224: Dr. Orbison is quoted from Transcript Vol. 3, pp. 1212–21.

p. 226: Dr. Mikels is quoted from Transcript Vol. 2, pp. 1157–71.

p. 229: More than half a century after Hickman's fantasy of product-tampering with poison, the nightmare came true in Chicago, with the still unsolved Tylenol murders of 1982.

pp. 230: Dr. Reynolds is quoted from Transcript Vol. 2, pp. 925–33.

p. 231: Dr. Shelton and Asa Keyes are quoted from Transcript Vol. 2, p. 790.

p. 232: Dr. Orbison is quoted from Transcript Vol. 3, pp. 1220–21.

p. 232: Ed's proposed speech is quoted from Transcript Vol. 3, pp. 1267–84.

p. 243: Dr. Orbison's exchange with Hickman is quoted from Transcript Vol. 3, p. 1285.

12. "We Looked upon Him as Brilliant"

p. 245: Judge Hardy's remarks are found in Transcript Vol. 1, p. 17.

p. 245: Asa Keyes's comment is quoted from the *New York Times*, January 26, 1928.

p. 245: Judge Hardy is quoted from Transcript Vol. 1, p. 19.

p. 245: Asa Keyes is quoted from Transcript Vol. 1, pp. 20–21.

p. 246: Dr. Skoog is quoted from Transcript Vol. 2, pp. 807–35.

p. 249: The exchange between Cantillon and Trabucco is quoted from Transcript Vol. 1, pp. 24–25.

p. 249: Dr. Mikels relates his observations in Transcript Vol. 2, pp. 1180–82.

p. 250: Jerome Walsh is quoted from the *New York Times*, January 28, 1928.

p. 250: Judge Trabucco is quoted from Transcript Vol. 1, p. 28.

p. 251: The exchange between Walsh and Trabucco is quoted from Transcript Vol. 1, p. 40.

p. 252: The intent of the defense is stated in Transcript Vol. 1, p. 52.

p. 252: Benjamin Bailey's deposition is found in Transcript Vol. 1, pp. 53–60.

p. 252: Thomas Lewis's deposition is found in Transcript Vol. 1, pp. 61–84.

p. 253: Irvin Harris's deposition is found in Transcript Vol. 1, pp. 86–92.

p. 253: Dr. Hunt's deposition is found in Transcript Vol. 1, pp. 92–102.

p. 253: Dr. Grigsby's deposition is found in Transcript Vol. 1, pp. 102–06.

p. 253: Sarah Slankard's deposition is found in Transcript Vol. 1, pp. 107–17.

p. 254: Ida Hickman's deposition is found in Transcript Vol. 1, pp. 117–23.

p. 254: Mrs. Artie Smith's deposition is found in Transcript Vol. 1, pp. 124–32.

p. 254: Mae Forrester's deposition is found in Transcript Vol. 1, pp. 133–48.

p. 255: Dr. Mikels relates his observations in Transcript Vol. 2, p. 1187.

p. 255: Spence Lane's deposition is found in Transcript Vol. 1, pp. 149–53.

p. 256: Stella Smith's deposition is found in Transcript Vol. 1, pp. 154–64.

p. 256: Dr. Brown's deposition is found in Transcript Vol. 1, pp. 165–90.

p. 256: Dr. Routh's deposition is found in Transcript Vol. 1, pp. 191–200.

p. 256: Don Johnstone's deposition is found in Transcript Vol. 1, pp. 221–56.

p. 257: Baylor Sutton's deposition is found in Transcript Vol. 1, pp. 261–90.

p. 257: Joe Tiffany's deposition is found in Transcript Vol. 1, pp. 291–310.

p. 257: Howard Hibbs's deposition is found in Transcript Vol. 1, pp. 311–21.

p. 257: John Proudfit's deposition is found in Transcript Vol. 1, pp. 321–32.

p. 258: C. M. McFarland's deposition is found in Transcript Vol. 1, pp. 338–42.

p. 258: Alfred Richmond's deposition is found in Transcript Vol. 1, pp. 342–57.

p. 258: Otto Dubach's deposition is found in Transcript Vol. 1, pp. 358–74.

p. 258: J. L. Laughlin's deposition is found in Transcript Vol. 1, pp. 375–83.

13. "An Average American Youth"

p. 260: Dr. Mikels's observation is quoted from Transcript Vol. 2, p. 1189.

p. 260: J. L. Laughlin's deposition is found in Transcript Vol. 1, pp. 384–94.

p. 260: Rebecca Tomlin's deposition is found in Transcript Vol. 1, pp. 395–416.

p. 261: Grace Hudson's deposition is found in Transcript Vol. 1, pp. 417–18.

p. 261: Mrs. Edwards's deposition is found in Transcript Vol. 1, pp. 418–44.

p. 261: Leslie Smith's deposition is found in Transcript Vol. 1, pp. 447–51.

p. 261: Edward Bainter's deposition is found in Transcript Vol. 1, pp. 451–54.

p. 261: James Parker's deposition is found in Transcript Vol. 1, pp. 458–60.

p. 262: Charles Edwards's deposition is found in Transcript Vol. 1, pp. 464–520.

p. 263: R. J. Lucas's testimony is found in Transcript Vol. 1, pp. 522–83.

p. 265: Lucas's testimony that Hickman "did not know Cramer" flatly contradicts published statements from both Edward *and* Cramer, who admitted knowing each other. Lucas was also incorrect in stating that police had found June Dunning.

p. 266: Walsh's confrontation with Mrs. Thoms was described in the *New York Times,* February 2, 1928.

p. 266: Chief Davis never did appear as a witness, apparently forgotten by Walsh in the course of the proceedings.

p. 266: Naomi Britten's testimony is found in Transcript Vol. 2, pp. 585–93.

p. 266: Mary Holt's testimony is found in Transcript Vol. 2, pp. 593–98.

p. 267: Herman Cline's testimony is found in Transcript Vol. 2, pp. 599–629.

p. 268: Dwight Longuevan's testimony is found in Transcript Vol. 2, pp. 629–33.

p. 269: Dr. Mikels's observation is quoted from Transcript Vol. 2, p. 1190.

p. 269: Welby Hunt's testimony is found in Transcript Vol. 2, pp. 634–44.

p. 270: Herman Cline's testimony is found in Transcript Vol. 2, pp. 645–46.

p. 270: Frank Peck's testimony is found in Transcript Vol. 2, pp. 650–56.

p. 271: Dr. Mikels's observation is quoted from Transcript Vol. 2, p. 1190.

p. 272: Alfred Hickman's testimony is found in Transcript Vol. 2, pp. 670–703.

p. 275: William Thomas Hickman's testimony is found in Transcript Vol. 2, pp. 704–33.

p. 280: Dr. Mikels's observation is quoted from Transcript Vol. 2, p. 1190.

p. 281: Eva Hickman's testimony is found in Transcript Vol. 2, pp. 734–44.

p. 281: Dr. Mikels's observation is quoted from Transcript Vol. 2, p. 1190–1.

p. 282: Dr. Fettes's testimony is found in Transcript Vol. 2, pp. 745–58.

p. 283: Dr. Shelton's testimony is found in Transcript Vol. 2, pp. 758–807.

p. 284: Dr. Mikels's observation is quoted from Transcript Vol. 2, p. 1191.

p. 287: Dr. Skoog's testimony is found in Transcript Vol. 2, pp. 807–88.

p. 292: Dr. Reynolds's testimony is found in Transcript Vol. 2, pp. 902–87.

p. 296: Dr. Mikels's observation is quoted from Transcript Vol. 2, p. 1191.

p. 298: Dr. Bowers's testimony is found in Transcript Vol. 2, pp. 988–1065.

p. 300: Dr. Mikels's observation is quoted from Transcript Vol. 2, pp. 1192–93.

p. 302: Dr. Schorr's testimony is found in Transcript Vol. 2, pp. 1066–77.

p. 302: Dr. Parkin's testimony is found in Transcript Vol. 2, pp. 1077–1107.

p. 303: Dr. Mikels's testimony is found in Transcript Vol. 2, pp. 1107–1200, and Volume 3, pp. 1202–3.

p. 304: Dr. Orbison's testimony is found in Transcript Vol. 3, pp. 1202–97.

p. 305: Dr. Williams's testimony is found in Transcript Vol. 3, pp. 1298–1346.

p. 307: Welby Hunt is quoted from Transcript Vol. 3, p. 1352.

p. 308: Walter Rappold is quoted from Transcript Vol. 3, p. 1354.

p. 308: Percy Beck is quoted from Transcript Vol. 3, p. 1364.

p. 308: Solomon Laykin is quoted from Transcript Vol. 3, p. 1385.

14. "The Touchstone of Common Sense"

p. 310: Forrest Murray's summation is found in Transcript Vol. 3, pp. 1443–68.

p. 315: Jerome Walsh's summation is found in Transcript Vol. 3, pp. 1469–96.

p. 319: Richard Cantillon's summation is found in Transcript Vol. 3, pp. 1497–1537.

p. 321: Asa Keyes's summation is found in Transcript Vol. 3, pp. 1538–74.

p. 324: Judge Trabucco's charge to the jury is found in Transcript Vol. 3, pp. 1577–86.

p. 325: Curiously, while Transcript Vol. 3, pp. 1587–88 notes that "the verdict was read" on each charge, it never states what the verdicts *were*.

p. 326: Walsh's motion for a new trial is found in Transcript Vol. 3, pp. 1590–93.

p. 328: Judge Trabucco's pronouncement of sentence is quoted from Transcript Vol. 3, pp. 1611–12. Hickman's demeanor at sentencing is described in the *New York Times*, February 15, 1928.

p. 330: Judge Craig's pronouncement of sentence is quoted from a transcript dated March 12, 1928, pp. 1–3.

15. "A Contrite and Humble Sinner"

p. 331: The deputies' paraphrase of Edward's remarks is quoted from the *New York Times*, March 18, 1928.

p. 332: Hickman's remarks to Dr. Stanley are quoted from Stanley's memoir, *Men at Their Worst* (New York: Appleton-Century, 1940), pp. 51–55.

p. 334: Buck Lieuallen is quoted from a *New York Times* editorial, March 22, 1928.

p. 334: An amicus curiae ("friend of the court") brief is accepted from noninvolved parties in certain cases, where the court feels additional opinions may be helpful in rendering a decision. Tuller's remarks are quoted from the brief he submitted to the California Supreme Court in May 1928, pp. 7, 9–10.

p. 336: In addition to the letters received in Sacramento, which are preserved in the California State Archives, Hickman also received an estimated two hundred letters a day at San Quentin. As unofficial correspondence, they were not preserved.

p. 336: Eva Hickman's undated letter is preserved in the California State Archives.

p. 337: William Herron's letter of October 16, 1928, is preserved in the California State Archives.

p. 337: M. V. Wardell's letter of July 4, 1928, is preserved in the California State Archives.

p. 338: D. C. Fretz's letter of October 11, 1928, is preserved in the California State Archives.

p. 338: The anonymous letter claiming that Marian Parker died during an illegal abortion is preserved in the California State Archives.

p. 338: Elizabeth Everett's letter of April 23, 1928, is preserved in the California State Archives.

p. 339: The letter from Alexis Dumas, dated October 15, 1928, is preserved in the California State Archives.

p. 340: Emory Lacy's letter of February 7, 1928, is preserved in the California State Archives.

p. 340: Ed's fight with Troche is described in the *New York Times*, July 3, 1928.

p. 341: The *New York Times* editorial is quoted from the August 19, 1928, edition. Today, death-row appeals consume an average nine years and seven months, with some dragging on for fifteen years or more.

p. 342: Jerome Walsh is quoted from the *New York Times*, September 21, 1928.

p. 342: Hickman's statement to the press is quoted from the *New York Times*, October 11, 1928.

p. 342: Ed's letter to Mrs. Thoms is quoted from the *Los Angeles Times*, October 17, 1928. Patrolman D. J. Oliver shot it out with Hunt and Hickman on Christmas Eve 1926. This issue of the *Times* carries the first mention of his being wounded in the gunfight.

16. "I Hope We Can Forget"

p. 344: Excerpts from Governor Young's statement were published in the *Los Angeles Times* and the *Herald* on October 11, 1928.

p. 345: Reverend T. J. Simpson is quoted from the *Los Angeles Times*, January 23, 1928.

p. 345: The *Miami Herald* editorial was published on October 17, 1928.

p. 346: Hickman's new confessions were detailed in the *Los Angeles Times*, October 14, 1928.

p. 346: The description of Hickman at the baseball game comes from the *Los Angeles Times*, October 15, 1928.

p. 347: Walsh's letter of October 16, to Governor Young, is preserved in the California State Archives.

p. 349: Edward's comments to the press are quoted from the *Los Angeles Times* and the *New York Times*, both of October 17, 1928.

p. 351: Elizabeth Martin enclosed a copy of her handbill in the letter she wrote to Governor Young on October 17, 1928.

Both are preserved in the California State Archives. The "two young men" alluded to in her conspiracy theory are presumably Marian Parker's brother and the unnamed surgeon's son mentioned in earlier rumors of a botched abortion.

p. 352: Perry Parker is quoted from the L.A. *Illustrated News*, October 17, 1928.

p. 353: Dr. Stanley is quoted from his memoirs, *Men at Their Worst*, p. 59.

p. 353: Ed Hickman's father is quoted from the *Los Angeles Times*, October 18, 1928. The paper speculated that Hickman had asked his father to reconcile with Eva, a questionable notion, since William Senior was remarried at the time.

p. 354: Hickman's dialogue with Welby Hunt is quoted from the *Los Angeles Times*, October 18, 1928. Edward had apparently changed his mind again on the subject of who shot Ivy Thoms—assuming, that is, that reports of his March 1928 confession were accurate.

p. 354: Hickman's comment to Walsh is quoted from the *Los Angeles Times*, October 18, 1928.

p. 355: Dr. McFall, Warden Holohan, and Jerome Walsh are all quoted from remarks to the *Los Angeles Times*, October 19, 1928.

p. 355: Hickman's letter to Chief Gurdane is quoted from the *Los Angeles Times*, October 19, 1928.

p. 356: Ed's note about death is quoted by Dr. Stanley in *Men at Their Worst*, p. 58. It must be said that Stanley's description of Hickman's last night—sleeping peacefully before and after he wrote the short message at 2:45 A.M.—is inconsistent with all other published accounts of his restless final hours.

p. 356: Hickman's conversation with Charles Alston is quoted from the *Los Angeles Times*, October 20, 1928. Hickman's reference to Scripture, however well intended, was inaccurate. The last three verses of Romans include no mention of "scoffers at God."

p. 358: The *L.A. Times* of October 20, 1928, names Patrolman D. J. Oliver—wounded in the shootout that killed Ivy Thoms—as a witness to Hickman's execution. So he may have been, but his name does not appear on Warden Holohan's list of witnesses, preserved in the California State Archives.

p. 358: Dr. Williams—misidentified in print as "Edwin"—is quoted from the *Los Angeles Times*, October 20, 1928.

Epilogue

p. 362: Interpretations of "bodily harm" under California's Little Lindbergh law have varied widely, with no case more controversial than that of Caryl Chessman, sentenced to death for kidnapping and sexual assault in 1948. Identified as L.A.'s Red Light Bandit, Chessman was accused of approaching couples parked on rural lover's lanes, robbing the men, and sometimes driving off with the women, who were forced to perform various sexual acts. No ransom was ever demanded, and no one was killed, but Chessman's trial judge sentenced him to die after the jury returned a verdict of guilty, with no recommendation for mercy. After twelve years of appeals and two bestselling books (smuggled out of his cell on death row), Chessman died in San Quentin's gas chamber on May 2, 1960.

p. 364: Harold Schechter has produced the definitive studies of Fish (*Deranged*, 1990) and Gein (*Deviant*, 1989), both published by Pocket Books. Other useful works on Albert Fish include Michael Angelella's *Trail of Blood* (1979) and Mel Heimer's *The Cannibal* (1971). Judge Robert Gollmar's quirky *Edward Gein* (1981) is also worth reading, for a jurist's personal insight into the case.

p. 366: The only book-length study of Kemper to date is Margaret Cheney's account, *The Co-ed Killer* (1976). Forensic psychiatrist Donald Lunde, who examined Kemper prior to trial, has also published observations on the case in *Murder and Madness* (1976).

p. 366: Herbert Mullin's case is covered by Donald Lunde and Jefferson Morgan in *The Die Song: A Journey into the Mind of a Mass Murderer* (1980). Dr. Lunde, who examined Mullin in his capacity as a forensic psychiatrist, also provides a thumbnail sketch of the case in *Murder and Madness*.

p. 367: For a more detailed examination of the Soto and Sears cases, see my own *Hunting Humans* (1990), or consult the *New York Times Index* for the relevant years.

p. 368: False claims of multiple personality are the most popular dodge for serial killers who attempt to beat the system on bogus insanity pleas. William Heirens set the precedent in 1946, blaming his Chicago murder spree on an alter ego named "George Murman" (short for "Murder Man"). Three decades later, John Wayne Gacy and Hillside Strangler Kenneth Bianchi both tried feigning multiple personalities, but their clumsy efforts were exposed by forensic psychiatrists. A more unusual case was that of David Berkowitz, New York's Son of Sam gunman, who briefly claimed to take his killing orders from an ancient demon, speaking through a neighbor's Labrador retriever. Prior to trial, however, Berkowitz gave up the game and admitted his scam to a court-appointed therapist.

p. 368: Unabomber Theodore Kaczynski is a prime example of those apparently deranged killers who insist they are perfectly sane. In 1998 Kaczynski vetoed his attorney's plan to offer an insanity defense at trial in Colorado, insisting on a plea bargain that consigned him to prison for life without the possibility of parole.